SOUTHERN LITERARY STUDIES
Fred Hobson, Editor

Martyn Bone

The Postsouthern Sense of Place in Contemporary Fiction

LOUISIANA STATE UNIVERSITY PRESS ⚜ BATON ROUGE

Published by Louisiana State University Press
Copyright © 2005 by Louisiana State University Press
All rights reserved
Manufactured in the United States of America
Louisiana Paperback Edition, 2014

DESIGNER: Barbara Neely Bourgoyne
TYPEFACE: Font Bureau Whitman

LIBRARY OF CONGRESS CATALOGING-IN-PUBLICATION DATA
Bone, Martyn, 1974–
 The postsouthern sense of place in contemporary fiction / Martyn Bone.
  p. cm. — (Southern literary studies)
 ISBN 978-0-8071-5634-6 (pbk. : alk. paper) — ISBN 978-0-8071-5635-3 (pdf) —
ISBN 978-0-8071-5636-0 (epub) — ISBN 978-0-8071-5637-7 (mobi)
 1. American fiction—Southern States—History and criticism. 2. American fiction—20th century—History and criticism. 3. Southern States—Intellectual life—1865– 4. Southern States—In literature. 5. Place (Philosophy) in literature. 6. Atlanta (Ga.)—In literature. 7. Local color in literature. 8. Regionalism in literature. 9. Setting (Literature) I. Title. II. Series.
PS261.B58 2005
813'.5093275—dc22

2004021169

The paper in this book meets the guidelines for permanence and durability of the Committee on Production Guidelines for Book Longevity of the Council on Library Resources. ∞

Contents

Preface   vii

PART 1. Capital, Land, and Place from Agrarianism to Postsouthernism

1. "Not a Mere Real Estate Development": Capital, Land, and the Agrarians' Proprietary Ideal   3
2. (Re)inventing the (Post)southern "Sense of Place"   25

PART 2. The Postsouthern Turn: Warren, Percy, Ford, and the Redevelopment of Place

3. Toward a Postsouthern Sense of Place: Robert Penn Warren's *A Place to Come To* and Walker Percy's *The Moviegoer*   55
4. Neo-Faulknerism or Postsouthernism?: Labor, Parody, and the Problem of Place in Richard Ford's *A Piece of My Heart*   75
5. Land and Literary Speculations: The Postsouthern World-as-Text in Richard Ford's *The Sportswriter*   93
6. New Jersey Real Estate and the Postsouthern Sense of Place: Richard Ford's *Independence Day*   117

PART 3. Placing the Postsouthern "International City": The Atlanta Conundrum

7. Locating a Nonplace: Atlanta's Absence from Southern Literature and the Emergence of a Postsouthern "International City"   139
8. Urban Renewal and Mixed-Use Developments: Place and Race in Anne Rivers Siddons's *Peachtree Road* and *Downtown*   170
9. Placing the Postsouthern "International City": Atlanta in Tom Wolfe's *A Man in Full*   192
10. Capitalist Abstraction and the Body Politics of Place: Toni Cade Bambara's *Those Bones Are Not My Child*   219

Epilogue: Against the Agrarian Grain, Taking the Transnational Turn   243

Bibliography   255

Index   269

Preface

It is a truth universally acknowledged among southern literary scholars that "the South" and "southern literature" have been characterized by a "sense of place." By 1996, the Natchez-born novelist Ellen Douglas could note, with a slight air of both bemusement and skepticism, that "Southern writers of fiction and poetry and the critics and academics of the literary world have been talking for a couple of generations about 'Place' and 'the Sense of Place.'" Indeed, "Place, Sense of" has been so integral to southern literary and cultural discourse that it was deemed worthy of its own entry in the monumental *Encyclopedia of Southern Culture* (1989). Historian Charles Reagan Wilson made a valiant attempt to explicate this ubiquitous but usually underdefined concept.[1]

In *The Postsouthern Sense of Place in Contemporary Fiction*, I take a historical-geographical materialist approach to the capitalist production and literary representation of "place" in the American South between the 1960s and the 1990s. I begin, however, by taking a lengthy backward glance at the Agrarians. This might not seem altogether original, given that southern literary critics have so often discussed the Agrarian group and, almost as frequently, distilled their own arguments through Agrarian ideas. But it is precisely the way in which the Agrarians and their neo-Agrarian literary-critical acolytes defined—or, to paraphrase Michael Kreyling, *invented*—southern literary "place" that interests me.[2] In Part One of this book, I suggest that, even now, the standard southern literary-critical conception of "place" derives substantially from the Agrarians' idealized vision of a rural, agricultural society. But more importantly—and more interestingly—I also want to recover an aspect of Agrarian theory that has been ignored or

---

1. Ellen Douglas, "Neighborhoods," in Marion Barnwell, ed., *A Place Called Mississippi: Collected Narratives* (Jackson: University Press of Mississippi, 1997), 456; Charles Reagan Wilson, "Place, Sense of," in William Ferris and Wilson, eds., *The Encyclopedia of Southern Culture* (Chapel Hill: University of North Carolina Press, 1989), 1137–38.

2. Michael Kreyling, *Inventing Southern Literature* (Jackson: University Press of Mississippi, 1998).

suppressed in later southern literary criticism: what historian Paul Conkin has called the Agrarians' "proprietary ideal." In Chapter 1, I reveal how, after 1930 (that is, after the publication of their most famous manifesto, *I'll Take My Stand*), the Agrarians increasingly conceived southern place as agricultural real property, apotheosized in the subsistence farm. John Crowe Ransom, Andrew Lytle, Allen Tate, et al. believed that the rescue and wider realization of this proprietary ideal offered the South's last best hope of surviving the vicissitudes of modern (finance) capitalism.

This increased emphasis upon the economics of place—upon the relationship between "capitalism and land," as Ransom once termed it[3]—had serious repercussions for the fate of Agrarianism itself. Increasingly between 1931 and 1936—the year that they contributed to *Who Owns America?* a second symposium that has received only a fraction of the attention scholars have lavished upon *I'll Take My Stand*—the leading Agrarians tried to transform their proprietary ideal into a social, political, and economic reality. However, this programmatic turn was ambushed by the actual farm policies of the New Deal, and the Agrarian movement disintegrated. Yet despite, or even because of, the resounding failure of practical Agrarianism, recognizing and recovering the original Agrarians' focus on the relationships among capital, land, and place have profound implications for our contemporary understanding of the invention of "southern literature," and the conventional practice of southern literary criticism. For the logic of the proprietary ideal implies that, if subsistence farming fails—if the South's agricultural society capitulates to a money economy, finance-capitalist land speculation, and large-scale real-estate development—then the South's unique sense of "place" expires too. In the second half of Chapter 1, I assess Allen Tate's southern literary criticism between 1935 and 1959, demonstrating how it is informed by exactly this sense that, as contemporary capitalism *dis*placed agricultural real property in the 1930s, so both "the South" and "southern literature" were doomed. This is not to say that, after *Who Owns America?* the ideal of the agricultural South disappeared entirely from social debate, or from literary narrative. I discuss William Faulkner's representation of Eula Varner in *The Hamlet* (1940) in terms of its distinctly Agrarian fantasy that the small-farm South's supposedly virgin land would remain impenetrable to the voracious forces of capitalist land speculation and real-estate development. I show, too, how Robert

---

3. This was the title of an unpublished manuscript written by Ransom in 1931.

Penn Warren's celebrated 1946 review-essay in *The New Republic*, which was instrumental in the reconsideration of Faulkner as a major modernist writer, celebrates and recapitulates this (to use Richard Godden's term) "aesthetics of anti-development" in Faulkner's work.

Nevertheless, when one considers the social, economic, and spatial transformations of "the South" during the 1930s and 1940s, the abject failure of the Agrarians' proprietary ideal, and the pessimism of Allen Tate's hugely influential southern literary criticism, one is compelled to ask how and why "sense of place" thrived as a key concept of southern literary criticism into and after the 1950s, and on identifiably Agrarian terms. As such, Chapter 2 explores the ways in which, as "southern literary studies" emerged and established itself as an academic field, its leading practitioners negotiated different "neo-Agrarian" conceptions of "place." From the 1950s through the 1970s, the doyen—one might even say founding father—of southern literary criticism, Louis D. Rubin, upheld an idealized "image" of the South. By contrast, two other critics who were central to the broadly neo-Agrarian formation of southern literary studies, Walter Sullivan and Thomas Daniel Young, took the grim logic of Tate's eschatological paradigm to its doom-laden limit, bemoaning the death by capitalism of the South, and offering a requiem for "southern literature" and its "sense of place."

No book-length study claiming to offer a critical reassessment of southern literary conceptions of place could ignore Eudora Welty. In the second part of Chapter 2, I assess Welty's own interventions in the discourse upon place, particularly through her critical essays "Some Notes on River Country" (1944) and "Place in Fiction" (1956), and her novel *Losing Battles* (1970). Just as important, though, is how and why critics have appropriated Welty's "aesthetics of place"—or aesthetics of antidevelopment—in order to support and perpetuate a particular neo-Agrarian sense of "the South." I argue that the case of Welty, and *Losing Battles* in particular, indicates the extent to which neo-Agrarian southern literary criticism has been conceptually unable, and ideologically unwilling, to consider seriously the material, geographical redevelopment of the region and the related representational shifts in fiction.

Chapter 2 concludes by theorizing a more contemporary, less conservative approach to reading "postsouthern geographies." Surveying and critiquing literary-critical work on the "postsouthern," from Lewis P. Simpson's coining of the term to its theorization in more recent essays by Kreyling and Scott Romine, I argue that a historical-geographical materialist reworking of this valuable concept can help us to recover the relation between postsouthern literature and the social reality of "place(lessness)" in a late capitalist post-South. I suggest, too, that the recent interdisciplinary boom in theories of place—as evinced in the work of Fredric Jameson, David Harvey, Edward Soja, and others—might be usefully applied to the postsouthern situation.

In Parts 2 and 3 I attempt to apply this theoretical framework as I embark upon what I hope are close readings of eight novels published between 1961 and 1999. I begin by turning in Chapter 3 to a text by one of the original Agrarians: Warren's *A Place to Come To* (1977). Arguing that Warren's last novel can be defined as a postsouthern, parodic interrogation of such foundational concepts as "the South," "southern literature" and "sense of place," I demonstrate that, in *A Place to Come To,* Agrarian signifiers and aesthetics of place, and of antidevelopment, no longer hold. Warren punctures neo-Agrarian nostalgia (not least his own) for agricultural real property by depicting not only the post-1930s decline of farming in the South, but also the way in which farming has become a forum for the conspicuous performance of "southernness" by upper-class socialites and academics. Through the narrator Jed Tewksbury's relationship to South Dakota and Chicago, Warren also deconstructs the familiar Agrarian and southern literary-critical binary opposition between "the South" and "the North," in which the latter is defined negatively as urban, industrial, and "placeless."

This theme links *A Place to Come To* with Walker Percy's *The Moviegoer* (1961). In this brilliant and complex novel, the narrator Binx Bolling initially embraces a postsouthern, suburban sense of place outside his family's historical geography, New Orleans' Garden District. This is not least because Binx himself is a land speculator. However, despite his own involvement in the speculative development of suburbia, Binx becomes seriously disturbed by the capitalist production of postsouthern geographies. Ultimately, and in contrast to Warren's Jed, Binx uses an excursion to "the North"—specifically, Chicago, which he narrates in familiarly negative, neo-Agrarian fashion as a "nonplace"—to recover an ideal "South," and to repress his fear that capitalist development is destroying the southern "sense of place."

Over the course of twenty years and three significant novels, the Mississippi-born novelist Richard Ford has offered the most impressively sustained and sophisticated critique of established notions of "the South" and its supposed "sense of place." In Chapter 4, I develop an in-depth reading of one of Ford's most neglected books, *A Piece of My Heart* (1976). Ford conceived this debut novel as an attempt to deconstruct and move beyond the standard assumptions and parameters of "southern literature." When *A Piece of My Heart* was dismissed by Larry McMurtry as an exercise in "neo-Faulknerism," Ford decided that he would never again write a novel set in the South. Against McMurtry, I argue that *A Piece of My Heart* deliberately parodies William Faulkner's southern literary geography. More than that, though, the novel challenges class-based assumptions about southern place through its representation of the itinerant laboring lives of its central protagonists. In order to explore fully the relationships among class, labor, and place, I compare *A Piece of My Heart* to *The Moviegoer*.

Chapter 5 is devoted to Ford's breakthrough book *The Sportswriter* (1986). In this novel, Ford gets beyond the (literary and geographical) limits of *A Piece of My Heart*—and indeed, "southern literature"—by relocating his narrator Frank Bascombe from Mississippi to New Jersey. One can read *The Sportswriter* in part as a satire on the privileged "placeness" afforded "the South" (over and above "the North") by Binx Bolling in *The Moviegoer*, and by Walker Percy throughout his work. However, Frank reads and writes his wider world as a text that blithely fails to query the production of place and sociospatial relations across "postsouthern America" (as Simpson was the first to call it). Drawing on Joseph Urgo's incisive analysis of the relationship between "land and literary speculation" in Faulkner's life and work, I explicate an equivalence between Frank's financial speculations in New Jersey real estate, and his textual-philosophical speculations in a certain way of seeing, writing and being in the world. This complacent worldview is severely destabilized when Frank encounters geographical uneven development and social inequality during a trip to Detroit and, later, while driving across New Jersey.

In 1995, Ford published a second Bascombe novel, *Independence Day*. In Chapter 6, I argue that, through his new job as a realtor, Frank finally achieves a sophisticated understanding of capitalist property relations, not least the fetishization of "place" as a commodity—a process which, I propose, has parallels to the fetishization of place in southern literary studies. Frank's postsouthern "sense of place" reconfigures Welty's canonical definition of that term, and problematizes Donald Davidson's original Agrarian conception of place as the antithesis of a "mere real estate development." Finally, Frank's revised theory of independence as a sociospatial practice facilitates his own self-placement in an intensely capitalistic postsouthern America.

There is one significant "southern" locus that, perhaps more than any other, has been conspicuously absent—with a couple of deeply ambiguous exceptions—from critics' mental map of "southern literature." As a city, and especially as a city that historically has embraced industrial capitalism on the "northern" and "New South" models, it attracted opprobrium from the Agrarians and their followers. Yet in the contemporary period, when "the South" increasingly is integrated into a dizzying network of global or "transnational" flows—not only of capital, but also of immigrants and their cultures—it seems to me more important to understand this city than ever before. This city—or as its boosters call it, this "international city"—is Atlanta, and Part 3 of *The Postsouthern Sense of Place* constitutes a kind of case study of Atlanta and its literary representations, especially those published in the last fifteen years.

I begin this case study in Chapter 7 by surveying Atlanta's historical-geographical development as an aggressively capitalist "New South" city, and I consider how and why this has contributed to Atlanta's anomalous status—what I call, with a consciously Percyan echo, its "nonplace"—in the canonical cartography of "southern literature." The first half of Chapter 7 also provides brief readings of the relationships among capital, land, and place in the two most prominent Atlanta fictions, Margaret Mitchell's *Gone with the Wind* (1936) and Flannery O'Connor's "The Artificial Nigger" (1955). I also, though, look at another text that is considerably less well known, arguably for reasons bound up with the neo-Agrarian cultural politics of southern literary canonization: Donald Windham's debut novel *The Dog Star* (1950). In the second half of Chapter 7, I consider the emergence since the 1960s of what I term the postsouthern "international city." I assess the scale of capitalist investment in, and redevelopment of, Atlanta, and the city's entry into the "space of flows" (Manuel Castells) of globalized financial exchange. Building upon the premise that Atlanta's burgeoning status as a global capital of capital makes it especially amenable to a postsouthern approach to place and its narrative representation, I suggest that such an approach might usefully range from the local to the global: from a critical analysis of the creative destruction and racial-spatial division of Atlanta's material geography, to what geographer Doreen Massey has termed a "global sense of place," a wider perspective that (among other things) takes into account the city's more abstract role in the globalization of capital flows.

Ten years before the publication of Tom Wolfe's much-hyped "Atlanta novel" *A Man in Full*, the "popular" novelist and Atlanta resident Anne Rivers Siddons published a sweeping historical novel, *Peachtree Road* (1988), that powerfully depicts the shift from the "New South" city of the 1930s to the postsouthern metropolis of multinational capital and mixed-use developments that emerged between the 1960s and the 1980s. In Chapter 8, I turn my attention to *Peachtree Road* as well as to a subsequent Siddons novel that constitutes a peculiar (or as I call it, "palimpscestuous") sequel of sorts, *Downtown* (1995). I argue that, for all its value as a powerful narrative map of Atlanta's postsouthern, "international" redevelopment, *Peachtree Road* constructs a distinctly idealized vision of the city's historical-geographical development. *Peachtree Road*'s selective rendering of Atlanta is driven by a hagiographic image of the white, upper class, civic-corporate "power structure" that presided over the city until the early 1970s. In both *Peachtree Road* and *Downtown,* this ideological bias is manifested in Siddons's (non-)representation of inner city "urban renewal" in the 1960s and the large-scale commercial redevelopment of Atlanta—under local black political leadership—in the 1980s.

A Man in Full, published in 1998, drew attention to Atlanta as had no other novel since *Gone with the Wind*. Like Mitchell, Wolfe represents capitalist land speculation and real-estate development through the actions and perspective of the novel's protagonist (in Mitchell's case, the lumber merchant Scarlett O'Hara; in Wolfe's, the property developer Charlie Croker). In Chapter 9, drawing especially on the theoretical work of Jameson and Castells, I demonstrate how, in *A Man in Full,* capitalist abstraction—as mediated through mixed-use developments, and as manifested in the finance-capitalist "space of flows"—produces a "sense of placelessness," a feeling that, in Marx's and Engels's seminal phrase, "all that is solid melts into air."[4] But the novel also encompasses less glamorous loci that exist within or on the borders of the "international city." In doing so, *A Man in Full* reveals (though not without exhibiting certain formal and ideological limitations of its own) the harsh realities of class and labor that survive in the postsouthern metropolis and identifies the immigrant population of "Chambodia" as an alternative "international" Atlanta.

Toni Cade Bambara's posthumously published *Those Bones Are Not My Child* (1999) is an epic meditation upon the Atlanta Child Murders of 1979–1981. Bambara (like Wolfe) also emphasizes and explicates the power of capitalist abstraction in the "international city." In Chapter 10, I reveal how *Those Bones* maps the tensions between the global and the local: between Atlanta's global economic status and its local, material realities of spatial and

---

4. Karl Marx and Frederick Engels, *The Communist Manifesto* (1848; reprint, London: Verso, 1998), 39.

racial inequality. Drawing on the classic theoretical formulations of Mikhail Bakhtin and the recent work in southern literary studies of Patricia Yaeger, I demonstrate how Bambara develops a grotesque body politics of place to interrogate and indict purely economic definitions of international Atlanta. Central characters in *Those Bones* resituate Atlanta in a much more critical global framework, relating the so-called international city to other global urban sites of economic and racial inequality. In the process, both the characters and Bambara herself enact the global sense of place theorized by Massey.

Of the novels discussed in *The Postsouthern Sense of Place*, two in particular, *A Man in Full* and *Those Bones Are Not My Child*, bring into focus the transnational flows of capital and immigrants into the region that we have known as "the South." In a short epilogue, I ponder more explicitly the relationship between postsouthernism and transnationalism, and I offer a provisional (though, I hope, not prescriptive) assessment of the advantages that might accrue from a "transnational turn" in southern literary studies. Noting that a transnational turn in the South must extend its critical gaze beyond Atlanta, I make a modest attempt to analyze the role of transnational capital and labor relations in contemporary rural Kentucky, as depicted in Barbara Kingsolver's *Prodigal Summer* (2000). The emphasis here on Kingsolver's representation of the rural, agricultural South also emerges out of another issue considered in the epilogue: the danger that revisionist, postsouthern readings of place uncritically reproduce the city-centric bias of postmodern spatial theory. I attempt to resolve this conundrum, without having recourse to neo-Agrarian southern literary(-critical) representations of the region, by reading *Prodigal Summer* and Harry Crews's memoir *A Childhood: The Biography of a Place* (1978) as texts that reconstruct rural, agricultural "place" in ways that go against the Agrarian grain.

This book emerged out of a doctoral dissertation undertaken at the University of Nottingham in England but mostly written while living and working in Copenhagen, Denmark. I would like to thank my supervisors at the University of Nottingham, Professor Richard H. King and Professor Peter Messent, for intellectual guidance and generous sacrifice of time (albeit more often involving e-mail exchanges across the North Sea than "face time"). I also want to extend my appreciation to those other scholars in England, the United States, and Denmark who read and commented on various parts of this project at different stages of its development: David Murray, Richard Godden, Sharon Monteith, Drew Whitelegg, Paul Grainge (my best man in more than one sense), Suzanne Jones, Scott Romine, and Martin Leer. Of course, any over-zealousness or sheer wrong-headedness in the argument that follows is mine alone. Also deserving of a shout out are those friends and Ph.D. peers at Nottingham who endured discussions of this project and/or provided comic relief at crucial moments: Paul Grainge again, James Lyons, Helen Oakley, John Place, and Luca Prono.

I wish to acknowledge the generous financial support of the Arts and Humanities Research Board in England. Also much appreciated was additional funding from the AHRB and the University of Nottingham that allowed me to undertake a research trip to Atlanta. Further funding from Nottingham, and from the University of Copenhagen, allowed me to present papers based on parts of this book at various conferences in the United States, Great Britain, and Denmark. I would also like to extend my thanks to the staffs of the following libraries for their diligent assistance: the Hallward Library at the University of Nottingham; Det Kongelige Bibliotek in Copenhagen; the Margaret Mitchell Library in Atlanta; and the British Library in London for supplying interlibrary loans. I wish to thank various members of the Louisiana State University Press editorial staff past and present—John Easterly, Maureen Hewitt, Sylvia Frank Rodrigue, and George Roupe—for their interest and encouragement. As copyeditor, Ruth Laney went a long way to rectifying the stylistic and grammatical weaknesses of the manuscript; any outstanding failings are my fault alone. Fred Hobson and a second, anonymous reader provided generous and cogent commentary on the manuscript.

Parts of this book have been published in different form elsewhere. Early versions of sections from Chapters 3 and 5 were published as "The Postsouthern Sense of Place in Walker Percy's *The Moviegoer* and Richard Ford's *The Sportswriter*" in *Critical Survey*, volume 12, number 1 (2000). I thank Berghahn Journals for permission to reprint that material here. An earlier version of Chapter 6 was published in a special "southern issue" of *American Studies in Scandinavia*, volume 33, number 2 (2001); the Nordic Association of American Studies gave me its permission to reprint. A different version of Chapter 9 was published in *South to a New Place: Region, Literature, Culture* (Baton Rouge: Louisiana State University Press, 2002), edited by Suzanne Jones and Sharon Monteith. An edited version of Chapter 10 was published in *Journal of American Studies*, volume 37, number 2 (August 2003), for which I thank Cambridge University Press for its permission to reprint.

* * *

Finally, and most importantly, I thank my parents Janet and Raymond; my wife Anna Mia; and my children Samuel and Rosa. My parents have provided emotional and (at key moments) financial support beyond the call of familial duty. Anna Mia was with me, though not yet my wife, when this project started; Samuel came along nearly two years into the Ph.D.; Rosa was born when final revisions to the book manuscript were under way (that is, dragging out). I'm not entirely sure that it's healthy to divide my family life according to the progression of this project. But I do know that, whether in Nottingham or Copenhagen, the presence of my wife and children has brought home to me the wise words of those seminal spatial theorists Teenage Fanclub: "Your love is the place I come from." Tusind tak for det hele, I tre.

PART ONE

Capital, Land, and Place from Agrarianism to Postsouthernism

1. "Not a Mere Real Estate Development": Capital, Land, and the Agrarians' Proprietary Ideal

In "The Irrepressible Conflict," his contribution to *I'll Take My Stand: The South and the Agrarian Tradition* (1930), historian Frank Owsley wrote that "[w]hen America was settled, the tradition of the soil found hospitable rootbed in the Southern colonies, where climate and land combined to multiply the richness of an agrarian economy.... Thoughts, words, ideas, concepts, life itself, grew from the soil." Here, Owsley presents a traditional South, and an economic system, that was at one with nature. The "richness" of the region's "agrarian economy" fairly burst forth from the South's fecund loam. But Owsley and his fellow Agrarians never—any more than the early colonists Owsley describes—"discovered a 'natural' order" in the South's physical geography. As Michael Kreyling has observed, they themselves invented this supposedly "natural," "organic" South. Thus the Agrarian construction of "the South" is often as notable for what it excludes as for what it includes. To cite only one glaring example, when Owsley refers to southerners' "endless enjoyment of the fruits of the soil," he fails to mention the slave labor often involved in farming these "fruits." For Owsley to maintain his image of a "natural" society, this strategic exclusion is a structural and ideological necessity.[1]

Throughout *I'll Take My Stand*, both slavery and postbellum race relations jeopardize the Agrarians' collective effort to construct "the South and the Agrarian Tradition" as natural and benevolent. John Crowe Ransom attempts to slide smoothly from "the social organization" of "squirearchy" into the supposedly natural relations of master and slave: "people were for the most part in their right places. Slavery was a feature monstrous enough in theory, but, more often than not, humane in practice." In "The Briar Patch," Robert Penn Warren provides rhetorical sanction for racial segregation by arguing that "the small town and farm" was the natural, biological, even metaphysical, "place" for "the Southern negro." Warren concludes: "That is where he

1. Frank Owsley, "The Irrepressible Conflict," in Twelve Southerners, *I'll Take My Stand* (1930; reprint, Baton Rouge: Louisiana State University Press, 1977), 69; Kreyling, *Inventing Southern Literature*, 6.

still chiefly belongs, by temperament and capacity; there he . . . is likely to find in agricultural and domestic pursuits the happiness that his good nature and easy ways incline him to as an ordinary function of his being." Ransom and Warren's essays exemplify the pernicious way in which, as Charles Reagan Wilson has noted, "southern whites [have] frequently used *place* to indicate the status of blacks."[2]

The Agrarians' "natural" rhetoric also failed to obscure what Richard Gray has called the "doubleness" running through *I'll Take My Stand*'s representation(s) of "the regional tradition." The Twelve Southerners' vision of "the South and the Agrarian Tradition" is divided between the antebellum plantation and, more usually, the yeoman farm—or, in some cases, it includes an unconvincing admixture of both. Stark Young claims that "our traditional Southern characteristics derive from the landed class." This class bias led Young to confront the thorny issue of slavery more explicitly than Ransom did; he acknowledged that "we are talking largely of a certain life in the Old South, a life founded on land and the ownership of slaves." In stark contrast to Young, who damns the "respectable and sturdy" yeomanry with faint praise and scorns the "shiftless" poor whites, Andrew Lytle sees the South's man at the center as the small farmer. Somewhere in between, Owsley describes a South that, presumably by virtue of being "close to the soil," could naturally encompass both the plantation *and* the small farm.[3]

These divisions and elisions in Agrarian thought circa 1930 have been well documented by Gray and other scholars. I have touched on them here in order to make an important point that serves as the springboard for the argument that follows. My point is that, whatever the fraught and flagrant problems regarding the place of "race" (or the race of "place"), and however difficult the farm/plantation dichotomy, the Twelve Southerners were compelled to construct "the Agrarian Tradition" along these complicated and often contradictory lines because they feared the impact of modern capitalism upon the contemporary South. In this opening chapter, I will argue that Agrarian images of southern "place" were conceived primarily as

---

2. John Crowe Ransom, "Reconstructed but Unregenerate," *I'll Take My Stand,* 14; Robert Penn Warren, "The Briar Patch," *I'll Take My Stand,* 260–61; Wilson, "Place, Sense of," 1137.

3. Richard Gray, *The Literature of Memory: Modern Writers of the American South* (London: Edward Arnold, 1977), 50; Stark Young, "Not in Memoriam, but in Defense," *I'll Take My Stand,* 337, 336; Owsley, "The Irrepressible Conflict," 71. Gray explicates these divisions in both *Literature of Memory,* 50–54, and *Writing the South: Ideas of an American Region* (1986; reprint, Baton Rouge: Louisiana State University Press, 1998), 134–38.

a bulwark against capitalism and the threat it posed to the region's relatively stable, largely rural social geography—or perhaps more pertinently, to the *idea* of such a "southern" geography. Especially *after* the publication of *I'll Take My Stand,* the Agrarians conceived (or invented) their "South" as a site of resistance to capitalism's destruction of "place" through land speculation, real-estate development, urbanization, and industrialism. Taking a cue from historian Paul Conkin, I want to recover the Agrarians' specific, economic vision of "place" as agricultural real property. Increasingly in the 1930s, the Agrarian sense of place was of a rural, self-sufficient and nigh-on precapitalist locus focused upon the small farm, operating largely outside the cash nexus, and absent large-scale land speculation. As Conkin observes, this "proprietary ideal" is an important element of Agrarianism that "has received scant attention from historians and literary critics."⁴

Agricultural Real Property: The Agrarian Aesthetics and Politics of Antidevelopment, 1930–40

The underlying link between anticapitalism and the Agrarians' "naturalization" (that is, ideological construction) of "the South and the Agrarian Tradition" in *I'll Take My Stand* becomes more transparent when one considers, as Richard Gray does, how the Twelve Southerners' rhetoric regularly opposes an "organic," "spontaneous," and "rooted" region to the "artificial, mechanical" characteristics of an urban, industrial society. Whether this urban, industrial society is identified as the North or the New South, it supposedly denies "all bonds and connections other than the economic." In a typical example, *I'll Take My Stand*'s introductory "Statement of Principles" contrasts the South's culture of the soil with "nature industrialized, transformed into cities and artificial habitations, manufactured into commodities . . . no longer nature but a highly simplified picture of nature."⁵

Through this overarching antipathy to a city-centered "industrialism"—"Agrarian *versus* Industrial," in the introduction's basic binary opposition—the Twelve Southerners' various images of a rural, agrarian South attain some cohesion. Yet it is notable that the Agrarians rarely criticize capitalism per se in *I'll Take My Stand.* Ransom identifies a "poverty of the contemporary

4. Paul K. Conkin, *The Southern Agrarians* (Knoxville: University of Tennessee Press, 1988), 90.

5. Gray, *Literature of Memory,* 46, and *Writing the South,* 154; "Introduction: Statement of Principles," *I'll Take My Stand,* xlii.

spirit . . . located at [society's] economic base," but attributes it to "industrialism," not capitalism.⁶ Such rhetorical obfuscation may partly explain why scholars have fudged, finessed, or simply failed to perceive the Agrarians' anticapitalist impulse. However, it also indicates that the Agrarians were not *absolute* anticapitalists. They were against industrialization, urbanization, and land speculation as manifestations of, in Richard King's words, "the modern economy of industrial and financial capitalism." As King observes, while the Agrarians were "not explicitly anticapitalist," they took their stand against modern forms of capitalism— industrialism and finance capitalism—by promoting the vision of "an agrarian order based upon personal private property and held together by the cooperation of planter and yeoman."⁷

In *I'll Take My Stand*, Owsley's antebellum agrarian society is a place "where land, water, and timber were practically free." The cash nexus and land speculators were not merely absent: they were not required. It is in this sense—as part of a nonspeculative, land-centered South contrasting with the "abstract" property relations of contemporary capitalism—that the Agrarians could celebrate the plantation *alongside* the small farm, in the process obscuring the divisive "doubleness" *between* the planter and the yeoman farmer. Having said that, *I'll Take My Stand*'s anti-"industrialism" is filtered chiefly through a celebration of the farmer's "place" in the South, over and above the planter's. For all that Ransom cites a hierarchy of "right places," he concentrates primarily upon the yeoman and his "farm or native province." Ransom expresses his concern that this "substantial" (albeit small-scale), rooted, and localized form of southern social relations will be abstracted out of existence in the marketplace: "a pile of money, a volume of produce, a market, or a

---

6. "Introduction: Statement of Principles," *I'll Take My Stand*, xliii. Though Donald Davidson and Andrew Lytle were also assigned to write the introduction, the final version was almost entirely Ransom's. Both Ransom and Davidson had been using "the term 'industrialism' as a sweeping label for all the evils that threatened the South" since 1927 (Conkin, *The Southern Agrarians*, 36).

7. Richard H. King, *A Southern Renaissance: The Cultural Awakening of the American South, 1930–1955* (New York: Oxford University Press, 1980), 52. As Mark Jancovich notes, the Agrarians also "drew upon critiques of capitalist relations produced by the pre-capitalist social classes of the South." This historical, ideological source helps to account for the Agrarians' idealized representations of the region (past and present) as a rural, agricultural, even precapitalist locus. See Jancovich, *The Cultural Politics of the New Criticism* (Cambridge: Cambridge University Press, 1993), 12, and Gray, *Writing the South*, 147–58, on the relation between the Agrarians and earlier proslavery, anticapitalist advocates.

credit system. It is into precisely these intangibles that industrialism would translate the farmer's farm."[8]

The southern small farmer is most celebrated, and the antipathy to capitalist (not just "industrial") land speculation is most explicit, in Lytle's "The Hind Tit." Here, Lytle advocates subsistence farming as the South's last best hope of remaining outside a "money economy" that threatens to transform landowning farmers into mere tenants, "abstract selves" ripe for exploitation by the "absentee-landlordism of capitalism." Lytle even expresses disdain for the southern planter, arguing that antebellum cotton snobs who "bought freely from England and the North" were responsible for opening the South to a money economy. According to Lytle, this led to "the farming South, the yeoman South, that great body of free men, [who once] had hardly anything to do with the capitalists and their merchandise," losing their farms to land speculators and absentee landlords. The second section of "The Hind Tit" is the symposium's most strident attempt to evoke everyday life in an agrarian locus outside the cash (or credit) nexus, and beyond the scope of land speculators. Richard Godden has brilliantly explicated Lytle's detailed description of sallet, an authentic Tennessee country crop (as opposed to "the fancy-tin can salads" of "industrialism"), in terms of a "Southern aesthetic of antidevelopment" whose "magic defends it from capitalist rationality." A similar magical—or mystifying—aesthetic informs Lytle's aphoristic celebration of corn as an anticommodity that epitomizes and apotheosizes the subsistence farm, thereby somehow ensuring a rooted, organic, "natural" sense of place outside the abstract and rational (that is, *un*natural) capitalist marketplace: "A farm is not a place to grow wealthy; it is a place to grow corn."[9]

Lytle's call to resist the "absentee-landlordism" of real-estate speculators through subsistence farming testifies to what Godden calls the Agrarians' "literary preoccupation with land ownership." Though this preoccupation emerged more clearly later in the decade, cohering around what Conkin calls the "proprietary ideal," one can find other examples among the less famous contributions to *I'll Take My Stand*. For example, Owsley suggests that the Old South felt an affinity with the Roman farmers "of the early republic, before land speculators . . . had driven men from the soil to the city slums." The

---

8. Owsley, "The Irrepressible Conflict," 88; Ransom, "Reconstructed but Unregenerate," 20.

9. Andrew Lytle, "The Hind Tit," *I'll Take My Stand*, 243, 208, 226; Richard Godden, *Fictions of Capital: The American Novel from James to Mailer* (Cambridge: Cambridge University Press, 1998), 143–44; Lytle, "The Hind Tit," 205.

implication is that an even more onerous form of their spiritual ancestors' fate threatens self-sufficient farmers of the South in 1930. Meanwhile, Herman Nixon describes how the Civil War had "destroyed real-estate values, not only with serious damage to pre-war owners, but with a consequential jungle of speculation, promotion and 'booms.'" Nixon warns that "[t]he South's passive indifference to industrialism is not adequate to withstand realtors' activities" and that, "unless the traditional leanings toward agrarianism are reinforced," the shift in the "Southern perspective toward a bourgeois materialism" will be irreversible.[10]

It is highly debatable whether such images of a traditional agrarian South standing firmly rooted against the abstracting, displacing tendencies of capitalist land speculation had any historical basis. In *Old South, New South* (1986), economic historian Gavin Wright points out that southern slave owners were *human* capitalists: their investment was concentrated chiefly in slaves rather than land. As such, many slaveholding planters were in fact highly mobile; *pace* Stark Young, they were only secondarily "founded on land." Wright comments that "[t]his is the economic essence of the distinction between real and personal property, slaves almost always having been classified as the latter. . . . Slavery generated a weaker and looser connection between property holders and the land they occupied." Hence, Wright argues, because "[s]laveholding farmers and planters moved from place to place so often they seldom had time to sink roots," so "the passionate southern attachment to the soil" must be regarded as "a post–Civil War phenomenon." What is more, any such postbellum attachment to the soil must have been grounded in the *economic* shift from human property to real property. Because Emancipation destroyed human capitalism, landowners (large *and* small) turned to "raising land yields and land values in particular localities." So, whereas Lytle sees the shift from subsistence farming to cash cropping as a pernicious influence of an unnatural, nonsouthern money economy, Wright notes that this change—usually from corn to cotton—resulted from "the effort of landlords to raise the value of their land's product." Similarly, whereas Owsley implies that "land speculators" threatened a supposedly precapitalist, property-based, rural "South," Wright insists that, after 1865, both farming and town building were basically real-estate ventures. Owsley presents the speculators as outsiders; Wright reveals that these ventures were initiated by southern landowners themselves,

---

10. Godden, *Fictions of Capital*, 140; Owsley, "The Irrepressible Conflict," 70; H. C. Nixon, "Whither Southern Economy?" *I'll Take My Stand*, 188, 199, 189.

and designed to boost the value of their own real estate. All told, *Old South, New South* helps to reveal how *I'll Take My Stand*'s history of southern property relations is, to put it mildly, selective.[11]

It can be argued—as we shall see in Chapter 2, it *has* been argued by Louis D. Rubin—that the divergences between *I'll Take My Stand*'s "South(s)" and historical-geographical reality are irrelevant. One might argue (as Rubin does) that the Agrarians' image of their region is a poetic form of polemic. However, there is a basic flaw to such an argument. For after *I'll Take My Stand* appeared, the Agrarians themselves went on to formulate a far more programmatic sense of southern place concentrated upon the kind of small subsistence farms vividly evoked in "The Hind Tit." As Conkin has observed, "[o]ut of this would develop a true agrarian program, one tied to land reform and property restoration. By the most precise use of the terms, a southern agrarian movement was born only in 1933 and burned itself out over the next four years." In answer to Scott Romine's pointed question—"were farms necessary" to "the Agrarian mythology of place"?—I would suggest that they were, very much so, as the centerpiece and bulwark of what Conkin calls the "proprietary ideal." Romine rightly notes that the Agrarian critique of capitalism could never countenance a "causal relationship between base and superstructure" (it would have been perilously close to Marxism). Nonetheless, I want to emphasize that the Agrarian sense of southern "place" as land was not based only upon vaguely religious "[t]ropes of organic emergence." Increasingly after 1930, Agrarian theory featured a key economic component focused on the relations of capital, land, and place. Stung by accusations that they were merely armchair critics, yet feeling vindicated by the Wall Street crash, the Agrarians tied their programmatic turn to a more explicit critique of the destabilizing, displacing influences of "finance capitalism" or "monopoly capitalism" (no longer merely "industrialism").[12]

In 1935, Donald Davidson admitted that "our programme for the farm was not much particularized in the book [*I'll Take My Stand*] itself." However, Davidson insisted, "most of the contributors, through whatever media have

---

11. Gavin Wright, *Old South, New South: Revolutions in the Southern Economy since the Civil War* (1986; reprint, Baton Rouge: Louisiana State University Press, 1996), 17, vii, vi, 34, 36. On the extent to which slave property value outstripped real property value in antebellum southern states, see Wright, 19.

12. Conkin, *The Southern Agrarians*, 89–90; Scott Romine, "Where Is Southern Literature?: The Practice of Place in a Postsouthern Age," *Critical Survey* 12, no. 1 (spring 2000): 12–13.

been open to them, in recent years have pushed the principles of agrarianism far beyond the point represented in *I'll Take My Stand* and have made proposals about as specific as could be expected from men who do not have the good fortune to be members of Congress or of the Brain Trust." In particular, Davidson pointed to John Crowe Ransom, who "throughout 1930 and 1931 argued for a kind of subsistence farming." If, as Conkin claims, a true Agrarian movement coalesced only in 1933, then Ransom was very much in the vanguard. In 1931, he read some back-to-the-land books written during the early Depression, and was sufficiently inspired to write his own (ultimately unpublished) economic treatise, "Capitalism and Land." In 1932, *Harper's* printed Ransom's article, "Land! An Answer to the Unemployment Problem." Here, Ransom criticized "the substitution of the capitalistic or money economy for the self-subsistent or agrarian economy" during World War I.[13]

Again, one might question the historical accuracy and ideological bent of such a statement. As Wright reveals, the "substitution" of cash crops for subsistence farming had been well under way since the end of the Civil War. Nonetheless, Ransom's rubric recognizably has altered to enable a more direct attack on capitalist land-use. Moving further away from his earlier "South" of hierarchical "right places," Ransom emphasizes the deleterious impact of "capitalistic farming," with its excessive devotion to "money crops," upon a "self-subsistent" way of yeoman farming. Rearticulating Lytle's vision of small subsistence farms operating largely outside the cash nexus, "Land!" invokes "generations of men who . . . lived in what they often regarded as comfort and dignity on the soil without the use of a great deal of money for purchasing goods upon the market." Ultimately, Ransom calls for no less than an "agrarian agitation" intended to "re-establish self-sufficiency as the proper economy for the American farm." If this form of sociospatial relations would not be entirely pre- or anticapitalist, it would be close enough.[14]

The varying Agrarian visions of "the South" were rapidly converging on the "proprietary ideal . . . land or other means of production under the full

13. Donald Davidson, "*I'll Take My Stand:* A History," *American Review* 5 (1935): 317–18; Ransom, "Land! An Answer to the Unemployment Problem," *Harper's* 165 (July 1932): 219. See also Conkin, *The Southern Agrarians*, 100–101.

14. Ransom, "Land!" 219, 221. Ransom does not, however, call for complete subsistence farming. Ransom's moderation on this point was also evident in 1933 when he stated, "Agrarianism means old-fashioned farming; or the combination of a subsistence farming of the first place with a money farming of the second." See Ransom, "Happy Farmers," *American Review* 1 (October 1933): 527–28.

managerial control of the individual owners."[15] If this had been implicit in *I'll Take My Stand,* it now became, as Ransom's "Land!" essay anticipated, absolutely central—so much so that, in his 1936 essay "The South Is a Bulwark," Ransom acknowledges the somewhat "wearisome iteration" of subsistence farming as *the* proprietary ideal in recent Agrarian essays.[16] The culmination and apogee of practical Agrarianism—particularly its conception of agricultural real property as a bulwark against finance-capitalist land speculation and abstraction—came in 1935, with the publication and genuine political influence of Frank Owsley's "The Pillars of Agrarianism." In order to safeguard "[s]ubsistence farming [as] the first objective of every man who controls a farm or plantation," Owsley suggests that the state should offer landless tenants eighty acres and two mules (plus two cows and living expenses). Owsley adds that, if subsistence farming is to succeed, "[i]t must become impossible for land to be sold to real estate and insurance companies or banks."[17] As Conkin observes, "The Pillars of Agrarianism" was "the closest the [Agrarian] group ever came to endorsing specific remedies for agricultural distress in the South." Owsley's essay was distributed to and lauded by Alabama senator John Bankhead, whose Bankhead-Jones Farm Tenancy Act of 1936 provided loans enabling tenants to buy their own land.[18]

The extent to which the Agrarians now conceived of the agricultural proprietary ideal as a safeguard against "alienation of the soil"[19] resulting from finance-capitalist land speculation is consistently apparent in *Who Owns America?* (1936). This was a second symposium featuring eight of the original Twelve Southerners, Agrarian sympathizers George Marion O'Donnell and Cleanth Brooks, and some Distributists. *Who Owns America?* also reveals

---

15. Conkin, *The Southern Agrarians,* 106.
16. Ransom, "The South Is a Bulwark," *Scribner's* 99 (May 1936), 302.
17. Owsley, "The Pillars of Agrarianism," *American Review* 4 (March 1935), 539, 537, 539.
18. Conkin, *The Southern Agrarians,* 113. As renegade Agrarian cum New Deal advocate Herman Nixon observed enthusiastically in 1936, the Bankhead-Jones bill "was designed to transform worthy tenants, croppers, and farm laborers into land-owning farmers under government financial sponsorship with low rates of interest and long terms for payment." It is striking and surprising—given the more familiar Agrarian (in particular, Davidsonian) view of the state as "Leviathan"—that "The Pillars of Agrarianism" shares Nixon's taste for state intervention. See Herman Nixon, "From Tenancy to the Forefront" (1936), in Emily Bingham and Thomas Underwood, eds., *The Southern Agrarians and the New Deal: Essays after "I'll Take My Stand"* (Charlottesville: University Press of Virginia, 2001), 169.
19. Owsley, "Pillars of Agrarianism," 539.

just how comprehensively the Agrarians had excised Young's aristocratic plantation in favor of Lytle's small subsistence farm.[20] Much as "The Hind Tit" attacked *ante*bellum planters for exposing the South to a "money economy," O'Donnell's "Looking Down the Cotton Row" criticizes *post*bellum "Big Business" planters for "deserting the agrarian economy deliberately in order to share in the great profits of a money economy dominated by finance-capitalism." In O'Donnell's essay, as throughout the volume, the small farm is configured as a self-sufficient site of resistance to the cash nexus and finance-capitalist land speculation. For O'Donnell, as for Lytle, an agrarian economy was not about profit; rather, it was "the economy of men who love the land and who derive their whole sustenance from it." As such, it was best expressed by the subsistent yeoman farmer who "possesses liberty based on property—the only true liberty."[21]

20. Indeed, "the South" per se was deemphasized in *Who Owns America?* as the Agrarians attempted to establish the "alliances with sympathetic communities everywhere" mooted earlier in *I'll Take My Stand*'s "Statement of Principles" (xxxix). Already in 1934, Ransom had adumbrated a more general "aesthetic of regionalism" that referred to New Mexico Indians rather than white southerners. But this aesthetic saw the Indians in familiar terms, as subsistence farmers living largely outside the cash nexus: "So this was regionalism; flourishing on the meanest capital . . . they have sufficient means, and they are without that special insecurity which white men continually talk about, and which has to do with such mysterious things as the price of wheat." Ransom, "The Aesthetic of Regionalism," *American Review* 2 (January 1934): 291. Writing elsewhere in 1936, Ransom explicitly acknowledged the "Americanization" of the previously "Southern" proprietary ideal: "[t]he new book *[Who Owns America?]* is not written with peculiar reference to the South . . . it advances doctrines 100 per cent pure American." But, of course, such doctrines remained especially "congenial to Southern habits of mind." Ransom, "The South Is a Bulwark," 301.

21. George Marion O'Donnell, "Looking Down the Cotton Row," in Herbert Agar and Allen Tate, eds., *Who Owns America?: A New Declaration of Independence* (1936; reprint, Wilmington, Del.: ISI Books, 1999), 212–13, 215, 221. Reminding us that the Agrarians were not against capitalism per se but monopoly- or finance-capitalism, O'Donnell acknowledges that even the yeoman subsistence farmer was a capitalist "since he owns his own land, and since he may have a tenant or so." But O'Donnell added the qualification that the farmer was not a capitalist "since his main concern is not to exploit his capital and his labor for a money income but to use them in making a living in goods" (220–21). Subsistence farming is thus valued to the degree that the cash nexus or "money economy" is minimized.

There is an irony lurking within Agrarianism's equation of liberty with property: the echo of nineteenth-century *northern* republicanism—though, as Gavin Wright notes, the idea that liberty came with property had largely been abandoned in the North by this point (Wright, *Old South, New South,* 113). The republican rhetoric of liberty through property enabled the

In "The Small Farm Secures the State," Lytle himself lays down the key tenet of the Agrarian proprietary ideal: "It [the small farm] is the norm by which all real property may be best defined." Much as the agrarian South was shown to be more "natural" than urban, industrial society in *I'll Take My Stand*, so in *Who Owns America?* self-sufficient farms, the epitome of real property, are more "real" than capitalist real estate. Although Lytle's small farm "norm" was more Agrarian textual ideal than social reality, the ruthless (and rigid) binary pattern of Agrarian rhetoric was effective in defining agricultural real property as the "concrete" antithesis of unnatural, "abstract" capitalist real estate. Robert Penn Warren and Allen Tate's contributions to *Who Owns America?* follow Lytle's advice in full. Warren argues that "real property" guarantees "the relation of man to place," unlike the "abstract property" relations of finance capitalism. Tate, like Lytle, refers to the "familiar, historical" small farm as "real private property." A "thirty-acre farm in Kentucky" (the southern agricultural example is hardly accidental) is a "tangible" and "genuine" material geography. It stands in contrast to "giant corporate property," which is very often not even real in any material sense, but something abstract, such as "a stock certificate in the United States steel corporation." The stockholder's tenuous relation to his property as an intangible commodity on the market has replaced the farmer's individual ownership of his land, and the use-value of that land. The farmer has been uprooted and alienated from his "stable basis" in agricultural society by a "finance-capitalism [that] has become . . . top-heavy with a crazy jigsaw network of exchange-value." This critique of finance-capitalist property speculation echoes Lytle's earlier attack on the "money economy" and "absentee-landlordism" in "The Hind Tit." The difference is that, like Ransom in "Land!" Tate attempts to go beyond the largely rhetorical binaries familiar from *I'll Take My Stand* (i.e., abstract "industrialism" versus concrete agrarianism) to begin engaging with economic and social theory.[22]

By 1936, then, the Agrarians had developed a much more stringent critique of monopoly- and finance-capitalism, bolstering this critique with

---

Agrarians to deemphasize their "southernness" (see also note 20) and portray themselves as the true heirs of Jeffersonian "Americanism."

22. Lytle, "The Small Farm Secures the State," in *Who Owns America?* 310; Warren, "Literature as a Symptom," in *Who Owns America?* 354; Tate, "Notes on Liberty and Property," in *Who Owns America?* 112–13, 115. Tate cites two recent studies of capitalism and corporate property. On Ransom's liking for "ruthless binary thinking," see Kreyling, *Inventing Southern Literature*, 12, 20.

a more concentrated and consistent argument for the practical restoration of subsistence farming. Explicitly emphasizing the economic-geographic difference that distinguished the South (and other agrarian cultures) from urban, industrial America, the Agrarians were less likely to have recourse to hazy "natural" rhetoric. At one point in "Land!" Ransom notes wryly that "[i]t is tempting to write like a poet . . . about the aesthetic and spiritual deliverance that will come when the industrial laborers with their specialized and routine jobs and the business men with their offices and abstract preoccupations become translated into people handling the soil with their fingers and coming into direct contact with nature." Such a sentence reads like an ironic indictment of *I'll Take My Stand*'s aesthetics of antidevelopment.[23]

However, the more rigorous, socioeconomic focus put the Agrarian idea of the South in a perilous position. The programmatic turn in *Who Owns America?* implies that if the redemption of the small farm fails, the South as a distinct entity is doomed to death by finance- capitalism. The Agrarian argument had reached a high pitch at which the contrast between a rooted, rural society and abstract, urbanizing land speculation could not be reconciled, either practically or poetically. The South, with its supposed "relation of man to place," would survive on agricultural real property, or it would succumb to capitalist land speculation and development. There was no middle ground, whether material or metaphorical.

For all the Agrarians' "desperate optimism," as Alfred Kazin once called it, their practical proposals proved to be futile.[24] The Great Depression of the 1930s made the prospect of establishing a Jeffersonian republic of self-sufficient small farms bleaker than ever. In "The Pillars of Agrarianism," Owsley observed that "[t]he majority of the planters do not really own their lands; the real owners are the life insurance companies or the banks."[25] In 1932 alone—the year Ransom published "Land!"—the twenty-six largest insurance companies in the country acquired fifteen thousand farms. A 1935 report by the Land Tenure Section of the Bureau of Agricultural Economics found that in the seven Cotton Belt states, "between 60 and 70 percent of the

23. Ransom, "Land!" 221–22.

24. Alfred Kazin, *On Native Grounds* (1942; reprint, Garden City, N.Y.: Doubleday Anchor, 1956), 329.

25. Owsley, "Pillars of Agrarianism," 533–34. Strangely, Owsley here passed over the similar experience of the subsistence farmer, the Agrarians' own (post–*I'll Take My Stand*) man at the center.

value of the farm real-estate belonged to persons or agencies other than the farm operator." These "persons or agencies" were usually credit companies, banks, and mortgage corporations.²⁶

Many of the Agrarians (notably Owsley and Ransom) had been cheered when, during the early New Deal, a Division of Subsistence Homesteads was established, leading to the foundation of thirty small, largely self-sufficient farming communities.²⁷ Moreover, the relative practical political success of "The Pillars of Agrarianism" had given the Agrarians some cause to believe that their proprietary ideal might yet be realized. But as Gavin Wright observes, New Deal benefit payments to impoverished small farmers "were of more value to more people than the lamented land distribution schemes could ever have been."²⁸ More generally, as Pete Daniel has discussed, the New Deal—whether in the form of the Resettlement Administration or its successors, the Farm Security Administration and the Farmers' Home Administration—never really worked to turn displaced tenants into landowners, as Owsley had hoped. Instead, New Deal plans to save and revolutionize southern agriculture focused upon larger, more efficient units of production, at the expense of small subsistence farms.²⁹ Between 1940 and 1945, between 20 and 22 percent of the South's agricultural population, more than three million people, left the land. Between 1940 and 1950, the number of southern farm operators declined by 350,000; between 1950 and 1959, this number plummeted by a further one million plus. All told, between 1935 and 1970, thirteen million people abandoned the southern agrarian way of life.³⁰ Donald Davidson later propagated the simplistic view that only during the New Deal did the "traditional society" ("poor in money and what money will buy, but rich in what money can never buy") accede to the cash nexus. Yet there is something to be said for Davidson's opinion that "it was not until the latter part of the Roosevelt administration that the South began to receive the full shock of modernism."³¹

---

26. See Pete Daniel, "Federal Farming Policy and the End of an Agrarian Way of Life," in Paul D. Escott and David Goldfield, eds., *Major Problems in the History of the American South*, vol. 2, *The New South* (Lexington, Mass: D. C. Heath, 1990), 403.

27. See Conkin, *The Southern Agrarians*, 102.

28. Wright, *Old South, New South*, 232.

29. See Daniel, "Federal Farming Policy," 400–401.

30. Statistics from Wright, *Old South, New South*, 241, 245, and Numan V. Bartley, "The New Deal as a Turning Point," in Escott and Goldfield, *Major Problems*, 394.

31. Davidson, "Why the Modern South Has a Great Literature," in Lewis P. Simpson, ed.,

I have focused upon *Who Owns America?* as much as the ostensibly more "southern" (and certainly more celebrated) *I'll Take My Stand* to emphasize the Agrarians' sense of crisis as rural, agricultural "place" became ever more exposed to the cash nexus, finance-capitalist land speculation, and real-estate development. I do not mean to suggest that, if the Agrarians' "South" died during the 1930s, the racialized sense of place sketched by Warren in "The Briar Patch" disappeared too. Moreover, it is arguable whether subsistence farming was really *the* peculiar institution that defined the South's agricultural identity until the 1940s. After all, during those decades there was another, perhaps even more significant shift in southern sociospatial relations: sharecropping was being replaced by wage labor, not least in the burgeoning urban centers. Following Wright and Jon Wiener, Godden cites sharecropping, not subsistence farming, as "the South's singular regime of accumulation." For Godden, the end of sharecropping and the region's low-wage economy destroyed "the basis of the region's distinctiveness." But whether one regards subsistence farms or sharecropping as the most distinctive or dominant form of southern social, economic, and regional identity, both were less prevalent than ever circa 1940.[32]

In the late 1930s, the Agrarians abandoned their agricultural program. Tate, Warren, and Ransom turned to creative writing and literary criticism, while Davidson tried to deny and dismantle the political, practical element of Agrarianism that had culminated in *Who Owns America?* As we have seen, in 1935 Davidson had insisted that "in recent years [the Twelve Southerners] have pushed the principles of agrarianism far beyond the point represented in *I'll Take My Stand*" by positing "very specific proposals" focused upon subsistence farming and state-sponsored land redistribution. Yet, only four years later, Davidson was downplaying the "proper economics and politics" of *Who Owns America?* and insisting that, as in *I'll Take My Stand*, "the emphasis is still upon principles rather than practice." Davidson did not abandon Agrarianism; indeed, his commitment to the cause hardened (and narrowed) in the 1940s, and he became increasingly embittered at the backsliding of his erstwhile colleagues. Davidson, however, preferred dramatic rhetorical flourishes—vivid invocations of "principles"—to practical economic proposals. One witnesses both Davidson's continued advocacy of Agrarianism, and his taste for simplis-

---

Still Rebels, Still Yankees and Other Essays (1957; reprint, Baton Rouge: Louisiana State University Press, 1972), 175.

32. Godden, *Fictions of Capital*, 142.

tic binary rhetoric, in a 1940 address to the Tennessee Folklore Society. Here, Davidson celebrates a family-centered "folk" that is "securely established on the land" and a "stable community which is really a community, not a mere real estate development."[33]

Davidson's attempt to maintain and advance the "principles" of Agrarianism, while simultaneously muting the movement's practical side, should not distract us from the specific economic and political bent of the Agrarian essays that appeared in the mid-1930s. Even if self-sufficient, agricultural real property was less a southern historical reality than an ideologically loaded ideal, most of the leading Agrarians were seriously engaged by the socioeconomic redevelopment of place in the South and the nation. However, after 1936, not only Davidson was confronted by the burden of *Who Owns America?*'s logic. The failure to realize the proprietary ideal implied that the South itself—in the Agrarians' own definition, an agrarian society of subsistent, even precapitalist real property surviving outside the cash nexus and untarnished by land speculation—must finally cease to exist as a unique social geography. It was not least this recognition that prompted the general Agrarian turn away from the South to literature and criticism. Ransom especially changed course, going back to aesthetics instead of the land. More generally, as Gray has trenchantly observed, those Agrarians who became New Critics sought "in works of literature . . . what they had once sought for in historical institutions: a harmonious system, an organism in which there was a place for everything and everything was in its place." Davidson was left alone to claim that "agrarianism in 1938 has no politics" even as his colleagues were abandoning the movement—their "very specific proposals" for real property rendered redundant by history.[34]

Allen Tate, Flem Snopes, and the Last Years of "the South"

As Agrarianism departs the political scene, it leaves me to pose an important question. If "the South" ceases to be a distinctive socioeconomic geography, what happens to "southern literature"? I want to turn to Allen Tate for one possible and persuasive answer—not the Tate of "Notes on Liberty and Property," but Tate the southern literary critic. As Conkin notes, literary criticism was the mode through which Tate "continued to affirm his agrarian

33. Davidson, "*I'll Take My Stand:* A History," 318; "Agrarianism and Politics," *Review of Politics* 1 (April 1939): 116; "Current Attitudes toward Folklore," in *Still Rebels, Still Yankees*, 136.
34. Gray, *Writing the South*, 163; Davidson, "Agrarianism and Politics," 125.

philosophy" from 1937 until his death. What is really interesting, though, is that Tate's literary-critical essays between 1935 and 1959 are informed by the sense that, as the cash nexus and land speculation finally overcame the resistance offered by agricultural real property, so the South did indeed die. What is more, Tate suggests that southern literature, too, had expired along with the region's traditional, agrarian economy.[35]

In "The Profession of Letters in the South" (1935), Tate recapitulates certain "merits of the Old South" that are familiar from *I'll Take My Stand*: "its comparative stability, its realistic limitation of the acquisitive impulse, [and] its preference for human relations compared to relations economic." Like Owsley before him, Tate blithely ignores the "acquisitive impulse" driving land seizure by the original planter-settlers, the less-than-human relations of slavery, and the mobility of antebellum human capitalists and their "personal property." Echoing Lytle's aphoristic, corn-centered sense of place in "The Hind Tit," Tate asserts that "[a]n environment is an abstraction not a place; Natchez is a place but not an environment." So far so familiar, but the argument takes an unexpected turn when Tate observes that, for all the positives of life in the Old South, its *literature* was decidedly lacking. Tate disputes Ransom's essay of the previous year, "Modern with the Southern Accent," in which Ransom put forward the particularly reactionary view that modernity per se was a disaster for the South. Against Ransom, Tate posits that the power of contemporary southern writing derives precisely from the modern economic transformation of the region, as that process is mediated by the writers' "historical consciousness" of the South's traditional social relations.[36]

Yet there is another twist before the essay ends. It becomes clear that, whatever the "considerable achievement of Southerners in modern American letters," Tate remains distinctly antagonistic toward the capitalist redevelopment of the region, and highly skeptical about its long-term impact upon southern literature. The contemporary southern novelist may have "left his mark upon the age; but it is of the age. From the peculiarly historical consciousness of the southern writer has come good work of a special order; but the focus of this consciousness is quite temporary." Tate concludes by wondering whether the wellspring of modern southern writing will be able

---

35. Conkin, *The Southern Agrarians*, 128.

36. Tate, "The Profession of Letters in the South," in *Essays of Four Decades* (Chicago: Swallow Press, 1968), 527, 533. See also Ransom, "Modern with the Southern Accent," *Virginia Quarterly Review* 11 (April 1935), 184–200.

to maintain a historical recall of premodern place, or simply accede to "[t]he prevailing economic passion of the age." It is an appropriately melancholic, even apocalyptic conclusion to an essay that traces a metahistory of the literary artist's removal from his "place" in a feudal, "organic society" to the mire of "finance-capitalism" and "the cash nexus" (Tate uses the latter term four times in the final third of the essay). Most important for my purposes, "The Profession of Letters in the South" reveals Tate's serious doubts that the South, or by extension southern literature, can survive being "dominated by capitalism, or 'economic society.'" This is a distinctly despondent view, especially considering that it comes a year *before* his spirited attack on finance capitalism in *Who Owns America?*[37]

Tate's perspective on the future of southern letters is even more pessimistic in "The New Provincialism," published in 1945, by which time the proposals outlined in the Agrarian-Distributist symposium must have seemed a mere pipe dream. The body of this essay argues that, in the modern period of Marxism and capitalism, "we have been the victims of a geographical metaphor, or a figure of space"—an ahistorical world "provincialism," in Tate's titular term. According to Tate, globalized industrial capitalism and "Utopian" socialism on a worldwide scale are replacing localized economies and communities. Put another way, this fallacious "world community or world region" has superseded authentic regionalism, "that consciousness or that habit of men in a given locality which influences them to certain patterns of thought and conduct handed to them by their ancestors." Unsurprisingly, Tate cites the traditional South as an authentic site of regionalism that contrasts favorably with the world-systems of Marxism and modern capitalism. In an "Epilogue on the Southern Novel," Tate offers his famous theory that the South's "backward glance" resulted in "a literature conscious of the past in the present." Finally, he recapitulates his earlier argument that "the peculiar historical consciousness of the Southern writer"—his or her awareness of the socioeconomic transformation of the South itself—produced the literature of the Southern Renascence. Tate concludes that, nearly ten years later, he finds "no reason to change that view."[38]

More interestingly, though, "The New Provincialism" also shows that Tate is even less certain than he was in 1936 that the Renascence or the South itself has survived the seismic shift from regionalism to world provincialism.

37. Tate, "Profession of Letters," 533, 534, 519, 534.
38. Tate, "The New Provincialism," in *Essays of Four Decades*, 538, 539, 545, 546.

In the very first paragraph, Tate asserts bluntly that "the Southern literary renascence . . . is over." When subsequently Tate invokes his "traditional" and "classical-Christian" South of "regional consciousness" and "limited acquisitiveness," it is in contrast with the "corrupt . . . South today," a New South of "cynical materialism." The "backward glance" to a better time and place—to a historical and regional consciousness—may have been available at the end of World War I but not, it seems, at the end of World War II. The cumulative effect of "The New Provincialism" is of one prominent southern writer's sense that "the South" no longer serves as a social reality that guarantees the relation of man to place.[39]

In "A Southern Mode of the Imagination" (1959), Tate again talks of the Southern Renascence in the past tense. He invokes the usual idealized Agrarian image of the Old South as a "premodern" and "preindustrial society [that] meant, for people living in it, that one's identity had everything to do with land and material property, at a definite place, and very little to do with money." Critiquing the sociospatial transformation (decline) of this society, Tate cites the "dislocated external relations" of modern characters in the fiction of Lytle and William Faulkner, "men [who] had missed their proper role, which was to be attached to a place." Tate then observes tartly that "Southern literature in the second half of this century may cease to engage the scholarly imagination; the subject may eventually become academic, and buried with the last dissertation." He is implying that southern literature can no longer engage our interest because, unlike Lytle and Faulkner, emerging writers do not have the historical consciousness to gauge the modern destruction of the South (let alone an unmediated knowledge of the premodern South). Hence, not only southern literature but also southern literary criticism becomes, at best, a retrospective affair.[40]

I do not want to challenge Tate's (or Donald Davidson's) belief that the Southern Renascence flourished within the context of the region's social destruction and redevelopment.[41] Aside from Tate's examples, Renascence fiction furnishes abundant examples of the socioeconomic transformation of older

39. Tate, "The New Provincialism," 535, 545, 544.
40. Tate, "A Southern Mode of the Imagination," in *Essays of Four Decades*, 581–82.
41. Davidson agreed that "the modern South has a great literature" precisely *because* modern capitalism caused the South's "traditional society" to come into "self-consciousness." See Davidson, "Why the Modern South," 172.

southern geographies. In a fine essay, Joseph Urgo reveals how "[a] series of land transactions regarding a single piece of property effectively structures [Faulkner's] *The Hamlet* [1940] along a real-estate continuum." Urgo argues that Flem Snopes performatively invests the Old Frenchman's Place with a fictional, inflated exchange-value, and that this process results in the highly profitable transfer of the property to Armstid, Ratliff, and Bookwright.[42] One might add that, confronted by capitalist speculation in, and despoliation of, the rural South, Faulkner was not averse to indulging a neo-Agrarian "aesthetics of anti-development." Richard Godden identifies the inverted delta symbol in *Go Down, Moses* (1942) as Faulkner's iconic site of resistance to the economic violation of the Mississippi Delta. This gendered icon, complete with hymen and pudenda, "preserve[s] the impenetrability of the land" as it "isolates the land within a natural female function."[43] In a similar fashion, Eula Varner in *The Hamlet* becomes a gendered figure of southern virgin land. When Flem Snopes tries to possess Eula through patriarchal marriage and the "power of money," it becomes analogous to his ownership of "a field . . . the fine land rich and fecund and foul and eternal." However, having always rejected the "exchange value" and "puny asking-price" of male love, even after marrying Flem Eula remains "impervious to him who claimed title" to her personal (and personified real) property. Faulkner's neo-Agrarian fantasy is that, if Eula is never penetrated (possessed) by Flem, so too the small-farm South will—at some sublimated sallet- or hymen-like level—remain impervious to the voracious land speculation and crude credit system that characterizes "Snopesism."[44]

In a 1946 review-essay on Faulkner published in the *New Republic*, Robert Penn Warren concurred that "nature can't, in one sense, be 'owned.'" Warren cites approvingly the way in which Eula, "a kind of fertility goddess or earth goddess," repudiates Flem's philosophy of "ownership." Warren also quotes at length Ike McCaslin's theory (in "The Bear") that land ownership through the cash nexus has, at some metaphysical or religious level, forever

---

42. Joseph Urgo, "Faulkner's Real Estate: Land and Literary Speculation in *The Hamlet*," *Mississippi Quarterly* 48, no. 3 (summer 1995): 443. Urgo also wonders whether "Faulkner may have found inspiration in the history of land speculation in Mississippi" (455n). Certainly, in *Requiem for a Nun*'s virtuoso metahistory of Yoknapatawpha, Faulkner points out that "land speculators" appeared alongside "traders in slaves" at the genesis of the European's colonial, genocidal New World. Faulkner, *Requiem for a Nun* (1951; reprint, New York: Vintage, 1975), 188.

43. Godden, *Fictions of Capital*, 154–55.

44. William Faulkner, *The Hamlet* (1940; reprint, New York: Vintage, 1964), 118–19.

dispossessed mankind from the land. Both Faulkner and Warren likely allude to Thomas Paine's notion of "natural property" (created by God, unlike "artificial property," which is "the invention of men"). But Faulkner's more specifically "southern" aesthetic of antidevelopment (and antiownership) must have been especially enticing to a lapsed Agrarian. Indeed, Warren works hard to distinguish the Faulknerian-southern small farmer from Flem Snopes, emphasizing "the assault made on a solid community of plain, hard-working small farmers by Snopeses and Snopesism."[45] Like many other critics, Warren fails (or refuses) to recognize that Flem's father-in-law and predecessor as local landlord, Will Varner, hardly offers a pre- or anticapitalist "alternative to Snopesism."[46] The New Critical tendency to avoid distasteful social changes by seeking consolation in art also seems evident here. Like "the sole owner and proprietor" of Yoknapatawpha himself, Warren finds solace in Faulkner's *literary* South in the very period that Agrarian proposals for a *practical* return to subsistence farming—and hopes for any kind of rural, small-farm economy—were being rejected, or simply ignored.

Faulkner knew better, however, than to hold to a neo-Agrarian aesthetics of antidevelopment in order to ignore the reality of sociospatial change. As such, we witness the transformation of "the entire old Compson place"—as Godden puts it, from "immovable property (Compson land) into movable property (a sum of money)"—in *The Sound and the Fury* (1929) and again in *The Mansion* (1959), by which time "the bulldozer and the dragline [w]ould

45. Robert Penn Warren, "William Faulkner," in Frederick J. Hoffman and Olga Vickery, eds., *William Faulkner: Three Decades of Criticism* (1960; reprint, New York and Burlingame: Harbinger, 1963), 116, 120. Warren's essay-review of Malcolm Cowley's *The Portable Faulkner* first appeared in the *New Republic,* 12 and 26 August 1946. See also Thomas Paine, "Agrarian Justice" (1795), quoted in Christopher Duncan, *Fugitive Theory: Political Theory, the Southern Agrarians, and America* (Lanham, Md.: Lexington Books, 2000), 26.

46. Frederick Karl, *William Faulkner: American Writer* (1989; reprint, New York: Ballantine, 1990), 288. Before Flem Snopes's arrival and ascendancy, Varner exemplifies the postbellum landlord capitalist described by Gavin Wright. Thus I question Urgo's claim that "Varner is, above all else, a resident of Frenchman's Bend with no speculative skills," sentimentally tied to the Old Frenchman's Place as a domicile (Urgo, "Faulkner's Real Estate," 457). One might even argue that not only Snopes and Varner, but also Frenchman's Bend's small farmers, have sullied the South's virgin land. If so, Eula Varner really signifies nothing (or at best, a mystical *pre*proprietary ideal). Ultimately, it may be more balanced to say that *The Hamlet* maps land ownership and speculation in *relative terms* that are similar to the Agrarians': petty-bourgeois land ownership is positively virtuous when compared to Snopes's large-scale, speculative violation of "the fine land rich and fecund." (Compare notes 14 and 21 above.)

not only alter but efface geography." The Compsons' old homestead has been radically redeveloped as Flem Snopes's subdivision, Eula Acres, complete with a "new arterial highway" and a "filling station." *The Hamlet*'s gendered, ahistorical aesthetic of antidevelopment has failed: posthumously, the "eternal" earth goddess Eula has finally been "claimed" by Flem—as the "title" of a real estate development.[47]

A writer rather less favored by the Agrarians, Thomas Wolfe, also critically represented the speculative redevelopment of the South's social geography. Much as Urgo relates Faulkner's real-estate aesthetics to the author's other role as a property owner in Oxford, Richard Reed has traced "Real Estate in *Look Homeward, Angel*" back to Wolfe's mother's "relentless speculation" during the property boom and bust in and around 1920s Asheville. To the degree that "Wolfe employed real estate for the value of its contrast to the life of the spirit," he echoed the Agrarian aesthetics of antidevelopment. Yet unlike the Agrarians or even Faulkner, Wolfe's fiction emphasized the speculative development of an *urban* South. Coming home again, George Fairchild observes how "[e]veryone bought real estate; and everyone was 'a real estate man' either in name or practice. . . . Along all the streets in town the ownership of the land was constantly changing; and when the supply of streets was exhausted, new streets were feverishly created in the surrounding wilderness; and even before those streets were paved or a house had been built upon them, the land was being sold, and then resold, by the acre, by the lot, by the foot, for hundreds of thousands of dollars."[48]

One could add more examples from the literature of the Renascence, but that is not my main purpose here. Instead, I want to conclude this chapter by further examining the serious implications of Tate's literary-critical essays for "the South," "southern literature" and the supposed southern (literary) "sense of place." As we have seen, Tate sees the "real" ("real property") South as a premodern, almost precapitalist, agricultural society. Yet as early as 1935 Tate is stating that such a society no longer exists, except in the collective memory of Southern Renascence writers. By 1945, Tate is suggesting that the representational authenticity, even the very possibility, of "southern

47. William Faulkner, *The Mansion* (1959; reprint, New York: Vintage, 1965), 328; Richard Godden, *Fictions of Labor: William Faulkner and the South's Long Revolution* (Cambridge: Cambridge University Press, 1997), 46; Faulkner, *The Mansion*, 334, 333.

48. Richard Reed, "Real Estate in *Look Homeward, Angel*," *Southern Literary Journal* 19, no. 1 (fall 1986): 48, 50; Thomas Wolfe, *You Can't Go Home Again* (1940), excerpted in Escott and Goldfield, eds., *Major Problems*, 471.

literature" ended with the Renascence—itself valued primarily for its vivid, doom-laden depiction of the South becoming dis-placed, de-realized, by capitalist redevelopment. By 1959, Tate dismisses even the *study* of contemporary (post-Renascence) southern literature.

All this raises three important interrelated questions. If we consider that Tate, nonpareil in his influence as an Agrarian and southern literary critic, sounded the death knell of "the South" and "southern literature" in 1935, 1945, and 1959, how did southern literary studies flourish, on distinctly Agrarian terms, during and after the 1950s? Why did the term "sense of place" begin to appear so frequently in southern literary criticism after 1961? And why was this "sense of place" almost always seen as positive and benevolent, in contrast to Tate's own devastating assessment (in 1959) of the "dislocated external relations" of Renascence men who have become detached from "place"? It is tempting simply to cite Hegel's maxim that "the owl of Minerva spreads his wings only with the falling of the dusk" and declare that we cannot comprehend a historical period until it is coming to a close. From this premise, one might argue that southern literary critics of the 1950s and 1960s were simply struggling to understand and define "the South" and "the Southern Renascence" in the aftermath of the time and (sense of) place itself. I want to suggest, however, that the issues are rather more complex and ideological. With reference to the decline-and-death narrative that drives Tate's essays, Romine has identified "an overdeveloped eschatological sense" informing "the southern literary tradition. The southernness of place, it seems, is always in danger of expiring." Always in danger—yet "sense of place" has endured as an organizing, even foundational idea of southern literary studies. In Chapter 2, I argue that one reason for the survival of a "neo-Agrarian" sense of place is that few southern literary critics have really confronted the socioeconomic implications of Tate's eschatological paradigm—or of the failure of the Agrarians' proprietary ideal. I will try to show how and why certain southern literary critics maintained a neo-Agrarian "image" of a rural, small-town "South"—even as the material transformation of the region reached levels the Agrarians could only have imagined when they wrote *Who Owns America?*[49]

---

49. Hegel's *Philosophy of Right* quoted in Francis Wheen, *Karl Marx* (London: Fourth Estate, 1999), 119; Romine, "Where Is Southern Literature?" 9.

2. (Re)inventing the (Post)southern "Sense of Place"

Fred Hobson has identified "the origins of modern southern literature as an academic discipline in a volume published in Baltimore in 1953, *Southern Renascence,* edited by Louis D. Rubin, Jr., and Robert D. Jacobs." Hobson goes further, positing that, by defining a canon of modern southern literature, "Rubin and Jacobs, nearly as much as Faulkner and Tate and Warren, were 'responsible' for the 'Southern Renascence.'" While I concur with Hobson's perceptive remarks, I would add that a backward glance at *Southern Renascence* reveals not only the "responsibility" of Rubin and Jacobs themselves but also the continuing critical influence of the Agrarians. Two of the original Twelve Southerners, Andrew Lytle and Donald Davidson, actually contribute essays. As the preface acknowledges, Davidson also had a hand in choosing other contributors. The most prominent disciple of the original Agrarians, Richard Weaver, is featured, and as many as ten other pieces deal with the Agrarians as artists and/or critics.[1]

In "How Many Miles to Babylon," Andrew Lytle restates his unreconstructed stand: "Twenty years is a short time as history goes, but I see no reason to withdraw the assumption upon which the Agrarians based their warning" about the dystopian impulse of "Industrialism." True to his word, Lytle reheats the anti-industrial, profarm property thesis expounded in "The Hind Tit" and "The Small Farm Secures the State." Yet, as we saw in Chapter 1, even ten years—from 1930 to 1940—was "short time" enough to revolutionize the socioeconomic geography of the South. By 1953, there is an even stronger sense that Lytle is harping upon a received Agrarian idea of the region rather than referring to any substantial social reality.[2]

Weaver's contribution largely recapitulates Lytle, and the more general Agrarian notion of a "natural" South that also has resisted the cash nexus and

---

1. Fred Hobson, "Surveyors and Boundaries: Southern Literature and Southern Literary Scholarship after Mid-Century," *Southern Review* 27, no. 4 (winter 1992): 743–44.

2. Andrew Lytle, "How Many Miles to Babylon," in Louis D. Rubin and Robert D. Jacobs, eds., *Southern Renascence: The Literature of the Modern South* (Baltimore: Johns Hopkins University Press, 1953), 31–32.

finance-capital. The reader is assured that it is a "blessing that the South has never had much money" because "it has retarded the spoiling of the South." Because capital has been concentrated in the land itself (like Owsley and Tate before him, Weaver elides the human capitalist relations of slavery), the region's "rural working people" have avoided the "peculiar degenerative effects of the possession of wealth" and remained "in close contact with the natural environment." In rhetoric that echoes Lytle's pithy aphorisms and Ransom's rigid binary oppositions, Weaver contrasts this organic, natural, nigh precapitalist South with the artificial, abstract, finance-capitalist North: "whereas the South has the farms, New England has the insurance companies." The problem, though, is that Weaver's essay seems just as anachronistic as Lytle's: the work of a latecomer *reinventing* an Agrarian "South" that, in the wake of the region's socioeconomic transformation during the 1930s and 1940s, seems more rhetorical than ever. Weaver claims—in a clear echo of Lytle—that "words are among the fixed things which has kept the South conservative," and contrasts this semiotic and social stability with the modern moral relativism lurking in the perilous gap "between the word and the thing signified." But arguably, by attaching his own words to old Agrarian tropes, it is Weaver's "South" that signifies nothing, that fails to refer to social reality.[3]

As we shall see in this chapter, Lytle and Weaver were not the last critics of an Agrarian bent whose "South" has seemed more rhetorical than referential. In the first part of Chapter 2, I try to demonstrate how, after 1953, other "neo-Agrarian" literary and cultural critics promulgated an increasingly anachronistic and idealized image of "the South" and southern "place" that propped up and even propelled the ideological project of southern literary studies. In particular, I will consider the critical work of Rubin who, besides coediting the epochal *Southern Renascence* and a subsequent, similarly important collection of essays, *South: Modern Southern Literature in Its Cultural Setting* (1961), wrote two influential introductions to reprints of *I'll Take My Stand*. I shall also assess another strand of neo-Agrarianism, exemplified in the work of Walter Sullivan and Thomas Daniel Young, which took Allen Tate's eschatological paradigm (as discussed in Chapter 1) to its logical conclusion. In contrast to and even in open conflict with Rubin, Sullivan and

---

3. Richard Weaver, "Aspects of the Southern Philosophy," in *Southern Renascence*, 27, 19. Compare Lytle on "[t]he very meaning of language, that men and nations mean what they say (that is, words)" and the manner in which modernity has destroyed this traditional, stable relationship between sign and referent ("How Many Miles to Babylon," 32).

Young mourned the death by capitalism of the South and offered a requiem for its literature—a literature that, they believed, could no longer claim to refer to any agrarian (or Agrarian) reality.

Inventing Southern Literature's "Sense of Place"

Eight years after *Southern Renascence* appeared, the Louis Rubin–Robert Jacobs editorial axis presided over the publication of *South: Modern Southern Literature in Its Cultural Setting*. In an important and frequently incisive introduction, Rubin and Jacobs recognize that it has become necessary to reconsider the South and its literature within the context of the region's social, spatial, and racial transformations. At a time of massive racial strife in the region, it is to Rubin and Jacobs's great credit that they (unlike the Agrarians in *I'll Take My Stand*) criticize the "place" that blacks occupied in this "old, agrarian society" as "hewers of wood and drawers of water, to till the fields and wait upon table and otherwise perform the role of a peasantry." They also observe that "with the passing of segregation there must also pass important features of a pattern of life based upon a fixed, closely knit rural and small-town society," replaced "by a cosmopolitan, fluid industrial society in which social status and economic stratification are constantly changing." Rubin and Jacobs conclude on this striking note:

> [T]o the extent that the Southern novel has always presupposed a strong identification with a place, a participation in its life, a sense of intense involvement in a fixed, defined society, the best work of the leading younger Southern writers is not in these respects "Southern." Just as the South has changed until it has lost much of its old, closely knit, small-town and rural character, so its most recent novelists have lost their sense of community, of involvement within a limited, bounded universe. The kind of community that was Yoknapatawpha County, created by a known and felt history, marked off into distinct, recognizable parts, each with its proper function and its proper relationship to the others, is gone. Towns have become cities, cities have become huge metropolises. . . . Now the fixed center is gone, and the younger Southern writers, as Walter Sullivan declares, must look for something else to take its place.[4]

If there is a tinge of nostalgia for Tate's premodern South of "people in their proper role . . . attached to a place" (one notes here the simplistic suggestion that everyone and everything in Faulkner country is each in its ordered

---

4. Louis D. Rubin and Robert D. Jacobs, Introduction to Rubin and Jacobs, eds., *South: Modern Southern Literature in Its Cultural Setting* (Garden City, N.Y.: Dolphin Books, 1961), 16, 15–16, 24–25.

place), nonetheless this is a radical conclusion. Like Tate's literary-critical essays, the introduction to *South: Modern Southern Literature in Its Cultural Setting* seems to have profound implications for the South and southern literature. Rubin and Jacobs appear as witnesses, even doomsayers, of the fate that Tate foretold. As the small-town and rural South, with its "strong identification with a place," becomes extinct, so too dies "southern literature" as we have known it. At the very least, the coeditors concur with Walter Sullivan: a coherent, "fixed," and "rooted" literature has been severely *displaced*.

On closer inspection, however, Rubin and Jacobs's definition of "place"—both what southern place was, and what that "something else to take its place" will be—remains rather airy. To the extent that the traditional South is seen as "small town and rural in character," and as threatened by "huge metropolises," there are clear echoes of the Agrarian worldview. However, traditional southern "place" is not given the specific identity that it was by the Agrarians between 1931 and 1936: agricultural real property owned and operated by subsistence farmers. It is only in a general sense, then, that Rubin and Jacobs confirm the implication in *Who Owns America?* and Tate's essays that southern place will cease (*has* ceased) to exist as a distinctive entity. I want to suggest that this failure (or refusal) to focus upon the socioeconomic processes and property relations that destroyed the agrarian South later allowed Rubin and other neo-Agrarian critics to maintain a *literary-critical* "image" of southern "place" even in the midst of massive *sociospatial* change.[5]

The publication of *South: Modern Southern Literature in Its Cultural Setting* also marked the emergence of the term "sense of place" as a distinctive signifier in and of southern literary studies. The term can be traced back directly to the Agrarians: in 1933, Donald Davidson, discussing the importance of "sectionalism" for regional life and culture, observed that "powerful research into the past is paralleled by a new sense of place." Davidson proceeded to

---

5. Rubin had already contributed an essay to *Southern Renascence* on place (and time) in Thomas Wolfe's work. In one sense, as Michael Kreyling has noted, this essay diverged from Agrarian orthodoxy simply by considering Wolfe—no favorite of the Agrarians—seriously. Yet Rubin configures Wolfe as a southern writer within recognizably Agrarian parameters, lauding him for a sense of rhetoric, a sense of time and place, and an antipathy toward abstraction. Like the introduction to *South*, "Thomas Wolfe in Time and Place" does not attempt to understand southern place in terms of property, as the Agrarians did in the 1930s, and, as Richard Reed has demonstrated, as Wolfe himself did in both his life and his fiction. See Rubin, "Thomas Wolfe in Time and Place," in *Southern Renascence*, 290–305; Kreyling, *Inventing Southern Literature*, 40–41; Reed, "Real Estate in *Look Homeward, Angel*," 46–55.

observe that regionalist writers "openly profess allegiance to a place and its tradition."[6] And without using the specific term "sense of place," Robert Penn Warren argued in *Who Owns America?* that "real property" guaranteed "the relation of man to place," unlike the "abstract property" relations of finance-capitalism. But Frederick Hoffman's essay "The Sense of Place" in *South: Modern Southern Literature in Its Cultural Setting* exemplifies how Agrarian-influenced southern literary criticism both ignored the original movement's anticapitalist proprietary ideal—as detailed in Ransom's "Land!" and Owsley's "The Pillars of Agrarianism," as well as throughout *Who Owns America?*—and failed to refer to contemporary sociospatial reality. Hoffman does echo the earlier Owsley of *I'll Take My Stand* (as well as Weaver in *Southern Renascence*) by suggesting that "[t]he history of the Southern place is essentially one of human agreements made with nature." However, this hoary "natural South" rhetoric sidelines the Agrarians' post-*I'll Take My Stand* emphasis on land as agricultural real property—not to mention Rubin and Jacobs's introductory emphasis on the place of race/race of "place" in the South circa 1961. Hoffman's "South" is not merely precapitalist or premodern: it is prelapsarian.[7]

It takes the following essay, James Dickey's "Notes on the Decline of Outrage," to expose Hoffman's ahistorical dream of Arcady by reemphasizing some of the specific social, economic, and racial difficulties that impinge upon any definition of southern "place" circa 1961. Dickey admits his distaste for "the empty money-grubbing and soul-killing competitive drives of the Northern industrial concerns" that threaten "the *sense* of this place," the rural South. However, he rejects outright the possibility that "the South [could], in fact, have remained a farming region": the subsistence farm is no longer a (proprietary) ideal, let alone a social reality. What is more, Dickey sees contemporary white southern identity as based solely upon the effort to keep the black southerner "in *his* 'place.'" For Dickey in 1961, all that remains of Robert Penn Warren's briar patch is its racist sense of "place."[8]

6. Donald Davidson, "Sectionalism in the United States" (1933), in Bingham and Underwood, eds., *Southern Agrarians and the New Deal*, 64–65.

7. Frederick Hoffman, "The Sense of Place," in *South*, 67. Hoffman recast this essay as part of the first chapter of his *The Art of Southern Fiction: A Study of Some Modern Novelists* (Carbondale and Edwardsville: Southern Illinois University Press, 1967). In the conclusion to that book, Hoffman once again figures southern place chiefly in terms of Nature—"of weather, of landscape, of changes in the seasons, of the textures of leaves, mold, birds, animals, the lowering and raising of the water level, etc." (165).

8. James Dickey, "Notes on the Decline of Outrage," in *South*, 81, 85, 87, 85.

Louis Rubin's Neo-Agrarian Image of the South

Around this time, Harper and Brothers, planning to republish *I'll Take My Stand*, commissioned Louis Rubin to write a new introduction. Rubin begins by noting that the symposium had long been out of print (indeed, the 1962 printing was the first since the original edition), and acknowledges that "[i]n the years that followed *I'll Take My Stand*'s publication, the South and the nation cannot be said to have heeded its economic, political and social counsels to any startling effect." By sketching the extent to which the South has been transformed—"[t]he importance of farm life in the South has steadily diminished" so that "today one-half of all Southerners live in an urban environment"—Rubin again reveals his readiness to confront the changing historical and geographical reality of the region. However, he is also eager to emphasize what he believes to be the continuing value of *I'll Take My Stand*. Focusing upon "the four leading Fugitive poets"—Ransom, Warren, Tate, and Davidson—Rubin argues that "as poets they were given to the metaphor, and they instinctively resorted to an image for their critique of American society. They saw in the history of their own section the image of a region which had clearly resisted the domination of the machine, persisting in its agricultural ways . . . and only now beginning to capitulate fully to the demands of American industrial society."[9]

Here we encounter a conundrum that is, as Michael Kreyling has observed, recurrent in Rubin's southern literary criticism: an attempt to reconcile the harsh realities of the region's "history" with a frankly neo-Agrarian "image" (the term is Allen Tate's) of "the South." Having openly acknowledged the historical and geographical realities that seem to have made redundant *I'll Take My Stand*'s representation of a rural, self-sufficient agrarian society, Rubin yet sets out to rescue the Agrarians' "South" as a poetic "image" of "the good life." Kreyling remarks that, for Tate and the other original Agrarians, "[i]mages constitute the vocabulary of the stable, traditionalist, religious community," but that such "images do not bond well with the contingent grammar of history." In Rubin's 1962 introduction, this tension between image and history—and between image and material, historical "place"—becomes apparent in an oxymoronic phrase like "the tangible image of the South." Rubin valorizes the Agrarians' representation of the South because it is rooted in a "tangible" historical geography, yet he also admits that "[t]he image of the old agrarian South in *I'll Take My Stand* was the image of a society that

---

9. Louis Rubin, Introduction to Torchbook Edition (1962) of *I'll Take My Stand*, xxvi, xxv.

perhaps never existed." Rubin thus concedes that the "agrarian South" was less a historical, material reality than an abstraction. A phrase like "tangible image" cannot resolve rhetorically this historical-geographical conundrum. This conundrum is apparent again when Rubin posits that "[t]he image of the agrarian South provided the essayists with a rich, complex metaphor, giving body to their arguments, anchoring their perceptions in time and place." Once more, "the agrarian South" is both a poetic construct and an actual, spatiotemporal entity, but the putatively material "anchor" becomes subservient to the Agrarian—or Rubin's own—poetic figure. Much like history, so too place melts into image and metaphor. The historical-geographical South gives way to the imag(in)ed South.[10]

A fundamental problem here is that Rubin ignores Tate's and the other Agrarians' own programmatic, economic emphasis—their focus upon agricultural, subsistence-based real property. Were Rubin to refer to the proprietary ideal, a (neo-) Agrarian "South" would seem even more anachronistic in 1962 than it did in 1930, 1936, or 1953, when Lytle and Weaver contributed to *Southern Renascence*. Rubin himself openly considered this problem in 1977, in a second introduction to *I'll Take My Stand* for another new edition published by Louisiana State University Press. This time around, Rubin admits that it was "misleading" to stress "the 'metaphoric' element of *I'll Take My Stand*." He recognizes "that at the time the book was being written the [Agrarian] enterprise was envisioned as a literal and practical program, a specific course of action" by many of the contributors. Rubin also acknowledges that Ransom turned to "agrarian economics" after the publication of *I'll Take My Stand*. Most notably, Rubin confesses that no less an authority than Donald Davidson strongly criticized the 1962 introduction for focusing upon the poetic "image" rather than "a literal and practical program, a specific course of action." Rubin retrospectively explains his motives circa 1962: "There was the chance, even the likelihood, that, as in the early 1930s, the obvious impracticalities of a return to subsistence farming in the age of the tractor, the supermarket, and the television set . . . might serve to distract the symposium's readers from what was and is the book's real importance: its assertion of the values of humanism and its rebuke of materialism."[11]

10. Rubin, Introduction to Torchbook Edition, xxxii, xxxiv; Kreyling, *Inventing Southern Literature*, 37; Rubin, Introduction to Torchbook Edition, xxxi.
11. Louis Rubin, Introduction to Library of Southern Civilization Edition (1977), xvi–xviii. Considering that, in the wake of the Agrarian program's political failure, Davidson himself tried to shift the focus back from "practice" to "principles" (see Chapter 1), it seems a bit rich

Yet having made this admirably frank confession, Rubin reasserts his original opinion that "a return to a preindustrial farming society was unfeasible, but that this was the least of what the Agrarians had to say." This remains misleading. I do not mean to suggest that Rubin's consistent focus upon the image is "wrong" in any absolute way: clearly, the image was important to the Agrarians, and to Tate in particular. Nor does the fact that Rubin's own interpretation of the image cleaves so closely to Tate's preclude the potential for valuable insights, even if such insights inevitably tend to recapitulate Agrarian–New Critical logic. The real problem here has to do with the repeated, even stubborn, emphasis on image. This emphasis requires that the Agrarians' "literal and practical program" is repeatedly downplayed and dismissed, despite the fact that, as we saw in Chapter 1, the Agrarians came to believe that getting back to the farm *was* feasible, and perhaps even the South's last best hope for survival. If Rubin is somewhat more willing to recognize the implications of his position in 1977 than in 1962, he nonetheless continues to slough off the Agrarians' more practical initiatives in an attempt to redeem the "concrete imagery" of the Agrarians' "South" as a more flexible—but also less radical—rebuke to "the social effects of capitalism and industrialism."[12]

Historian Paul Conkin surely had Rubin in mind when he suggested that the focus upon *I'll Take My Stand* has distorted our understanding of Agrarianism. Whereas Rubin repeatedly emphasizes image and metaphor in that famous first symposium, Conkin observes that the Agrarian movement

---

to condemn Rubin for focusing on metaphor or image over a "literal and practical program."

12. Rubin, Introduction to Library of Southern Civilization Edition, xix, xv, xviii. Other essays and books that Rubin published between 1975 and 1982 follow this line. In "Fugitives as Agrarians: The Impulse behind *I'll Take My Stand*" (1975), Rubin again defines the Agrarians' "South" in terms of "symbol" and "metaphor," and as "imaging human experience." But once more there are hints of the contortions necessary to deemphasize the Agrarians' small-farm focus. Rubin claims that "[t]hose who read the volume as an attempt to will back into existence the historical Old South by a deliberate turning back toward mass subsistence-farming miss the point" but parenthetically admits that "it must be said that several of the essays in the book encourage such a misreading." See Rubin, *William Ellis Shoots a Bear: Essays on the Southern Literary Imagination* (Baton Rouge: Louisiana State University Press, 1975), 157–59. See also Frederick J. Hoffmann and Olga Vickery, "The American South: The Continuity of Self-Definition," in Rubin, ed., *The American South: Portrait of a Culture* (Baton Rouge: Louisiana State University Press, 1980), 13 ("really a pastoral metaphor rather than a program for economic action"); and *The Wary Fugitives: Four Poets and the South* (Baton Rouge: Louisiana State University Press, 1978), especially the section titled "Agrarianism and Farming," 207–28.

of the 1930s, with its political program to transform the "proprietary ideal" into practical reality, has "received scant attention from historians and literary critics." More recently, Paul Murphy has named names, noting that, along with other "neo-Agrarians," "Rubin was not willing to take seriously the Agrarian hope that the social and economic structures of industrial capitalism could be resisted." In their valuable introduction to *The Southern Agrarians and the New Deal: Essays after "I'll Take My Stand"* (2001), editors Emily Bingham and Thomas Underwood echo Murphy by criticizing Rubin's emphasis on a metaphoric reading of Agrarianism, and count Rubin among a collection of "neo-Agrarians" who have produced an "abstracted version of agrarianism [that] was often ahistorical in its disassociation from the political, economic, and social context of the South during the New Deal."[13]

Traditionally, scholars have tended to define as "neo-Agrarian" those cultural and literary critics like Weaver and Hoffman who depict a traditional, even static image of "the South" and its "sense of place": rural, agricultural, even "natural." I do not want to dismiss this definition of neo-Agrarianism, for there is a clear link to what Frank Owsley and others were doing in *I'll Take My Stand*. However, even Rubin's ostensibly more historicized neo-Agrarianism has obscured that political element of the original movement that came to the fore between the publication of "Land!" in 1932 and *Who Owns America?* in 1936. Eudora Welty once appreciatively termed Rubin a "mapmaker . . . able to invent, to reinvent, a country." Inadvertently, Welty's words might also seem to allude to Rubin's role in the invention of southern literature—

---

13. Conkin, *Southern Agrarians*, 90; Paul V. Murphy, *The Rebuke of History: The Southern Agrarians and American Conservative Thought* (Chapel Hill: University of North Carolina Press, 2001), 224; Bingham and Underwood, eds., *Southern Agrarians and the New Deal*, 10. I have not drawn further on *The Rebuke of History* or the introduction to *Southern Agrarians and the New Deal* as these books were published when this chapter was substantially completed. However, as I have observed elsewhere, these two fine pieces of scholarship go a long way toward explaining, and correcting, the lack of attention to Agrarian thought post–*I'll Take My Stand*, and to the proprietary ideal in particular. See my review-essay "Were Farms Necessary?: The Agrarian Question," *Mississippi Quarterly* 56, no. 3 (summer 2003): 421–37.

Also pertinent here is Michael O'Brien's pointed observation that "*I'll Take My Stand* was edited into metaphor, as though John Crowe Ransom had never written that party politics were necessary." Substitute "subsistent farms" for "party politics" and you have a concise summation of my point. See O'Brien, "A Heterodox Note on the Southern Renaissance," in *Rethinking the South: Essays in Intellectual History* (Baltimore: Johns Hopkins University Press, 1988), 168.

more specifically, in mapping a neo-Agrarian aesthetics of place that fails to attend to the Agrarians' own emphasis on agricultural real property.[14]

Having de-emphasized the proprietary ideal, it is perhaps inevitable that Rubin's neo-Agrarian "image" of "the South" does not take into account the profound implications of this ideal. As we saw in Chapter 1, the implication that emerges from *Who Owns America?* is that if finance-capitalism defeats the proprietary ideal, the South itself will cease to exist as a distinct social geography. Taking this logic a step further, Tate's southern literary criticism between 1935 and 1959 implies that "southern literature" too must then expire as a distinctive aesthetic form. By contrast, throughout his career Rubin has tended to emphasize the "continuity" of, rather than "changes" in, "the South" and "southern literature." There is, though, another strand of neo-Agrarian literary criticism that, taking Tate's eschatological paradigm to its logical conclusion, argues more or less explicitly that "the South" and "southern literature" did, in fact, die along with the agrarian society itself. Walter Sullivan and Thomas Daniel Young best represent this perspective. In the late 1960s and 1970s, Sullivan in particular engaged Rubin in an ongoing debate over the current status—indeed, the very survival—of "the South" and its literature.

Walter Sullivan, Thomas Daniel Young, and the Tate Paradigm

Early in his 1975 Lamar Memorial Lectures, published as *A Requiem for the Renascence* (1976), Walter Sullivan states that he accepts the traditional view "on southern regionalism and the sense of place [articulated] by Louis Rubin, Robert Heilman, Richard Weaver, Frederick Hoffman, and many other critics," and notes that such critics took their cue from the Agrarians. However, when Sullivan in *Death by Melancholy* (1972) sketches what he sees as the neo-Agrarian, southern literary critical perspective, it actually diverges somewhat from both Rubin's metaphorical "South" and Hoffman's "natural" sense of place: "It has been our custom, and rightly so, following some of the most perspective critics of our time, to think of the South in which the Southern Renascence was rooted largely in Agrarian terms. The people, being farmers, had lost the Civil War, and therefore they knew about the tragedy of life: living close to the land, they understood the inscrutable quality of providence. Dealing with mules and boll weevils rather than with stocks and bonds, they

---

14. Eudora Welty, "Louis Rubin and the Making of Maps," *Sewanee Review* 97, no. 2 (spring 1989): 258.

had a firmer grip of reality than their city counterparts." This last sentence suggests that Sullivan's own neo-Agrarian sympathies are, in fact, rather more closely identified than Rubin's or Hoffman's with that particular emphasis (in "The Hind Tit" or "Land!" or "Notes on Liberty and Property") upon the small farm as a site of resistance to finance-capitalism. In this, Sullivan follows Allen Tate. One should qualify here that, like Tate, Sullivan is interested in the South mainly for religious, rather than economic or geographic, reasons: "reality" primarily has to do with Providence, and only secondarily with southern farming (which only provides a *perspective* on Providence, one supposedly denied to the Wall Street broker). It is also telling that Sullivan cites Tate's "Notes on the Southern Religion" ("that essay which remains astonishingly vital after more than forty years") before lamenting the South's failure to formulate an appropriate theology. However, Sullivan also follows Tate in finding some secular solace in the region's traditional agrarian makeup, and in the "farmer's way of looking at reality." Resigned to the belief that the South's religion is fundamentally flawed, both Tate and Sullivan shift at least part of their emphasis to economics: from the transcendent-metaphysical to the historical-geographical. In both *Death by Melancholy* and *A Requiem for the Renascence*, much of the Tate-esque burden of Sullivan's argument is that only with the material survival of the farmer's reality could the South—and by extension, southern literature—survive. As the evocatively eschatological titles suggest, Sullivan feels that southern literature *has* perished along with the agrarian South itself.[15]

Sullivan's essay "Allen Tate, Flem Snopes, and the Last Years of William Faulkner" initially is quite positive. Sullivan suggests that, at the end of *The Hamlet*, and despite their exploitation by Flem Snopes, the small farmers of Frenchman's Bend are "redeemed by love." Indeed, this is more optimistic than my own or Joseph Urgo's readings of *The Hamlet* through real-estate speculation (see Chapter 1). However, Sullivan subsequently argues that the shift in focus from Frenchman's Bend to Jefferson in *The Town* and *The Mansion* is fatal for an agrarian society based on rural, agricultural real property. He states adamantly that "Jefferson is not the country, and even in a small town, land and livestock lose their significance, property tends toward abstraction, and the symbol becomes not the farm or the house but the bank."

15. Walter Sullivan, *A Requiem for the Renascence: The State of Fiction in the Modern South* (Athens: University of Georgia Press, 1976), xiv; *Death by Melancholy: Essays on Modern Southern Fiction* (Baton Rouge: Louisiana State University Press, 1972), 10, 11, 116.

Not only does the Snopes trilogy depict the destruction of "the agrarian community" by abstract finance-capitalism, but it also reveals Faulkner's fateful displacement from the source of his best fiction. Unlike Warren in 1946 (writing before *The Town* and *The Mansion* were published), Sullivan does not have recourse to some Agrarian-Faulknerian aesthetic of antidevelopment that might magically (i.e., textually) save the South. Rather, Sullivan's view that small farmers have failed to resist Snopesism seems to conform to and confirm the ominous prophecy of the original Agrarians in *Who Owns America?* that finance-capitalism sounds the death knell of southern agricultural real property.[16]

Sullivan asks: "But what happens when the old procedures of the land are reduced by mechanized farming, and the woods are destroyed by the lumber companies, and the city establishes its hegemony over the countryside?" That Sullivan even views the small town (Jefferson) as a danger to the "agrarian community" really makes this a rhetorical question. By 1972 (the year that *Death by Melancholy* was published), the wide-ranging and deep-reaching process of regional redevelopment to which Sullivan alludes had long been underway. In 1940, when the Agrarians were finally abandoning their advocacy of the proprietary ideal, 65 percent of the population of the South remained rural (as opposed to 36 percent in the non-South). By 1960, "over half of the [southern] population were living in cities"; by 1970, the figure had reached 65 percent. In 1940, 36 percent of southern labor remained agricultural; by 1960, the figure had plunged to 10 percent. Of course, these are the kinds of sociological indices that the Agrarians—Davidson especially—loathed. Nevertheless, by 1971 sociologists John McKinney and Linda Bourque could justifiably observe that there was now "far stronger" evidence to support the opinion expressed in 1936 by Davidson's nemesis, Howard Odum, that "[t]here is no longer any single entity which may be designated as 'the South.'" To the large extent that their own ideal came to focus upon agricultural real property, the Agrarians would have been forced to agree that "the South" died some time between 1936 and 1971.[17]

16. Sullivan, *Death by Melancholy*, 5, 7.

17. Sullivan, *Death by Melancholy*, 11; John C. McKinney and Linda Bourque, "The Changing South: National Incorporation of a Region," *American Sociological Review* 36, no. 3 (June 1971): 401, 404, 410; some of my statistics were also taken from John Egerton, *The Americanization of Dixie: The Southernization of America* (New York: Harper and Row, 1974), 168. Interestingly, the political liberal Egerton echoes Agrarian warnings about finance-capitalist land speculation. In a chapter on land, Egerton asserts, "if there ever was a distinction to be made

The revolutionary nature of these sociospatial changes drives Sullivan's relentless decline-and-death narrative. Moreover, Sullivan's Tate-esque eschatology brought him to literary-critical loggerheads with Louis Rubin. This disagreement is explicitly announced in the preface to *Death by Melancholy*, and noted by Michael Cass in the foreword to *A Requiem for the Renascence*.[18] The debate over the continuity (Rubin) or destruction (Sullivan) of "the South" and "southern literature" also arose during a 1972 conference session in Chapel Hill. During that discussion, Thomas Daniel Young sided with Sullivan, positing the similar argument that "the sense of community you're talking about, as we see it in Frenchmen's [sic] Bend, is the last vestige of this kind of unity."[19] In *The Past in the Present* (1981), Young again echoes Sullivan by taking Tate's paradigm as his main tool for a bleak assessment of the contemporary South and recent southern fiction. Young's debt to Tate is apparent in the title, and he reiterates various Agrarian arguments throughout the book. But Young's neo-Agrarianism is also similar to Tate's or Sullivan's in that, despite the critic's primarily metaphysical beliefs, it takes a materialist turn. Young's claim that southerners "placed great emphasis on land and material property, on a definite place, and very little on money" is drawn straight from Tate's portrayal of Kentucky in "A Southern Mode of the Imagination." Young also utilizes "The Hind Tit" to portray place as the loamy locus that substantiates Lytle's iconic anticommodity: "Land is not a place, as Lytle has noted, where one grows wealthy; it is a place where one grows corn." More generally, if less explicitly, Young's vision of place appears to be related to the proprietary ideal of pre- or anticapitalist subsistence farming portrayed by the original Agrarians in the mid-1930s. Ultimately, Young follows Sullivan by presuming that industrial- and finance-capitalism has seriously damaged, if not totally

---

between land use and misuse in the South and in the rest of the country, that distinction no longer obtains" (50). Egerton quotes from a recent report that ten thousand companies, ranging from small-scale subdividers of family farms to mass-scale corporations, were turning rural land sale across America into a five-billion-dollar annual business. *The Americanization of Dixie* should remind us that, in the 1970s, not only conservative, overtly neo-Agrarian literary critics like Sullivan worried that "the South is just about over as a separate and distinct place" (xxi).

18. Sullivan, *Death by Melancholy*, x; Michael Cass, Foreword to *A Requiem for the Renascence*, ix.

19. Young is quoted in the chapter titled "Twentieth-Century Southern Literature" in Louis D. Rubin and C. Hugh Holman, eds., *Southern Literary Study: Problems and Possibilities* (Chapel Hill: University of North Carolina Press, 1975), 148.

destroyed, the South's "emphasis on land and material property, on a definite place." This feeds directly into Young's mournful conclusion that "[m]uch of contemporary literature, in the South as elsewhere, is a literature of no specific place."[20]

Shortly I will assess the implications of Sullivan and Young's Tate-like arguments for contemporary southern literature. More immediately, however, I want to mediate my argument through a brief consideration of the way in which Eudora Welty's oft-cited "sense of place" has been adopted and adapted by southern literary critics, Sullivan among them.

Aesthetics of Place or Aesthetics of Antidevelopment? Eudora Welty

There is an inadvertently auspicious moment in "The Sense of Place" when Frederick Hoffman quotes from Eudora Welty's essay "Place in Fiction" (1956). Hoffman hereby inaugurates a southern literary critical tradition in which this essay in particular, and Welty's work as a whole, has become the classic explanation and exemplar of the southern "sense of place." As James Justus has observed, "Place in Fiction" has been second only to "The New Provincialism" as "the revered text that ratified the critical consensus." It is not a little ironic, then, that Welty herself sounds a note of skepticism at the start of "Place in Fiction," identifying place only as "one of the lesser angels" of literary production. Nonetheless, in "Eudora Welty's Sense of Place" (another *South: Modern Southern Literature in Cultural Setting* essay, based on a piece from *Southern Renascence*), Robert Daniel concluded that "[t]he presiding genius of her work is her sense of place." So what exactly constitutes Welty's "sense of place"—or perhaps more pertinently, the critics' sense of Welty's "sense of place"?[21]

Arguably, it was not a literary critic but a historian, C. Vann Woodward, who did most to establish a markedly neo-Agrarian conception of Weltyan place. In the seminal essay "The Search for Southern Identity" (1958), Woodward cites his friend Robert Penn Warren's argument that southerners have a "fear of abstraction." He then proceeds to cite Welty's "experience" as the

---

20. Thomas Daniel Young, *The Past in the Present: A Thematic Study of Modern Southern Fiction* (Baton Rouge: Louisiana State University Press, 1981), 7, 9, 8.

21. Hoffman, "The Sense of Place," 61; James Justus, Foreword to Jeffrey Folks and James Perkins, eds., *Southern Writers at Century's End* (Lexington: University Press of Kentucky, 1997), xi; Eudora Welty, "Place in Fiction," in *The Eye of the Story: Selected Essays and Reviews* (New York: Random House, 1979), 116; Robert Daniel, "Eudora Welty's Sense of Place," in *South: Modern Southern Literature in Its Cultural Setting*, 286.

southern antithesis of a standard American "insignificance of place, locality, and community." In this now-familiar formulation—recapitulated as recently as 1994 in Jan Gretlund's "common-sense reading"—Welty's "sense of place" takes its stand against abstraction. However, Woodward never considers the opposition between "abstraction" and "place" in the specific form that the Agrarians themselves conceived it in the 1930s: the opposition between the abstract property relations of finance-capitalism, and agricultural real property that guarantees (as Warren once stated it) "the relation of man to place." To put it another way, Woodward figures Welty's sense of place in vaguely neo-Agrarian terms, but avoids the more specific socioeconomic critique developed through the Agrarians' proprietary ideal. This is not to score Woodward for failing to identify, in those few influential paragraphs, the Agrarians' specific mid-1930s focus upon subsistence-based small farms. It is simply to cite Woodward as the most famous of many (mostly literary) critics who have configured the Weltyan "sense of place" along Agrarian lines, without recognizing or acknowledging that it might be an anachronistic ideal.[22]

It is notable that neither "Place in Fiction" nor the essay in which Welty first used the term "sense of place," "Some Notes on River Country" (1944), refers directly to the radical sociospatial transformation of the South during the (post–New Deal, post-Agrarian) period they were written. Instead, at the end of "Some Notes on River Country," Welty implies that "sense of place" transcends economics: "[p]erhaps it is the sense of place that gives us the belief that passionate things, in some essence, endure . . . regardless of commerce." Yet one might argue against Welty that the historical economic decline of Rodney's Landing that "River Country" describes proves precisely that "place," and the practice of place in everyday life, is always profoundly influenced by the "vagrancies" of capital. Arguably, it is the *withdrawal* of capital, followed inevitably by outward migration, that has produced the unpopulated "natural" landscape that Welty rhapsodizes over in terms approaching the pathetic fallacy. Given the transformation of the South in the 1940s, one might ask whether "River Country" indulges not only what Gretlund calls an Agrarian "aesthetics of place," but also (to cite Richard Godden again) the Agrarians' "aesthetics of anti-development." As we saw in Chapter 1, Andrew

22. C. Vann Woodward, "The Search for Southern Identity," in *The Burden of Southern History: Enlarged Edition* (1969; reprint, Baton Rouge: Louisiana State University Press, 1989), 23–24; Jan Nordby Gretlund, *Eudora Welty's Aesthetics of Place* (Odense, Denmark: Odense University Press, 1994), vii.

Lytle transformed sallet and corn into magical anticommodities. Similarly, Welty homes in on the magnolia flower which "can be seen for several miles on a clear day" as an archetypal symbol of a "southern" Nature that supposedly has reestablished "for the third time, or the fourth, or the hundredth" its supremacy over human history—including "commerce."[23]

There is reason to believe that the broad, vague scope of "Place in Fiction" and the "natural" focus of "River Country" allowed certain neo-Agrarian critics to celebrate Welty's "sense of place" rather than recognizing that—according to the doom-laden logic of the Agrarians' own proprietary ideal—"the South" no longer existed. However, the referential gap, or time-space warp, between Welty's textual "sense of place" and sociospatial reality has not gone entirely unnoticed. In 1961, Daniel approvingly referred to the town of Morgana in *The Golden Apples* (1949) as "an organism, to which its people could feel that they belonged." But with some perturbation, Daniel noted that Welty writes "in the past tense: most of the incidents in *The Golden Apples* take place in 1910 or a little later." This warp is particularly apparent in *Losing Battles* (1970). In *Requiem for the Renascence*, Walter Sullivan pointedly observes that "the brilliant novel *Losing Battles* is a long look backward. The action is very carefully circumscribed in terms of time and place; it is set in the middle 1930s and consequently none of the agonies of our own situation in history are allowed to intrude." Sullivan's polemical point is that the best contemporary southern literature (in 1972, he had made similar remarks regarding Walker Percy and the "neo-Agrarian" Madison Jones) does not remotely refer to the present.[24]

Of course, Sullivan's own brand of neo-Agrarian nostalgia is evident here. Speaking alongside Sullivan at a conference in 1972, historian Norman Brown perceptively identified a certain ideological bias informing literary critics' celebration of *Losing Battles* as "the last good 'southern novel.'" Brown observed that such rhetoric revealed the extent to which critics "think of the southern novel as being rooted in the agrarian order." To take Brown's point further, I would suggest that Sullivan and other critics could see *Losing Battles* as the great latecomer of "southern literature" because Welty so vividly portrays

---

23. Welty, "Some Notes on River Country," in *The Eye of the Story*, 299, 297, 295. The famous line "I have felt many times there [in the Mississippi river country] a sense of place as powerful as if it were visible and walking and could touch me" (286) provides the most obvious example of the pathetic fallacy.

24. Daniel, "Eudora Welty's Sense of Place," 282–83; Sullivan, *Requiem for the Renascence*, 52. See also "Twentieth-Century Southern Literature" in *Southern Literary Study*, 141; on Madison Jones as a "neo-Agrarian," see *Death by Melancholy*, 97.

subsistence farming in the Mississippi hill country. One might term it a return of the critically repressed: sense of place as the Agrarians' proprietary ideal.[25]

In contrast to Jefferson or even Frenchman's Bend, the hill-country hamlet of Banner barely has been touched by the cash nexus, let alone a bank (Sullivan's central symbol of property "tend[ing] towards abstraction" under finance-capitalism). To be sure, there are occasional, oblique signs in *Losing Battles* that Banner has experienced socioeconomic change. For example, Curly Stovall has taken possession of the local store. However, for all his meanness, Stovall is no Flem Snopes. An ongoing source of comedy in the novel is the Renfro family's inability or refusal to reimburse "that billy goat [in] cash" for goods Stovall gives them begrudgingly on credit. On a somewhat larger scale, a lumber company has been and gone again: the destructive mill-owner Dearman "took over some of the country, brought niggers in here, cut down every tree within forty miles, and run it through a sawmill." Yet even Dearman is dismissed by the Renfros as merely a "glorified Stovall." Nor has the mill's withdrawal had any discernible impact upon a local labor market largely engaged in subsistence farming.[26]

There are hints, albeit oblique, that the Renfros' own farm is failing. Reference is made to the family's current reliance upon New Deal food programs for basic sustenance. However, as we saw in Chapter 1, the Depression (and the New Deal itself) devastated small farming as a widespread, identifiably southern way of life. Yet the gloomy prospects of the Renfro clan impinge not at all upon the polyvocal carnival conducted at Granny Vaughn's birthday reunion. Uncle Dolphus declares defiantly that "[f]armers still and evermore will be!" Hence, a critic such as Sullivan could see *Losing Battles* as a successful "southern novel" because (like *The Hamlet*) it demonstrates familial love redeeming an agrarian community that also, almost incidentally, resists finance-capitalism—something that the "South" of the early 1970s had conspicuously failed to do.[27]

If Sullivan's agonized awareness of the South's socioeconomic destruction motivates his celebration of novels that retain a residual sense of the region

---

25. Brown quoted in "Twentieth-Century Southern Literature" in *Southern Literary Study*, 156. In his *New Republic* review, Jonathan Yardley referred to *Losing Battles* as "the last 'Southern novel'—or should I say the last good one." See Gray, *Writing the South*, 217.

26. Eudora Welty, *Losing Battles* (1970; reprint, London: Virago, 1986), 39, 341, 342.

27. Welty, *Losing Battles*, 194.

as agrarian, he never loses sight of the anachronistic nature of Eudora Welty's (or Madison Jones's) fiction. Nonetheless, there remains a related problem. Sullivan's Tate-esque eschatological paradigm makes it all but impossible to talk about that recent literature that *has* depicted the region's postagrarian (or post-Agrarian) sociospatial reality. The same criticism can be made of Young, not to mention Tate himself. Young's adoption of Tate's southern decline (and death) narrative includes the axiomatic assumption that modern southern fiction has no real sense of place. As Young states explicitly, "it is difficult to differentiate between the contemporary southern novel and the fiction produced in New York, Chicago, or Paris." If Rubin's neo-Agrarian "image" of "the South" seems to be floating without reference to contemporary sociospatial reality, the "remarkably gloomy" worldview of Sullivan and Young's criticism is no more helpful to a nuanced understanding of contemporary "southern literature."[28]

That region we have known and narrated as "the South" may no longer be primarily agrarian—it may in fact have ceased to exist as a distinctive economic-geographical entity—but the social practice and production of place continues. Whether one likes it or not, capitalist land speculation and real-estate development play a major role in the *r*eproduction—the creative destruction—of traditional "southern" loci. How, then, can we theorize such sociospatial processes in literary-critical terms? Given the extent to which they have been constructed upon, and burdened with, Agrarian and neo-Agrarian beliefs, we may want to begin by reconfiguring the foundational terms: "South," "southern literature," and "sense of place."

Postsouthern Cartographies

In 1980, Lewis P. Simpson published an essay entitled "The Closure of History in a Postsouthern America." Simpson coined the term "postsouthern" to denote the emergence of a new and distinctive literary moment in which "[t]he history of the literary mind of the South seeking to become aware of itself"—a central aspect of Southern Renascence writing—no longer appeared to operate. As such, Simpson suggests, "[t]he epiphany of the southern literary artist will not be repeated. The Southern Renascence will not come again." Simpson concludes on a somewhat more optimistic note than Tate or Sullivan, however, positing that "the postsouthern America"

---

28. Young, *The Past in the Present*, 24; on the "remarkably gloomy" worldview of Sullivan, see O'Brien, "A Heterodox Note on the Southern Renaissance," 159.

presented by Walker Percy might yet yield "a return to a participation in the mystery of history."[29]

Though Simpson's initial definition of "postsouthern" was tentative, the neologism introduced into southern literary and cultural criticism an imperative to reassess the legitimacy of other established tropes, beliefs, and constructs. As Michael Kreyling suggests, "postsouthern" has been "an enabling word"—similar to and synonymous with "postmodern"—with which to reassess the meaning and legitimacy of such foundational terms as "South" and "southern." Of those other scholars who offered early definitions of "postsouthernism," Stephen Flinn Young most specifically related it to the "sense of place." Young begins by pondering whether "we may have even become prisoners of our own fascination" with sense of place, "for when change overtakes us and place, even the place we call the South, is not the place it used to be, anxiety strikes." Yet Young ultimately seeks a postsouthern art that retains the "pre-postmodern . . . sense of place." He finds it in contemporary sculpture that, for all its formal innovation, focuses its representative attention upon familiar rural figures and landscapes. Young ends up folding the new (Simpson's postsouthern America) into the established (a rural southern sense of place).[30]

It is Kreyling who has most incisively extended Simpson's enabling word as a critical tool through which to explicate recent fiction. Kreyling's version of the postsouthern is tied to postmodernist parody: a literary technique that, in the (post)southern context, liberates contemporary authors like Barry Hannah, Harry Crews, and Reynolds Price from a Faulknerian anxiety of influence (usually imposed upon them by literary critics). Scott Romine has helpfully noted that such a theory of postsouthernism does not refer to any "real South," i.e., to a contemporary, material geography. As Romine remarks, "[b]ecause parody takes as its primary object not a thing but a style or system of representations," the postsouthern text can only parody "previous imitations of place." I believe that there is cause for concern here. If postsouthernism is constituted purely at the level of self-reflexive textual representations

29. Lewis P. Simpson, "The Closure of History in a Postsouthern America," in *The Brazen Face of History: Studies in the Literary Consciousness of America* (Baton Rouge: Louisiana State University Press, 1980), 268–69.

30. Kreyling, "*The Fathers*: A Postsouthern Narrative Reading," in Jefferson Humphries, ed., *Southern Literature and Literary Theory* (Athens: University of Georgia Press, 1990), 186, and *Inventing Southern Literature*, 153–55; Stephen Flinn Young, "Post-Southernism: The Southern Sensibility in Postmodern Sculpture," *Southern Quarterly* 27, no. 1 (fall 1989): 4.

or signs, one might ask whether postsouthern literature can *ever* refer to, let alone try to represent, the "real South" (which, as Romine notes, is "a concept [Kreyling] does not reject entirely"). More pointedly, one might ask if literary postsouthernism, in all its ingenious intertextuality, ever refers to the real, and highly capitalist, geography of the *post*-South—to, in Gavin Wright's words, the "new economy [that] has moved into the geographic space formerly occupied by the old [rural, agricultural] one."[31]

At this point, it is worth considering a 1990 essay by Julius Rowan Raper. While Raper does not discuss the postsouthern per se, he offers a properly skeptical "postmodern view" as to why "the extraordinary sense of place . . . is a mainstay still of Modern Southern Fiction—but, less and less, of modern Southern life." Raper argues that, as contemporary southerners assert a more stable sense of *self*, rather than relying on a sense of *place*, so a postmodern southern literature will emerge. Liberated from "fidelity to description of place," this postmodern southern literature will have "a special role to play in keeping us *free* from the verisimilitude, the seeming truth, that 'controllers of reality,' the advertisers and ideologues of the age, have a distinct interest in foisting upon us." As Romine observes, Raper's "postmodern view" is "an antimimetic style that will not emerge *from* place, but *against* it in the form of postmodern subversions of verisimilitude." Again, though, one is compelled ask whether this kind of "playful . . . liberating" literature will even attempt to depict the sociospatial reality of the post-South. Raper himself notes that "the skylines of Atlanta, even Durham, show us that we are becoming the Postmodern South." But by turning to "the kingdom of imagination" and away from "the sociological and historical literature of memory," will Raper's postmodern southern literature—not to mention postmodern southern literary criticism—also look away from the capitalist reality of Atlanta's sense of place(lessness)?[32]

The most sophisticated assessment of the postsouthern sense of place is Romine's essay "Where Is Southern Literature? The Practice of Place in a Postsouthern Age," published in 2000. Romine asks whether the terms "southern" and "place" can endure "without mimetic reference at the economic or ideological levels." I have already argued that, even in the 1940s,

---

31. Romine, "Where Is Southern Literature?" 22; Wright, *Old South, New South*, 16.

32. Julius Rowan Raper, "Inventing Modern Southern Fiction: A Postmodern View," *Southern Literary Journal* 22, no. 2 (spring 1990): 9, 6, 10; Romine, "Where Is Southern Literature?" 15; Raper, "Inventing Modern Southern Fiction," 17–18.

what Romine calls the "overdeveloped eschatological sense" of place patented by Allen Tate and perpetuated by Walter Sullivan and Thomas Daniel Young strongly implied that "the South" could not survive capitalist redevelopment of agricultural real property. On these terms, it would seem that "southern" and "place" can no longer claim "mimetic reference" at the economic level—i.e., at a traditional, agricultural base. Romine himself vacillates as to whether "Tate's eschatology was correct, only premature; it may be premature yet." However, he also asserts that "it seems inevitable that the erosion of economic and ideological distinctiveness will radically alter the meaning of place." Echoing Raper, Romine states that "[a]lmost certainly, place as a marker of southern literary identity cannot continue under the aegis of verisimilitude and mimesis." In the final paragraph, he tentatively predicts that "southern literature will become less real," with *hyper*realists like Hannah and Lewis Nordan "generat[ing] their own worlds without especially borrowing from ours." As his ambivalence concerning Kreyling's theory of postsouthern parody suggests, Romine is skeptical about a postsouthern practice of place that exists only in "purely textual form." However, his concluding, Baudrillardian intimation that postsouthern fiction "might, in fact, dispense with reality altogether" leaves us in the same quandary as the theories of Kreyling and Raper. We face the prospect of a literary (and literary-critical) refusal to refer to, let alone represent, the social reality of "place(lessness)" in a late capitalist post-South.[33]

I want to suggest that a historical-geographical materialist approach might help us to recover the relation between postsouthern literature and the sociospatial reality of the contemporary (post-) South. It might even enable us to retrieve and update that aspect of the Agrarians' (and Sullivan's) work that has been largely ignored: their critique of (finance) capitalism and its role in the production and destruction of place. Romine provocatively juxtaposes Tate's theory of "provincialism" to Jean-François Lyotard's claim that "capitalism inherently possesses the power to derealize familiar objects, social roles, and institutions to such a degree that the so-called realistic representations can no longer evoke reality except as nostalgia or mockery." Romine thus implies that the postsouthern rejection of "the real South" relates in some fashion to the kind of derealization of place by capitalism that, in different periods, both Tate and Lyotard observed. Yet one might ask whether a (post)southern literary (-critical) turn away from sociospatial

33. Romine, "Where Is Southern Literature?" 11, 9, 23, 25.

reality into nonreferential narrative play merely mimics (and not parodically, but as pastiche) capitalist reification. To put it another way: if postmodern capitalism—particularly that form of finance-capitalism once identified by Tate—has derealized or abstracted familiar southern geographies, one might ask whether postsouthern hyperrealism risks uncritically recapitulating the (il)logic of late capitalism itself. Is there a danger that the parodic poetics of postsouthernism are neutered, even co-opted, by a socioeconomic system that has derealized the foundational sense of place more than hyperreal fiction ever could?[34]

This is where historical-geographical materialism comes in. Given capitalism's tremendous impact upon the material production of place in our time, it becomes all the more important to consider texts that *do* try to represent the sociospatial reality of the post-South. Postsouthern literature should not be hermetically sealed in some hyperreal hall of self-reflexive nonrepresentations. This does not mean that one must have recourse to some outdated (nostalgic, according to Lyotard) notion of mimetic "realism," or even of literature per se, as retaining some residual "truth-value" that, more than "any other signifying practice," resists and critiques capitalism. Postmodern literary theorists like Linda Hutcheon have taught us that fiction "actually refer[s] at the first level to other texts: we know the past (which really did exist) only through its textualized remains." Indeed, postsouthern parody is valuable precisely because it emphasizes the extent to which the *southern* past, and southern place, have been defined primarily through literary mediations or "images," rather than sociohistorical or sociospatial reality. So I do not want to dismiss the power and importance of postsouthern, intertextual parody. But I *do* want to insist that we must pay attention to the historical-geographical, material reproduction of place as real estate, and the creation, destruction, and mediation of place under capitalism more generally.[35]

34. Romine, "Where Is Southern Literature?" 23; see also Jean-François Lyotard, *The Postmodern Condition: A Report on Knowledge* (Manchester, U.K.: Manchester University Press, 1984), 74. See Fredric Jameson's distinction between parody and pastiche in *Postmodernism, or, the Cultural Logic of Late Capitalism* (London: Verso, 1991), 17.

35. Drew Milne, "Introduction Part II: Reading Marxist Literary Theory," in Terry Eagleton and Drew Milne, eds., *Marxist Literary Theory* (Oxford: Blackwell, 1996), 22; Linda Hutcheon, *A Poetics of Postmodernism* (London: Routledge, 1988), 119. I have discussed elsewhere how William Faulkner and, more recently, Barry Hannah use postsouthern parody to interrogate the textual production and mediation of neo-Confederate ideology in and as southern history and historiography. See "'All the Confederate Dead . . . All of Faulkner the Great':

As it happens, even as "place" has remained a received idea in southern literary criticism—the efforts of Raper and Romine notwithstanding—the concept has come under intensive scrutiny in postmodern theory spanning various academic disciplines. In *Postmodern Geographies* (1989), Edward Soja called for (and himself enacted) "the reassertion of space in critical social theory." From a spatial turn first taken by Henri Lefebvre and, more tentatively, Michel Foucault, much theoretical attention is now being paid to place. Soja regards postmodern geographies as the result of "successive eras of capitalist development" and calls for "a simultaneously historical and geographical materialism" that will allow us to fully comprehend these social processes. He posits that "the development of what I call postmodern geographies has progressed far enough to have changed significantly both the material landscape of the contemporary world and the interpretative terrain of critical theory." I hope that my own historical-geographical materialist approach to the capitalist production of place in the (post-) South might contribute to a new interpretative terrain through which we can understand postsouthern geographies—and postsouthern literary cartographies. Before proceeding to textual analysis, I want to conclude this chapter, and Part 1, with a brief assessment of some of the theoretical approaches to postmodern capitalist geographies that I will be incorporating into Parts 2 and 3.[36]

In *Inventing Southern Literature,* Kreyling quotes the leading left-wing theorist of the postmodern: "Fredric Jameson might say that 'southern' has fallen victim to the inexorable critical-economic process of commodification: 'Postmodernism is what you have when the modernization process [commodification] is complete and nature is gone for good.'" Kreyling thus quotes Jameson to iterate that foundational terms such as "southern" have been—to use Agrarian rubric in a suitably postsouthern, parodic fashion—"uprooted" by commodity fetishism to the extent that nothing seems "natural" any more. However, this is only a partial take on Jameson's theory of postmodernism as "the cultural logic of late capitalism." For Jameson, it is not simply the authority of semiotic referents such as "southern" that has been undermined by the commodification process. Capitalism's awesome power has resulted in

---

Faulkner, Hannah, Neo-Confederate Narrative and Postsouthern Parody," *Mississippi Quarterly* 54, no. 1 (spring 2001): 197–211.

36. Edward Soja, *Postmodern Geographies: The Reassertion of Space in Critical Social Theory* (London: Verso, 1989), 3, 12.

no less than the material "effacement of Nature [itself], and its precapitalist agricultures, from the postmodern." Indeed, one doubts whether Jameson would agree with Kreyling's claim that "capitalism" cannot (any more than "southern") operate as a "totalizing and totally authoritative referent." For Jameson, late capitalism's hegemonic expansion into previously residual or resistant loci (including natural and agricultural spaces) is a defining feature of postmodernity.[37]

Jameson pays no particular attention to the South per se. However, his passing reference to Faulkner "inherit[ing] a social and historical raw material, a popular memory" that "inscribed the coexistence of modes of production in narrative form" echoes Tate's theory that Renascence writers' historical consciousness enabled them to record the shift between, and the juxtaposition of, precapitalist agriculture and the abstract property relations of modern finance-capitalism. If, as Jameson suggests, precapitalist agricultures have now been entirely effaced, what has become of "place" in Faulkner or the Agrarians' "South"? Jameson observes that "in that simpler phenomenological or regional sense, place in the United States no longer exists, or, more precisely, it exists at a much feebler level, surcharged by . . . the increasingly abstract . . . power network of so-called multinational capitalism itself." One can conceive of Tate grimly concurring with this assessment of a *post*southern America and its sense of place(lessness) within a wider capitalist worldsystem. Davidson, Ransom, Lytle, and Warren, too, might have agreed that, under contemporary finance-capitalism, "an older kind of existential positioning of ourselves in Being—the human body in the natural landscape, the individual in the older village or organic community—[becomes] exceedingly problematical." Where Tate had earlier insinuated and anticipated, Jameson likely would confirm that "the South"—not only the textual sign, but also the material and/or imag(in)ed place of precapitalist agricultures to which the Agrarians and Faulkner once referred—has indeed been destroyed by capitalism.[38]

The geographer David Harvey provides another valuable historical-geographical materialist approach to the postmodern capitalist production of place. In *The Condition of Postmodernity* (1989), Harvey gives a name to the acceleration and expansion of capitalism since 1973 that Jameson also describes: "time-space compression." Just as Jameson echoes the Agrarians, so Harvey too notes the increasingly "abstract," "de-materialized" nature

---

37. Kreyling, *Inventing Southern Literature*, 155; Jameson, *Postmodernism*, 366.
38. Jameson, *Postmodernism*, 405, 127.

of finance-capitalism, and of the money form per se, as "currency markets fluctuate across the world's spaces," apparently detached from "productive activity within a particular space." Harvey also attends to a more material-geographical phenomenon that he calls the "spatial fix," whereby excess capital and labor are rerouted into "the production of new spaces within which capitalist production can proceed." Harvey mentions the South as one among many "geographical centres of accumulation" created after 1945.[39]

In *Justice, Nature and the Geography of Difference* (1996), Harvey provides a couple of examples that suggest the paradoxes of abstract and material place relations in the contemporary South. Harvey quotes German theater director Johannes Birringer's response to the "unforeseen collapse of space" in two Texas cities, Dallas and Houston. Birringer remarks upon "the unavoidable fusion and confusion of geographical realities, or the interchangeability of all places, or the disappearance of visible (static) points of reference into a constant commutation of surface images." Birringer could be describing the spatial confusion of postsouthern capitalist cities that are not only built upon *local*, material oil extraction/production, but also bound up in the *global*, abstract flow and exchange of capital. Yet Harvey's other example stands in sobering contrast to the dematerialized networks of global capital. In Hamlet, North Carolina, in 1991, a chicken-processing plant run by the Imperial Foods Corporation caught fire, killing twenty-five workers. The chicken-processing industry has been dubbed "the latest industry of toil to reign in the [U.S.] South," a sobriquet which should remind us that, even today, there exists exploitation of labor that bears bleak comparison with what has gone before in the region.[40]

The above examples aside, Harvey gives little more direct attention to the (post-)South than Jameson does. However, I would repeat the speculative point that—in the tradition of "similarity between Agrarian and Marxist critiques of capitalism"—Tate, Ransom, and Lytle, together with the neo-Agrarian likes of Sullivan and Young, would likely agree with much of these contemporary, leftist critiques.[41] To the degree that the Agrarians during the

39. David Harvey, *The Condition of Postmodernity* (Oxford: Blackwell, 1989), 297–98, 183, 185.

40. David Harvey, *Justice, Nature, and the Geography of Difference* (Oxford: Blackwell, 1996), 243, 335.

41. Romine, "Where Is Southern Literature?" 13. Conkin comments on "the verbal similarities" between Tate and Ransom's essays and *The Communist Manifesto* when the two Agrarians "occasionally substituted capitalism for industrialism" (*Southern Agrarians*, 76–77). Conkin also observes Tate's exposure to "the critique of capitalist society mouthed by leftist friends"

1930s formulated a radical conservative critique of capitalism, they have more in common with contemporary leftists than neoconservative idolaters of the free market. The likes of Soja, Jameson, and Harvey provide a critical framework through which to approach a post-Agrarian social geography in which agricultural real property has been displaced by what Tate termed the abstract property relations of finance-capitalism. The critical difference is that, unlike the Agrarians and many of their neo-Agrarian literary-critical followers, these contemporary theorists try to understand how people live in a world in which the usual platitudes of "place"—whether as precapitalist proprietary ideal, or literary-critical "image"—no longer hold. A Jamesonian critique of Agrarianism might emphasize the way in which it remained tied to that "right-wing critique of capitalism" which portrays "a 'fall' into civilization"—a fall out of place into a nostalgic yearning for (to quote Faulkner) "a make-believe region . . . which perhaps never existed anywhere." The Agrarians' eschatological worldview prevented them from envisioning the future in anything but dystopian terms. We have seen how Tate's literary-critical vision of the South operated as a decline narrative that, by Walter Sullivan's time, had become a requiem for the renascence. The challenge, then, is to apply the theories of Jameson, Harvey, Soja and others in a manner that might take us beyond the defunct Agrarian/neo-Agrarian "South," and into the contemporary post-South in which people still live—and authors still write.[42]

As we have seen, Harvey continues to refer to "the U.S. South." However, many other commentators, not to mention boosters, have preferred the term Sun Belt to describe the regional boom since the 1970s. As a semiotic sign referring to the radical economic redevelopment of the region previously known as "the South," "Sun Belt" might be seen as a specifically economic synonym for "*post*southern." However, I would argue that "*post*southern" is a more useful critical term because, unlike "Sun Belt," the word (specifically, the prefix) does not simply erase the historical-geographical continuities

---

(44) in New York during the late 1920s. See also Gerald Graff's essay "American Criticism Left and Right," which cites Tate circa 1939 on "the iniquity of finance-capitalism," and challenges the reader to distinguish Davidson from Marx or Georg Lukács! Graff in Sacvan Bercovitch and Myra Jehlen, eds., *Ideology and Classic American Literature* (Cambridge: Cambridge University Press, 1986), 97, 118–19.

42. Jameson, *Postmodernism*, 337; Faulkner, unpublished 1933 manuscript quoted in Fred Hobson, *Tell about the South: The Southern Rage to Explain* (Baton Rouge: Louisiana State University Press, 1983), 3.

of uneven development—of which the chicken-processing industry is an example. Too often, "Sun Belt" has been a highly performative sign, barely referring to, or at best obfuscating, the sociospatial inequality that remains. If I generally want "postsouthern" to signify a radical *break* with our familiar ideas of "the South," the etymological retention of "southern" can also point up historical-geographical continuities—much as Harvey and Soja emphasize that *post*modern geographies arise out of capitalist modernity and "successive eras of capitalist development."

Jameson insists that one can counter postmodern capitalist abstraction through "the practical reconquest of a sense of place" (and not only within a local geography, but also the "global system" defined by capitalist social relations). Soja articulates a similar sensibility, a "spatialized ontology," whereby individuals and groups undertake "an ontological struggle to restore the meaningful existential spatiality of being" *within* postmodern capitalist geographies. Meanwhile, Harvey emphasizes that "[c]oncern for both the real and fictional qualities of place increases in a phase of capitalist development in which the power to command space, particularly with respect to financial and money flows, has become more marked than ever before." He goes further, insisting that "[t]he preservation or construction of a sense of place is then an active moment in the passage from memory to hope, from past to future."[43]

If "the South" no longer survives as a material, sociospatial reality, or even as part of the Agrarian political-poetical imagination, this does not mean that postsouthern geographies exhibit no sense of place. Nor does it mean that the practice of everyday life is futile. The books that I discuss in subsequent chapters are variously set in suburban New Orleans circa 1960; Mississippi in the 1970s and 1980s; Atlanta in the 1980s and 1990s; and even pre-millennial New Jersey. In various ways and to varying degrees, Walker Percy, Richard Ford, Anne Rivers Siddons, Tom Wolfe, and Toni Cade Bambara all construct postsouthern cartographies in which suburban and urban land speculation and development is commonplace. "Cents of place" may well have been substituted for "sense of place." [44] Yet at important points in most of these novels, we witness characters undertaking the active and hopeful (if necessarily con-

---

43. Jameson, *Postmodernism*, 51; Soja, *Postmodern Geographies*, 7; Harvey, *Justice, Nature, and the Geography of Difference*, 247, 306.

44. Stephen Smith, "The Rhetoric of Southern Humor," in Jefferson Humphries and John Lowe, eds., *The Future of Southern Letters* (New York: Oxford University Press, 1996), 173.

tingent) reconstruction of a spatialized ontology, a revised sense of place, that allows them to live within their respective postsouthern worlds. It is precisely because the familiar southern "sense of place" is defunct that "the scholarly imagination," as Tate termed it, should be engaged with the "real and fictional qualities of place" manifested in postsouthern life and literature.

PART TWO

The Postsouthern Turn: Warren, Percy, Ford, and the Redevelopment of Place

3. Toward a Postsouthern Sense of Place: Robert Penn Warren's *A Place to Come To* and Walker Percy's *The Moviegoer*

When Lewis Simpson introduced the term "postsouthern" to the literary-critical lexicon, he had in mind the work of Walker Percy. Chiefly concerned with the fate of the "literary mind of the South" in the post-Renascence period, Simpson focused upon the desperate struggle of "the southern consciousness" depicted in Percy's *The Last Gentleman* (1966). But in positing that "Walker Percy suggest[s] we are beginning to live in a postsouthern America," Simpson identified Percy's concern with the transformation not only of the South's literary mind but also of its social space. Perhaps more eloquently and explicitly than any other post-Renascence writer, Percy observed the perniciously lingering, purely literary influence of such foundational, canonical "southern" spaces as "Faulkner country," "O'Connor country," and "Welty country." It was Percy who implored that the contemporary southern writer should "not try to become a neo-Agrarian."[1]

The main part of this chapter explicates Percy's debut novel, *The Moviegoer* (1961), in terms of its significance and its limits, as a proto-postsouthern literary representation of a changing social geography. But I want to begin by reading "place" in a novel by one of the original Agrarians: Robert Penn Warren's *A Place to Come To* (1977). I argue that Warren's last novel enacts its own postsouthern turn. The one-time contributor to *I'll Take My Stand* and *Who Owns America?* offers a subtly parodic interrogation of "the South," "southern literature," and "sense of place"—complexly commingled with a residual antipathy toward the capitalist reproduction of "the South."

Most importantly for my purposes, the sense of place presented by Warren's character-narrator Jediah (Jed) Tewksbury affords a useful comparison to that exhibited by Percy's character-narrator John Bickerson (Binx)

---

1. Simpson, "The Closure of History in a Postsouthern America," 268–69; Walker Percy, "Novel Writing in an Apocalyptic Time," in Patrick Samway, ed., *Signposts in a Strange Land* (London: Bellew, 1991), 166–67.

Bolling. This sense of place is manifested as Jed and Binx experience and narrate not only the capitalist reproduction of familiar "southern" sites but also the built spaces of "the North"—particularly Chicago and the small-town Midwest. There are two significant "southern" sequences in Warren's novel—Jed's youth in rural, small-town Alabama in the 1930s, and his young adult, academic life in Nashville in the early 1950s. As we will see, during the 1950s (as narrated in the 1970s), Jed develops a skeptical, ironical attitude toward implicitly Agrarian conceptions of "the South" as agricultural real property. By contrast, and despite initially seeming content with life in the burgeoning suburbs of New Orleans circa 1960, Binx has a deeply troubled relationship to the capitalist development of postsouthern geographies. This anxiety arises not least because Binx himself is involved in the material reproduction of, and financial speculation in, familiar "southern" places: urban New Orleans and rural bayou country. In order to redeem some residual, authentic "South" from (sub)urban real-estate development, Binx invokes the kind of purely rhetorical contrasts between "North" and "South" that no longer serve for Warren's postsouthern philosopher of "place(lessness)," Jed Tewksbury.

Jed Tewksbury in Alabama

A Place to Come To begins with Jed Tewksbury recounting the outlandish death of his father, Buck, back when Jed himself was a boy still living on the family farm in the Heaven's Hope neighborhood of Dugton, Alabama, in the early 1930s. Almost immediately, though, Jed acknowledges that such a scene "does not seem real. It is like something I might have read in one of those novels about the South, if I had been old enough back then in the time they were being written."[2] In archetypal postmodern fashion, literary representations have come to precede the "real." Jed realizes that (to cite Linda Hutcheon's formulation) "the past (which really did exist)" is primarily known "through its textualized remains": in this case, the canonical texts of the Southern Renaissance written "back then" in the 1930s. Yet I would suggest that Jed—or rather Warren—is making more than a fashionable postmodern literary-technical point or a general observation about the legacy of southern literary history. The narrative indicates that the 1930s rural South of Jed's youth, and of Warren's own Agrarianism, no longer carries that "con-

---

2. Robert Penn Warren, *A Place to Come To* (London: Secker and Warburg, 1977), 7. All further page references will be incorporated into the main text.

crete" sense of place as agricultural real property upon which the Agrarians felt that they could ground their proprietary ideal.³

In 1930, in "The Hind Tit," Andrew Lytle constructed his textual aesthetic of antidevelopment with the conviction that it referred to a rural, social reality—even if that aesthetic tended to imbue suitably earthy symbols of southern agriculture (sallet, corn) with a mystical anticapitalist repellent. Even in 1953, despite worrying that modernity imperiled "[t]he very meaning of language, that men and nations mean what they say (that is, words)," Lytle could still assert with confidence (or bravado) that "I see no reason to withdraw the assumption upon which the Agrarians based their warning" about the grim fate of an industrialized South.⁴ But for Warren in 1977, signifiers of "southernness"—place-based anticommodities in the Agrarian grain of Lytle's corn and sallet—have not just lost their agricultural referent, or their magical aura: they have become actually and textually extinct. In *A Place to Come To*, Warren does not quite make Michael Kreyling's postsouthern move of "put[ting] quotation marks around the real" to signal the textual mediation of any such "reality." However, it is notable that Jed feels he must *explain* to his reader that "buttermilk was hung in the well—a method used in that time and place to keep milk cool" (12). Here, Jed can just about convey an authentic but defunct Southern (agri)culture through its "textualized remains." But by explicating the historical-geographical specificity of the word "buttermilk," Jed implicitly acknowledges that the contemporary reader lacks any such sociolinguistic source of reference, and is therefore unable to make southern agrarian words mean what they (used to) say. Jed subsequently observes in passing that "trading" was "the old rural word" (14), thus implying that, though capitalist exchange-value was present in the 1930s South, the cash nexus was not (yet) the dominant mode of exchange. However, the fact that Jed again has to clarify the meaning of this "rural word" further emphasizes that the agricultural and small-town southern economy to which "trading" once referred is now defunct, and that the word itself is redundant. Speaking more generally of agricultural real property as the socioeconomic base of his birthplace, Jed observes dryly that not only the "citizens of the Heaven's Hope neighborhood, Claxford County, Alabama," but also those citizens' small farms, were "really alive then and [are] really dead by now." Here, even as he

3. Hutcheon, *A Poetics of Postmodernism*, 119.
4. Lytle, "How Many Miles to Babylon," 32. See also Chapter 2 above.

reports that the agrarian "real" (or Agrarians' ideal) has been effaced, Jed once more has to *explain* this dead reality to us, his latecomer readers. In these syncretic examples, then, we see how Jed's narrative quickly becomes less a mimetic representation than a rhetorical mediation of a historical geography that "in God's truth" (10) really existed, but which has been derealized, *displaced*, by capitalist development.[5]

Doggedly trying to demonstrate that Dugton folk were not simply "characters in a piece of [grotesque Southern] fiction," Jed invokes a distinctly Agrarian binary opposition between rural, southern, concrete experience and northern, urban, finance-capitalist abstraction. He depicts the locals as "sustained by hope and irony but in a few years to enter a time of long hunger and despair as the consequence of something that was to happen in New York City, which they had vaguely heard about, in the stock market, which was something they had never before heard about or, if they had, thought was a place where people bought and sold cattle and work stock" (10).[6] Here, Jed attributes the Depression-era destruction of the southern small farmer to a northern or national market economy. However, Jed's narrative is not structured around a simple neo-Agrarian nostalgia for a "real" South of subsistence farms. He recounts how, after Buck's death, his mother sold the (already diminished) family farm, moved into town, and took a job "in the new canning factory." Though this was "the only industrial development that, even by the bait of no taxes and no unions, ever got lured to Dugton before World War II" (17), it signals the sociospatial shifts underway in the rural South during the 1930s. Moreover, the main reason Jed's mother works so hard is so she can relocate him "to a real city a thousand miles from this-here Dugton" (323). As she tells him regularly during his youth, there "[a]in't nothing here for you . . . Yores is waiting for you, somewheres" (32). Indeed, Jed leaves Dugton in 1935 and is in Chicago by 1940. Given this background, it is unsurprising that Jed's own relationship with Alabama, and "the South" more generally, is experientially limited and philosophically skeptical.[7]

5. Kreyling, *Inventing Southern Literature*, 155.

6. Compare this, for example, with the passages from Allen Tate's "Notes on Liberty and Property" quoted in Chapter 1, contrasting real agricultural property, exemplified by a "thirty-acre farm in Kentucky," with the abstract property of the stock market.

7. See James C. Cobb's *The Selling of the South: The Southern Crusade for Industrial Development, 1936–1990*, 2nd ed. (Urbana and Chicago: University of Illinois Press, 1993), 5–34, for an account of how small southern towns battled to attract industry with the bait of low taxes and no unions.

Jed in Nashville

The other southern site featured heavily in *A Place to Come To* is Nashville, where the young Jed gets a position as a university lecturer in the early 1950s. Before Jed's departure from the University of Chicago, his self-appointed mentor smugly assumes that, "like Antaeus," Jed needs to "go back to your native earth" (117)—even though Alabama-born Jed "had never even seen the place [Nashville] before, had never harbored even a fleeting twinge of curiosity about it." Jed identifies Dr. Sweetzer as an "innocent Indiana victim of Thomas Nelson Page and *Gone with the Wind* and the Lost Cause" (118). Here, Jed clearly is satirizing northerners' textually mediated (distorted) conception of a monolithic "South." It is all the more notable, then, that the Nashville sequence itself is characterized by a subtle postsouthern skepticism toward certain other intertexts closer to Warren's own experience: the Agrarian writings of the 1930s.

Jed describes Nashville as "a thriving middle-size commercial city of the Buttermilk Belt" (123). In doing so, he immediately distinguishes Nashville from Dr. Sweetzer's "South" of Tara and Ole Virginia. But Jed also indicates a divide between the modern, urban capitalist city where the Nashville Agrarians were based, and the rural, agricultural loci that they celebrated in their texts. Jed does become friendly with a Nashville farmer by the name of Bill Cudworth. However, for all that his very surname seems a magical signifier of agrarian values, Cudworth is not the subsistence farmer valorized in "The Hind Tit" or *Who Owns America?* Though Bill now lives in the very farmhouse he was born in, he was most recently a lawyer in New York City. Indeed, Bill's coming home again has been negotiated through the "northern" cash nexus: he has bought back the old farm with money he made in New York. What is more, Bill's southern agrarian credentials are seriously compromised by the fact that he has hired tenants who help take care of his daily duties. All told, Jed is torn between admiration for the ostensibly "simple completeness of their [the Cudworths'] life," and "ask[ing] myself what their world meant: a charade of the past" (146). With reference to the Baudrillardian schemata cited by Scott Romine in his essay on the postsouthern practice of place, one might say that Jed is perceptive enough to ask whether the Cudworths' farm is a simulated "image" that "masks the *absence* of a basic reality"—authentic (subsistence) farming. But even Bill himself is self-consciously concerned that perhaps "nothing I'm doing is even real" (174).[8]

[8]. Jean Baudrillard, *Simulations* (New York: Semiotext(e), 1983), 11; see also Romine, "Where Is Southern Literature?" 24, and Chapter 2 above.

In *A Place to Come To*, the apogee of postsouthern skepticism toward the Agrarian conception of place as agricultural real property comes when Bill tells Jed that "there's a really nice farm coming up for sale right here, overlapping me on a corner. Right price, any terms desired. Part of an estate being wound up. You're a Southerner, why not come home like me, settle down? . . . Mix farming and professoring" (175). Bill thus implies that being a southerner is essentially, even existentially, related to agricultural labor. But to make this case for "farming and professoring" he necessarily ignores not only his earlier doubts over his own role as a part-time pseudofarmer, but also the precipitous post–Wall Street crash decline in southern agriculture. As we saw in Chapter 1, this decline destroyed the Agrarian claim that farming was (or could be again) the basis of a distinctive "southern" identity. What is more, the Cudworths and their ilk seem to be supplanting the last of the genuine farmers. Bill appears blithely unconcerned about the fate of the tenant who runs the bankrupt farm that Bill has implored Jed to buy on the cheap. Relating how the tenant "had a farm once, his own . . . Not much of a place, but something. He lost it" (178), Bill attributes the man's fate to alcoholism. Bill never considers a reversal of cause and effect: that the repossession of his own farm (hardly unusual in the 1930s and 1940s, as we saw in Chapter 2), followed by a slide into servile tenancy, might have led the farmer to drink. It is Jed who, while assessing the property, becomes disturbed by the presence of "the tenant of the farm," the haunted eyes of whom, "bloodshot and defeated, glare in outrage at me" (177). Whatever the exact reasons for the tenant's gloomy situation, the presence of this lifelong farmer throws Jed's own halfhearted plans to play "southern" into sharp relief, and he does not buy the farm.

In *A Place to Come To*, the Nashville farm owners (owners, rather than farmers per se) are those who can still afford it: the former New York lawyer Bill Cudworth and the artist-socialite Lawford Carrington, who farms not at all (125). To varying degrees, they use their farms to perform "southernness," a romanticized simulation of the southern agrarian way of life. The Cudworths' and Carringtons' preexisting wealth allows them to combine farming and socializing without worrying about the grim economic reality of southern agriculture in the 1930s. Only Jed really sees through this "charade of the past." In the process, he rejects the opportunity to "mix farming and professoring"—a combination once felt by the Agrarians as something of an obligation but which to Jed seems just as self-conscious as mixing farming and socializing. Ultimately, Jed's life in Nashville narrows into the "timeless sexuality" of his relationship with Rozelle Carrington. For Jed, the supposed abolition of time and space through sex with Rozelle at least means that "I did not ever have to play with the pretense or the self-delusion of joining Nashville, or any other goddamned place, [or] of being Southern" (209).[9]

Jed in Chicago and Ripley

Both before and after 1951, Jed Tewksbury moves in a social world that extends far beyond Nashville: a social world that, following Simpson, we might call postsouthern America. When Jed studies and later teaches in Chicago, Warren disrupts familiar Agrarian oppositions between the rural South and the northern (or midwestern) metropolis. During the 1930s, this Agrarian binary opposition had become almost axiomatic for Donald Davidson, and it included a tendency to conflate Chicago and New York as "the North" in extremis. For example, in 1934 Davidson scorned "the university laboratories of Chicago or New York"; the following year, he decried the sociological threat to the South "arriving almost daily from the slum-laboratories of Chicago and New York." By contrast, late in *A Place to Come To* Warren's Jed, now an old man, expresses a conclusive attachment to and knowledge of Chicago that outstrips any putatively "southern" sense of place that he might be expected to harbor: "I knew Chicago better than any place in the world, and I suppose I loved it" (318).[10]

But the most notable example of Jed's embracing the North is to be found in his relationship with Ripley City, South Dakota, the place where his first wife, Agnes, came from. During his first visit to Ripley, Jed initially expresses a reflexively "southern" view that the midwestern geography, including the big sky, is the objective correlative of "a new kind of loneliness." Jed remarks of Ripley's sky and landscape that "the distance is fleeing away from you, bleeding away from you, in all directions, and if you can't stop the process you'll be nothing left except a dry, transparent husk" (93). Yet by the end of that first visit, Jed admits that, "though I had approached Ripley City with dire misgivings, I now looked back on my stay with elegiac pleasure." He realizes that Ripley is "[n]ot isolated. Not lost"; rather, it is "perfectly self-contained, self-fulfilling, complete." Ripley does not quite realize the most

---

9. The original Agrarians were often mocked for their efforts to reconcile agriculture and academia. For example, see the 1933 satirical cartoon of "three little Agrarians [Tate, Ransom, and Davidson] in their chosen element" reprinted in Conkin, *Southern Agrarians*, 60.

10. See Davidson, "Dilemma of the Southern Liberals" (1934), in Bingham and Underwood, eds., *Southern Agrarians and the New Deal*, 77; "I'll Take My Stand: A History," 305.

extreme version of the Agrarian proprietary ideal: it is not a self-sufficient community of subsistence farms flourishing beyond the cash nexus, for the railroad that takes away the wheat provides "fine filaments of [commercial] connection with the outside world" (95). Nevertheless, for Jed, Ripley contrasts favorably with Dugton or Nashville; indeed, it may well be that Ripley, not Dugton, is the "place to come to" of the novel's title. When Agnes dies and is buried in her hometown, her father, the priest, promises Jed that "a place will always be kept waiting by her side." Despite initially and sardonically noting the differences between Dugton and Ripley—thus invoking a "southern" sense of homeplace that he does not actually live out—Jed subsequently acknowledges that "it was nice to know that there was, somewhere, a place to come to" (114). As it transpires, Jed repeatedly returns to Ripley before he ever goes down home to Dugton.

Jed Back in the South

This eventual return to Dugton, after twenty-five years' absence and a few months after his mother's death, generates the novel's final sequence. However, there is no sense that Jed's return to his southern, rural hometown provides closure—either to the narrative or to his life. Though Jed's mother kept "a place fer him in my heart," she never wanted him to return to Dugton: "he shore better stay out of town" (391). Now that he has returned, Dugton stands as totemic testimony to the death not only of his mother but also of the old agrarian South—or the Agrarians' "South." Jed cannot help but notice that "there was already a real development started" (397). Indeed, he discovers that the site of his father's ignominious and notorious death has been "drained for the new development and the untarnished mortgages" (400). Along with Dugton's old social geography, so, too, the people "were long since gone, or had transmogrified themselves into another kind of people" (397).

This late scene in Warren's last novel fleshes out the author's observation, made in an interview with Louis Rubin from the same period, that by the 1970s capitalist land speculation was so intense and ubiquitous that the South had acquired a new moniker. As Warren put it, "this term 'Sun Belt' is a realtor's term, and that captures the whole story." But in *A Place to Come To*, Warren works *through* the fulfillment of the old Agrarian fear that "place," even "the South" itself, would be abstracted, displaced, by finance-capitalist land speculation and development. By this, I mean that Warren goes *beyond* Allen Tate's eschatological vision of the death of the South to map what has replaced it. Much as the alien, abstract New York stock market once superseded local, tangible "cattle and work stock" as the central determinant of Dugton life, so now agricultural real property has been replaced by (in Donald Davidson's words) "a mere real estate development."[11]

Tjebbe Westendorp has observed that Jed's stepfather "Perk is more 'real' to him [Jed] than most people he has met in the arty or academic worlds of Nashville or Chicago." One duly notes that Jed does consider living out his life with Perk in his mother's old house. However, there is little evidence that Jed really will retire to Dugton. Indeed, the novel ends not in Alabama, but with Jed back in Chicago, writing a hopeful letter of reconciliation to his second wife. It is possible that Jed's embrace of any place, even Chicago, has and will remain semidetached because, as he tells his friend Stephan Mostoski, "hating the South, I had fled it. . . . I had fled but had found nowhere to flee to" (347). It might be argued, then, that Jed never finds his "place to come to"—certainly not in Dugton, but not in Chicago or Ripley either. Mostoski's role in the final third of the novel seems to be to express the kind of grand philosophical theme of which Warren was so fond: in this case, the notion that Jed's peripateticism expresses "the first pangs of modernity . . . the death of the self which has become placeless" (348). Westendorp notes that "Jed Tewksbury's diagnosis of cultural crisis . . . goes beyond Nashville and its environs, beyond even the South and the American continent, to take in the entire Western world." On one hand, such a totalizing conception of modernity's apparently all-pervasive sense of placelessness threatens to overwhelm the local focus on Dugton, Nashville, or anywhere else featured in the novel. On the other hand, Warren's monumental sense of "cultural crisis" refuses to redeem "the South" as some residual "place," taking its stand as a last bulwark against capitalist (post)modernity.[12]

I have tried to show how, in *A Place to Come To*, the "southern" narrator cannot come home again, either to the small-farm community of his 1930s youth, or to the inauthentic farmhouses of the Agrarians' Nashville. By juxtaposing Nashville and Chicago, small-town Alabama and small-town South Dakota, Warren interrogates Agrarian binary oppositions between "the North" and "the South." In examining *The Moviegoer*, I want to demonstrate how

---

11. Warren quoted in "The South: Distance and Change; A Conversation with Robert Penn Warren, William Styron, and Louis D. Rubin, Jr.," 309; Davidson, "Current Attitudes toward Folklore," 136.

12. Tjebbe Westendorp, "A Place to Come To," in Richard Gray, ed., *Robert Penn Warren: A Collection of Critical Essays* (Englewood Cliffs, N.J.: Prentice-Hall, 1980), 127, 130.

Binx Bolling attempts to rescue a "southern" sense of place by reconstructing the very North/South opposition that *A Place to Come To* dismantles.

Binx Bolling in New Orleans and Gentilly

It is a critical commonplace that the narrator of *The Moviegoer*, Binx Bolling, has seceded from his Aunt Emily's southern stoical ethos.[13] However, by "living the most ordinary life imaginable, a life without the old longings; selling stocks and bonds and mutual funds," Binx not only rejects his aunt's mythical idea of southern history and identity,[14] he also begins to establish a sense of place that diverges from his great aunt's by relocating himself outside her social geography. Binx was raised in Emily and Jules Cutrer's "gracious house in the Garden District" (6) of New Orleans, but, now approaching his thirtieth birthday, he refuses his aunt's advice to enter medical school and return to live in his "old garçonnière in the carriage house" (52). Having also become disenchanted with the French Quarter, where he had lived for two years, Binx has spent the last four years as a stock and bond broker in "Gentilly, a middle class suburb." As Binx observes, "one would never guess it was part of New Orleans. . . . But this is what I like about it. I can't stand the old world atmosphere of the French Quarter or the genteel charm of the Garden District" (6).

By moving Binx from the more established and exclusive areas of New Orleans into a newly built space that has no traditional "southern" identity, Walker Percy initiates a subtle parody of established southern literary images of place. Put another way, Percy confronts "southern literature"—not least the familiar conceptions of "literary New Orleans" (and especially the French Quarter) as "exotic," "languorous," and "atmospher[ic]"[15]—with the contemporary sociospatial reality of suburbia. *The Moviegoer* provocatively presents its narrator as someone who—initially at least—unashamedly embraces a suburban way of life that, in its divergence from and skepticism toward established definitions of the southern "sense of place," seems actively *postsouthern*. Binx notes that his own street, Elysian Fields, "was planned to be,

---

13. See, for example, Simpson, "What Survivors Do," in *The Brazen Face of History*, 249, and Gary M. Ciuba, *Walker Percy: Books of Revelations* (Athens: University of Georgia Press, 1991), 61–64.

14. Walker Percy, *The Moviegoer* (1961; reprint, New York: Vintage International, 1998), 9. All further page references will be incorporated into the main text.

15. Richard S. Kennedy, Preface to *Literary New Orleans: Essays and Meditations* (Baton Rouge: Louisiana State University Press, 1992), xiv–xv.

like its namesake, the grandest boulevard of the city" but that "something went amiss, and now it runs an undistinguished course from river to lake through shopping centers and blocks of duplexes and bungalows and raised cottages" (9). To Binx, Elysian Fields nonetheless "is very spacious and airy and seems truly to stretch out like a field under the sky" (9–10). Thus Binx continues to compare suburbia favorably with the pseudoaristocratic Francophilia of New Orleans's older locations.

However, the emergence of this new commercial and residential space is not as accidental or natural as Binx ingenuously implies. He soon allows as much, admitting that his interest in the erection of a new school next to his apartment is "less a religious sentiment than a financial one, since I own a few shares of Alcoa [the aluminum corporation]. How smooth and well-fitted and thrifty the aluminum feels!" (10). This rhapsody to commodity fetishism explicitly signals Binx's (usually more discreet) complicity in the capitalist production of suburbia and begins to explain just why he is so conspicuously positive about constructing a *post*southern sense of place.

Binx's own profitable involvement in the (literal) construction of suburbia is more clearly revealed when we learn that he is planning to sell his patrimony to the property developer Sartalamaccia. Believing that the land in St. Bernard Parish on which his father had a hunting lodge is a "worthless parcel of swamp" (71), Binx proposes to sell it for only eight thousand dollars. However, upon seeing the site for the first time in years, Binx realizes that its value has appreciated substantially: "A far cry from a duck club now, my patrimony is hemmed in on one side by a housing development" (90) owned by Sartalamaccia (93). Binx's "worthless" inheritance has become a prime piece of real estate.

In "Some Notes on River Country" (1944), Eudora Welty famously commented that "I have never seen . . . anything so mundane as ghosts, but I have felt many times there [Mississippi river country] a sense of place as powerful as if it were visible and walking and could touch me." Binx seems to imply that he feels just such a sensual, even supernatural attachment to Roaring Camp (as the defunct duck club is called) when he observes that his secretary, Sharon Kincaid, is *not* moved by "the thronging spirit-presence of the place and the green darkness of summer come back again and the sadness of it." But again, he is being disingenuous. As it turns out, Binx's postsouthern dissociation from his family's history and geography precludes any such poetic affiliation with his father's land. Binx eulogizes the ancestral-pastoral "spirit-presence of place" only because he believes (mistakenly, it transpires) that it will impress Sharon. Tellingly, Binx soon declares that Sharon "is right" (91) to be unconcerned with discovering a metaphysical *essence* of place, and he reverts to his initial perception of the patrimony as a mere commodity. When Sartalamaccia subsequently suggests that Binx should keep his land and "make the offsite improvements" while he "build[s] the houses," Binx decides to "enjoy the consolation of making money" (94) from real-estate development.[16]

Yet by this point *The Moviegoer* has already taken a significant turn in another direction. For Binx early on experiences an epiphany that subsequently causes him to become, at somewhat erratic junctures, distinctly *critical* of the ways in which "southern" sites in and around New Orleans are being transformed by land speculation and real-estate development. In the paragraph immediately following his ode to Alcoa, Binx remarks that "things have suddenly changed. My peaceful existence in Gentilly has been complicated. This morning . . . there occurred to me the possibility of a search" (10). Though Binx remains absorbed in his stock-market speculations (64), he also becomes increasingly troubled. The "search" impels Binx to reassess his sense of self. But he also begins to go beyond "vulgar" existentialism to ponder the material, sociospatial relations of his being-in-the-world. In Edward Soja's term, Binx begins to construct the "spatialized ontology" necessary to comprehend postmodern capitalist geographies. This becomes apparent when he starts taking nocturnal walks around his neighborhood. As he paces past "the bungalows and duplexes and tiny ranch houses" and on to "the fifty and sixty thousand dollar homes" (84), he agonizes over the meaning of this unfamiliar new milieu: "Instead of trying to sleep I try to fathom the mystery of this suburb at dawn. Why do . . . these new houses look haunted. . . . What spirit takes possession of them?" (86).[17]

Having previously celebrated his life in Gentilly, and even as he plots to profit from the redevelopment of his patrimony, Binx has begun to be troubled by the capitalist production of postsouthern space. But, crucially, Binx

---

16. Welty, "Some Notes on River Country," 286. See Philip E. Simmons, *Deep Surfaces: Mass Culture and History in Postmodern American Fiction* (Athens: University of Georgia Press, 1997), 33, for a perceptive analysis of the significance of the patrimony sale.

17. See Soja, *Postmodern Geographies*, 118–37; see also note 19 below.
In "Carnival in Gentilly," an excerpt from *The Moviegoer* published in 1960, Percy pegged the price of Gentilly's "fifty to sixty thousand dollar homes" at "forty to fifty thousand." Similarly, he put the patrimony value at only "[t]wenty-five dollars a foot" (it was fifty dollars a foot in the novel). That Percy made these changes and few others before "Carnival of Gentilly"

avoids answering his own question, "What spirit takes possession of them?" Binx evades the answer—and, in fact, mystifies the question itself—precisely because he is personally implicated in the construction of suburbia. Despite having rejected the poetic notion of a supernatural "spirit-presence of place" in order to treat Roaring Camp as a material commodity, he now claims a "spirit" has taken "possession" of Gentilly. This reemergent metaphysical terminology serves to obfuscate the materialist fetishization of place and Binx's own complicity in that capitalistic process. By rhetorically repressing the "spirit" of capitalism—both the abstraction of land into exchange-value and the material reproduction of space through the erection of new houses— Binx's narrative becomes what Fredric Jameson calls a "postmodern ghost story, ordered by finance-capital spectralities."[18]

Having repressed the revelation that the specter haunting and colonizing southern "place" is finance-capitalist land speculation, Binx is able to postpone the "search" and revert to, even extend, his own earlier role as a land speculator. He plans to use the capital accrued from the patrimony deal to build and operate a service station on a vacant lot at the corner of Elysian Fields and Bons Enfants. This prompts further fetishistic rapture: "It is easy to visualize the little tile cube of a building with its far flung porches, its apron of silky concrete and, revolving on high, the immaculate bivalve glowing in every inch of its pretty styrene (I have already approached the Shell distributor)" (112). What is more, by immersing himself in capitalist speculation, Binx does not only mean to neutralize his own urge to search. He also tries to convince his cousin, Kate Cutrer, that *her* existential crisis could be resolved if she joins him in a marital cum business partnership: "Did you know you can net over fifteen thousand a year on a good station?" (116).

Binx in Bayou des Allemands

Binx also tries to reinvigorate his "ordinary life"—which he also terms the "Little Way," as opposed to "the big search for the big happiness" (135–36)—by taking a tour of the Gulf Coast with Sharon. However, at Bayou

---

was (re)integrated into *The Moviegoer* suggests the precise nature of his concern with place as real estate. Indeed, one might say that this precipitous rise in the price of property in the year between "Carnival" and the novel itself suitably mimics the speculative appreciation of fictitious property "values." See Percy, "Carnival in Gentilly," *Forum* 3 (1960): 11, 14.

18. Fredric Jameson, "The Brick and the Balloon: Architecture, Idealism and Land Speculation," *New Left Review* 228 (March/April 1998): 46.

des Allemands, where his mother's family have a fishing camp, he again experiences an involuntary aversion to the postsouthern space that elsewhere he eulogizes. At first, Binx simply tries to enjoy the camp's seemingly pastoral sense of place: "here on Bayou des Allemands everybody feels the difference. . . . The splintered boards have secret memories of winter, the long dreaming nights and days when no one came and the fish jumped out of the black water and not a soul in sight in the whole savannah" (139). The next morning, however, he "awake[s] in the grip of everydayness." Though Bayou des Allemands has not been defiled by material redevelopment, Binx still believes this remote rural locus has been infiltrated by *something*. I suggest that Binx here employs the noun "everydayness" to refer, however obliquely, to the demoralizing existential *experience* of anonymous, mass-produced (sub)urban capitalist space. According to Binx, "everydayness" has expanded from its urban origins into even the bayou: "[t]he everydayness is everywhere now, having begun in the cities and seeking out the remotest nooks and corners of the countryside, even the swamps" (145). The implication is that industrial capitalism has extended its domain beyond mass-produced urban buildings; it is also culturally expressed through, and existentially experienced as, "everydayness." In other words, the sinister "spirit" of "everydayness" has enabled capitalism to move beyond the material production of city space into a kind of metaphysical colonization of the country. This theory seems well nigh neo-Agrarian when we consider that Donald Davidson similarly described industrial capitalism's insidious, immaterial impact upon being-in-the-(rural-southern)-world. In medical metaphors that quite eerily anticipated *The Moviegoer*, Davidson posited that modern man "cannot escape the infection of the cities by mere geographical remoteness. The skepticism and malaise of the industrial mind reach him anyway."[19]

If Binx believes that "everydayness" has infected even the obscure bayous of Louisiana, and that "malaise" has "infested" him and the other "handsome, well-fed and kind-hearted people" (166) visiting the Gulf Coast on a Sunday afternoon, it would seem that *no* place in the South can offer sanctuary from

---

19. Davidson, "A Mirror for Artists," in *I'll Take My Stand*, 58. See Edward G. Lawry, "Literature as Philosophy: *The Moviegoer*," *The Monist* 63, no. 4 (October 1980): 547–57, for a useful analysis of the existential nature of Binx's "everydayness" considered in relation to Martin Heidegger's use of the term. Lawry suggests that both Emily's "aristocratic Southern stoicism" (550) *and* Binx's "flight . . . into everydayness" (553) are what Heidegger calls "inauthentic" modes of "being-in-the-world." By contrast, the "search" is an existential quest for the authentic. Lawry also notes that critics often associate Heideggerian everydayness with

this debilitating existential disease that he associates, however imprecisely, with the specter of capitalist land speculation. How, then, can Binx possibly resist or escape this postsouthern dystopia—especially given the fact that he is implicated in its production? Almost immediately upon returning from the Gulf Coast, Binx has to travel to Chicago for a business convention. The excursion proves to be crucial because it enables Binx to invoke a binary opposition between "the South" and "the North" that reaffirms urban New Orleans (rather than rural Bayou des Allemands) as an authentic "southern" locus. This maneuver enables Binx to once again—and this time conclusively— repress his fear that capitalism has destroyed the foundational "South" in the process of developing a new *post*southern geography.

Binx in Chicago and Wilmette

Binx begins redeeming "the South" by redefining the previously ambiguous term "spirit-presence of the place" in a distinctly loaded fashion, with negative reference to "Northern" cities. Claiming that "it is my fortune and misfortune to know how the spirit-presence of a strange place can enrich a man or rob a man but never leave him alone" (99), Binx depicts Chicago as a specter threatening to snatch his body, even his (southern) self. He asserts that the city has already turned his traveling companion, Kate— Emily's stepdaughter and a belle of Garden District society—into "a regular city girl not distinguishable from any other little low-browed olive-skinned big-butted Mediterranean such as populates the streets and subways of the North" (202). He compounds this sweepingly racialized construction of the metropolitan "North" by remarking that Kate has been transformed into "a dark little Rachel bound home to Brooklyn on the IRT" (206). Thus, as he inflates the contrast between "the South" and "the North," Binx also—like Donald Davidson before him—conflates Chicago and New York.

Having implied the (white) South's ethnic purity, Binx invokes another archetypal signifier of "southernness," the Confederate dead. During his earlier visit with Sharon to the Confederate fortress Ship Island, Binx had as-

---

"middle-class conformity" (551). I depart from Lawry by arguing that Binx's *existential* everydayness is specifically and inextricably related to his "sense of place"—his material experience of the middle-class, urban-suburban form of "place" produced by capitalism. See Soja, 131–37, for an excellent discussion of "the Existential Spatiality of Being." Soja rejects merely solipsistic or "vulgar" existentialism (131) and extrapolates from Heidegger to emphasize that "being-in-the-world" is subject to social, spatial, and economic influences.

serted his dissociation from regional history and its memorial geography by stating that "[i]t is the soul of dreariness, this 'historic site' washed by the thin brackish waters of Mississippi Sound" (129). But now, in Chicago, Binx cites the "stubborn back-looking ghosts" that haunted Quentin Compson as a privileged southern means of understanding the modern, urban North: "Nobody but a Southerner knows the wrenching rinsing sadness of the cities of the North. Knowing all about genie-souls and living in haunted places like Shiloh and the Wilderness and Vicksburg and Atlanta where the ghosts of heroes walk abroad by day and are more real than people, he knows a ghost when he sees one" (202).[20]

Binx also introduces the elements into his North/South binary. He comments that, whereas "Lake [Pontchartrain] in New Orleans is a backwater glimmering away in a pleasant lowland. . . . Lake [Michigan] is the North itself: a perilous place from which the spirit winds come pouring forth all roused up and crying out alarm" (203). In this claim to some metaphysical or meteorological difference between "the North" and "the South," there is a distinct echo of *A Place to Come To;* specifically, of Jed Tewksbury's arriving in Ripley City and identifying the "new kind of loneliness" that leaves one "a dry, transparent husk."But, as we have seen, Jed abandons this self-consciously "southern" sense of self and place and comes to appreciate the "perfectly self-contained, self-fulfilling, complete" South Dakota town far more than his hometown in Alabama. By contrast, Binx's negative construction of "the North" does not even reach its highest pitch until he visits Wilmette, the small suburban town outside Chicago where his Korean War colleague Harold Graebner now resides. As Binx puts it, Harold lives in "a place called Wilmette which turns out not to be a place at all since it has no genie" (206). While Chicago at least has a "spirit-presence" (albeit a "strange" and terrifying one), Binx sees suburban Wilmette as the vanishing point of the northern void, vindicating the southerner's existential fear of becoming "No one and Nowhere" (99)—that is, like the "dry, transparent husk" initially evoked by Jed.

Thomas Daniel Young claims that Binx "suffer[s] from the 'new provincialism'" because he "belong[s] to no specific place" and that *The Moviegoer* "could just as well have been set in a suburb of Rochester." This is too simplistic: Young's view is tied to the Tate paradigm and as such cannot get beyond the eschatological view that the South and its supposedly unique sense of

---

20. William Faulkner, *Absalom, Absalom!* (1936; reprint, New York: Vintage International, 1990), 7.

place have been expunged by industrial- and finance-capitalism (see Chapter 2). Young's reading fails to register how, rather than simply accepting the "essentially characterless" homogeneity of postsouthern America, Binx uses the trip to Illinois to redeem a distinctly "southern" sense of place. Binx simply cannot allow New Orleans to be made equivalent to Chicago; similarly, he refuses to accept that his pre-search everyday life in Gentilly could just as well have been set in a suburb of Illinois. Binx's melodramatic expression of horror at this supernatural vacuum called "the North" far supersedes his earlier repressed anxiety that a similarly spectral, suburbanizing "spirit" of capitalism has "take[n] possession" of "the South." It is crucial to Binx's redemption of "the South" that he expresses his antinorthern attitudes only in metaphysical terms. Upon arriving in Chicago, Binx bemoans his ignorance of such "local space-time stuff" as "who built the damn [railway] station, the circumstances of the building, details of the wrangling between city officials and the railroad" (201). But by depicting Chicago in vague, metaphysical language, rather than analyzing it as a local, materially produced place, Binx can deride "the North" without having to ponder possible *similarities* with the redeveloped (sub)urban "South." Arguably, this is why Binx never identifies Chicago's malevolent spirit-presence of place in more explicit terms as the "spirit" of urban industrial- and finance-capitalism. For to directly identify the specter of finance-capital in Chicago might indirectly demystify the possessive "spirit" that Binx felt, but fudged, in Gentilly. Ultimately, in reinventing "the South" by contrasting it with a negation named "the North," Binx can repress his earlier terror of capitalist land speculation and its cultural logic ("everydayness"). And in doing so, he once again abjures his own involvement in the speculative production of *post*southern geographies.[21]

Binx Back in the South

Appropriately, Binx's northern exposure ends with a telephone call from Aunt Emily. Upon returning to New Orleans, he visits the Cutrers' Garden District home. Emily reaches a crescendo of southern stoical rhetoric as she castigates Binx for taking his sick cousin to Chicago: "More than anything I wanted to pass on to you the one heritage of the men of our family, a certain quality of spirit, a gaiety, a sense of duty, a nobility worn lightly, a sweetness, a gentleness with women—the only good things the South ever had and the only things that really matter in this life. . . .But how did it happen that none

---

21. Young, *The Past in the Present*, 8, 24.

of this ever meant anything to you?" (224). In dramatizing how Binx has "default[ed]" (220) from his inherited position among the "gentlefolk" (222), Emily elides the social reality of racial hierarchy and spatial segregation upon which her privileged "South" is constructed. She claims that, by contrast with the derelict Binx, she has at least "some slight tradition in common" with Cothard, "that Negro man walking down the street" (221). But as an African American manual laborer—Binx calls him "the last of the chimney sweeps" (226)—Cothard has a strictly delineated "place" in Garden District society. Emily might admit him into the privileged private space of her home as a worker but never as a social (or stoical) equal. Revealingly, it is Cothard whom she subsequently identifies as the "prize exhibit" of a declining "human race" (224)—the epitome of the modern "common man" (223) she so despises.

By contrast with Cothard, the banished Binx is quickly welcomed back into his aunt's aristocratic-stoical worldview—and into her local social geography. Having returned home to Gentilly after Emily's verbal mauling, Binx has already concluded that "[m]y search has been abandoned; it is no match for my aunt, her rightness and her despair" (228) when Kate arrives and informs him that she has told Emily of their impending marriage. The nuptials effect a rapid rapprochement between Emily and Binx. Their reconciliation is symbolically and spatially expressed in Emily's readiness to readmit Binx to her home; as Kate tells Binx, "[s]he [Emily] only hoped that you might come to see her this afternoon" (232).

Critics have argued that the "search" is at least partly fulfilled as Binx makes a Kierkegaardian "leap of faith" and achieves "community with Kate" or "communion of consciousness with Lonnie," his half-brother.[22] Such readings leap over another lacuna exposed by the "search," one that remains unresolved by *The Moviegoer*'s awkward ending: Binx's repressed knowledge of the capitalist production of postsouthern geographies. But at least two critics have identified Binx's yearning, as *The Moviegoer* concludes, for an identifiably "southern" traditional culture—that is, a culture of the kind he derided earlier in the narrative. Anne Goodwyn Jones notes that, "[a]t the end of the novel," both Binx and Kate "are climbing into the shell of southern tradition in the hope of surviving the middle of the twentieth century." More

---

22. Simpson, "What Survivors Do," 249; Max Webb, "Binx Bolling's New Orleans: Moviegoing, Southern Writing, and Father Abraham," in Panthea Reid Broughton, ed., *The Art of Walker Percy: Stratagems for Being* (Baton Rouge: Louisiana State University Press, 1979), 20; Ciuba, *Walker Percy*, 78.

recently, Phillip Simmons has observed that "Binx Bolling eventually finds his way out of mass culture and back into the history of his family's and society's decline."[23] Refracting these astute analyses of Binx's attempt to recover "the South" through a spatialized critical lens, I suggest that Binx finds his way out of the postsouthern suburbs and the metaphysical fog of capitalist mass-cultural "everydayness" by getting back to the Garden District. By surrendering the "search" and marrying his cousin—thereby recovering the sexualized, racialized Kate of Chicago as a submissive white Southern Lady—Binx also effects a reconciliation with his aunt and reentry to her "South" (which is, after all, the "South" in which Binx himself grew up). In the epilogue, the reader is abruptly informed that Binx has left his job and apartment in Gentilly to enter medical school (tellingly, in accordance with Emily's earlier wish). Though Binx does not move back into his old garçonnière, he has returned to his aunt's ideological and geographical sphere of influence: Kate has found the newlyweds "a house near her stepmother, one of the very shotgun cottages done over by my cousin Nell Lovell" (236).

Binx's reentry into the Bolling-Cutrer-Lovell family circle, and to his aunt's "South," is eased by the fact that the whole clan is more implicated in capitalist land speculation than Emily would ever care to admit. Binx and Kate's marital home is only one example of the Lovells' speculative involvement in gentrification: cousin Nell and her husband Eddie are "forever buying shotgun cottages in rundown neighborhoods and fixing them up . . . and selling in a few months for a big profit" (20–21). Even Emily is not immune: her ledger tantalizingly lists her inherited "properties," including "sundry service stations" (recalling Binx's own proposed deal with Shell) and even "Canadian mines" (226). Despite Emily's rhetorical distinction between "integrity" and the "market place" (31), the Bolling-Cutrer-Lovell clan's profitable involvement in the sociospatial transformation of "the South" helps Binx to bridge the apparent gap between his own bourgeois "Little Way" and Emily's pseudoaristocratic Southern Way of Life.

Ultimately, it is doubtful that Binx's postsouthern incredulity toward Emily's "South" was ever radical enough for him to undertake a serious spatialized "search" between the established southern and emerging postsouthern spaces in and around New Orleans. Despite Binx's move to Gentilly, the Garden District has remained his foundational locus and sanctuary; he has

23. Anne Goodwyn Jones, *Tomorrow Is Another Day: The Woman Writer in the South, 1859–1936* (Baton Rouge: Louisiana State University Press, 1981), 7; Simmons, *Deep Surfaces*, 39–40.

never fully distanced himself from either Emily or Jules Cutrer. Although Binx moved to and worked in Gentilly, he remained in the employ of Uncle Jules, a man who (like the father of pseudofarmer Lawford Carrington in *A Place to Come To*) combines the image of the "Old South" with the capitalist impulse of the "New South"—"old-world charm and new-world business methods" (31)—to impressive and profitable effect.[24] In the end, we might usefully project back through time and place—past Wilmette and Chicago, past Bayou des Allemands, past Binx's anxiety-ridden walks around Gentilly—to the novel's first meeting between Binx and his aunt. Even that early, Binx admits: "In a split second, I have forgotten everything, the years in Gentilly, even my search. As always we take up again where we left off. This is where I belong after all" (26).

At the start of *The Moviegoer*, Walker Percy sympathetically renders Binx Bolling's revolt against the mythical "South" and wryly satirizes canonical constructions of the southern "sense of place" by relocating Binx in Gentilly. By mapping various loci from Gentilly via Roaring Camp to Bayou des Allemands, *The Moviegoer* moves us toward a postsouthern sense of place—an awareness of capitalism's material and experiential reproduction of traditional or supposedly "natural" southern loci. Finally, however—and despite exposing Emily's aristocratic southern stoicism as an anachronistic, rhetorical construct—*The Moviegoer* envisions no escape from the "spirit" of postsouthern capitalist space other than returning Binx to his aunt's upper-class enclave. Perhaps what Simpson once termed Percy's own "troubled experience of life as a member of the southern patriciate" impelled him to dismiss the possibility of a postsouthern sense of place or way of life *within* the mass-produced, middle-class suburbs. Whether or not we refer to the author's own life, Binx's rhetorical redemption of New Orleans as an authentic, aristocratic "Southern" sanctuary concludes *The Moviegoer*'s (anti-)climactic retreat from postsouthern literary cartography.[25]

---

24. Lawford's father, like Binx's uncle, incorporates the image of the "Old South" into the capitalist impulse of the "New South," and harnesses that image in economic relations with "the North": "Nicholas Carrington . . . well knew the value of the Old South as a facade for the New Order, especially when he was dealing with money from Chicago" (Warren, *A Place to Come To*, 229).

25. Simpson, *The Fable of the Southern Writer* (Baton Rouge: Louisiana State University Press, 1994), 197.

4. Neo-Faulknerism or Postsouthernism?: Labor, Parody, and the Problem of Place in Richard Ford's *A Piece of My Heart*

In a 1977 review-essay entitled "Walker Percy: Not Just Whistling Dixie," Richard Ford observed pointedly that "Percy has been telling us for a long time what most of us may be just realizing: that southern regionalism as a factor in the impulse that makes us write novels . . . has had its day." At the time, Ford must have felt especially strongly about taking his stand with Percy. He had recently published *A Piece of My Heart* (1976), a debut novel in which, as Ford confided twenty years later, "I thought I was writing about the South in a way that nobody would ever recognize as being southern." "The heartbreaking thing," Ford observed, was that critics still wrote about *A Piece of My Heart* "as a piece of, if not Gothic, at least southern writing." Preeminent among these critics was fellow novelist Larry McMurtry who, in the *New York Times Book Review*, scored Ford's "neo-Faulknerism" and opined that "[t]he South—dadgummit—has struck again, marring what might have been an excellent first novel."[1]

I see *A Piece of My Heart* differently: as the opening salvo in Ford's ongoing fictional *interrogation* of "the South," especially as it has been represented or invented in "southern literature." *Pace* McMurtry, Ford's debut novel utilizes postsouthern parody: the self-conscious narrative performance of "southernness" via which the text, in Michael Kreyling's words, "adjusts or lightens the burden of southern literariness it must necessarily carry in the presence of 'Faulkner' triumphant." It is true, though, that *A Piece of My*

---

1. Richard Ford, "Walker Percy: Not Just Whistling Dixie," *National Review* 29 (13 May 1977), 561–62; R. J. Ellis and Graham Thompson, "Interview with Richard Ford," *Over Here: A European Journal of American Culture*, 16, no. 2 (winter 1996): 114; Larry McMurtry, review of *A Piece of My Heart* in the *New York Times Book Review*, 24 October 1976, 16. McMurtry's charge of "neo-Faulknerism" adds contextual spice to Ford's barbed observation that "'southern writer' [is] an expression which limps from one 'critic' to the next, but which almost always is pejorative, hazy in its essentials, and frequently born out of a simple poverty of wit, and which generally means simply *like Faulkner*" (Ford, "Walker Percy," 561).

Heart's postsouthernism is not altogether successful; Ford himself later came to feel that, despite his best intentions, his first book remained too "indebted to Faulkner [and] to Flannery O'Connor." Thus this chapter will also ponder the limitations of postsouthernness, particularly with regard to "place," in *A Piece of My Heart*.[2]

McMurtry's critique of *A Piece of My Heart* is largely founded on the claim that "the men who carry the narrative invariably discover that they are also carrying the burden of Southern history." Evidently McMurtry is referring here to Ford's two central protagonists, Robard Hewes and Sam Newel; four sections of the novel focus on Robard, and three on Newel. Yet on this key point McMurtry's criticism can be rebutted. I will come to the strange case of Sam Newel a little later, but first I want to argue that Robard Hewes is not weighed down by "the burden of Southern history"—quite the opposite. Moreover, in properly historical-geographical terms, Robard does not exhibit a southern sense of place—at least, not as "sense of place" has usually been defined in southern literature and literary criticism.

Class, Labor, and "Sense of Place": Robard Hewes

At the start of the novel, we learn that Robard has been living in California for eight years; we join him as he embarks upon a return journey to the South—destination, Helena, Arkansas, by way of Hazen, a nondescript small town in the same state. Robard had moved west after three years spent working in Hazen for a landowner called Rudolph. Interestingly, Matthew Guinn has compared this "rapacious farmer" to Faulkner's Thomas Sutpen. One might ask, however, whether Ford constructs Rudolph less as a "Faulknerian shade" than as a deliberate *parody* of not only Sutpen the plantation owner but also another figure from Faulknerian *and* Agrarian mythology, the yeoman farmer. Like Sutpen, who descends upon Yoknapatawpha from Virginia via Haiti, Rudolph is not a local. He arrived in Arkansas from Nebraska, at which point he "drove all over the country between Little Rock and Memphis looking for cheap land," eventually buying "eight hundred acres of swamp fifteen miles back out of Hazen, land that no farmer had even thought to abandon, much less cultivate."[3] But at a very basic level,

---

2. Kreyling, *Inventing Southern Literature*, 161; Ellis and Thompson, "Interview with Richard Ford," 114.

3. Richard Ford, *A Piece of My Heart* (1976; reprint, London: Harvill, 1996), 48–49. All subsequent page references will be incorporated into the main text.

Rudolph differs from Sutpen in that his capital is concentrated largely in—to invoke Gavin Wright's distinction—real property (his "cheap land") rather than human property (slaves). Nor is the land itself some Sutpen's (Eight) Hundred. Far from building a mansion out of the swamp on the backs of others, Rudolph does not even see his land as a farm per se, let alone a plantation. Rather, this supposed "rapacious farmer" makes most of his money from duck hunting—from which his former employee, Robard, used to earn his wages.[4]

Here, like Faulkner and Percy before him, Ford charts a post-Agrarian vision of southern rural land use. As we saw in Chapter 3, in *The Moviegoer* Binx Bolling transforms his father's patrimony—once the site of a duck-hunting club, but which has apparently become a "worthless parcel of swamp"—into a highly profitable housing development. But in *A Piece of My Heart*, the land is of little value as either farmland or real estate. It is duck hunting itself, not a derelict duck-hunting club, that brings in the money. Yet it is not quite that simple. Rudolph is canny enough to realize that, although his swampland is unsuitable for farming, it has an indirect economic value, and not only as an inert backdrop for duck hunting. For it is the artificially "natural," even precapitalist, aura of Rudolph's land, and not just the thrill of the hunt, that attracts wealthy customers to Hazen. Richard Godden has argued that, in *The Wild Palms* (1939), Faulkner depicts formerly "natural" and industrial landscapes (the Mississippi Gulf Coast, Utah, and Wisconsin) that have been deliberately "shaped into a wilderness" by entrepreneurs. These artificial wildernesses are marketed to tourists who yearn to escape the social relations of modern capitalism—the very relations with which they are complicit in their everyday lives and labor. Apparently, Rudolph has marketed his own personal "wilderness" in a similar fashion. He rents out his land—or more properly, he rents out its artificial authenticity—to professionals from Memphis, Gulfport, Pass Christian, and Port Arthur who willingly pay a "thousand dollars a head" (7) to simulate the traditional "southern" (that is, "natural" and rural, rather than blue-collar and urban) pastime of hunting.[5]

In *Go Down, Moses* (1942), Faulkner charts the destruction of what Ike McCaslin calls "the ruined woods," and of hunting as a southern way of life. Yet in "The Bear" and "Delta Autumn," Sam Fathers's life (and death) as a

---

4. Matthew Guinn, *After Southern Modernism: Fiction of the Contemporary South* (Jackson: University Press of Mississippi, 2000), 113–14; Wright, *Old South, New South*, 17.

5. Godden, *Fictions of Labor*, 208.

hunting guide retains a residual mythic quality. In stark contrast, Robard's life and work as a hunting guide in Hazen is mundane, even banal; he recalls "watching [Rudolph's] sluice gates and sitting out winters in the little shotgun house" while waiting "for the duck hunters" (47). Indeed, this tedium was the catalyst for Robard's flight to California, "where he felt enough distance was opened between him and the shack and the fields and the whole life there that it would be too hard to go back" (8).[6]

Returning to Arkansas from California in the novel's present (1971), Robard does go back to Hazen. However, rather than demonstrating any nostalgia for, or "burden of," the past, this brief visit only confirms that Robard has no reason to go home again on a permanent basis. Even the material geography of Robard's personal history in Hazen has been effaced, for Rudolph has "put soybeans in there right where [Robard] lived" (53). This also indicates that, since Robard departed, Rudolph has managed to make over at least some of his swampland for large-scale commercial farming (perhaps assisted by advances in agricultural technology). However, Rudolph himself has atrophied to a degree even the postbellum Sutpen never did, having spent more than eleven years sitting and brooding over the collapse of his romance with Edwina, the owner of Hazen's R. E. Lee hotel. Eventually, Robard realizes that "he was making a mistake acting like he wanted to see the old man when he didn't want to at all" (51). Having deduced that Hazen "didn't mean anything to him" (54), Robard simply leaves. All told, then, it seems unlikely that Hazen is the site or source of any "burden of Southern history" that Robard could have been carrying while living in California. His life in Hazen was defined by mundane manual labor; having returned, he has no desire to take up the role of a modern-day Wash Jones to Rudolph's pseudo-Sutpen.

Nor does Robard feel any peculiarly southern "sense of place" or "burden of history" when he eventually rolls into Helena, his destination and the hometown of his cousin Beuna, with whom he plans to rekindle an old affair. On this point, I disagree with Kenneth Holditch, who has argued that "with the southerner's typical attachment to the place from which he came, Robard, despite having inured himself against dependence on people or locations, is convinced that Helena, Arkansas, because it was his birthplace [sic], will allow him to fulfill his quest." It is true that, by returning to Helena, Robard puts faith in "the reliance that the place *would* hold him up long enough to do what he

---

6. William Faulkner, "Delta Autumn," in *Go Down, Moses* (1942; reprint, New York: Vintage, 1973), 364.

came to do, pay him, in a sense, for having been born there." But, as Holditch himself acknowledges, this is out of character: by having recourse to this "reliance" upon Helena itself, Robard feels he is reneging on "all he had schooled himself to believe" (44). Undermined by his own hard-nosed skepticism, Robard's uncharacteristically romantic "attachment to place" cannot hold.[7]

In order to comprehend further the reasons for Robard's incredulity toward southern "place," we might usefully ponder Holditch's passing association between *A Piece of My Heart* and *The Moviegoer*. Citing Robard's belief that life is full of "beginnings" between which "there would be vacant moments when there was no breathing and no life" (8), Holditch compares this with Binx's theory "that it was difficult just to get through an ordinary Wednesday." However, Holditch makes a qualification that he does not explore: "Walker Percy's character certainly lacks the total cynicism of Robard." *Why* does Robard seem even more cynical than Binx? Holditch rightly observes that Robard's "philosophy of life" is expressed in the maxim "[o]ne minute don't learn the next one nothin" (230). But what might be the *source* of such a belief?[8]

I believe that Robard's labor drives the "total cynicism," the extreme sense of contingency, expressed in his "philosophy of life"—and in his philosophy of place. Much as he once went to Hazen just for work, Robard only boarded in Helena (with his mother's cousin) because it was a convenient short-term base while he worked the switches on the Missouri Pacific Railroad. That Robard spent a mere fifteen days in Helena, in 1959, and that he can barely remember it, is reason enough to doubt he has a "southerner's typical attachment" to the town. But it also becomes clear that Hazen and Helena both are part of a larger, itinerant pattern in Robard's laboring life. His job satisfaction and security have not notably improved since he departed Arkansas: "From the first, eight years ago, when he had left Hazen and transported himself and her [his wife Jackie] across the country, and had started to pick work where he could up the Sierras, he had been as desperate as anybody, and every bit as panicked when a job shut down, and had gone off to wherever there was

---

7. W. Kenneth Holditch, "On the Fine Edge of Disappearing: Desperation and Despair in *A Piece of My Heart*," in Huey Guagliardo, ed., *Perspectives on Richard Ford* (Jackson: University Press of Mississippi, 2000), 36. Robard's hope "that the place *would* hold him up . . . for having been born there" apparently refers to Arkansas more broadly, as he was not born in Helena itself (as Holditch claims) but in Cane Hill (124, 200).

8. Holditch, "On the Fine Edge of Disappearing," 37.

another one opened" (14). It is true that Robard does not seem *conscious* that the temporary nature of his work defines his short-term worldview ("one minute don't learn the next one nothin"). Nonetheless, he does summarize "those years of running desperation and internal commotion getting jobs and being anxious" in a telling simile of mechanized manual labor: "a lot of useless barging around, like a man with his sleeve in a thresher" (15).

Upon recalling his tedious working life in Hazen, Robard becomes doubtful about "relying" irrationally on Arkansas. He recognizes that "there wasn't any reason to believe the place or anybody in it would turn out any better or kinder or any more understanding than they had when he tried to make it honest, working for old man Rudolph" (43). Why, then, does Robard take yet another temporary job upon arriving back in Arkansas? Indeed, the job, guarding Mark Lamb's island, is much like the one he performed for Rudolph eight years before. I suggest that Robard takes the work not because he feels a special attachment to the state, but because he is acting subconsciously upon a familiar sense of place—and life itself—as being defined by temporary, itinerant work. Robard realizes bemusedly that, "[w]ithout even intending, he had gone straight for a job, just like finding one was bone-hard necessity. It was aggravating" (57).

Bearing in mind this link between itinerant manual labor and place(lessness) in Robard's life, I want to flesh out Holditch's speculative comparison between Binx and Robard. In the previous chapter, we saw how Binx undertakes an abortive "search" of "the South" because he is troubled by the speculative, suburban redevelopment of the region's historical geography. With a nod to McMurtry, the "search" could be construed as Binx's own "burden of Southern history" (or historical geography). But Binx eventually finds (or invents) signs of historical-geographical uneven development that signify the survival of an older, more genteel "South." In contrast, Ford's Robard has no historical, familial, or financial investment in "the South" that could compel him to even start out on this kind of search for place. Robard's quest is rather more quotidian, with none of the upper-class, angst-ridden resonance of Binx's "search"—Robard merely wants work and a wage. Nor is this quest limited to "the South": Robard has never known anything other than mundane manual labor, whether in Arkansas or California.

It is this contingent experience of supposedly distinct "regions" (the South and the West) that, in terms of labor conditions, are more similar than dissimilar, that really determines Robard's better instinct that he cannot expect Arkansas to "pay him, in a sense, for having been born there." The wage metaphor is revealing: at base, and however little he reflects upon the fact, Robard knows that his sense of place has been inextricable from, and limited to, financial necessity. For Robard to put his faith in Arkansas simply because it is his birthplace would be fallacious. Despite trying to work up a sense of "reliance" on Helena, Robard knows that there is no Weltyan "sense of place" in this "weedy cotton plant on the skin of the delta" (43) that might mystically vindicate his return. Hence, to speak of "the southerner's typical attachment to place" is to invoke essentialist notions of "southernness" and "the South" that elide the social realities of class and labor. The only reason for Robard's return to the South is Beuna, his cousin: they plan to rekindle the lustful fling that started in Helena in 1959. Singularly focused upon the sexual thrill promised by Beuna, Robard has no other reason or inclination to search for his place in the South. Indeed, Robard's mind-set recalls that of Jed Tewksbury, who rejects time, space, consciousness, and even "being Southern" during his Nashville sex sessions with Rozelle Carrington (see Chapter 3).

The Search for Place and Postsouthern Parody: Sam Newel

If there *is* a man "carry[ing] the narrative" of *A Piece of My Heart* who also appears to be "carrying the burden of Southern history," it is Sam Newel. At the time of the novel's present, Newel is living in Chicago, where he is reluctantly training to be a lawyer while having an affair with *his* cousin, fellow Mississippi expatriate Beebe Henley. When we first encounter Newel, he is planning a return trip to Mississippi to come to terms with his southern past. Newel's nocturnal conversations with Beebe, however, reveal that he does not really know *why* he wants to go home again. It becomes apparent that Newel is working through certain received notions of southern identity—including "history" and "place"—that have little bearing on his own personal experience.

Newel's talks with Beebe in the cold Chicago room rather inevitably recall, as Guinn has noted, Quentin Compson in garrulous dialogue with Shreve McCannon in the freezing dorm at Harvard. Newel seems possessed by a need that Fred Hobson sees apotheosized in Quentin: the "Southern rage to explain," to "tell about the South." Yet Newel seems to be self-consciously seeking, and even inventing, the kind of dramatic, neurotic love-hate relationship with the South that was second nature to Quentin. At one point, Beebe asks Newel whether "fucking me lets you get back sneakily at your past" in Mississippi. Though Newel believes that "[p]assions have to come from someplace," he is forced to conclude that his past in Mississippi is "not good enough" (73) reason. In other words, Newel well knows that there is no sublimated version of southern history or place being played out in their sexual relationship (any more than there is in Robard and Beuna's affair, or than there was in Jed and Rozelle's), however much he wills it to be so.[9]

In a more sympathetic moment, Beebe identifies the one event that just might explain Newel's raging focus on the past: the death of his father, decapitated by a rogue load of corrugated pipes while driving through Bastrop, Louisiana (77). However, even Newel himself is unwilling to see this (suitably grotesque) primal scene as the reason for his return to the South: "Do you want me to say that happened to *him*, and I couldn't cope with my past because it was so awful? . . . My father isn't finally important. He's just adhesive for everything" (78–80). Yet one might usefully ask *why* Newel disregards his father's role in his past—why, on this occasion, this melodramatic young man uncharacteristically passes up the opportunity to inflate his personal history into a synecdochic expression of southernness and its discontents. An explanation begins to emerge if one considers the differences between Newel's background, and those of Quentin Compson or Binx Bolling. For Newel's personal history, like Robard's, maps a "South" that is literally another place, and populated by another class. Newel's father was a traveling salesman who often covered "[o]ne hundred miles a day, [across] seven states—Mississippi, Arkansas, Louisiana, Tennessee, Alabama, Florida, part of Texas." Newel recalls how

> We'd drive to some big warehouse and he'd go inside and talk to a man . . . and write up an order. Then he'd leave. Maybe he wouldn't sell anything. That was it. Then he'd go someplace else. . . . He loved it so much, I think, it seemed fun to him. And that wasn't the worst. The worst was sitting in all those goddamned rooms, in Hammond, Louisiana, and Tuscaloosa, with nothing at all in them, for *years*. Just come in late in the afternoon, have a drink of whiskey, go down and eat your dinner in some greasy fly-speck café, smoke a King Edward in the lobby, and go back to the room, and lie in bed listening to the plumbing fart, until it was late enough to go to sleep. And that was *all*. (80–81)

I quote at some length here because these words begin to reveal Newel's problem. He is unable to find the kind of Faulknerian literary drama in his father's life and labor—and his family's "sense of place" or history—that could turn him into a Quentin, or even a Binx. Newel's "And that was *all*" has none of the ironic bathos that Faulkner injected into his fiction by using that phrase at moments of extreme tension, at the terminus of seemingly endless

---

9. Guinn, *After Southern Modernism*, 113; see also Hobson, *Tell about the South*.

paragraphs. Newel *means* it: he can see nothing noteworthy in his father's itinerant working life across the South. Newel cannot believe that his father could have "loved it [his labor] so much." If Robard exhibits little consciousness about his class-specific or "southern" identity, Newel's paradox is that he *wants* to feel a Quentin-like alienation from (yet connection to) "the South," but he sees his father's working-class life as too trivial, too absurdly "fun," to fulfill the tragic Faulknerian sensibility.[10]

In a telling scene between Newel and Beebe, Newel remembers how, when he was a child, "we had a flat tire right on the bridge at Vicksburg" and that "my mother grabbed me and held me so tight I couldn't breathe, until he [his father] had fixed the tire. She said she was afraid of something happening." Here, Newel rather heavy-handedly hints that his mother was afraid his father might kill them all. But Beebe's response is skeptical, even sarcastic: "That's very romantic, but what does it have to do with you?" (82). Beebe is beginning to realize that Newel is rhetorically performing a pseudoliterary idea of "the South"—that he is trying desperately to dramatize a personal burden of southern history. Beebe exposes the disjunction between Newel's actual experience, and his exaggeration, or invention, of a tragic familial and regional experience. Indeed, Beebe's incredulity toward her cousin's self-conscious southern discomfort subsequently prompts Newel to admit the performative nature of his past-in-the-present: "So it has to do with me because I say it does" (83). Newel's rage to explain his very own burdens of southern history and place has become a rather petulant act.[11]

10. Among southern literary intertexts, one also recalls Eudora Welty's "Death of a Traveling Salesman," a story that Jan Nordby Gretlund rightly identifies as "Welty's clearest statement in support of basic Agrarian ideas." "[D]esperately dislocated" and unable to relate to "country people who ignore his usual cash approach," the traveling salesman Bowman is "the antithesis" of the subsistence farmer Sonny and his wife. That Newel's father was no Bowman—that Newel Sr. *loved* his itinerant sales job—challenges the neo-Agrarian "aesthetics of place" of Welty's story. The contrast also anticipates later works in which Ford questions the Weltyan worldview: see Chapter 6. Eudora Welty, "Death of a Traveling Salesman," in *A Curtain of Green* (1943; reprint, Harmondsworth: Penguin, 1947), 168–83, and Gretlund, *Eudora Welty's Aesthetics of Place,* 49–51, 56.

11. Ford's own father was a traveling starch salesman, and the Ford family was similarly peripatetic. Ford's 1987 essay "My Mother, In Memory" recounts a scene that is strikingly similar to, yet significantly differs from, Newel's memory of the flat tire on the Vicksburg bridge: "A flat tire we all three had, halfway across the Mississippi bridge at Greenville. High up there, over the river. We stayed in the car while my father fixed it, and my mother held me so tightly to her I could barely breathe. I was six. She always said, 'I smothered you when you

Richard Ford quite deliberately constructs Newel as a *parody* of southern literature's familiar (whether Faulknerian or Percyan) white, male, upper-class figural hero. When McMurtry diagnosed *A Piece of My Heart* as a case of "neo-Faulknerism," he failed to distinguish that it is Sam Newel, rather than Richard Ford, whose narrative strategy follows the familiar Faulknerian tropes. It is Newel whose "passion for rhetoric" refers less to his own experience than to what Michael Kreyling has called "the Faulkner-Quentin model." Contra McMurtry's criticisms, the Chicago scenes between Beebe and Newel reveal how Ford subtly undermines Newel's "Quentissential" identity and discourse through postsouthern parody.[12]

There is, though, one way in which Newel manages to construct a distinctive sense of "the South" before leaving Chicago on the "lunatic trip [to Mississippi] he couldn't even understand the good sense of" (68). It is also here that Newel's sense of place has something in common with Binx Bolling's. For like Binx, Newel rhetorically reasserts his "South" by contrasting it with Chicago. When Beebe declares herself an acolyte of urban scholar Jane Jacobs and asserts that "[t]he city is put here to solve our problems" (69), Newel responds that "[y]ou should try it on the south side before you make up your mind." To this, Beebe retorts that "I get along with the boogies just fine" (70). This should not simply be taken as the racist remark it appears to be. Rather, Beebe is slyly parodying, and provocatively challenging, Newel's own image of Chicago as a racialized site of violence. Newel explicitly expresses this image of Chicago shortly afterwards, contrasting it with a (relatively) favorable vision of the South: "[Mississippi's] not any more threatening than it is out there. . . . There's goddamn whores right in this building, right below us. When they're around things can get real *special,* you might say, especially if they're coons, which these ladies certainly are. There's plenty of everything

---

were little. You were all we had. I'm sorry.' . . . But I wasn't sorry. It seemed fine then, since we were up there. 'Smothering' meant 'Here is danger,' 'Love protects you.'" Ford recalls the *love* that his family members felt and expressed to one another, for all their economic and geographic instability. In the novel, Newel dramatizes the similar scenario as a nightmare of (his own) southern history. Ford, "My Mother, In Memory," *Harper's*, August 1987, 48.

12. McMurtry, review of *A Piece of My Heart*, 16; Kreyling, *Inventing Southern Literature*, 110. In the context of her interesting discussion of "the rhetorical failure of language" in the novel, Elinor Ann Walker rightly notes that Newel exhibits "a sensibility that verges on the affected." However, Walker's subsequent reference to Newel's "problematic New South voice" does not allow for the self-consciously Quentissential nature of Newel's rhetoric, or the textual operation of postsouthern parody. See Walker, *Richard Ford* (New York: Twayne, 2000), 42.

right there, if you want to be scared. Some poor Pakistani managed to get his throat cut standing in the middle of Kenwood Avenue. That's fairly outrageous" (78).

If Newel does not go so far as Binx, who feared Kate's mutation into a "little low-browed olive-skinned big-butted Mediterranean such as populates the streets and subways of the North," Newel follows Binx by invoking an oblique sense of southern whiteness. When Newel (like Binx a decade before) at last escapes Chicago on a southbound train, his lingering impression of the city is motivated by his general conception of Chicago as a nonwhite locus of crime and chaos. Just before departing, having briefly left his bag on a station platform, Newel returns to find it gone. He asks a little boy, one of a "group of well-dressed Negroes," where the bag is. The boy tells him that the "[p]o-lice done got it" (68) but, upon boarding his train, Newel shoots "an accusing look at the Negroes." Though "[n]one of them was holding his bag," Newel still watches as the blacks "grow smaller in the station until they were absorbed" (69)—absorbed back into Newel's imagined heart of darkness.[13]

Disembarking from the train in Memphis, Newel begins a vaguely Binx-like search for place and "southern" identity. Realizing that "he had never felt the [Mississippi] river," Newel walks down to the water, driven by a sense that the river "seemed now like a vast and imponderable disadvantage, and made him feel like he needed to know" (87). It is surely this sentence that McMurtry had in mind when he wrote that "the burden of southern history . . . squashes them [Ford's main protagonists] into a mulch of pronouns and pulpy adjectives, of which 'imponderable' is the one I personally have come to dislike the most. If it's so imponderable why must everyone keep pondering it, in a fashion at once so tedious and so vague?"[14]

It would seem, then, that Newel's "imponderable" speculations upon the Mississippi River are a perfect example of "neo-Faulknerism." I want to continue arguing against McMurtry, however, that Ford is actually *parodying* the Faulknerian figural hero. Unsatisfied with "feeling" the river by simply dipping his hand in it, Newel wades into the water and is dragged down by the current. Again, any reader familiar with the southern literary tradition will likely recall the Quentissential intertextual moment: Quentin's suicide in the Charles River. However, having halfheartedly flirted with a suitably southern

13. Percy, *The Moviegoer*, 202.
14. McMurtry, review of *A Piece of My Heart*, 18.

literary suicide, Newel realizes that he is "risking self-annihilation without even willing it so" (87). The scene becomes less tragic than comic as Newel realizes "that his shorts were now gone and he was floating with his privates adangle in the cold current, prey to any browsing fish" (88). Eventually, Newel is rescued by two bargemen who, although they seem like stereotypes from a primer on the southern grotesque, appear less ridiculous than Newel himself. The comedy is repeated as farce when Newel again almost drowns while staying on Mark Lamb's island (184). On both occasions, Newel's self-conscious fascination with the "imponderable" Mississippi river shows him acting out the "learned behavior" of which, Kreyling observes, "Quentin's 'experience' of the South and Southern history is authorization." Ford's intertextual parody implies that the tropes of southern (literary) history and place legitimized and naturalized by "the Faulkner-Quentin model" are no longer tenable. For despite his neo-Faulknerian efforts, such familiar fictional figures are in fact irrelevant to Newel's own experience.[15]

These pseudo–suicide attempts also suggest that Newel is behaving in a way he has "learned" from Walker Percy. In a pioneering essay on Ford's third novel, *The Sportswriter* (1986), Edward Dupuy applied Percy's concept of the "ex-suicide" to that book's narrator, Frank Bascombe. Yet Percy's theory can be applied more literally to Newel. Percy adumbrates his "ex-suicide" hypothesis in *Lost in the Cosmos* (1983):

> Suppose you elect suicide. Very well. You exit. Then what? What happens after you exit? Nothing much. Very little, indeed. After a ripple or two, the water closes over your head as if you had never existed . . .
>
> Now, in the light of this alternative, consider the other alternative. You can elect suicide, but you decide not to. What happens? . . . Where you might have been dead, you are alive. The sun is shining.
>
> Suddenly, you feel like a castaway on an island. You can't believe your good fortune . . . cast upon a beach . . .[16]

We have already seen how Newel flirts with and then rejects "self-annihilation" in the Mississippi River. Subsequently, however, he diverges from Percy's ex-suicide in that, rather than feeling "good fortune" after (twice)

---

15. Kreyling, *Inventing Southern Literature*, 106.

16. Edward Dupuy, "The Confessions of an Ex-Suicide: Relenting and Recovering in Richard Ford's *The Sportswriter*," *Southern Literary Journal* 23, no. 1 (fall 1990): 95 and passim; Walker Percy, *Lost in the Cosmos: The Last Self-Help Book* (1983; reprint, London: Arena, 1984), 77–78.

escaping death by water, he regresses into a listless funk while staying on Lamb's island. This intertextual allusion to Percy's theory of the ex-suicide, with its extended "castaway" metaphor, is also useful in that it helps to flesh out Holditch's tentative comparison between Newel and Binx Bolling. In *The Moviegoer*, Percy portrays Binx's awakening to the "search" in terms similar to the ex-suicide's regeneration. Binx feels "as if I had to come to myself on a strange island" and describes himself as a "castaway" who "pokes around the neighborhood and . . . doesn't miss a trick." And as we saw in Chapter 3, Binx begins his sporadic search for place in the South by critically reexamining his own neighborhood (Gentilly) before moving into older southern spaces (Bayou des Allemands, the Garden District). But the ex- (or pseudo-) suicide Newel lacks even the erratic, compromised drive of the cynical Binx. Confining himself to Lamb's island during his stay in Mississippi, Newel never really searches for (his) place in the larger "South." Nor does the island itself yield anything that might make his past usable or unburdened. Eventually, Newel decides that Mississippi is "boring as shit" (229) and simply returns to Chicago.[17]

At the moment of this bathetic epiphany, Ford attaches to Newel an extended metaphor that once again recalls Percy's "castaway." However, the metaphor merely confirms that, if Newel is now a "castaway," the South is not his "strange island," his sanctuary, any more than it is the burdensome site of his southern personal history. Instead, Newel's metaphorical beach proves to be, of all places, Chicago: "It was the day to leave, without doubt. Get the bus to Memphis and be on the late train. . . . There was a squeamish serenity in that, of choosing the only thing left. . . . It was the compromise satisfaction a person got, he thought, when he is washed up on the beach of some country after spending weeks floating around on a tree limb, too far from home ever to hope to be deposited *there,* and satisfied to be on land, no matter really which land it happened to be" (225). Finally, then, Newel abandons his attempt to perform a Quentissential identity and to enact a Binx-like "search" for place. More broadly speaking, as the pseudosuicide cum pragmatist prepares to go back to Memphis and on to his bittersweet home in Chicago, so the narrative trajectory of *A Piece of My Heart* inverts and parodies the foundational trope of southern literary place that involves coming home again from the urban, placeless North—a trope that operates in both Faulkner's *The Sound and the Fury* and, as we have seen, Percy's *The Moviegoer.*

17. Percy, *The Moviegoer,* 13.

"This Little Cut-Off Tit of Nothing": Mark Lamb's Island and the Problem of Place

So far, I have tried to show that, rather than neo-Faulknerism, there is a sophisticated *postsouthernism* operating in *A Piece of My Heart*. Ford focuses upon one working-class protagonist whose sense of place is peripatetic and contingent upon his labor, and another whose sense of place and burden of history serves to parody Faulkner and Percy. One might still ask, however, why Ford's debut ultimately is an unsatisfying novel. Guinn has called Ford's debut his "weakest effort"; like McMurtry, Guinn bemoans the pernicious influence of Faulkner. More inclined than Guinn to see postsouthern parody operating in *A Piece of My Heart*, I want to suggest other reasons for the novel's failings.

Ford maroons not only Newel, but also the novel itself, on Mark Lamb's island. To be sure, Ford does seem to want to use the island to raise interesting issues: specifically, the relationship between capital, land, and place, and the increasingly untenable opposition between "North" and "South" in a postsouthern America. (These are interesting issues because, as we shall see in Chapters 5 and 6, they become central to Ford's later fiction.) Lamb—Newel's host, Robard's employer, and ostensibly the island's sole owner and proprietor—has bribed the Corps of Engineers to erase the island from its maps. In doing so, Lamb believes that the island "has ceased to exist for the rest of the world" (164). This cartographic erasure also enables Lamb to claim that the island is part of his own home state of Mississippi, rather than Arkansas. But Lamb also constructs a familiar and more telling opposition: between "the South" and "the North." Lamb scorns Newel as "a fish" who "belong[s] back up in Lake Michigan where it's cold and wet, not down here where people's got blood" (216). This attack is not a little ironic given Newel's own earlier attempt to distinguish Mississippi from Chicago; it also echoes Binx's smugly partisan contrast between Lake Pontchartrain and Lake Michigan ("the North itself"). However, Lamb's antipathy toward the North is, like Binx's, driven by an ulterior motive. For it transpires that Lamb does not own the island at all: he rents it from a company called "Chicago Pulp and Paper" (168). Sounding like a grotesque amalgam of Binx and Newel deriding the "Mediterraneans" and "coons" of Chicago, Lamb rails at the "wops" and "greasy dagos" (169) who run Chicago Pulp and Paper. He splutters that "[i]t's an in-dignity to suffer their presence on this island, like this was some part of Detroit or one of them other hellish places" (170). Lamb thus follows Donald Davidson, as well as Binx Bolling, by conflating northern cities—albeit in his case the targets are Chicago and Detroit, not Chicago and New York. But more important, these racist epithets also reveal Lamb's repressed fear that, at (the economic) base, the island is not southern at all—that it effectively belongs to, is part of, the North. Lamb's emphasis on the island's status as part of Mississippi turns out to have been entirely performative. That Chicago Pulp and Paper owns and regularly surveys the island shows that Lamb's power over the island was only ever textual, written on to—or rather, written out of—the Corps of Engineers' maps. By contrast, Ford's narrative cartography suggests that, in the last instance, sense of place is more contingent upon property rights than the regionalist rhetoric of a local resident like Mark Lamb.

But in spite of all that, as a central locus in the narrative, the island does tend to mire *A Piece of My Heart* in the southern literary tradition that Ford so deftly parodies elsewhere in the novel. In his thoughtful discussion of Ford's work, the English author Nick Hornby indicts "critics, particularly English critics," for stereotyping *A Piece of My Heart* as the work of a "Southern writer," but then admits that, "without wishing to squeeze Ford uncomfortably into any tradition, [Mark] Lamb is the kind of Southern grotesque that literary critics would seize upon." Well, I would seize upon Lamb's surreal death—he is electrocuted while trying to fish with a peculiar battery device—as the most obvious example of Ford's gratuitous use of the grotesque. This stylized grotesquerie also appears on the island in the form of glass-eyed Fidelia, and through tales of Fidelia's mad brother John (218). The irony then is that, like Newel, Ford himself finally seems to have succumbed to a form of southern literary "learned behavior." The narrative's turn toward this hermetic realm of the grotesque feels like going south to a very old place.[18]

Ultimately, perhaps the island's most significant role is to prevent Newel from discovering what "the South" is *really* becoming circa 1971. The narrative provides one vivid hint that, elsewhere in Mississippi, there has been dramatic sociospatial change. In one of the last and more interesting exchanges between the two central characters, Newel's continued stubborn insistence that one's (southern) past impacts upon one's present prompts Robard to launch into an unusually voluble tirade: "Shit! If the only thing you can bear is just coming back to this little cut-off tit of nothing, somebody ought to tell you something. . . . If you *did* really want to come down here to live, some-

---

18. Nick Hornby, *Contemporary American Fiction* (New York: SMJ, 1992), 94.

where, you wouldn't choose this place, cause everything's trapped right here, and I'm positive you wouldn't recognize nothin else. Down in Jackson there ain't nothing but a bunch of empty lots and people flying around in Piper Comanches looking for some way to make theirselves rich. It wouldn't feel nothing at all anymore, to *you*" (230). A "little cut-off tit of nothing": Robard's choice words identify just why the island tells Newel little about "the South" circa 1971. For all the pseudoliterary tropes through which Newel rages to explain or invent his "southernness," his putative search for place is doomed to meaninglessness because the "baronial and ridiculous" island can shed no light on either his itinerant working-class family history or the redevelopment under way elsewhere in present-day Mississippi.

Confined to this "cut-off tit of nothing," Newel's search (such as it is) necessarily runs down. All that remains is for him to come to the bathetic realization that Mississippi (or rather, Mark Lamb's performative "Mississippi," which is all that Newel experiences) is "boring as shit," and cast himself back to Chicago. Frank Shelton argues optimistically that "because he [Newel] recognizes the futility of searching for meaning in the South and his Southern past, [he] may be freed to make life for himself." Yet there is no real sense that Newel has solved what Percy would call his "predicament of placement"; at best, he has achieved a "compromise satisfaction." When Robard asks whether "[y]ou like Chicago better now," Newel responds, "I don't care" (229).[19]

With Newel gone, the reader is left alone with Robard. If Newel's southern literary self and search for place disintegrated during his time on the island, Robard seems to have been entirely unmarked by the experience. Leaving the island after Lamb's death, to Robard "[i]t all seemed like someplace he hadn't ever been but knew about, something away from his life altogether now" (279). Here we have another example of Robard's minute-by-minute philosophy of life, and his highly contingent sense of place. Like Hazen, where he worked for Rudolph, the island, where he worked for Lamb, means nothing to him afterward. However, because Robard is so willfully unconscious of the social relations (class and labor) that dominate his life, the narrative finally narrows down to his sexual relationship with Beuna. The brutal denouement of this affair leads indirectly to Robard's murder. Finally then,

---

19. Frank W. Shelton, "Richard Ford (1944–)," in Joseph M. Flora and Robert Bain, eds., *Contemporary Fiction Writers of the South: A Bio-Bibliographical Sourcebook* (Westport, Conn.: Greenwood Press, 1993), 150.

the sly and funny parody that Ford filtered through Newel is swamped by what Hornby calls the "grim nihilism" of Robard's death. It is possible, though, that Ford knew of the problem with *A Piece of My Heart* before anyone else. Reviewing Percy's *Lancelot* in 1977, the year after *A Piece of My Heart* was published, Ford observed that "if it is true that *Lancelot* is written as parody, it's true only part of the time, and I'm afraid I lose the thread of intention." Ford could have been critiquing his own recent debut novel: as postsouthern parody succumbs to grim nihilism, and as the working-class geographies of postsouthern America give way to the grotesque island, one loses the thread of intention in *A Piece of My Heart*.[20]

Yet there lingers the puzzle of Robard's uncharacteristically voluble and perceptive critique of Jackson's transformation. Robard's diatribe points to another Mississippi that Ford might have introduced into the novel. If Ford wanted to write "about the South in a way that nobody would ever recognize as being southern," why did he portray a "cut off tit of nothing" that pastiches Faulkner and O'Connor, rather than mapping the dramatic sociospatial change in and around his birthplace? An explanation might be found in Ford's "An Urge for Going: Why I Don't Live Where I Used to Live" (1992). In this essay, Ford writes that: "Place . . . is supposed to be important to us Southerners. . . . But where I grew up was a bland, unadhesive place—Jackson, Mississippi—a city in love with the suburban Zeitgeist the way Mill was in love with utility, a city whose inert character I could never get interested in." Here, Ford offers another skeptical interrogation of the South's supposed sense of place, but with a more specific emphasis on capitalist redevelopment. If "An Urge for Going" thus provides a more explicit take on Robard's critique of Jackson, it also echoes Ford's 1977 essay on Percy, in which he made a wider point about the redevelopment—even destruction—of southern place: "The south has become the regrettable 'Sunbelt,' in case you haven't noticed. And I'm afraid the Sunbelt is buckled on to stay, and the jury is not even impaneled yet that will judge the literature that such a strange new territory will produce.

20. Hornby, *Contemporary American Fiction*, 97; Ford, "Walker Percy," 564. Similarly, the structural prominence and recurrence of the italicized (and stylized) "flashback" sections, in which Newel recalls (supposedly) key moments in his childhood, tends to undercut the novel's use of Newel's sub-Quentin self-absorption to parody such southern literary tropes as "the burden of southern history" and "the rage to explain." Ford perhaps became aware of this problem, as he subsequently parodied the "flashback" in *The Sportswriter;* see Chapter 5, especially Note 5.

. . . The south is not a place any more: it's a Belt, a business proposition, which is the nearest thing to anonymity the economy recognizes."[21]

In "An Urge for Going" and "Walker Percy: Not Just Whistling Dixie," Ford implies that the reproduction, or erasure, of "place" by Sun Belt capitalism has produced a "strange new territory" that is not even *interesting*. As Ford identifies and indicts this *post*-South, one begins to understand why he never wrote about Jackson in *A Piece of My Heart*. Indeed, it seems that, having been accused of "neo-Faulknerism" despite *parodying* the southern literary "sense of place," Ford became even less inclined to write about "the regrettable 'Sunbelt'" in his subsequent fiction. Instead, after *A Piece of My Heart*, Ford decided "to get my work out of the South as much as I possibly could." When McMurtry counseled Ford to "weed his garden of some of the weeds and cockleburs of his tradition," the Texan could hardly have anticipated that Ford would abandon his native southern garden altogether. By locating his later books beyond "the South," however, Ford ensured that his postsouthern interrogation of southern literary shibboleths like "sense of place" became far more radical. For all its faults, *A Piece of My Heart* is engaging not least because it anticipates the more sophisticated and successful postsouthernism played out in *The Sportswriter* (1986) and *Independence Day* (1995). The next two chapters will consider these two novels, and how Ford maps in detail the capitalist geographies of postsouthern America.[22]

21. Ford, "An Urge for Going: Why I Don't Live Where I Used to Live," *Harper's*, February 1992, 61; "Walker Percy," 562.
22. McMurtry, review of *A Piece of My Heart*, 18.

5. Land and Literary Speculations: The Postsouthern World-as-Text in Richard Ford's *The Sportswriter*

When *The Sportswriter*'s narrator Frank Bascombe begins by stating, "I am a sportswriter. . . . My life . . . has not been and isn't now a bad one at all," he echoes quite eerily Binx Bolling's comment that "I am a stock and bond broker. . . . It is not a bad life at all." Indeed, a number of critics have identified *The Moviegoer* as an influence upon *The Sportswriter*. However, it can be argued that *The Sportswriter*'s often elusive and elaborate skepticism toward literary constructions of "the South" enacts a significant *shift* in the postsouthern sensibility first mapped by Walker Percy. In *The Sportswriter*, Ford extends his postsouthern project beyond the (formal and spatial) limits of *A Piece of My Heart*, and in doing so he produces a complex intertextual critique of the southern "sense of place" presented in *The Moviegoer*. Frank Bascombe's coming of age in Mississippi diverges from familiar southern literary geographies, including Binx Bolling's.[1]

"No Particular Sense of Their Place": Frank's Family in Biloxi

Early in *The Sportswriter*, just before recounting his childhood in the South, Frank Bascombe makes a disarming disclaimer: "All we really want is to get to the point where the past can explain nothing about us and we can get on with life. Whose history can ever reveal very much? In my view Americans put too much emphasis on their pasts as a way of defining themselves, which can be death-dealing. I know I'm always heartsick in novels . . . when the novelist makes his clanking, obligatory trip into the Davy Jones locker of the past" (30).

We encounter here a self-reflexive narrative strategy that operates on two

---

1. Richard Ford, *The Sportswriter* (1986; reprint, London: Harvill, 1996), 9–10; Percy, *The Moviegoer*, 9. On the relation between these two novels, see Hornby, *Contemporary American Fiction*, 97, and Fred Hobson, *The Southern Writer in the Postmodern World* (Athens: University of Georgia Press, 1991), 55. All subsequent page references to *The Sportswriter* will be incorporated into the main text.

levels. First, as the supposed producer of the text entitled "*The Sportswriter*," Frank preemptively undercuts any attempt on the reader's part to define him according to his southern history and homeplace. Secondly, Richard Ford begins to extend his own, omniscient-authorial interrogation of "southern literature," initiated in *A Piece of My Heart*, through the mediating figure of his character-narrator. For despite the wider reference to "Americans," and beyond the self-conscious *anti*literary attitude, Frank's opening gambit disrupts the conventional sense of southern (literary) identity. In notable contrast to Sam Newel, Frank does not feel at all obliged to define his "southernness" according to such familiar tropes as "the past in the present" or "the burden of southern history."[2]

Even the protopostsouthern experience of Binx Bolling is alien to Frank. Anticipating a similar point I made (in Chapter 4) with reference to Newel and Robard Hewes, Jeffrey Folks has noted that "Frank's own heritage (and Ford's as well)" is working-class, and therefore "contrasts markedly with the privileged milieu of Walker Percy's fiction." Frank observes that his parents had "no particular sense of their *place* in history's continuum." Whereas Aunt Emily in *The Moviegoer* harps on the stoical heroism of the Bolling clan since the Civil War, Frank's parents were "without a daunting conviction about their own consequence," which to Frank "seems like a fine lineage to me still" (30). In fully historical-*geographical* terms, one can also say that Frank's parents had no "sense of their *place*" in the historical geography of the South. They were born in rural Iowa and passed through Davenport, El Reno, and Cicero before settling in Biloxi on the Mississippi Gulf Coast. In *The Moviegoer*, Binx observes that his uncle combines the "old-world charm" of Garden District society with the "new-world business methods" of his stockbroking partnership. In *The Sportswriter*, Frank comments that his father worked in the post–World War II military-industrial complex, "plating ships with steel at the Ingalls ship-building company" (31) in Biloxi. Moreover, whereas Binx is able to recover, or cynically simulate, a "spirit-presence" at his father's old duck club, Frank cannot conjure any such metaphysical aesthetics of place from his memories of Gulf Pines military school. Frank writes: "What I remember of the place was a hot parade grounds surrounded by sparse pine trees . . . a stale shallow lake where I learned to sail, a smelly beach and boat house,

---

2. If there is a (post)southern literary echo here, it is, as Fred Hobson has noted, of Percy's epigraph to *The Last Gentleman*: "If a man cannot forget, he will never amount to much" (Søren Kierkegaard). See Hobson, *The Southern Writer in the Postmodern World*, 55.

hot brown stucco classroom buildings and white barrack houses that reeked with mops" (32). Through Frank's reminiscence, Ford suggests a working-class "ordinary, modern existence" (30) in Biloxi that contrasts with (but occurs in the same period as) Binx's petty-bourgeois "ordinary life" in Gentilly. Like Robard and Newel, Frank Bascombe grew up in another "South."[3]

However, Frank's life, like Newel's, has since gone north toward home. When Frank was fourteen, his father died, and his mother "went to work in a large hotel called the Buena Vista in Mississippi City as the night cashier." Here, she met and married a jeweler from Chicago and moved to a "strangely suburban ranch-style house" in a Jewish neighborhood of Skokie, Illinois. As in *A Piece of My Heart*, here Ford interrogates the typological opposition in southern literature (and southern literary criticism) between "the North" and "the South"—not least as Binx constructs that opposition in *The Moviegoer*. For Frank's youthful experience of Illinois stands in stark contrast to Binx's northern exposure to the same state. Though Frank notes that it was "a town where I had no attachments," he never scorns Skokie in the manner that Binx attacked Wilmette as the vanishing point of the northern "Nowhere." In fact, once his mother relocated to Skokie, Frank had no more attachments in Mississippi. Hence, upon graduating from the military school in Gulfport, he simply left the South and "enrolled at the University of Michigan" (34). As we shall see, it is to Michigan that Frank makes a sentimental homecoming in *The Sportswriter*. Just as the "place to come to" of Warren's Jed Tewksbury

3. Jeffrey Folks, "The Risks of Membership: Richard Ford's *The Sportswriter*," *Mississippi Quarterly* 52, no. 1 (winter 1998–99): 80; Percy, *The Moviegoer*, 31, 91. As Folks hints, and as with the figure of Sam Newel in *A Piece of My Heart*, autobiographical traces can be identified in Ford's depiction of Frank. In his essay "My Mother, In Memory," Ford distinctly echoes Frank's description of his parents' "ordinary, modern existence." He states that "[w]e were not a family for whom history had much to offer," before proceeding to describe the kind of son-of-a-traveling-salesman life that Newel agonized over. Ford writes: "I think they [his parents] were just caught up in their life, a life in the South, in the thirties, just a kind of swirling thing that didn't really have a place to go. There must've been plenty of lives like that then. It seems a period now to me. A specific time, the Depression. But to them, of course, it was just their life." Ford, "My Mother, In Memory," 44, 46.

One downside of Frank's coming of age in Mississippi during the late 1950s/early 1960s is his failure to relate to, or textually refer to, the civil rights movement. Only his observation that "[o]ne Negro even taught" (32) at Lonesome Pines obliquely suggests the fraught social context of civil rights–era Mississippi. Though Frank's experience reveals a different (post-) South, he is (and will be throughout *The Sportswriter*) withdrawn from the public political sphere.

was South Dakota, not Alabama, so Frank returns to Detroit, rather than Mississippi.

The Sportswriter starts interrogating the binary opposition between northern "nonplaces" and the southern "sense of place" even *before* Frank recounts his youthful relocation to Illinois and Michigan. In the opening chapter, Frank and his ex-wife (literally referred to as "X" throughout) are visiting the grave of their son, Ralph, who died two years before the novel's present. X picks this moment to tell Frank that he has not been "well enough armored for the unexpected." As Frank recounts it, X believes this is "because I didn't know my parents very well, had gone to a military school, and grown up in the south, which was full of betrayers and secret-keepers and untrustworthy people, which I agree is true, though I never knew any of them. All that originated, she said, with the outcome of the Civil War. It was much better to have grown up, she said, as she did, in a place with no apparent character, where there is nothing ambiguous around to confuse you or complicate things, where the only thing anybody ever thought seriously about was the weather" (19).

Here, X echoes Binx's definition of "the South" and its sense of place to the degree that she contrasts it with a northern "Nowhere"—her own (home) "place with no apparent character" in Michigan. But Ford, making his first postsouthern move, has X slant this comparison in a distinctly *anti*southern fashion. She insinuates that the implicit "placeness" of "the South" is that of a dysfunctional, even sinister society still burdened by Appomattox. To the extent that X affirms the virtues of the North/Midwest, she sounds less like Binx than Jed Tewksbury in *A Place to Come To* celebrating Ripley City, South Dakota, as the "self-contained, self-fulfilling, complete" antithesis of Dugton, Alabama. But Ford executes a second postsouthern twist. Though Frank laconically agrees with X's negative assessment of the South, he adds the proviso that he never knew any southerners like those his ex-wife evokes. Frank is ready to concur with X's criticism, but accepts neither its influence upon him, nor its applicability to his own lived experience of the region. Whereas Jed had to struggle with the story of his father's death appearing less "real" than a scene "in one of those novels about the South," Frank has never even experienced this kind of rural, grotesque "South." Whereas Jed can still recall the rural site of his father's demise, even though the site has become a housing development, Frank's only moderately vivid memory of *his* father is on the golf links at Biloxi's air force base (31). If there is a (post)southern literary echo here, it is of Percy's claim that, whereas "Faulkner and all the rest of them were always going on about this tragic sense of history. . . . My South was always the New South. My first memories are of the country club, of people playing golf."[4]

At this point, it is worth discussing another dizzying dimension to *The Sportswriter*'s postsouthern practice. This dimension, both self-reflexive and intertextual, emerges when Frank recounts his brief career as a novelist. It transpires that, despite his own "ordinary, modern existence" as a boy in Biloxi, Frank went on to write fiction that regurgitated a veritable gumbo of southern literary clichés. Frank recalls how in 1967, returning to college after being discharged from the marines owing to a serious illness, he began to consider writing a novel. Evidently, this novel *Night Wing* involved the outlandish embellishment of thinly veiled autobiography—the story of "a bemused young southerner who joins the Navy but gets discharged with a mysterious disease, goes to New Orleans and loses himself into a hazy world of sex and drugs and rumored gun-running and a futile attempt to reconcile a vertiginous present with the guilty memories of not dying alongside his Navy comrades, all of which is climaxed in a violent tryst with a Methodist minister's wife who seduces him in an abandoned slave-quarters, though other times too, after which his life is shattered and he disappears permanently into the Texas oil fields. It was all told in a series of flashbacks" (42).

Frank's summary suggests that he wrote *Night Wing* under the anxiety-ridden influence of Faulkner. To use Harold Bloom's terms, *Night Wing* sounds like a "weak" rewriting—rather than a strong "misreading"—of Faulkner's *Flags in the Dust*. In the figure of the "bemused young southerner" returning to his native region burdened by "the guilty memories of not dying alongside his Navy comrades," Frank seems to allude, wittingly or not, to John Sartoris, the traumatized World War I veteran in Faulkner's novel. When the "bemused young southerner" in *Night Wing* confronts his "past in the present," one senses a weak, stylized take on the Faulkner-Tate theme. To put it another

4. Warren, *A Place to Come To*, 95, 7; Percy quoted in Lewis Lawson, *Still Following Percy* (Jackson: University Press of Mississippi, 1996), 14–15. Frank, however, would have no truck with Percy's upper-class country club. As Folks notes, Frank disapproves of "the country club milieu" (Folks, "The Risks of Membership," 85) of X's (Michigan) family. There may also be an echo of the Compson Place's transformation in Faulkner's *The Sound and the Fury* (see Chapter 2). However, development of the golf course in *The Sportswriter* proceeds under the auspices of the national military-industrial complex, not as the private form of "New South" leisure-class land speculation witnessed by the Compsons and Walker Percy.

way, Frank plays out in fiction the Faulknerian figural heroism that, in *A Piece of My Heart,* Sam Newel so self-consciously performed on his supposedly auspicious return to the South.[5]

All in all, Frank appears to have written a "southern" novel according to certain traditional tropes, with scant reference to his own "ordinary, modern" experience. Fred Hobson has commented astutely that Frank's juvenilia seems "nearly a parody of the usual racially charged, Christ-haunted southern production." But, to qualify Hobson's point, from Frank's own perspective in 1967, *Night Wing* was never parody but rather—to invoke Fredric Jameson's distinction—pastiche, "the imitation of a peculiar or unique, idiosyncratic style . . . without any of parody's ulterior motives." The postsouthern *parody* —the knowing indication and interrogation of shopworn southern literary tropes—emerges from Frank's (or Ford's) wry précis of *Night Wing* in the present narrative, "*The Sportswriter.*"[6]

When Frank begins to recount how, as a budding young author, he moved to Haddam, New Jersey, Ford extends his postsouthern dialogue with Percy. At this time (1970), Frank was working on another novel, *Tangier,* while living in New York. However, one morning he woke up with "a feeling we had to get out of town pronto so that my work could flourish in a place where I knew no one and no one knew me and I could perfect my important writer's anonymity." So Frank and his wife moved to "New Jersey: a plain, unprepossessing and unexpectant landscape, I thought, and correctly" (45). Frank recounts how he "wrote a piece in a local magazine about 'Why I Live Where I Live,' in which I talked about the need to find a place [i.e., Haddam] that is in most ways 'neutral'" (46). In a 1980 essay for *Esquire* entitled "Why I Live Where I Live," Percy describes his Louisiana hometown, Covington, in similar terms, though rather than calling Covington "neutral," Percy terms it a "nonplace." To this extent, Percy evinces a postsouthern skepticism toward "place"; he notes wryly that Covington "is in the Deep South, which is supposed to have a strong sense of place." Yet Percy still upholds "sense of place" as a special

---

5. Harold Bloom, *The Anxiety of Influence: A Theory of Poetry* (New York: Oxford University Press, 1973), 5 and passim. Frank's reference to *Blue Autumn*'s "flashbacks" signals another level of postsouthern, intertextual parody: Ford is acknowledging the failings of *his* debut. Undermining *A Piece of My Heart*'s parody of Newel's pseudoliterary "burden of southern history" is Ford's mannered use of modernist, Faulknerian "flashbacks"—although, as Hobson has noted (*The Southern Writer in the Postmodern World*, 44), this technique owes as much to Ernest Hemingway's *In Our Time* (1925).

6. Hobson, *The Southern Writer in the Postmodern World*, 52; Jameson, *Postmodernism*, 17.

"Southern" value by emphasizing Covington's "nearness to New Orleans," which he says is "very much of a place." Percy also presumes that a "Southern writer" who has relocated to "a nondescript Northern place" will still want to write about the South.[7]

By contrast, Frank Bascombe begins to appreciate New Jersey on its own terms, not just as a writer's "neutral" retreat or as "a nondescript Northern place." Frank even quits writing fiction altogether and takes a job as a sportswriter.[8] Having tried to cultivate New Orleans's Gothic mystery in *Night Wing*, Frank now uses his nonfictional narrative to celebrate Haddam instead: "a town like New Orleans defeats itself. It longs for a mystery it doesn't have and never will, if it ever did. New Orleans should take my advice and take after Haddam, where it is not at all hard for a literalist to contemplate the world" (54). Frank's refusal to regard New Orleans as unique expresses something of Ford's own postsouthern incredulity toward both the privileged "placeness" afforded New Orleans and the prejudice directed at northern "nonplaces" in Percy's work. When Huey Guagliardo asked about Frank's antipathy toward New Orleans, Ford explicitly stated his quarrel with Percy and drew attention to the socioeconomic reality of "the Big Easy": "That's an answering knell to one of Walker's characters in *The Last Gentleman*, who says the place where I was living when I read those books—Ann Arbor—was a *non-place*. That was me, basically, lobbing a salvo back over Walker's wall. . . . New Orleans steeps itself in its history and obfuscates all of its fundamental urbanness and modern problems by turning its head. . . . The fact is that it's a great big urban complex with a theme park in the middle, and everything else about New Orleans is just like every other city in America."[9]

So far, my reading of *The Sportswriter* has been chiefly concerned with the ways in which Ford's postsouthern parody interrogates received textual constructions of "the South" and its "sense of place." To adapt Michael Kreyling's formulation, we have seen how Ford's text adjusts or lightens the burden of southern place it must necessarily carry in the presence of Faulkner's Mississippi or Percy's Louisiana. But to assess further how Ford depicts the material production and social reality of place in *The Sportswriter*, one must turn away from Frank's boyhood memories of the South, and focus more closely upon

7. Walker Percy, "Why I Live Where I Live," in Patrick Samway, ed., *Signposts in a Strange Land* (London: Bellew, 1991), 3–6.
8. In the early 1980s, Ford himself wrote briefly for *Inside Sports* magazine.
9. Huey Guagliardo, "A Conversation with Richard Ford," *Southern Review* 34, no. 3 (summer 1998): 617.

the *postsouthern* America in which Frank now lives, works, and owns property. By considering Frank's everyday life in Haddam, New Jersey, it is possible to see how Ford further critiques the Percyan image of "the North." However, unlike Frank, Ford does not uncritically celebrate everyday life in the capitalist (sub)urban landscapes of New Jersey—no more than Percy, as distinct from Binx, celebrates land speculation and real-estate development in Louisiana. Rather, Ford employs a subtle irony to expose the socioeconomic realities that Frank omits from his narrative cartographies of postsouthern America.[10]

Frank in New Jersey

As we saw in Chapter 3, Binx Bolling's "peaceful existence" in Gentilly is "complicated" by the possibility of a spatialized "search" that impels Binx to embark upon insomniac strolls amid the "splendid" but spectral new houses of his suburban neighborhood. On his own "after dark" walks through the "winding, bowery streets" of Haddam, Frank "looked in at these houses . . . the sound of laughing and glasses tinking and spirited chatter floating out, and thought to myself: what good rooms these are. What complete life is here" (57). Unlike Binx, Frank is not actively involved in the material construction of suburbia. Yet, whereas Binx at least thinks critically about capitalist land speculation and real-estate development in Gentilly, Frank has not even begun to question the production of place in his own hometown. Instead, he celebrates Haddam as an "Anyplace," comparable to "grinning, toe-tapping Terre Haute or wide-eyed Bismarck, with stable property values, regular garbage pick-up, good drainage, ample parking" (109–10). Once again, it is notable that Frank advocates the virtues of the archetypal "northern" small town that Binx contemptuously dismissed as "Nowhere." However, Frank's take on the "good rooms" and "complete life" of Haddam ignores—and his mental (and textual) map of the town and its environs tends to elide—the existence of other, less privileged loci.

Frank does seem aware that his hometown is a wealthy enclave. He notes the substantial presence of white-collar corporate professionals: "Editors, publishers, *Time* and *Newsweek* writers, CIA agents, entertainment lawyers, business analysts, plus the presidents of a number of great corporations that mold opinion, all live along these curving roads or out in the country in big secluded houses." He also notes that local Republicans emphasize "a conservator's clear view about property values" based upon "the rule that

---

10. Kreyling, *Inventing Southern Literature*, 161.

location is everything." Evidently, the high exchange-value of local real estate helps to maintain Haddam's exclusive status. Yet despite his own working-class background in Mississippi, Frank tends to skim over the divisions of class, labor, and race that exist in Haddam. He blithely incorporates local African Americans and other less privileged residents into a homogeneous imagined community of happy Haddamites: "Even the servant classes, who are mostly Negroes, seem fulfilled in their summery, keyboard-awning side streets down Wallace Hill behind the hospital, where they own their own homes" (56). Having said that, Frank does distance himself from both the "small, monied New England émigré contingent" and the "smaller southern crowd," claiming affiliation with "the other, largest group . . . who act as if we're onto something fundamental that's not a matter of money" (55). The problem here is that Frank has already admitted that his ability to partake of "the best of what New Jersey offers" is precisely determined by the "matter of money," mentioning in passing that his "sound house" in Haddam was bought with "movie money" accrued when a producer optioned his short-story collection *Blue Autumn* in 1970 (45).[11]

At this point, we encounter a succession of self-reflexive, postsouthern turns to the novel's representation of place. Though Frank never published *Night Wing* (the manuscript was lost in the mail), he did publish "a reduced version" in *Blue Autumn*. Earlier, I quoted Hobson's point that *Night Wing* seems to be a parody of the standard "southern [literary] production." Once mediated through Jameson's theory of pastiche as a particularly "postmodern cultural production" complicit with late capitalism, Hobson's term intones the *economic* motive that might have informed young Frank's "southern" literary labor. For there is a suspicion that, as a self-consciously "southern production," *Night Wing*/"Night Wing" exemplifies what Scott Romine calls "conspicuous southernness": the profitable literary (re)production of familiar, marketable "sign[s] of southernness."[12]

Following this line of enquiry, one discovers that "southern literature," postsouthern "place" and the cash nexus become inextricably entwined throughout *The Sportswriter*. Most obviously, the "conspicuous southernness"

---

11. The "southerner-in-exile" is memorably personified by Fincher Barksdale, the "slew-footed mainstreet change jingler in awful clothes" with his "New South" mink ranch in south Memphis (75).

12. Romine, "Where Is Southern Literature?" 20, and *The Narrative Forms of Southern Community* (Baton Rouge: Louisiana State University Press, 1999), 206.

of the revised "Night Wing" helped to generate the surplus value that Frank speculated in New Jersey property. But whether one regards Frank or Ford as the author of the text, *literary production* in and of *The Sportswriter* never operates in some purely aesthetic sphere; it is always inseparable from the *economic production* of place. For there is another twist: the link between Frank's literary production and his land speculation echoes Ford's own experience. In 1987, Ford told Kay Bonetti that he sold *A Piece of My Heart* "to the movies and made some money and bought a house in New Jersey." In his essay on Faulkner's *The Hamlet,* Joseph Urgo observes that "[t]he term *speculation* conjoins real estate and literary aesthetics into a seamless definition." Urgo's point seems borne out by the experiences of both Frank and Ford: their respective speculations in the literary market have become equivalent to, exchangeable with, their speculations in the property market.[13]

However, it is important to note that there are significant *differences* between Frank and Ford's attitudes toward place and its literary-economic production, speculation, and representation. In a telling moment, Frank admits that since trading fiction for sportswriting, he no longer "care[s] to risk speculating" upon "the large world." Instead, he simply accepts "[t]hat we all look at it from someplace," a Weltanschauung that, he believes, "isn't enough for literature" (57–58). Thus Frank effectively acknowledges that, since he stopped writing fiction, he has rejected what Urgo calls the "intellectual" definition of speculation (as *opposed* to the "real-estate term"): "the human capacity of ratiocination—testing human vision against the nature of reality." Instead, Frank has adopted a *post*literary worldview that he calls "literalist." In this literalist mode, Frank feels able to accept and enjoy the "mysteries" of everyday life, which a "factualist" like his ex-wife cannot (138–39). The problem is that, since limiting himself to literalism, immersing himself in "mystery," Frank has refused to recognize the capitalist sociospatial reality of the world around him. In other words, he no longer "care[s] to risk speculating" *intellectually* (i.e., critically) upon his own local, social geography because he has speculated *financially* in it. As such, Frank complacently lauds Haddam for being "as straightforward and plumb-literal as a fire hydrant, which more than anything else makes it the present place it is" (109). The "literalist" who scathingly criticized New Orleans yet finds "meaningful mystery" (54) in

---

13. Kay Bonetti, "An Interview with Richard Ford," *Missouri Review* 10, no. 2 (1987): 94; Urgo, "Faulkner's Real Estate," 452.

New Jersey, a place that, as we will see, actually *mystifies* its own geographical uneven development.[14]

In a thoughtful essay on *The Sportswriter*, Edward Dupuy argues persuasively that "Frank is a man who sees the world as a text to be read. Since he claims no system—no myth—to order his reading, he relents to the text of the world." Dupuy's suggestion that Frank "sees the world as a text" is plausible and useful: indeed, the literalist's own text reveals that he does indeed "read" the world around him. For example, driving along Route 33 in New Jersey, Frank asserts that "[a]n American would be crazy to reject such a place, since it is the most diverting and readable of landscapes, and the language is always American" (58). But in response to Dupuy, I would say that Frank is diverted from critically speculating upon (rather than financially speculating in) New Jersey's capitalist landscapes precisely because he uncritically "relents" to a superficial and selective "reading" of them. To the extent that Frank believes the New Jersey Turnpike is "beautiful" (183), his postsouthern worldview continues to challenge an Agrarian-southern aesthetics of place/antidevelopment. As Joel Garreau has observed, "[t]he view along the New Jersey Turnpike is so appalling that Dixie planners specifically mention that state as what they don't want to see their world become." However, Frank's "relenting" literalism prevents him from seeing *critically* the grim, uneven (post)industrial landscape that spreads out alongside the turnpike. He does not test his "human vision" against the true "nature of [capitalist] reality." Instead, Frank insists it is better to "[s]top searching" than "remain up in the dubious airs searching for some right place that never existed and never will" (59). Matthew Guinn "hear[s] the echo of Thoreau" in these words. I beg to differ and suggest instead that Frank sounds like no one so much as Binx Bolling: that is, the complacent Binx of the "Little Way," driving along the increasingly commercialized Gulf Coast, "past Howard Johnson's and the motels," trying to repress his impulse to "search" for something, somewhere, beyond the increasingly commercialized and suburbanized landscape that surrounds him. Only when reawakening to "the search" and its (albeit largely repressed) critique of capitalist production does Binx decide he can no longer bear "the anonymity of our little car-space" and "the malaise" of "ten thousand handsome cars" congesting the coast. But for now Frank, the literalist who has not even *started* "searching," remains content driving toward the

14. Urgo, "Faulkner's Real Estate," 452.

"caressing literalness of the New Jersey coastal shelf" (58), cruising through the Garden State "as indistinguishable from my fellow Jerseyites as a druggist from Sea Girt" (87).[15]

But Frank does not just "read" the world-as-text: he also writes that wor(l)d. As the readers of Frank's text, we should be skeptical when he begins to incorporate the "American" language of capitalist place production into his own narrative. In *The Moviegoer*, a defining sign of New Orleans' suburban redevelopment is the banner hanging over Gentilly's movie theater proclaiming "Where Happiness Costs So Little." In *The Sportswriter*, Frank observes a roadside billboard for a new housing complex on the outskirts of Haddam: "*An Attractive Retirement Waits Just Ahead.*" Unlike Binx however, Frank has lost all sense of ironic, critical distance. Apparently unconcerned by the way in which, as Ford has written elsewhere, "the language used to signify our pleasure is being re-referenced by the lexicographers of American business," Frank removes the quotation marks and recapitulates this "American" language in his own words: "An attractive retirement is Pheasant Run & Meadow" (59). Frank thus uncritically relents to a capitalist world(view) and lexicon in which place has been reduced to, re-referenced as, real estate.[16]

One might, then, usefully replace Dupuy's theory of Frank "relenting" to the world-as-text with another Percyan formulation, from *Lost in the Cosmos: The Last Self-Help Book* (1983). Ever since the death of his son, Ralph, and his subsequent divorce from X, Frank has tried to solve his existential "predicament of placement vis-à-vis the world" through what Percy calls an "immanence of consumption." Drawing also on Percy's essay "Why I Live Where I Live," one can say that Frank's specific "species of consumption" is the consumption of *places*. This frantic consumption of places ranges from local developments like Pheasant Meadow to the "literal and anonymous cities of the nation, your Milwaukees, your St. Louises, your Seattles, your Detroits, even your New Jerseys" (13). Without knowing for certain whether Frank plans to sell his latest, autobiographical manuscript to the publishers of *Blue Autumn*, one can say that, by consuming the ostensibly "readable" language of land speculation, both locally and nationally, and by incorporating it seam-

---

15. Dupuy, "The Confessions of an Ex-Suicide," 98; Joel Garreau, *The Nine Nations of North America* (New York: Avon, 1981), 65; Guinn, *After Southern Modernism*, 131; Percy, *The Moviegoer*, 135, 125, 166. In fact, Ford has offered very skeptical opinions about Thoreau and his "sense of place." See Bonetti, "An Interview with Richard Ford," 81, and Chapter 6 below.

16. Percy, *The Moviegoer*, 7; Ford, "Heartbreak Motels," *Harper's*, August 1989, 13.

lessly into his own narrative, Frank "speculates" textually in a capitalistic way of seeing and writing the wor(l)d.[17]

Ford, though, offers a subtle critique of Frank's world-as-text, and the way in which it is conjoined with the "American" language of land speculation. By emphasizing the *difference* between Frank and Ford as authors of, and narrative cartographers in, *The Sportswriter*—by noting how Ford's irony exposes the limited, literalist worldview expounded in Frank's sportswriterly text—I do not mean to imply that Ford, unlike Frank, holds to some notion that literature is "transcendent" (22). The fact that Ford alludes to the equivalence between his own land and literary speculations hardly suggests that he regards fiction as a privileged form of cultural production that always retains an essential or autonomous truth-value. Nonetheless, Ford's critique emerges through the lacunae in Frank's "own" text—lacunae that are there because Frank has refused both Binx-like "searching" in, and intellectual speculation upon, the "large world." Frank's world-as-text begins to unravel during a jaunt to one of the supposedly "literal and anonymous cities" that he cites, Detroit. Through Frank's representation of Michigan, Ford's skeptical, textual practice of place once again challenges Percy's prejudices, even while exposing the problems with Frank's postsouthern world-as-text.

Frank in Michigan

In contrast to Binx Bolling's terror upon disembarking in Chicago, Frank Bascombe is brimming with anticipation upon arriving in Detroit. Indeed, Frank seems to experience much the same "wonder" that Carrie Meeber felt a century earlier when first responding to the sign-systems of Chicago. However, Frank is more literate in the consumer semiotics of urban space than Theodore Dreiser's heroine: "The air in Detroit Metro is bright crackling factory air. New cars revolve glitteringly down every concourse. Paul Anka sings tonight at Cobo Hall, a flashing billboard tells us" (119).[18]

Hobson has rightly noted that Frank celebrates "the much maligned Midwest, the target of much of Walker Percy's satire." Indeed, Ford's postsouthern response to Percy perhaps reaches its peak when Frank advocates neither (to use John Egerton's well-known terms) "the Americanization of Dixie,"

17. Percy, *Lost in the Cosmos*, 113, 120, and "Why I Live Where I Live," 5: "There is a species of consumption at work here. Places are consumed nowadays."

18. Theodore Dreiser, *Sister Carrie* (1900; reprint, Harmondsworth: Penguin Classics, 1986), 9–10.

nor "the Southernization of America," but the midwesternization of America. As Frank puts it, "I have read that with enough time American civilization will make the midwest of any place, New York included. And from here that seems not at all bad. Here is a great place be in love; to get a land-grant education; to own a mortgage . . . friendly Negroes and Polacks pull their pants legs up, sit side by side, feeling the cool Canadian breeze off the lake. So much that is explicable in American life is made in Detroit" (121).[19]

Much as Frank celebrates "Anyplace" where Binx scorned "No where," so this ode to Detroit contrasts with Binx's vision of Chicago. Binx saw only "heavy and squarish" buildings and shadowy nonwhite women.[20] Frank sees a racially harmonious, bourgeois utopia, a city that is compatible with New Jersey's own "American" landscape. Frank can envision becoming a consumer in Detroit, "buy[ing] a new car every year right at the factory door. Nothing would suit me better in middle life than to set up in a little cedar-shake builder's-design in Royal Oak or Dearborn" (121). Whereas Binx derided Harold Graebner's life in Wilmette, Frank has no such reflexive southern prejudice toward consumer life in the midwestern suburbs. On the contrary, Frank fondly imagines a college friend, Eddy Loukinen, living "down in Royal Oak with his own construction firm. Possibly an insulated window frame outlet in the UP—trading cars every year, checking his market shares" (157).

But one must look more closely at this postsouthern, post-Percyan sense of place. For in this vision of Eddy, we encounter an inclination in Frank that becomes increasingly apparent as the novel progresses. If the literalist no longer "risk[s] speculating" about the "large world," he does indulge in flights of fancy about the possible lives of friends and acquaintances, and even about alternative lives for himself. Frank's fantastical speculations about Eddy seem to follow the "fictional" logic of finance-capitalist land speculation itself. For much as this "fond wonder" upon Eddy's life and suburban sense of place has no referential meaning beyond Frank's world-as-text, the kind of market speculation in which (Frank *imagines* that) Eddy indulges is a wondrous fiction. Like "land value," speculation in "market shares" is made up of "fictitious capital," which David Harvey defines as "a flow of money capital not backed by any commodity transaction" or productive labor. Frank's "fictitious" life of Eddy, with its juxtaposition of manual work and market

---

19. Hobson, *The Southern Writer in the Postmodern World*, 49; see also Egerton, *The Americanization of Dixie*.

20. Percy, *The Moviegoer*, 203.

speculation, both elides the contrasts and simplifies the connections between Wall Street and Royal Oak: between finance-capitalist "valuation" and speculation, and the material production of space through wage labor.[21]

We have further reason to wonder about Frank's world-as-text when he visits Walled Lake, a small commuter town "beyond the perimeter of true Detroit suburbia" (157). Frank is here to interview ex–football star Herb Wallagher. However, in the figure of Herb, Frank encounters a case of angst "in the old mossy existential sense" (151) that severely contravenes his own suburban (financial and textual) speculations. The sportswriter had presumed that athletes are usually "fairly certain about the world and are ready to comment on it." However, Herb expresses an anxiety-ridden empathy with Ulysses S. Grant's declaration of alienated selfhood: "I think I am a verb instead of a personal pronoun. A verb signifies to be; to do; to suffer. I signify all three" (163). From here on, Frank's sportswriterly text(s) cannot contain Herb's existential-semantic alienation. Herb's wor(l)ds both interpolate Frank's autobiographical narrative (*"The Sportswriter"*), and complicate the cozy magazine feature Frank is supposed to write. As Frank later admits, Herb "is no easy nut to crack, since he's obviously as alienated as Camus. . . . Some life does not give in to a sportswriter's point of view" (214–15).

Nick Hornby has noted that it is Frank who "occasionally appears as alienated and as dislocated as the hero of Camus' *L'Étranger.*" More than this, though, Frank's existential and narrative identity is inseparable from his consumer's self-placement in an intensely capitalist world. Edward Soja's *Postmodern Geographies* may be helpful here. Having criticized vulgar existentialism, the "pure contemplation of the isolated individual" ("excremental philosophy," in Henri Lefebvre's memorable definition), Soja emphasizes the "existential spatiality of being." Extrapolating from Martin Heidegger, Soja argues that "being-in-the-world" is always mediated through a nexus of social, economic, and spatial factors. As I have tried to show, Frank's own being-in-the-world is bound up with an uncritical celebration of, and immersion in, the kind of postmodern capitalist geographies that Soja discusses. Frank has displaced his existential anxiety about the "large world" on to the consumer-friendly language-landscapes of New Jersey and Detroit. As such, we should

21. David Harvey quoted in Jameson, "The Brick and the Balloon," 43. That Eddy supposedly has a construction firm can be seen not only as further subtle evidence of Frank's obsession with capitalist property relations, but also as an oblique acknowledgment that ultimately even the material production of "place" is, under capitalism, connected to the abstract and "fictitious" definition of land "values."

not be surprised that once Herb's fractured sense of *self* begins to trouble Frank—"I am sorry to hear Herb referring to his life in the past tense. It is not an optimistic sign" (160)—the sportswriter's complacent sense of *place* is also destabilized. His "spatialized ontology" in turmoil, Frank suddenly revises his way of seeing and writing Walled Lake too: "It is not a particularly nice place, a shabby summer community of unattractive bungalows. Not the neighborhood I'd expected for an ex-all-pro" (161).[22]

Frank even begins to connect his alienation quite explicitly with land speculation and real- estate development. As the interview goes from bad to worse, Frank characteristically projects outward from his subjective self on to objective place. However, unlike Pheasant Run & Meadow in New Jersey, where Frank "consumed" a language-landscape that signified successful capitalist speculation, Walled Lake offers no consolation. On the contrary: "A hundred years ago, this country would've been wooded and the lake splendid and beautiful. A perfect place for a picnic. But now it has all been ruined by houses and cars" (161). Leaving Walled Lake (and fleeing Herb) in Mr. Smallwood's taxi, Frank sees the charred remnants of the local casino, where he once gambled during his college days. Walled Lake Casino is a site that, to paraphrase John Carlos Rowe, once referred to and epitomized a speculative economy. However, in its present dilapidation, the site symbolizes the contingency of (land) speculation in a market economy, undermining further Frank's self-assurance: "No one, apparently, has thought to find a new use for the land. My past in decomposition and trivial disarray" (171). Frank's existential investment in the pleasure of a capitalist world-as-text has been exposed by the irruption of *real* (sub)urban decay into his life and narrative.[23]

Upon returning to Detroit, the alienation of Frank's existential-spatial being from his "American" language-landscape proceeds apace. Though Frank's traveling companion, Vicki Arcenault, is waiting for him, he cannot avert "the sad old familiarity from the dreamy days after Ralph died . . . lost in strangersville with a girl I don't know well enough" (174). Attempting to avert this dislocation, and to redeem Detroit as "*the* right place" (176), Frank and Vicki venture into the city. Folks has observed that, for Frank, "Detroit itself, with its unpredictable weather, is capable of inspiring hope as well as loss." This

---

22. Hornby, *Contemporary American Fiction*, 101; Soja, *Postmodern Geographies*, 131–32.

23. John Carlos Rowe, "The Economics of the Body in Kate Chopin's *The Awakening*," in Lynda S. Boren and Sara DeSaussure Davis, eds., *Kate Chopin Reconsidered: Beyond the Bayou* (Baton Rouge: Louisiana State University Press, 1992), 124.

is true, as far as it goes; one might add that, in his hopeful image of Detroit, Frank implicitly continues to reject Binx's (or, in *A Piece of My Heart*, Mark Lamb's) "southern" horror of the midwestern metropolis. Nevertheless, as at Walled Lake, the sociospatial reality of Detroit soon destroys Frank's hope. Indeed, venturing into the real Detroit also destroys Frank's earlier image of the city as a utopian, all-American melting pot. Frank and Vicki attempt to find a steakhouse on Larned but, as Frank admits, "when we had gone as far as Woodward, everyone we saw had become black and vaguely menacing, the taxis and police all unexplainably disappeared" (180). Due to urban-industrial decay and racial segregation—inextricably related to the development of those "white-flight areas" advancing toward and beyond Walled Lake and Lansing (157)—Woodward no longer offers even the seedy carnivalesque of Frank's college days (180–81). Replacing Frank's earlier imagined community of blacks and polacks, this racialized vision of Detroit comes closer to Binx or Newel's image of Chicago.[24]

Eventually, the dispirited couple retreat to their hotel room. Matthew Guinn observes perceptively that the room conforms to what architect Robert Venturi terms "commercial vernacular," "the characteristically postmodern approach of blending the motifs of high culture with the less lofty aim of commercial gain." Guinn also notes that the eleventh-floor room affords Frank a view of Renaissance Center, a "city-within-a-city" designed by John Portman, whose work Fredric Jameson has interpreted as the apotheosis of "postmodern hyperspace." It is possible to expand upon Guinn's useful points on a couple of counts. First, as Sharon Zukin notes in *Landscapes of Power: From Detroit to Disney World* (1991), Renaissance Center was bankrolled by the Ford Motor Company as part of a civic-corporate attempt to reverse Detroit's urban-industrial decay. Thus, even while Frank focuses his "fisheye view" upon "gaunt Ren-Cen" (126), the economic logic of this "postmodern hyperspace" alludes to downtown Detroit's wider "postindustrial" decline. The economic base of Renaissance Center intones the more pervasive urban blight. Second, Renaissance Center is not simply a "city within a city," as Guinn claims: to quote Jameson, it exists in "disjunction from the surrounding city." This may appear paradoxical—that a building can both allude to, and separate from, the surrounding city. But like Portman's Bonaventure Hotel in Los Angeles, Renaissance Center can be seen as, in Jameson's formulation, "a total space, a complete world" that "does not wish to be a part of the

24. Folks, "The Risks of Membership," 83.

city but rather its equivalent and replacement or substitute." Frank perhaps catches something of the center's disjunction from its built environment with the adjective "gaunt." What Charles Rutheiser has written of a third "Portman-teau," Peachtree Center in Atlanta, can also be applied to Renaissance Center: as an "analogous city," it is "uncontaminated by the 'congestion' and 'danger' of the streets." Hence, when Frank turns his consumer's gaze upon "Ren-Cen," he sees the reflection—and the capitalist spatial logic—of his own desire to escape the "menacing" poverty and segregation of that older urban space around Larned.[25]

Having returned to their hotel room, Vicki and Frank abruptly decide to catch the quickest flight back to New Jersey. Even now, Frank does not see either Walled Lake or Detroit as a northern nowhere. It is Vicki who implicitly includes Detroit alongside her hometown Dallas in a flippantly dystopian vision of a placeless postsouthern America (180). Nonetheless, it is telling that Frank's expedition to Detroit has ended almost as abruptly as Binx's excursion to Chicago. Ultimately, much as Binx's residual "southern" sense of place was revealed during his trip to Illinois, so the problem with Frank's *post*southern spatial ontology—his financial, existential, and textual investment in an idealized "American" language-landscape—has been exposed in Michigan. This should not be surprising if we consider that, in the 1980s, and contrary to Frank's fantasy of a multiracial utopia where cars go straight from the factory door to the suburban consumer, Detroit was devastated by downtown disinvestment and the precipitous decline of the automobile and steel industries. The harsh realities of capitalist space—uneven development and postindustrial decay—have burst through the lacunae in Frank's world-as-text.[26]

Frank in New Jersey Again

His literalist's vision of Detroit having failed, Frank subsequently attempts to reinforce his idealized image of New Jersey. He begins to do so even on the plane back from Detroit: it is at this point that Frank looks down upon the Turnpike and declares it "beautiful." However, Frank's world-as-text

---

25. Guinn, *After Southern Modernism*, 121–22; Sharon Zukin, *Landscapes of Power: From Detroit to Disney World* (Berkeley: University of California Press, 1991), 105; Jameson, *Postmodernism*, 40–41; Charles Rutheiser, *Imagineering Atlanta: The Politics of Place in the City of Dreams* (New York: Verso, 1996), 163.

26. By the late 1980s, central Detroit's unemployment rate was 36 percent, compared to 12 percent in the metropolitan area and a national average of 6 to 7 percent. See Zukin, *Landscapes of Power*, 105.

further unravels when he returns to ground in Haddam. No sooner has he literally distanced himself and his worldview from Herb Wallagher than "[i]n my house stands Walter Luckett" (186). Walter is a fellow member of Haddam's Divorced Men's Club who has come to Frank for advice after a homosexual encounter with a fellow Wall Street monies analyst. During and after this unwanted visit, Frank tries hard to avoid becoming embroiled in Walter's emotional travails. This evasion is of a piece with Frank's continued refusal of serious, critical engagement with the "large world." However, Frank's complacency is violently disrupted when, while he is spending Easter Sunday at the Arcenault family home in Barnegat Pines, X rings with news of Walter's suicide. This shock is soon followed by Vicki's violently ending their relationship.

With this extra irruption of personal trauma into Frank's worldview, his sociospatial ontology also becomes further strained. During the car ride to Barnegat Pines, New Jersey had lived up to its earlier definition as a legible "American" landscape. Indeed, according to Frank, New Jersey appears not just as "Anyplace" but as Everyplace, a generic industrial-commercial geography that can even benignly simulate the South:

> [Vicki's] directions route me past the most ordinary but satisfying New Jersey vistas, those parts that remind you of the other places you've been in your life....
> Much of what I pass, of course, looks precisely like everyplace else *in* the state.... Clean industry abounds. Valve plants. A Congoleum factory. U-Haul sheds. A sand and gravel pit close by a glass works. An Airedale kennel. The Quaker Home for Confused Friends. A mall with a nautical theme. Several signs that say HERE! Suddenly it is a high pale sky and a feeling like Florida, but a mile farther on, it is the Mississippi Delta—civilized life flattened below high power lines, the earth laid out in great vegetative tracts where Negroes fish from low bridges.... (245)

But now, on the return journey to Haddam, after Frank has heard of Walter's suicide and experienced the end of his relationship, the satisfactions of this "clean" (post)industrial panorama fail him completely. As he drives along the parkway, "there is no consoling landscape" on to which Frank can displace his emotional anxiety. Even the everyday capitalist signs once taken for wonders—"[a]n occasional Pontiac dealer's sign or a tennis bubble"—now seem "far too meager and abstracted" (304).

Typically, Frank attempts to redeem "mystery" when, "halfway through the town of Adelphia, New Jersey, on Business 524" (305), standing opposite the Ground Zero Burg burger bar, he puts in a call to Selma Jassim, an ex-girlfriend. Selma provides no solace, however, and Frank sustains minor injuries when, surreally, his phone booth is rammed by a car driven by a local youth. Dupuy has smartly observed that, at this point, Ground Zero Burg appears as "an appropriate objective correlative for his [Frank's] state of mind." However, one can go further and argue that, as at Walled Lake, there is a more deep-seated equivalence between Frank's disturbed existential being and the ailing capitalist geography itself. Frank's optimism is briefly reignited by the kindness of Debra Spanelis, the carhop; tellingly, he uses Debra's kindness in an attempt to dissociate his *existential* depression from Adelphia's *economic* depression: "Who would've thought a root-beer float could restore both faith and health, or that I would find it in as half-caste a town as this, a place wizened to a few car lots, an adult book store, a shut-down drive-in movie up the road—remnants of a boom that never boomed. From this emerges a Samaritan. A Debra" (313).[27]

Frank here shows an unusual willingness to acknowledge capitalist uneven development (albeit only implicitly, and expressed in a puzzling racial metaphor that perhaps refers insidiously to Debra's relationship with the African-American who rammed his car into the phone booth). However, the sociospatial reality of Debra's life cannot be reconciled with his literalist's optimism. Folks has stated that there is "an element of solidarity in Frank's unusual degree of sympathy with subaltern figures—his willingness to cross social boundaries, to empathize with the excluded, and to submit the class assumptions of his suburban community to critical examination." Frank's "sympathy with subaltern figures" seems apparent when Debra says that she wants to work in Yellowstone Park, reminding Frank that he had the same fantasy after his divorce. But Debra's hopes are hamstrung by the fact that she has a baby. Frank is forced to recognize that their respective sociospatial realities, their language-landscapes, are ultimately irreconcilable: "I might as well have been speaking French from the planet Pluto" (315). Unlike Debra, Frank can drive in and drive on back to Haddam. It is telling that, as Frank departs, he now describes Adelphia as "a bleak-looking place," and remarks that he "can't help thinking of Herb Wallagher's dream of death and hatred" (316). As at Walled Lake, Frank's latest attempt to lose himself in a capitalist world-as-text comes up against the reality of (sub)urban decay and social exclusion.[28]

27. Dupuy, "The Confessions of an Ex-Suicide," 102.
28. Folks, "The Risks of Membership," 83.

Reentering Haddam, Frank still hopes to redeem "a pastoral kind of longing" (318) from the suburbs. However, as Dupuy notes, Frank "must confront the empty fact of Walter's death." This grim fact impinges upon Frank's previously idealized cognitive map of Haddam. Where Frank could have been French or Plutonian to Debra in Adelphia, now he is the alien in Haddam: "I see again it can be a sad town, a silent, nothing-happening, keep-to-yourself Sunday town. . . . It is unexpectedly a foreign place, as strange as Moline or Oslo" (320). Beginning to *reread* his world-as-text, Frank sees that even mortality (something he should know all about, given Ralph's demise) is denied by the suburbs. Death becomes "a misreading, a wrong rumor to be forgotten" (325).[29]

Yet Frank still tries to seek some consolation by "driv[ing], an invisible man" through Haddam, a place that, even now, he regards favorably as "a first-class place for invisibility" (345–46). He heads for Haddam's railway station, where he seeks a characteristically limited human connection: "It is not bad to sit in some placeless dark and watch commuters step off into splashy car lights, striding toward the promise of bounteous hugs" (347). Once again, it is notable that Frank's open-minded attitude to a semipublic "nonplace" contrasts with Binx's attitude upon arriving at the Chicago railway station: "I will say it again, perhaps for the last time: there is mystery everywhere, even in a vulgar, urine-scented, suburban depot such as this" (348). When he thinks he sees Walter's grieving sister arriving and heading his way, however, Frank is panicked into boarding the train to New York. Now hastily dismissing Haddam as one of many "little crypto-homey Jersey burgs" (353), he desperately recasts his world-as-text to encompass the city that he previously has referred to pejoratively as "Gotham." It is indicative of his desperation that he even tries to incorporate New York into his earlier theory of the midwesternization of America (358).

Eventually, Frank does find some succor in New York, in the form of sportswriting intern Catherine O'Flaherty. Dupuy concludes his reading of *The Sportswriter* with Frank in "the city of flux . . . not disappointed," refusing (unlike Walter) to relent to death. Against Dupuy, I would argue that, having been confronted by the existential and socioeconomic suffering of others, Frank's own relenting, literalist identity and worldview have been seriously, even terminally damaged. Moreover, *The Sportswriter* ends not in New York, but in Florida. As such, any reading of Frank's "sense of place"—both his own

---

29. Dupuy, "The Confessions of an Ex-Suicide," 102.

spatialized ontology and his textual cartography—must consider the complexities of this final postsouthern turn.[30]

Frank in Florida

The shift to Florida enables Ford to provide a final flourish to *The Sportswriter*'s postsouthern parody of place. As we saw in Chapter 3, in the epilogue to *The Moviegoer,* Binx Bolling elliptically and abruptly announces his return to a relatively traditional southern locus: New Orleans's Garden District. Such an option is not open to Frank Bascombe at "The End" of *The Sportswriter.* We know by now that Frank has no Compson-like family waiting for him in Mississippi. Instead, rather more modestly, Frank finds in Florida "some cousins of my father's who wrote me in Gotham through Irv Ornstein (my mother's stepson)" (376). Fred Hobson has correctly observed that Frank's discovery of these distant relatives "parodies the idea of southern family" and occurs in "a setting not given to such discoveries in most southern novels." Echoing the earlier evocation of his own mother and father's "ordinary, modern existence" in postwar Mississippi, Frank declares the "Florida Bascombes" to be "a grand family of a modern sort." Empress Bascombe certainly does not share Aunt Emily's southern stoicism, and Buster and Empress's "big yellow stucco bungalow outside Nokomis" is decidedly different from Thomas Sutpen's "dark house" and even the Cutrer mansion. Empress does, though, share the Bolling-Cutrer family's fascination with land speculation. Frank sketches her as "a pixyish little right-winger" who "sells a little real estate on the side (though she is not as bad as those people often seem)" (376), a trait that recalls Emily's (albeit more secretive) dabblings in gas stations and Canadian mines.[31]

In contrast to Sam Newel, Frank embraces this extended family precisely because it does *not* represent "the burden of southern history," or the stale stuff of "southern literature": "And truthfully, when I drive back up Highway 24 just as the light is falling beyond my condo, behind its wide avenue of date palms and lampposts, I am usually (if only momentarily) glad to have a past, even an imputed and remote one. There is something to that. It is not a burden, though I've always thought of it as one. I cannot say that we all need a past in full literary fashion, or that one is much useful in the end. But a small one doesn't hurt, especially if you're already in a life of your own

---

30. Ibid., 103.
31. Hobson, *The Southern Writer in the Postmodern World,* 51.

choosing" (377). Thus Ford finishes *The Sportswriter* by taking still further the postsouthern parody initiated in *A Piece of My Heart* and extended earlier in Frank's narrative. For all that Florida is nominally in the South, Frank finds no traditional "community" historically rooted in "place." Indeed, Florida seems more like Frank's postsouthern, midwesternized America than Mississippi or even Binx Bolling's suburbanized Louisiana. Frank observes that "[p]eople in Florida, I've discovered, are here to get away from things, to seek no end of life. . . . Many people are here from Michigan. . . . It is not like New Jersey, but it is not bad" (373). And in what can be seen as another sly salvo against Percy's image of Michigan (and the Midwest generally) as a "nonplace," Ford has Frank define himself not as a native southerner but as "a good Michigander, get[ting] the sun on my face while somewhere nearby I hear the hiss and pop of ball on glove leather. That may be a sportswriter's dreamlife" (376).

But these final pages also reveal the same *problems* with Frank's postsouthern sense of place—the problems that became apparent during his trip to Michigan. We witness yet another example of Frank's complacent self-placement in the "large world," his conspicuous consumption of, and narrative "speculation" in, places themselves: after New Jersey, Detroit, and New York comes Florida. To be sure, "The End" of *The Sportswriter* opens with the promising sense that Frank might just revise his spatial ontology. He admits that "Walter's death, I suppose you could say, has had the effect on me that death means to have; of reminding me of my responsibility to a somewhat larger world." Though Frank avoids Walter's funeral in Coshocton, Ohio—"I could not feel that I had a place there" (372)—it is at Walter's behest that he arrives in Florida. In a suicide note addressed to Frank, Walter claims he has a secret daughter living in Florida; after "a good bit of sleuthing," Frank concludes that no such daughter ever existed. Yet the "goose chase" at first appears to have given Frank the impetus to embark upon a more serious, even Binx-like "search" of his own "larger world." It is all the more notable, then, that Frank's subsequent comments—not least his identification with Michiganders—lead us to suspect that he is simply inventing Florida as one more site for his "sportswriter's dreamlife," one more language-landscape to be included in his repeatedly revised, expanded, and ultimately escapist world-as-text. As Frank claims in familiar fashion, "[c]oming to the bottom of the country provokes a nice sensation, a tropical certainty that something will happen to you here. The whole place seems alive with modest hopes" (373).

At the close of *The Sportswriter*, Frank remains in Florida, musing: "Will I ever live in Haddam, New Jersey, again? I haven't the slightest idea" (380). In

1995, however, Richard Ford published a sequel, *Independence Day,* in which Frank returns to Haddam and undertakes a search for "responsibility" in the "larger world." In *Independence Day,* Frank becomes a real-estate agent with a critical philosophy of place as capitalist property that sets him apart not only from Empress Bascombe, but also from that other land speculator, Binx Bolling. This is the subject of the next chapter.

6. New Jersey Real Estate and the Postsouthern Sense of Place: Richard Ford's *Independence Day*

Some way into his second autobiographical narrative, Frank Bascombe acknowledges that "[i]t might be of some interest to say how I came to be a Residential Specialist, distant as it is from my prior vocations of failed short-story writer and sports journalist."[1] He recounts how "[f]ive years ago, at the end of a bad season" (91) he moved to Florida and thereafter to France. It appears that the "foreign but thrilling *exterior* landscape" (92) of France followed New Jersey, Detroit, New York, and Florida as—to use Walker Percy's terms again—one more place feeding Frank's spatial "species of consumption." But Frank does now (it is 1988) acknowledge that his move to Florida was part of a "major crisis" (91). Moreover, it soon becomes apparent that, since departing France, Frank has been striving far more seriously to solve his Percyan "predicament of placement vis-à-vis the world."[2] He has embarked upon an existential search for his own sense of place by returning to "Haddam itself, which felt at that celestial moment like my spiritual residence more than any place I'd ever been, inasmuch as it *was* the place I instinctively and in a heat came charging back to" (93).

Most important, though, Frank's New Jersey homecoming is not simply an attempt to achieve self-placement via a familiar, mystified ("celestial," "spiritual") faith in the material geography of "Haddam itself." Frank is also determined to reach out to other people: to put into practice that "responsibility to a somewhat larger world" he began to feel in Florida. As he puts it, he returned to Haddam "with a new feeling of great purpose and a fury to suddenly *do* something serious for my own good and possibly even others'" (93). Since *The Sportswriter*, then, Frank has moved beyond self-effacing immersion in, and consumption of, capitalist geographies; but he has also avoided what Edward Soja calls vulgar existentialism—the "pure contemplation of the

---

1. Richard Ford, *Independence Day* (1995; reprint, London: Harvill, 1996), 91. All subsequent page references will be incorporated into the main text.

2. Percy, "Why I Live Where I Live," 5, and *Lost in the Cosmos*, 113.

isolated individual." Instead, he has begun to reconsider his personal predicament in terms of social relations: "everything I might do had to be calculated against the weight of the practical and according to the standard considerations of: Would it work? and, What good would it do for me or anybody?" (94).[3]

In this chapter, I hope to show that Frank's new job as a "Residential Specialist" is crucial to his revised sensibility. It plays a defining role in allowing Frank to move, in Jeffrey Folks's words, "from solitude back to society" by providing him with the opportunity to "*do* something serious for my own good and possibly even others." Frank abandons his earlier land and literary speculations in and upon postmodern, capitalist geographies. As his job helps him to understand that (in Michel de Certeau's dialectical formulation) "space is existential" and "existence is spatial," Frank enacts Soja's "spatialized ontology." This involves "the active emplacement and situation of being-in-the-world"—specifically, Frank's own "larger world" in and beyond Haddam. Working with real estate allows Frank to see how capitalist property relations impact upon the economic *and* existential production of (a sense of) place. Ultimately, having worked through these sociospatial realities, Frank formulates his own theory of independence as a practice that enables his self-placement—albeit contingent—in postsouthern America.[4]

Frank's New Philosophy of Place

Early in *Independence Day*, we encounter the kind of sly but clearly disparaging reference to the South that Frank frequently made in *The Sportswriter*. Evidently, Frank still favors New Jersey's sense of place over Mississippi's. He asserts that: "Of course, having come first to life in a true *place*, and one as monotonously, lankly *itself* as the Mississippi Gulf Coast, I couldn't be truly surprised that a simple *setting* such as Haddam—willing to be so little itself—would seem, on second look, a great relief and damned easy to cozy up to" (93). This characteristic skepticism toward the South introduces (albeit only implicitly at this point) a central tenet of Frank's new philosophy of place. This tenet is that one should not fetishize the material locus in "*itself*," as if physical geography has some intrinsic power or meaning independent of human action. Frank's view that Mississippi's celebrated, supposedly

---

3. Ford, *The Sportswriter*, 372; Soja, *Postmodern Geographies*, 131.

4. Folks, "The Risks of Membership," 87; Michel de Certeau, *The Practice of Everyday Life* (Berkeley: University of California Press, 1984), 117; Soja, *Postmodern Geographies*, 131, and 118–37, passim.

"natural" sense of place subsumes the identity of the native individual echoes Julius Rowan Raper's theory that "in the South, the *people (ethnos)* and the place *(edos)* tend to become one." As Raper argues, this leads to a problematic situation in which the "sense of place takes on a role better played by a sense of self." Having tended in *The Sportswriter* to displace his subjective identity on to the geographies of New Jersey and Michigan, Frank in *Independence Day* takes on a revised *post*southern role in which he refuses to conflate self and place.[5]

Frank's revised theory of the self's relation to "place" and "community" in postsouthern America becomes more explicit when he details his move from sportswriting to real(i)ty. Five years after the events of *The Sportswriter*, Frank's wife Ann (X has a name this time) has remarried and moved, with their two children, to Connecticut. Combined with Frank's occupation of Ann's own "postdivorce" (151) house, this move has generated "the geography of divorce" (103). It is during the sale of the former family home on Hoving Road, however, that the acting agent, Rolly Mounger, offers Frank the chance to become a residential specialist. Ironically, it is precisely Frank's prior detachment from *any* form of social relations in Haddam that informs Rolly's belief that the ex-sportswriter will make an ideal realtor. As Frank admits, "I didn't seem to have a lot of attachments in the community, a factor that made selling houses one hell of a lot easier" (109). Once Frank has accepted the job offer, Rolly offers his new colleague the platitudinous advice that: "This is realty. *Reality's* something else." But unlike the complacent Rolly—and *pace* the southern Agrarians, with their binary opposition between authentic, concrete real property and capitalistic, abstract real estate—Frank becomes acutely aware that realty *is* the (socioeconomic) reality underlying Haddam's sense of place. Hence his aside, "my personal take on the job probably wouldn't be just like Rolly's" (115).

In *The Sportswriter*, we learned that Haddam is an affluent, suburban small town populated largely by wealthy, white-collar professionals. In the opening lines of *Independence Day*, the socioeconomic privilege prevalent throughout Haddam appears nearly "natural": "In Haddam, summer floats over tree-softened streets like a sweet lotion balm from a careless, languor-

---

5. Raper, "Inventing Modern Southern Fiction: A Postmodern View," 10, 3. Given Frank's own tendency in *The Sportswriter* to displace his existential, social, and economic anxieties on to capitalist geographies, there seems to be a rather ironic point of comparison between the southern fetishization of place observed by Raper and the commodity fetishism of place in postsouthern America. Elinor Ann Walker makes a similar point, though without the economic emphasis. See Walker, *Richard Ford*, 165.

ous god, and the world falls in tune with its own mysterious anthems." From the first paragraph, it could be construed that the town is an inherently well-ordered, even "organic" community. Frank provides a narrative panorama that takes in the men in "the Negro trace" who "sit on stoops, pants legs rolled above their sock tops, sipping coffee in the growing easeful heat," to the varsity band practicing for Haddam's Independence Day parade. But rather disturbingly, these beneficent images recall Frank's failed textual invention of Detroit as a multiracial utopia populated by happy-go-lucky "Negroes and Polacks." Indeed, as in *The Sportswriter,* the realities of race and class now begin to leak into Frank's narrative. When he says, "We're repaving this summer . . . using our proud new tax dollars," his use of the personal and possessive pronouns inadvertently points up a socioeconomic gap between the capital and property owned by Haddam's residents and the reified hired labor of the "Cape Verdeans and wily Hondurans from poorer towns north of here" (3) who actually do the repaving.[6]

But where Frank's first narrative labored with increasing desperation to maintain the illusion of Haddam's "pastoral longing," this time he early and explicitly acknowledges that Haddam is *not* simply some self-contained paradise: "all is not exactly kosher here." Employing a meteorological metaphor, Frank explains that Haddam's "second nature"[7] of socioeconomic privilege is in unexpected and pervasive crisis: "falling property values now ride through the trees like an odorless, colorless mist settling through the still air where all breathe it in, all sense it" (4). Though the metaphor inclines to mist-ification, Frank here begins to signal that "sense" of place in Haddam is subject to market forces. Notably, Frank proceeds to note more explicitly the extent to which property values define sociospatial relations—not just in Haddam but across the United States: "it must mean *something* to a town, to the local *esprit,* for its values on the open market to fall. (Why else would real estate prices be an index to the national well-being?)" (5).

Frank's current clients, Phyllis and Joe Markham, have discovered just how Haddam's "local *esprit*" is mediated by "real estate prices." Having lived in Vermont since the early 1970s, the Markhams are comically ignorant of

---

6. Ford, *The Sportswriter,* 121.

7. In *Postmodern Geographies,* Soja notes how Henri Lefebvre distinguished between "[n]ature as naively given context and what can be termed 'second nature,' the transformed and socially concretized spatiality arising from the application of purposeful human labor" (80). But as we have already seen, the "purposeful human labor" of the Cape Verdean and Honduran immigrants has been reified as part of the "second nature" of Haddam.

how much their ideal house with "mysterious-wondrous home possibilities" (39) would actually cost. The population of Haddam may have "ballooned from twelve to twenty thousand" during the early 1980s, but in terms of market value and social status, the newer properties built during the boom are regarded as inferior to Haddam's coveted older houses. While the original eighteenth-century settlement has been tellingly "rechristened 'Haddam the Pleasant' by the village council" (23), local "realty lingo" (132) refers to the newer developments more prosaically as "the Haddam-area."

Inevitably, the Markhams are unable to afford a house in "Haddam the Pleasant." Among the more affordable properties Frank shows them is Mallards Landing, yet even the residential specialist himself admits that this new development "looks like a movie façade where a fictionalized American family would someday pay the fictionalized mortgage" (83). Frank perhaps hints here at the "fictitious" nature of his own narrative speculations in and upon Haddam's new developments, or Eddy Loukinen's Royal Oak, in *The Sportswriter*. From this intertextual perspective, it is telling that Frank does *not* now show Pheasant Meadow to the Markhams. In *The Sportswriter*, it was at Pheasant Meadow that, while uncritically "relenting" to the "readable," "American" language-landscape, Frank incorporated the developers' advertising slogan—"*An Attractive Retirement Waits Just Ahead*"—into his own world-as-text.[8] But by 1988, Pheasant Meadow has succumbed to the economic downturn, "not old but already gone visibly to seed"—"dilapidated sign" and all (141). Even more gloomily, Frank's fellow realtor and former lover, Clair Devane, was murdered here. As in *The Sportswriter*, Frank recapitulates the "realty lingo" of Pheasant Meadow in his own narrative. This time, however, Frank brings a critical sense of irony to the linguistic logic of late capitalism. In the process, he not only critiques the uneven geographical development within Haddam but also looks beyond national borders to another country with a more inclusive social system that stands as an implicit indictment of Reagan's America and its laissez-faire economics: "The best all-around Americans, in my view, are Canadians. I, in fact, should think of moving there, since it has almost all the good qualities of the states and almost none of the bad, plus cradle-to-grave health care and a fraction of the murders we generate. *An attractive retirement waits just beyond the forty-ninth parallel*" (191; my emphasis).

Frank also takes the Markhams to see a house in Penns Neck, on the outskirts of Haddam. This house presents an illusion of precapitalist, agricultural

---

8. Ford, *The Sportswriter*, 58–59.

real property that appeals to the Vermont-based couple—it has the "out-of-place look of having been the 'original farmhouse' when all this was nothing but cow pastures and farmland . . . and real estate meant zip" (60). But as Frank's quotation marks indicate, the building's rustic pseudoauthenticity is precisely its selling point in a district that "realty lingo" has reinvented as part of "the Haddam-area." Frank endures a trying time as agent to the insufferable Markhams. Joe, in particular, retains a belief in authentic rural-agricultural property untainted by the commercial imperatives and language of real estate, bemoaning the supposed absence, beyond Vermont, of any (to quote Robert Penn Warren's Agrarian-era turn of phrase) "relation of man to place": "I don't want to live in an area. . . . The Boston area, the tristate area, the New York area. Nobody ever said the Vermont area. . . . They just said the places" (59). Frank, however, scathingly criticizes the Markhams' romanticized vision of Vermont, especially their residual faith in what he calls "Vermont's spiritual mandate," which "is that you don't look at your*self*, but spend years gazing at everything *else* as penetratingly as possible in the conviction that everything out there more or less stands for you" (89). There is an interesting and somewhat unexpected Agrarian echo here. In his essay "Still Rebels, Still Yankees" (1938), Donald Davidson celebrated Vermont's "genius of place," arguing that it transformed the natives into "the image of what they contemplated . . . the landscape." For Davidson, this fusion of people and (agrarian) place was to be celebrated; despite the North/South divide, rural Vermont complemented and even mirrored Georgia's "genius of place." But for Frank, by "contemplating the landscape" of Vermont, the Markhams have only elided their own existential being. As Frank sees it, the Markhams have gone beyond making themselves over into the "image" of the "*exterior* landscape"; they have turned Vermont into a fetishized *substitute* for their selves. Their (Davidsonian) bad faith in Vermont's "spiritual mandate" resembles Frank's own earlier tendency, evident in *The Sportswriter,* to displace his existential anxiety about the "large world" on to the capitalist landscapes of New Jersey and Michigan, and also repeats that failing Raper identifies in the South: *edos* subjugates *ethnos*, the fetishized "sense of place takes on a role better played by a sense of self."[9]

Frank sees beyond his clients' bad faith and numerous neuroses to identify capitalist property relations as the root of the couple's frustrations. He

---

9. Warren, "Literature as a Symptom," 354; Davidson, "Still Rebels, Still Yankees," in *Still Rebels, Still Yankees*, 232–34.

observes that the Markhams "have failed to intuit the one gnostic truth of real estate (a truth impossible to reveal without seeming dishonest and cynical): that people never find or buy the house they say they want." Clarifying his own mystical rhetoric, Frank identifies this "gnostic truth of real estate" as the material reality of a "market economy." He states bluntly (but realistically, rather than cynically) that this market economy of place "is not even remotely premised on anybody getting what he wants. The premise is that you're presented with what you might've thought you didn't want, but what's available, whereupon you give in and start finding ways to feel good about it and yourself" (41). Frank reiterates this realtor's understanding of the spatial (il)logic of capitalism, and its impact upon the "relation of man to place," when it becomes clear that Joe wants a house that will provide "perfect sanction, a sign some community recognizes him." Frank observes that "the only way communities ever recognize anything [is]: financially (tactfully expressed as a matter of compatibility)" (51–52). Frank here echoes the point made by sociologist Robert Bellah and his colleagues in *Habits of the Heart* (1985): that so-called communities are often "lifestyle enclaves" where people live because "the housing prices there happen to fit their budgets."[10]

Frank's newly skeptical philosophy of place really comes to the fore during a trip to his girlfriend Sally Caldwell's house in South Mantoloking. Frank is overcome by a need to feel nostalgic for this place he hardly knows. But he recovers himself—and his sense of self—by recalling "a patent lesson of the realty profession, to cease sanctifying places—houses, beaches, hometowns." Frank insists that: "We may feel they [places] *ought* to, *should* confer something—sanction, again. . . . But they don't . . . as the Markhams found out in Vermont and now New Jersey" (151–52). In southern letters' seminal definition of "sense of place," Eudora Welty famously revered Mississippi River Country for "a sense of place as powerful as if it were visible and walking and could touch me." As we saw in Chapter 3, even Walker Percy's suburban property speculator Binx Bolling could still invoke, albeit rather cynically, a metaphysical "thronging spirit-presence of . . . place" at the derelict site of his father's duck club in rural Louisiana. By contrast, Frank Bascombe insists that "[p]lace means nothing" (152). In postsouthern America, both the Agrarians' proprietary ideal *and* the Weltyan "sense of place," with its debt to the pathetic fallacy of romantic pantheism, have been superseded by the capital-

---

10. Robert Bellah et al., *Habits of the Heart: Individualism and Commitment in American Life* (1985; reprint, New York: Perennial, 1986), 72, 11.

ist fetishization of place as a commodity. Hence, Frank refuses to attribute "mysterious-wondrous home possibilities" to mass-produced "Haddam-area" houses because, as geographer David Harvey suggests, to talk or "write of 'the power of place,' as if places . . . possess causal powers is to engage in the grossest of fetishisms." To fetishize the "power" or "sense" of place is to risk reproducing the commodity logic (and the "realty lingo") of late capitalism itself.[11]

Yet in a lengthy review of *Independence Day*, Barbara Ehrenreich claims that Frank's life and text do just that. Ehrenreich argues that, for Frank, "physical structures are easier to deal with than their residents. Realty beats reality." According to Ehrenreich, Frank engages in what "[s]eems like a case of ordinary commodity-fetishism, in which dead objects loom larger than persons." Meanwhile, with a postsouthern theoretical twist, Matthew Guinn claims that "real estate is an extension of Frank's penchant for the commodified mystery he once found in catalogs." I have already argued that Frank's new job helps him to understand just how the market economy of realty *is* (or at least produces) contemporary sociospatial reality. But this is not the same as saying that Frank willingly or cynically *accepts* capital's hegemonic role in the production of place. Rather, Frank's aphoristic negation ("Place means nothing") begins to negotiate a way *between* the pathetic fallacy and commodity fetishism, creating an opportunity to rework the theory and praxis of "place." *Pace* Ehrenreich and Guinn, Frank focuses upon human, sociospatial relations, rather than place in and of "itself."[12]

Frank's role as the Markhams' realtor offers him an immediate opportunity to put into practice his desire to "*do* something serious" for other people. He strives to help the couple avert "spatial dislocation" (90) and "a potentially calamitous careen down a slippery socio-emotio-economic slope" (44) by emphasizing that it *is* possible to live a fulfilling everyday life *outside* a privileged site like "Haddam the Pleasant." To cite de Certeau again, Ford's narrator insists that consumers can "reappropriate the space organized by techniques of sociocultural production" (among which capitalist techniques de Certeau includes "urban development"). In conversation with Phyllis, Frank emphasizes the existential value of human action, rather than the economic value of Haddam in and of "itself": "You *are* best off coming as close as you can and

---

11. Welty, "Some Notes on River Country," 286; Percy, *The Moviegoer*, 91; Harvey, *Justice, Nature, and the Geography of Difference*, 320.

12. Barbara Ehrenreich, "Realty Bites," *New Republic*, 18–25 September 1995, 50; Guinn, *After Southern Modernism*, 134.

trying to bring life to a place, not just depending on the place to supply it for you" (76). It is true that Frank subsequently calls this "a form of strategizing pseudo-communication I've gotten used to in the realty business," as opposed to the "[r]eal talk . . . you have with a loved one" (76–77). Such an aside does make one wonder to what extent Frank is, as Ehrenreich suggests, uncritically recapitulating the logic and lingo of commodity fetishism. Nonetheless, Frank is trying to make the Markhams understand the extent to which their (neo-Agrarian) proprietary ideal comes up against the market economy of realty, which *is* the reality, both materially and linguistically: "They can't afford their ideal. And not buying what you can't afford's not a compromise; it's reality speaking English. To get anywhere you have to learn to speak the same language back" (90). In this talk with Phyllis, Frank adumbrates a spatial ontology and usable language for everyday life amid the capitalist reality of realty: a sense of self-placement that neither precludes one's self, nor fetishizes "place."[13]

Race, Property, and "Community": Wallace Hill

Frank offers one more house to the beleaguered Markhams: one of his own rental properties in the black neighborhood called Wallace Hill. Frank purchased the two houses upon returning from France with the feeling that he had "contributed as little to the commonweal as it was possible for a busy man to contribute without being plain evil," especially having "lived in Haddam [for] fifteen years [and] ridden the prosperity curve right through the roof" (25–26). For all the civic goodwill informing Frank's investment in Wallace Hill, it uncomfortably evokes the specter of southern white paternalism. There is also an intertextual irony: in *The Sportswriter,* Frank blithely stated that Wallace Hill's residents "own their own homes." Furthermore, Frank admits to his own financial self-interest: "I hadn't been in the realty business long and was happy to think about diversifying my assets and stashing money away where it'd be hard to get at" (27). To this degree, Frank is himself a land speculator; here, he exhibits the "capitalistic interest in the commercial value of location" that Guinn describes. Or, as Frank himself puts it, he is "looking after Number One" (112).[14]

Nevertheless, Frank also wants to "do for others" (112): not only the Markhams, but also the black residents. He hopes his personal intervention

---

13. De Certeau, *The Practice of Everyday Life,* xiv, xii.
14. Ford, *The Sportswriter,* 56; Guinn, *After Southern Modernism,* 134.

in Wallace Hill will help prevent more predatory property speculators from drastically redeveloping the neighborhood. Ostensibly, Wallace Hill seems like an African American version of Donald Davidson's "stable community which is really a community, not a mere real-estate development." As Frank notes, "[r]eliable, relatively prosperous middle-aged and older Negro families have lived here for decades" (24).But for all Wallace Hill's *physical* "permanence"—a "relatively stable configuration of matter and things," in David Harvey's definition—Frank notes that its "sovereign protectors" have never had a corresponding *social* "sense of belonging and permanence" (27). Having previously (in *The Sportswriter*) included Wallace Hill's "servant classes, who are mostly Negroes" in his imagined community of happy Haddamites, Frank now recognizes the extent to which Haddam's historical geography has been defined by racial segregation. Wallace Hill's residents have always had a subordinate role in the town's social and labor relations. As Frank observes ruefully, the neighborhood's current denizens "and their relatives might've been here a hundred years and had never done anything but make us white late-arrivers feel welcome at their own expense" (28). Now, in 1988, black Haddamites' ability to achieve a "sense of belonging and permanence" is further imperiled by real-estate developers eyeing Wallace Hill as a prime location within "Haddam the Pleasant" (24–25). Frank believes he can "at least help make two families feel at home" (28) by "providing affordable housing options" (27).[15]

As we have seen, Frank will gain financially from investing in the "integrity" of Wallace Hill. That Frank himself refers to this as "reinvesting in my community" (27) recalls the tension in the opening paragraph's pronouns between capitalist property ownership and the sociospatial realities of race and class. Perhaps most intriguing, though, is Frank's suggestion that he will not be alone in making a profit from Wallace Hill properties: "as in-town property becomes more valuable (they aren't making any more of it), all the families here will realize big profits and move away to Arizona or down South, where their ancestors were once property themselves, and the whole area will be gentrified by incoming whites and rich blacks, after which my small investment . . . will turn into a gold mine" (25). If we feel uneasy about Frank's profitable ownership of two houses in a historically black neighborhood, I would argue that the narrative here raises a larger dilemma: the extent to

---

15. Davidson, "Current Attitudes toward Folklore," 136; Harvey, *Justice, Nature, and the Geography of Difference*, 55; Ford, *The Sportswriter*, 56.

which Wallace Hill's African American residents can really be said to constitute a "community" at all—especially a Davidsonian "stable community."

For in contrast to their ancestors, it appears that the black populace of Wallace Hill does not necessarily *seek* a "sense of belonging and permanence." In *The Practice of Everyday Life,* de Certeau argues that "as local stabilities break down," people are "no longer fixed by a circumscribed community." Instead, they become "immigrants in a system," albeit one which is "too vast to be their own, too tightly woven for them to escape it." Apparently, Wallace Hill's residents are becoming mobile "immigrants" within a national "system" of capitalist space, a "larger world" stretching from New Jersey through the South to Arizona. As such, home owning and renting become, in de Certeau's terminology, "spatial practices" through which (some) black consumers can manipulate the market economy of real estate to escape the traditional segregated geography, the "circumscribed community," of Wallace Hill. We thus arrive at a notable irony, and a contradiction of capitalism: whereas land speculation produces uneven development elsewhere in "the Haddam area," gentrification promises to reduce, even erase, the racial segregation of Wallace Hill.[16]

To suggest that there is no longer a "circumscribed" or "stable community" in Wallace Hill is not to say that there are no social relations between the residents. Neither does the arrival of the (white) Markhams necessarily mean that the "integrity" of this "established black neighborhood" (24) will be destroyed. It is true that Frank originally planned to rent his properties to African Americans. Frank is optimistic, however, that the white couple will "join the PTA, give pottery and papermaking demonstrations at the block association mixers, become active in the ACLU or the Urban League" (416) and find "common ground regarding in-law problems with Negro neighbors" (423). He hopes that the Markhams can find "a sense of belonging," if not "permanence," through "the satisfactions of optional community involvement" (431). But in the end they, like their black neighbors, might also transform themselves into migrants within the capitalist geographies of postmodern America, able to "do in New Jersey exactly what they did in Vermont—arrive and depart—only with happier results" (416). Eventually, whatever the "race" of the residents, Wallace Hill will likely be transformed from a "stable" or "circumscribed" (i.e., segregated) community, into a liminal, "optional community"—if we still want to call it a "community" at all.

16. De Certeau, *The Practice of Everyday Life,* xx, and on "spatial practices," Part III, passim.

To be sure, Frank's projection of the Markhams' future in and beyond Wallace Hill and elsewhere can seem romantic, ominously echoing those dreamy "speculations" upon his own and others' possible alternative lives in *The Sportswriter*. And one should qualify that certain sectors of Wallace Hill's populace *cannot* escape the historical continuities of uneven development and social inequality. Even those with the ability to migrate, to practice what Frank calls "demographic shifting," are restricted by the fact that "there aren't that many places for a well-heeled black American to go that's better than where he or she already is" (25). Nevertheless, in *Independence Day*, Frank's previously abstract musings are mediated by his realtor's understanding of the ways in which so-called consumers *can* practice their everyday lives within the market economy of place; how they can refuse to be rigidly constrained by either capitalist development, or outmoded ideas of "community" and "integrity." At the same time, though, Frank's own intervention in the property relations of Wallace Hill fulfils his intention to "do for others" by recognizing that not all local residents are "well-heeled" enough to become mobile manipulators of (the market)place. By renting the two Clio Street properties, Frank helps maintain—albeit at a minor and provisional level—a neighborhood that otherwise is being transformed into merely one more locus of capitalist land speculation.

Capital, "Compatibility," and the Fallacy of Continuous Community: Ridgefield, Deep River, and Cooperstown

A substantial proportion of *Independence Day* is devoted to Frank's preholiday trip with his son Paul to Cooperstown. This extended set piece can be seen as the structural and thematic equivalent of Frank's journey to Detroit in *The Sportswriter* or Binx Bolling's trip to Chicago in *The Moviegoer*. But while Frank witlessly celebrated the postindustrial language-landscape of Detroit, the journey to Cooperstown furthers his understanding of the capitalist production of place in the "larger world." Most important, the trip reconfirms Frank's philosophy that, despite the supposed decline of "community" and "place," social relations are the key to establishing one's own spatialized ontology within the capitalist geographies of postsouthern America.

On his way to pick up Paul in Deep River, Frank exits the New Jersey Turnpike in order to avoid "miles and miles of backup on the Cross Bronx (myself dangled squeamishly above the teeming hellish urban no-man's land below)" (195). This route takes him through Ridgefield, Connecticut, a small town like "Haddam, New Jersey—only richer." Ridgefield, even more than

Haddam, is less a community than a lifestyle enclave defined by economic "compatibility." Frank notes wryly that "anyone living below the Cross Bronx would move here if he or she could pay the freight" (196). Trying to find overnight accommodation, Frank criticizes the pervasive aura of exclusivity: "don't expect a room. Ridgefield's a town that invites no one to linger, where the services contemplate residents only, but which makes it in my book a piss-poor place to live" (197).

Ann's new hometown, Deep River, supersedes even Ridgefield as an enclave constructed and populated according to economic "compatibility." Upon arriving, Frank endures the attentions of a zealous "rent-a-cop" (233), a member of the private security force that has been employed to drive around Deep River surveilling nonresidents. Though it is no surprise that Frank dislikes Ann's second husband, Charley O'Dell, such personal antipathy does not fully account for Frank's sense that Deep River "is not such a great place to think of your children living (or your ex-wife)" (230). Frank contrasts his own sense of place with that of Charley the architect. Fleetingly he admits an "unexpected admiration toward meisterbuilder O'Dell's big blue house on the knoll; and to what a great, if impersonal, true-to-your-dreams *home* it is—a place any modern family . . . ought to feel lamebrained not to make a reasonably good go of life in." Frank ruefully recalls his own inability to shrug off "a sense of contingency" back when "we all were a tidy family in our own substantial house in Haddam" (283–84). Pursuing this contrast, however, Frank attacks Charley's literal[17] design for life: "It always seemed to me enough just to know that someone loved you and would go on loving you forever . . . and that the *mise-en-scène* for love was only that and not a character in the play itself. Charley, of course, is of the decidedly *other* view, the one that believes a good structure implies a good structure. . . . This, in Charley's view, constitutes life and no doubt truth: strict physical moorings" (284).

For all the personal animosity, Frank's critique of Charley's philosophy is entirely consistent with his wider critique of the capitalist fetishization of place. Though Frank continues to wonder whether it would be better if he were able to "speak [to Paul] from some more established *place*" (285), he eventually reaffirms his sense that human relations, however contingent, are more important than finding the "fixed point" of a fetishized "*place*." In

---

17. Frank terms O'Dell a "literal-as-a-dictionary architect" (99) and calls Ann a "bedrock literalist . . . which is I'm sure why she married Charley" (103). Evidently, Frank favors literalism less in *Independence Day* than he did in *The Sportswriter*.

contrast, Charley exemplifies de Certeau's "strategist" who believes that, through "the establishment of a place of power (the property of a proper)," one can exert control over social relations—even at the quotidian level of the family.[18]

Upon arriving in Cooperstown, Bascombe admits to a suspicion "that the town is just a replica (of a legitimate place), a period backdrop to the Hall of Fame . . . with nothing authentic (crime, despair, litter, the rapture) really going on no matter what civic illusion the city fathers maintain" (293). To this degree, Cooperstown exemplifies those towns that have been, in Soja's words, "recreated as simulacra, exact copies for which the original no longer exists." In his brief analysis of *Independence Day*, Guinn observes that Cooperstown is the endpoint of "a trip through a commercial landscape of almost unbelievable crassness." Yet Frank is pleased to see that, "[u]nlike stolid Deep River and stiff-necked Ridgefield, Cooperstown has more than ample 4th of July street regalia." Frank further qualifies his initial dismay at Cooperstown's apparently inauthentic sense of place. He decides that it is "still a potentially perfect setting in which to woo one's son away from his problems and bestow good counsel" (293). Thus, despite its "unbelievable crassness," Cooperstown's capitalist carnivalesque is preferable to the lifestyle enclave that is Deep River. It becomes the "legitimate place" for Frank and Paul to redefine a family life undermined by "the geography of divorce."[19]

The trip to Cooperstown also provides Frank with one final opportunity to elucidate his theory that so-called community has become inextricable from economic "compatibility." This opportunity arises, somewhat surreally, after Paul is injured in a batting cage at the Baseball Hall of Fame. A passerby offering assistance turns out to be Irv Ornstein, Frank's stepbrother. The two men have not seen one another in years and Irv, having recently felt "detached from his own personal history" (388), now experiences a transcendent sense of life's continuity. Irv's "*true interest*, one that makes his happy life a sort of formal investigation of firmer stuff beyond the limits of simulation"—he designs flight simulators—is a search for authentic, continuous "community." This leads him to suggest that Frank, being "in the realty business," must constantly encounter people's desire for "continuity . . . in the community sense" (386). Awaiting the diagnosis of Paul's eye injury outside a hospital in Oneonta, Frank takes this incongruous opportunity to restate his realtor's

18. De Certeau, *The Practice of Everyday Life*, 38.
19. Soja, *Postmodern Geographies*, 177; Guinn, *After Southern Modernism*, 132.

sense that, like "place," "community" has become contingent upon the market economy: "I don't really think communities are continuous, Irv. . . . I think of them—and I've got a lot of proof—as isolated, contingent groups trying to improve on an illusion of permanence, which they fully accept as an illusion. . . . Buying power is the instrumentality. But continuity, if I understand it at all, doesn't really have much to do with it" (386).

Here, even in the midst of a minor family crisis, Frank argues coherently and insistently that the concept of "community" is, like that of "place," less "transcendent" than subject to immanent economic reality ("buying power"). In this context, Irv's continuous community sounds eerily like Davidson's "stable community which is really a community, not a mere real-estate development." With his accumulated realtor's "proof" that real-estate speculation is the "instrumentality," Frank exposes Irv's ideal as an anachronism and a fallacy. The man who designs flight simulators is also simulating a sense of "community" for which, like the Agrarians' proprietary ideal, "the original no longer exists"—if it ever did.[20]

Independence as a Sociospatial Practice: Frank in Haddam on Independence Day

Having recognized that "sense of place" and "sense of community" have been rendered redundant, or at least highly contingent, by capitalism, Frank instead formulates his own sense of independence. The concept of independence first comes to the fore when Frank sends his son "The Declaration of Independence" and Ralph Waldo Emerson's "Self-Reliance" in preparation for the trip to Cooperstown. Frank believes that "independence is, in fact, what he [Paul] lacks—independence from whatever holds him captive: memory, history, bad events he struggles with, can't control, but feels he should" (16). But Frank's conception of independence goes beyond this notion of negative freedom, beyond vulgar individualism. In an interview with *Salon,* Ford stated that in *Independence Day* he wanted to redefine the "conventional sense" of independence as "putting distance between yourself and other people." Ford wondered "if independence could in fact mean a freedom to make contact with others, rather than just the freedom to sever oneself from others." In the novel, Frank utilizes a sense of independence

20. Frank states explicitly: "'Community' is actually one of those words I loathe, since all its hands-on implications are dubious" (386).

in this revisionary mode to finally "make contact with others." By doing so, Frank achieves semiautonomy—if not Irv-esque "transcendence"—from the everyday immanence of selling real estate.[21]

Frank puts his theory into practice during the final section of the novel, in which he (eventually) joins in Haddam's holiday celebrations. Initially, he is doubtful about the meaning of the Fourth of July, feeling "as though independence were *only* private and too crucial to celebrate with others." Furthermore, Haddam's Fourth of July festivities are (as in Cooperstown) a distinctly commercialized form of carnivalesque, located as they are in Haddam's Central Business District (CBD), transitory home of Benetton/Foot Locker and Laura Ashley/The Gap. Frank believes that this privatized space should be put to more public use: "I, in fact, wouldn't be sad or consider myself an antidevelopment traitor to see the whole shebang fold its tents and leave the business to our own merchants in town; turn the land into a people's park or a public vegetable garden; make friends in a new way" (425). Feeling alienated from this commodified landscape in a way he never was in *The Sportswriter*, Frank leaves the CBD and drives toward his old family home on Hoving Road. This return to the site of his $1 million-plus house nearly causes Frank to regress briefly into the familiar, fetishistic fantasy of place: "it's worth asking again: is there any cause to think a place—any place—within its plaster and joists, its trees and plantings, in its putative essence *ever* shelters some spirit ghost of us as proof of its significance and ours?" Finally though, Frank conclusively refuses the alluring "sanction," the mystical "essence" of place. The fact that Frank's former house is unrecognizable, having been converted into a conference center, only confirms that, under capitalism, material "place" is prone to instability, to creative destruction. Instead, the brief diversion to Hoving Road helps Frank to reaffirm his faith in the sociospatial practice of everyday life. Frank recognizes that interaction with "other humans" is what makes existential meaning: "We just have to be smart enough to quit asking places for what they can't provide, and begin to invent other options—the way Joe Markham has . . . as gestures of our . . . independence" (442).[22]

21. Sophie Majeski, "Richard Ford: The *Salon* Interview," http://www.salon1999.com/weekly/interview960708.html.

22. In a short essay titled "Sense of Place," Ford has written: "I would say against Thoreau that places—mountains, street corners, skylines, riverbanks—do not speak, have no essences which can be 'captured,' heard. They are intransigent, mute, specific, and that is enough." See Ford, "S.O.P.," *Aperture* 127 (spring 1992): 64.

Frank himself is reoriented to social relations when he encounters his old associate Carter Knott. Carter is not a close friend—indeed, in *The Sportswriter*, Frank's awkward relationship with Carter prompted him to comment that "the suburbs are not a place where friendships flourish." Nonetheless, "[b]y using Carter's presence," Frank now staves off the sense of "sadness, displacement, lack of sanction" provoked by his yearning for the Hoving Road house (445). This brief encounter with Carter gives Frank the will to rejoin the festivities in Haddam CBD, where he makes a significant "gesture" toward his revised sense of independence. In the last lines of *Independence Day*, we witness Frank "narrow that space . . . that separates people" and "make contact with others" in the middle of the Fourth of July crowd: "The trumpets go again. My heartbeat quickens. I feel the push, pull, the weave and sway of others" (451).[23]

Richard Ford's Postsouthern Sense of Place

In *The Southern Writer and the Postmodern World* (1991), Fred Hobson ingeniously but, I think, misguidedly tries to recover *The Sportswriter* as a "southern" novel. Hobson attempts this recovery partly on the premise that Frank Bascombe "has a great desire, nearly a compulsion, to link with place, whether the place is suburban New Jersey or Detroit." Despite acknowledging that Ford's work reveals no "particular allegiance to geographical place, southern or otherwise," Hobson subsequently suggests that because Frank is "keenly attuned to place," he is essentially "southern." But the sportswriter's peripatetic (to recite Percy's term) "immanence of consumption" in the capitalist landscape of postsouthern America differs from anything in the "southern literary tradition"—not only the (neo-) Agrarian tradition that has emphasized the rural "stable community," but also the "non-Faulkner" Percyan tradition to which Hobson refers. In *The Sportswriter*, Frank exhibits, in John Crowe Ransom's disapproving definition, "the character of our urbanized, anti-provincial, progressive, and mobile American life that . . . is in a condition of external flux." But the second Bascombe book goes further by showing just how thoroughly the Agrarian proprietary ideal has been displaced by finance capitalist real estate. Moreover, in *Independence Day* it is clearer than ever that Frank cannot follow Binx Bolling by resurrecting some residual idea of "the South," or by returning to a sanctuary like the Garden District. In the

---

23. Ford, *The Sportswriter*, 85; Ford quoting Emerson in Majeski, "Richard Ford."

residential specialist's postsouthern America, such "southern" metaconcepts as "place" and "community," to the extent that they mean anything, are contingent upon land speculation and development.[24]

And yet *Independence Day* is finally more hopeful than *The Sportswriter*—not to mention *A Piece of My Heart,* Ford's debut novel that moved from postsouthern parody to grim nihilism. During the course of his second narrative, Frank gains a genuine understanding of the flux and inequality that characterizes capitalist geographies. More than that, he also resolves his own "predicament of placement" (as well as the Markhams'), while recognizing the contingency of such a resolution. As we have seen, in *The Moviegoer* Binx was so horrified by the capitalist production of place as (sub)urban real estate that he rhetorically displaced the very phenomenon from Louisiana to Illinois. By contrast, and nearly thirty years later, Frank Bascombe remains optimistic that one can achieve a "sense of place"—however provisional—through the practice of everyday life *within* the capitalist spatial economy of postsouthern America.

If Hobson's critical approach to *The Sportswriter* is problematic, it cannot hold when transferred to *Independence Day.* Imitating Hobson's approach to the first Bascombe novel—trying to identify a subterranean "southern" sense of place or community in the sequel—proves unfruitful. As we have already seen, Frank dismisses Mississippi's supposedly essential sense of place by comparing it to Haddam's "simple setting." Later, Frank does claim that Wallace Hill "could be a neighborhood in the Mississippi Delta." But he adds the qualification that "the local cars at the curb are all snazzy van conversions and late-model Fords and Chevys" (119). Hence, this casual, comparative reference to the South subtly implies that, however much Wallace Hill has been segregated from the rest of Haddam, it remains a more prosperous black "community" than those generally found in Mississippi. It is true that Frank believes Wallace Hill's black residents may yet move "down South," thereby suggesting that the region yet retains a powerful pull for *black* Americans (and an attraction stronger than anything our narrator feels for his birthplace). But by adding that the South is "where their ancestors were once property themselves," Frank reminds us that, for all the Agrarian emphasis on agricultural real property, the region's peculiar identity was premised upon the *human* property relations of slavery. In the end, Frank's very few "southern" citations

---

24. Hobson, *The Southern Writer in the Postmodern World,* 50, 42, 50, 57; Percy, *Lost in the Cosmos,* 120; Ransom, "Reconstructed but Unregenerate," 5.

serve to remind us that, as Charles Reagan Wilson observes, "place" has often been a code word in southern discourse "to indicate the status of blacks" in a hierarchical society. It proves impossible to excavate some positive, absent presence of "the South" and its "sense of place" from *Independence Day*. Rather than having recourse to some residually "southern" sense of place or community, Frank resolves his predicament of placement—his earlier immersion in the capitalist geographies of postsouthern America—through his revised sense of independence.[25]

Ultimately, it is perhaps only within the context of *A Piece of My Heart*, *The Sportswriter* and some of Ford's essays that one can even perceive how *Independence Day* extends the author's postsouthern critique of "the South" and the "southern literary tradition." Having said that, *Independence Day*'s final reference to "the South" is a somewhat clearer case of postsouthern, intertextual parody. Frank reveals that he is considering being buried in Cut Off, Louisiana, because it is a place that has "minimum earthly history." Larry McMurtry might be surprised, but Frank is anything but burdened by this Deep South site; it is, he feels, even more of a nonplace than Esperance, New York (439). There is something else going on here, though: by slyly echoing Shut Off, Louisiana, as featured in Percy's *The Last Gentleman* (1966), Ford sounds another subtle "answering knell" to the antinorthern, antiurban prejudice often evident in Percy's novels.[26]

Although Richard Ford's fiction critiques the production of postmodern capitalist geographies, it never returns to a foundational "South." In a 1979 conversation with Louis Rubin, Robert Penn Warren stated his belief that "this term 'Sun Belt' is a realtor's term, and that captures the whole story." Not surprisingly for someone who once professed the Agrarian proprietary ideal, Warren thus blamed real-estate development and the resulting resignification of "the South" for the degradation of the region's sense of place. In 1977, in his essay on Percy, Ford similarly remarked that "[t]he south is not a place any more; it's a Belt, a business proposition, which is the nearest thing to ano-

25. Wilson, "Place, Sense of," 1137. Frank also refutes the myth—perpetuated by the black twins Everick and Wardell, who do manual work for the realty firm—that a white southerner like himself will inevitably "possess a truer instinct for members of their race than any white northerner could ever approximate" (33).

26. For Shut Off, Louisiana, see Percy, *The Last Gentleman* (1966; reprint, New York: Ivy, 1989), 273. See Chapter 5 for Ford's explanation that *The Sportswriter*'s scathing criticism of New Orleans was "an answering knell" to *The Last Gentleman*'s implication that Michigan is a "non-place."

nymity the economy recognizes." Yet Ford's Frank Bascombe shares none of the nostalgia that Warren and Welty evidently felt for "the South" as it was before the advent of the Sun Belt and its (in Welty's pejorative term) "real estate people." As we have seen in the last three chapters, Ford's literary cartographies differ from even the protopostsouthern (non)places depicted in Walker Percy's work. In his review-essay of *Lancelot*, Ford observed that: "For Percy, the south is simply the landscape he knows . . . firm, if temporary, ground from which to see and speak to the rest of the country."[27] Since he published *A Piece of My Heart* in 1976, Ford himself has rejected "the South" on even those limited terms, indicting the "indefensible restrictions of an outdated geography" imposed by "Southern literature."[28] Frank Bascombe—born in Mississippi, but realtor-resident of New Jersey—speaks to us from the late capitalist landscape of postsouthern America.

27. Warren quoted in "The South: Distance and Change," 309; Ford, "Walker Percy," 562; Welty quoted in "Growing Up in the Deep South: A Conversation with Eudora Welty, Shelby Foote, and Louis D. Rubin, Jr.," in Rubin, ed., *The American South*, 77; Ford, "Walker Percy," 561.

28. This final quotation is from Ford's contribution to "A Stubborn Sense of Place," *Harper's*, August 1986, 43. Among the "southern writers" participating, Ford was by far the most skeptical about "southern literature," "the South," and its supposed "stubborn sense of place."

PART THREE

Placing the Postsouthern "International City":
The Atlanta Conundrum

7. Locating a Nonplace: Atlanta's Absence from Southern Literature and the Emergence of a Postsouthern "International City"

On 19 July 1996, the *Atlanta Journal-Constitution* published an essay by the novelist Ellen Douglas. Douglas's short piece was written ostensibly in honor of the Olympics, the international sporting jamboree that Atlanta was about to host. Douglas began, though, by noting that southern writers, literary critics, and academics "have been talking for a couple of generations about 'Place' and 'the Sense of Place.'" Douglas expressed some skepticism toward this literary-critical consensus, asserting that "[a]ll this sometimes seems to me blown out of proportion." In passing—and sounding similar to Eudora Welty in "Some Notes on River Country"—Douglas did acknowledge the "solid" and "permanent" quality of nature in her own "South": "green black magnolia trees with leaves as thick as shoe leather, dark cedars weighed down with moss." But Douglas proceeded to focus "not [on] the changing South," but on the Earth as a whole, "our neighborhood—the only place we have." She worried that this planetary "Sense of Place" was imperiled by "the final choking dose of poison, the weight of too many billion people, the loss of too many billion trees."[1]

By shifting the focus from "the South" to the world, Ellen Douglas advanced an eco-critical perspective that (in its more optimistic conclusion) also affirmed the Olympian ideal of a global community or "neighborhood." The essay can also be loosely defined as an example of literary postsouthernism to the extent that Douglas queries the provincial "Sense of Place" that traditionally has been privileged in "southern literature." Yet it is curious that Douglas makes no reference to the Olympic host city itself. After all, the (sub)urban sprawl of metropolitan Atlanta strikingly differs from the Weltyan, rural-natural "Sense of Place" that Douglas briefly recites. Moreover, Atlanta also epitomizes a rather different "worldly" perspective than the one that Douglas eventually offers. I am referring to the city's burgeoning role in the

1. Douglas, "Neighborhoods," 456–57.

finance-capitalist world-system. Over the last few decades, this "southern" city has increasingly situated and defined itself in relation to what sociologist Manuel Castells calls the "space of flows," the dizzyingly abstracted "global network" through which commodities and capital itself are circulated, traded, speculated, and multiplied. When Douglas observes that we "have gotten dislocated in our time in a large and different way," she is referring to how, "since we first saw the pictures of Earth from space," we have reconceived our regional "Sense of Place" from a cosmic perspective. Yet in another context, Douglas's words could have been referring to the sense of dislocation—what anthropologist Charles Rutheiser has called the "sense of placelessness"— engendered by a hypercapitalist city that exists in a (cash) nexus between the local and the global, between material geography and abstract monetary flows. Douglas might have been describing the "generic urbanism" of a self-styled "international city" that is built and occupied by multinational corporations, and acts as a banking center for the technologically mediated transnational circulation of capital.[2]

In Part 3 I hope to show that Atlanta's spatial (re)production and narrative representation—not only by novelists, but also by boosters—is of interest and importance when one considers the contemporary reality and transformation of place in that region we have known as "the South." Anne Rivers Siddons's *Peachtree Road* (1988) and *Downtown* (1995), Tom Wolfe's *A Man in Full* (1998) and Toni Cade Bambara's *Those Bones Are Not My Child* (1999) depict the postsouthern "international city" and its sense of place—or sense of placelessness, as the case may be. First, though, this chapter takes a skeptical backward glance in order to assess Atlanta's historical absence from the canonical cartography of "southern literature." Ellen Douglas perhaps necessarily demurs from analyzing the Olympian locus in order to expound her ecological worldview. More generally, though, Atlanta's status as a "nonplace" in southern letters is, I suggest, inextricable from its long-established role as the locus classicus of the urban, capitalist "New South."

Agrarianism and Atlanta as a New South Nonplace

In 1864, Union General William Tecumseh Sherman ordered the annihilation of Atlanta; the following year, the Confederacy suffered its final defeat. But it was not long before native politicians and businessmen began

---

2. Manuel Castells, *The Informational City* (Oxford: Blackwell, 1989), 6, 311; Rutheiser, *Imagineering Atlanta*, 163.

to reinvent Atlanta, materially and rhetorically, as the center of a "New South" based upon the North's urban, industrial capitalist model. Rutheiser observes that, even in the 1870s, Atlantans were beginning to term their city "the New York or Chicago of the South (the choice, presumably, depending on which group of Northern businessmen they were courting)." Atlanta's pioneering adoption of what Paul Gaston has termed the "New South Creed" soon brought the city to national attention. In 1886, the editor of the *Atlanta Constitution*, Henry Grady, stood before a New York audience of bankers and industrialists—including Atlanta's nemesis Sherman, whom Grady jokingly chided "for being a little careless with fire"—and made his notorious "New South" speech. Grady advocated southern economic progress empowered by northern capital.[3]

Subsequent generations of Atlanta boosters perpetuated the capitalist ethos underpinning Grady's "New South" vision. In 1925, the city's Chamber of Commerce conceived a marketing campaign, "Forward Atlanta," with the aim of selling the city to national corporations. As well as coining the concept, oft-cited ever since, of an "Atlanta Spirit," Forward Atlanta subsidized a book, *Atlanta from the Ashes* (1928), written by the Chamber of Commerce president, Ivan Allen. But as William Gleason notes, "[t]he 'Atlanta Spirit' of the 1920s" caused many southerners to ponder "what rough beast was slouching toward Atlanta to be born." Indeed, Allen's tome, "the perfect embodiment of the Atlanta Spirit in action," was challenged, albeit indirectly, by another text that appeared two years later: the Agrarian manifesto *I'll Take My Stand*. As Rutheiser observes, "the 'Nashville Agrarians' delivered a stinging ruralized riposte to the urbanized, industrializing ethos of the New South Creed and, by way of association, to Atlanta as well." Rutheiser rightly qualifies this statement by adding that *I'll Take My Stand*'s critique of Atlanta was only implicit.[4] Only retrospectively did the most unreconstructed Agrarian, Donald Davidson, state explicitly the Fugitive-Agrarian opposition to those businessmen who were less interested in art than "the price of cotton or the value of real estate in Atlanta." Nevertheless, when John Crowe Ransom in "Reconstructed but Unregenerate" charged that "[t]he urban South, with its heavy importation of regular American ways and regular American citizens, has nearly capitulated" to northern industrial capitalism, he might as well have identified

---

3. Rutheiser, *Imagineering Atlanta*, 22.

4. William Gleason, *The Leisure Ethic: Work and Play in American Literature, 1840–1940* (Stanford: Stanford University Press, 1999), 309–10; Rutheiser, *Imagineering Atlanta*, 31, 36.

Atlanta directly; when Ransom scorned "the local chambers of commerce [that] exhibit the formidable data of Southern progress," he likely had Allen and his cohorts in mind.[5]

During the 1920s and 1930s there was, then, a distinctive narrative divergence between the Agrarians' representation of southern place as anti-urban, anti-industrial, and (implicitly) anti-Atlanta, and the city boosters' simultaneous promotion of Atlanta as the New South's commercial hub. To put it another way, the Agrarians' formulation of the proprietary ideal (see Chapter 2), which was centered upon "concrete," agricultural real property, came up against the abstract, economic "value of real estate in Atlanta." This narrative divergence becomes more noteworthy if one considers that the Agrarian-inflected southern literary renascence occurred even as Atlanta was declaring—and achieving—economic eminence within both region and nation. For despite Atlanta's regional and national rise, it remained, at best, marginal to a canonical literary-critical cartography of "the South" in which Welty's Mississippi River Country or Faulkner's hand-drawn map of Yoknapatawpha was sited and recited as (the rural) ground zero. Of course it would be fallacious and crudely deterministic to suggest that a city's economic ascendancy must necessarily be accompanied by a coterminous growth (or decline) in its literary representations. As we shall see, for complex reasons, major fictional works about Atlanta have been few and far between.[6] Nevertheless, it is notable that in the same year, 1936, that *Absalom, Absalom!* appeared (complete with Faulkner's map), Margaret Mitchell published the phenomenally popular *Gone with the Wind:* the most famous literary representation of Atlanta of all, yet one that is rarely located within the Southern Renascence. I maintain that Atlanta's anomalous status in "southern literature" derives at least partly from, and is exemplified by, *Gone with the Wind* and its ideological challenge to (neo-)Agrarian ideas of southern identity and place.

Atlanta Real Estate and Tara's Sense of Place: Margaret Mitchell's
Gone with the Wind

In the first part of *Gone with the Wind*, set in the immediate antebellum period, it becomes clear that the heroine, Scarlett O'Hara, has an ambiguous

5. Donald Davidson, *Southern Writers in the Modern World* (Athens: University of Georgia Press, 1958), 1; Ransom, "Reconstructed but Unregenerate," 20, 17.

6. I shall return to the debate over the relative paucity of "Atlanta literature," and the relationship between economic power and literary representation, in Chapter 9, for this debate reemerged in 1998 with the publication of Tom Wolfe's *A Man in Full*.

relationship to her family's plantation, Tara, and to the planter-class society of Clayton County. To be sure, Scarlett enjoys the social whirl of balls and garden parties, and she is never required to recognize that this leisurely existence is founded upon slave labor. But Scarlett cannot comprehend her father's core belief that "[l]and is the only thing in the world that amounts to anything ... the only thing worth working for, worth fighting for—worth dying for."[7]

If Scarlett exhibits an indifferent sense of homeplace, she is overtly hostile to established southern cities such as Savannah and Charleston, both of which she visits after the death of her first husband Charles Hamilton. It is only when she moves to Atlanta in May 1862 that Scarlett achieves a personal sense of place. For Scarlett, Atlanta stands in favorable contrast to both the "rural leisure and quiet" (145) of Clayton County and the "serene and quiet old cities" (150) of the South: "Scarlett had always liked Atlanta for the very same reasons that made Savannah, Augusta and Macon condemn it. Like herself, the town was a mixture of the old and new in Georgia, in which the old often came off second best in its conflicts with the self-willed and vigorous new" (141). Scarlett identifies with Atlanta's "new" urban vigor—a modern vitality evident even before the war is over. But she speculates far more, financially and personally, in the fortunes of *post*bellum Atlanta. As Kenneth O'Brien observes (and Louis Rubin and Richard King concur) in *Recasting: "Gone with the Wind" in American Culture* (1983), Scarlett's "successes are all associated with Atlanta, and its rebirth during Reconstruction as the business capital of the Lower South." When Scarlett returns to a devastated Atlanta shortly after the war, she is "cheered by the sight of new buildings going up all along the street." Admiring Atlanta's endurance, she anticipates the city's resurgence: "They couldn't lick you. You'll grow back just as big and sassy as you used to be!" (540). Scarlett's own involvement in the literal "reconstruction" of Atlanta—the redevelopment of the city's real estate—is tangible and profitable. She shrewdly invests in two sawmills that are ideally located to supply the lumber needed to rebuild the city. With a lack of scruples that astounds Atlanta's keepers of the Lost Cause, she even sells lumber to the "Carpetbaggers and Scallawags" who are "building fine homes and stores and hotels with their new wealth" (654).[8]

7. Margaret Mitchell, *Gone with the Wind* (1936; reprint, London: Pan Books, 1974), 38. All subsequent page references will be incorporated into the main text.

8. See Kenneth O'Brien, "Race, Romance, and the Southern Literary Tradition," in Darden Asbury Pyron, ed., *Recasting: "Gone with the Wind" in American Culture* (Miami: University Presses of Florida, 1983), 164. See also, in the same volume, Louis D. Rubin Jr., "Scarlett

Rubin rightly notes that "the breakdown of the old plantation society serve[s] to liberate Scarlett." Yet *Gone with the Wind* still manages to eulogize the plantation-based Old South—a mythical time and place apotheosized in Tara—even while celebrating the rising of Atlanta from the ashes of war. Rubin observes that "Mitchell's depiction of prewar plantation society is romanticized and false." But it is only upon achieving financial success in *postwar* Atlanta that *Scarlett* (rather than Mitchell) romanticizes Tara. Moreover, Scarlett's own "romanticized and false" simulation of the Old South—her postbellum recreation of Tara as a site of neo-Confederate nostalgia, despite her antebellum skepticism toward Gerald's transcendent vision of southern land-value—is mediated by a complex nexus of (as Frank Bascombe might term it) "socio-emotio-economic" investments.[9]

Scarlett first feels her father's sense of homeplace upon returning to Tara during the siege of Atlanta. In a passage that anticipates Ike McCaslin's metaphysical aesthetics of place in Faulkner's "The Bear," Scarlett discovers that "[s]he could not desert Tara; she belonged to the red acres far more than they could ever belong to her. Her roots went deep into the blood-colored soil and sucked up life, as did the cotton" (411). Returning to Atlanta in 1866, Scarlett struggles to reconcile herself to the fact "that Atlanta and not Tara was her permanent home now" (599). She feels "the ache that was even stronger than fear of losing the mills, the ache to see Tara again. . . . She loved Atlanta but—oh, for the sweet peace and country quiet of Tara, the red fields and the dark pines about it!" (670). There would seem to be an irreconcilable tension here between Scarlett's bourgeois capitalist association with the material reconstruction of Atlanta, and her metaphysical romanticization of Tara as a remnant of antebellum life. But this apparent tension is resolved because Scarlett embodies the New South Creed. As King observes by way of Gaston, while "the New South advocates . . . sanctioned industrial devel-

---

O'Hara and the Two Quentin Compsons," 90; and Richard H. King, "The 'Simple Story's' Ideology: *Gone with the Wind* and the New South Creed," 170–71. During the war itself, Scarlett inherits (from Charles Hamilton) real estate in and beyond Atlanta: "half of Aunt Pitty's house but farm lands and town property as well. And the stores and warehouses along the railroad track near the depot, which were part of her inheritance, had tripled in value since the war began" (152–53). It is not clear what happens to the "farm lands and town property." But Scarlett's postwar wealth derives from producing and selling construction materials rather than from property ownership per se.

9. Rubin, "Scarlett O'Hara and the Two Quentin Compsons," 89, 94; Ford, *Independence Day*, 44.

opment under the dispensation of laissez-faire capitalism," they also "celebrated the antebellum South." By this equation, Scarlett is an exemplary New Southerner: though she becomes a prominent businesswoman in Atlanta, she gradually moderates her notorious disdain for the Confederate cause and nurtures a nostalgic yearning for her Clayton County roots.[10]

It is entirely appropriate, therefore, that the very capital that Scarlett acquires from Atlanta's New South redevelopment facilitates the creation of Tara's Old South sense of place. Initially, Scarlett's career in Atlanta is partly determined by the realization that, after the war, the farm-cum-plantation economy of Clayton County is no longer self-sufficient. She experiences an epiphany "in the midst of [the] ruins" at the Wilkes family plantation, Twelve Oaks: "[t]here was no going back and she was going forward" (418–19). Yet Scarlett still hopes that Tara and the Old South itself will rise again: "Tara had risen to riches on cotton, even as the whole South had risen, and Scarlett was Southerner enough to believe that both Tara and the South would rise again out of the red fields" (447). It takes Will Benteen, the "Cracker" who runs Tara in Scarlett's frequent postwar absence, to tell her that "[t]his section won't come back for fifty years—if it ever comes back.... Tara's ... a farm, a two-mule farm, not a plantation" (950). It is Atlanta that proves resurgent—and ultimately it is Atlanta that maintains Tara. When Scarlett's first mill begins to make money, "[m]ost of it went to Tara and she wrote interminable letters to Will Benteen telling him just how it should be spent" (622). Thus, it is the profit from Atlanta's urban development that, transferred to Tara, enables Scarlett's ideological fetishization of the antebellum homeplace as an Old South haven. In the last instance, Tara's (meta)physics of place are inextricable from Scarlett's economic investments in Atlanta.[11]

Toward the end of the novel, Scarlett's old flame Ashley Wilkes admits that he "want[s] the old days back again." In response to Ashley, Scarlett explicitly states, "I like these days better" (901). Though she wavers momentarily when she remembers the "lazy days and warm still country twilights! The high soft laughter from the [slave] quarters," Scarlett is New Southerner enough to realize that the Cotton Kingdom will not rise again. She well knows

10. King, "The 'Simple Story's' Ideology," 170.
11. I do not mean that she fetishizes Tara in the Marxist sense—i.e., as a commodity. Rather, despite her oft-stated distaste for the Lost Cause, Scarlett romanticizes Tara as a remnant of antebellum life in much the same way ex-Confederates turn the cause itself into "a fetish" (856) (objectified through graves, battlefields, flags, sabers, letters, and even the veterans themselves).

that, whether she "like[s] these days better" or not, it is Atlanta's profitable redevelopment that enables Tara's survival (albeit in simulated form). At the very end of the novel, needing a "quiet place to lick her wounds" (1010) after the showdown with Rhett Butler, Scarlett goes home again. But *Gone with the Wind*'s famous last words, "to-morrow is another day" (1011), suggest that even now Scarlett will not remain at Tara—not only because she wants Rhett back, but also because she must return to Atlanta to make the money that maintains Tara as a monument to "the old days."[12]

I have already observed that *Gone with the Wind* is rarely considered as a canonical Southern Renascence text. Of course, critics have held the novel's very popularity against it. Richard Dwyer cites the measly biographical entry on Margaret Mitchell in Rubin's *A Bibliographical Guide to Southern Literature* (1969) as typical of the critical attitude. Faulkner's advocate Malcolm Cowley initiated this tradition of critical disdain in the year of the novel's publication. It should be clear by now that Cowley was simplifying somewhat when he claimed that "*Gone with the Wind* is an encyclopedia of the plantation legend." But as Darden Pyron has observed, Cowley's attitude "helps to illuminate the mystery of *Gone with the Wind*'s place, or 'non-place,' in American letters."[13]

The novel's popularity and its image as a romantic plantation novel also go some way to explaining the novel's "nonplace" in *southern* letters—but not, I think, the whole way. It is worth considering what the Agrarians would have made of Mitchell's novel. It is somewhat surprising that John Crowe Ransom, in his brief assessment of *Gone with the Wind* for the *Southern Review* in the autumn of 1936, expressed distaste for Mitchell's "painfully Southern" bias. What is more, Ransom's review exhibits only oblique hints of disdain for "modern Atlanta," and for Scarlett as the embodiment of the city. So, while

---

12. Scarlett is a much more successful "New Southerner" than the wartime mercenary Rhett who, at the end of the novel, declares, "I'm going to hunt in old towns and old countries where some of the old times must still linger. I'm that sentimental. Atlanta's too raw for me, too new" (1009). Rhett is primed to return to his family in Charleston—tellingly, one of those "Old Southern" cities that Scarlett so disliked. It is also notable that, unlike Scarlett, Rhett has no material attachment to Atlanta real estate (except their gaudy marital home). Because "[y]ou can't hide real estate very easily" (837), Rhett had put his money in to bonds rather than property.

13. Richard Dwyer, "The Case of the Cool Reception," in Pyron, ed., *Recasting*, 29; Malcolm Cowley, "Going with the Wind," in Pyron, ed., *Recasting*, 19 (originally published in the *New Republic*, 16 September 1936, 161–62); Pyron, preface to *Recasting*, ix.

Ransom does express his preference for Melanie as "the paragon of Southern ladies" and wonders whether Scarlett's apparent stupidity arises from a lack of wit "in old Atlanta," he couches this criticism within a wider regional-historical context. Echoing Tate's critique of the Old South's thin culture in "The Profession of Letters in the South" (published a year earlier, and itself partly a response to Ransom's own overly romanticized vision of the Old South in "Modern With the Southern Accent" from 1934), Ransom confesses his fear that the South has *always* been deficient in "wit," in "conversational brilliance," even "in the handsome gatherings of the Southern forebears."[14]

Nonetheless, while Ransom's review of *Gone with the Wind* expresses only mild antipathy toward "modern Atlanta," he and the Agrarians generally had cause to be rather more perturbed by the novel than the review allows: perturbed less by the excessive Old Southernism flagged in the review than by Mitchell's very evident *New* Southernism. Given Ransom's impassioned support (expressed in *I'll Take My Stand* six years previously) for the unregenerate southerner who "look[s] backward rather than forward," he could hardly have concurred with Scarlett's transparently New South belief that "[t]here was no going back and she was going forward" (419)—that "[n]o one could go forward with a load of aching memories" (901). It is also important to understand that *Gone with the Wind* does not only represent Reconstruction-era Atlanta as what King calls the *"locus classicus* of the New South spirit"; it also affirms the "Atlanta Spirit" of the 1920s that, as we have seen, the Agrarians opposed. When Ivan Allen and his civic-corporate cohorts proclaimed "Forward Atlanta," they would simply have confirmed Ransom's jaundiced view of chambers of commerce. But it was surely more surprising, even alarming, for an Agrarian to come across a contemporary *artist* who depicted a heroine "going forward" to Atlanta to be reborn through real estate. This perhaps explains the rather cutting closing remark in Ransom's review, which implies that present-day Atlanta, and the novel itself, are the logical outgrowth of the supposedly witless "young, pushing Atlanta" that emerged "before, during, and after the Civil War": "The trouble is that she [Mitchell] deeply committed herself to the mentality of her Scarlett. Or is the wit more lacking in modern Atlanta than elsewhere?" One surmises that "elsewhere" here refers to the rural, agrarian South.[15]

---

14. Ransom, "Fiction Harvest," *Southern Review* 2 (autumn 1936): 407–8.
15. Ransom, "Reconstructed but Unregenerate," 1; King, "The 'Simple Story's' Ideology," 170; Ransom, "Fiction Harvest," 408.

But whatever Ransom may have thought of the connection between "old" and "modern" Atlanta, *Gone with the Wind* quite deliberately develops a distinctly positive analogy between the forward-thinking New Southernism of Reconstruction-era Atlanta, and the present-day "Atlanta Spirit." Via the process that Georg Lukács calls "modernization," Mitchell's narrative becomes inextricable from the boosterism of its author's own time and place. Like her protagonist, Mitchell takes her stand for what Donald Davidson would one day witheringly dismiss as "real estate in Atlanta," and against—whether consciously or not—the Agrarian aesthetics of antidevelopment. Ultimately, Mitchell's highly favorable image of Atlanta as the archetypal site of New South capitalism must have rankled with the Agrarian and neo-Agrarian arbiters of "southern literature" rather more than her romanticized depiction of Tara. *Gone with the Wind*'s pro-New South, pro-urban, and procapitalist ethos challenges the rural, traditional visions of place propounded in *I'll Take My Stand* and *Who Owns America?* (published in the same year as Mitchell's novel). Indeed, one wonders whether Atlanta's peculiar status as a "nonplace" in "southern literature" is related to the fact that, for the Agrarians and for many neo-Agrarian critics, a capitalist city is by definition a nonplace. Employing Pierre Macherey's theory of constitutive absence, Richard Gray has argued that *I'll Take My Stand*'s general silence on the subject of slavery is a conspicuous lacuna that "helps us locate the vision of the world . . . that underpins all the essays in the symposium." Considering Atlanta's social significance from Reconstruction through the 1920s to the present, one might similarly suggest that the city's absence from (neo-)Agrarian mappings of "southern literature" reveals the ideological criteria behind, and the lacunae within, the southern literary-critical "sense of place."[16]

Despite the evasions of literary critics (and, one should be clear, despite the ghastly racism of *Gone with the Wind* itself), Margaret Mitchell's representation of Scarlett's Atlanta as the New South's capital of capital remains vivid and relevant. This representation of Atlanta anticipates, in different ways, the narrative cartographies I discuss in Chapters 8 to 10. *Gone with the Wind*'s example suggests that the contemporary writer—whether novelist or critic, neo-Agrarian or "Left Winger" (Mitchell's own scornful term)—cannot just ignore Atlanta's continuing status as a place defined by capitalist property relations.[17]

16. Georg Lukács, *The Historical Novel* (1962; reprint, Harmondsworth: Peregrine Books, 1969), 66 and 218–45; Gray, *Writing the South*, 145.

17. Mitchell quoted in Rutheiser, *Imagineering Atlanta*, 295, note 120.

Anti-Agrarianism and Coca-Cola: Flannery O'Connor's Atlanta

Almost two decades after Mitchell's novel was published, Flannery O'Connor critiqued Atlanta's peculiar commercial status as a Confederate shrine—an image that derived largely from the movie version of *Gone with the Wind*. As Rutheiser observes, David Selznick's 1939 film has given "[u]ntold millions of persons . . . a misleading impression of Atlanta as a city of the Old South, not unlike Charleston and Savannah." Scarlett O'Hara, so derisive toward these more established cities, might have been amused by this cinematic revisioning of Atlanta; Margaret Mitchell actually "yelped with laughter" at the film's "gentrification" of her novel. Nevertheless, when Atlanta's boosters seized upon Selznick's simulacrum of an Old South city, they too were acting in accordance with the New South Creed: the movie's aristocratic, antebellum Atlanta provided an unprecedented opportunity to promote the modern capitalist city. Hence, Mayor William Hartsfield brought the movie premiere to Atlanta despite his personal distaste for the Old South mythology of "magnolias and beautiful ladies and soft nights." As Frederick Allen has noted, Hartsfield felt that although "Hollywood might have distorted the Atlanta of the Civil War era . . . at least its impresarios and stars were endorsing the Atlanta of 1939 as a place of glamour and cosmopolitan taste."[18]

In O'Connor's 1953 story "A Late Encounter with the Enemy," the fake Confederate hero, General Tennessee Flintrock Sash, cannot actually remember the Civil War. He does, however, proudly recall his role in the Atlanta movie premiere. According to Sash, there "wasn't a thing local about it"—it was a "nashnul event" featuring "beautiful guls" from "Hollywood, California." The narrative subtly indicates what is not apparent to Sash himself: that the *Gone With the Wind* "preemy" was a mediated spectacle in which neo-Confederate nationalism was incorporated to the marketing of modern Atlanta as a city of "nashnul" significance. "A Late Encounter with the Enemy" not only suggests that the South's collective memory has become cinematically and commercially mediated. O'Connor's story also asks whether contemporary (1950s) capitalism pays *any* deference to Old South tradition, as did the earlier practitioners of the New South Creed. In the closing lines, the story suggests that Confederate iconography has given way to commodity fetishism. When Sash dies during his granddaughter's graduation ceremony,

---

18. Rutheiser, *Imagineering Atlanta*, 41; Pyron, "The Inner War of Southern History," in Pyron, ed., *Recasting*, 186, and preface to *Recasting*, ix; Frederick Allen, *Atlanta Rising: The Invention of an International City, 1946–1996* (Atlanta: Longstreet Press, 1996), 27.

the young boy entrusted with caring for the old man waits with the corpse next to a vending machine dispensing contemporary Atlanta's most famous commodity: Coca-Cola.[19]

Clearly, "A Late Encounter with the Enemy" is less favorable toward Atlanta than *Gone with the Wind*. Simply by acknowledging the looming presence of the New South city, however, the story can be seen as part of O'Connor's quite radical critique of a (neo-)Agrarian literary-critical cartography that has privileged and idealized the rural South. In the novella *Wise Blood* (1952) and various short stories, O'Connor depicts the startling spatial disjunction between Atlanta and the surrounding rural and small-town South. O'Connor's most concentrated textual map of this urban-rural opposition is "The Artificial Nigger" (1955). In this story, one Mr. Head takes his grandson Nelson to Atlanta, where the boy was born, to show him "that the city is not a great place."[20] Having reared Nelson in a rural county from which blacks have been banished, Head now wants to destroy the boy's pride in his birthplace. The old man begins by representing Atlanta as a place "full of niggers" (252). But when Nelson gazes into the "store windows, jammed with every kind of equipment—hardware, drygoods, chicken feed, liquor," his fascination with Atlanta only increases. Indeed, whereas the commodity overload of the central business district enraptures Nelson, Head is terrified—on a previous visit to Atlanta, he literally lost all sense of place while walking through a labyrinthine department store (258).

Head attempts to reassert his authority over Nelson by describing the city's sewers in such a manner that the boy "connected the sewer passages with the entrance to hell and understood for the first time how the world was put together in its lower parts" (259). When Head and Nelson subsequently blunder into a black residential neighborhood, Head declares the city a "nigger heaven" (261), implying that the racial-spatial otherworldliness of Atlanta constitutes a (white man's) hell on earth. As Head and Nelson wander further away from the railway station and central business district, the disoriented grandfather attempts to "teach [the] child a lesson" (264) about urban alienation. Head hides from Nelson, but his plan goes calamitously wrong

---

19. Flannery O'Connor, "A Late Encounter with the Enemy," in *The Complete Stories* (1971; reprint, London: Faber and Faber, 1990), 136.

20. O'Connor, "The Artificial Nigger," in *The Complete Stories*, 251. All subsequent page references will be incorporated into the main text.

when the frantic boy, believing himself abandoned, knocks down an elderly woman, causing a minor public scandal. Plagued by guilt, the grandfather now sees Atlanta as his personal gateway to hell—"if he saw a sewer entrance he would drop down into it and let himself be carried away" (267))—and as the site of his own judgment day: "He knew that if dark overtook them in the city, they would be beaten and robbed. The speed of God's justice was only what he expected for himself, but he could not stand to think that his sins would be visited upon Nelson" (266).

Yet Head manages to avert this sense of impending damnation, and to reassert his anti-Atlanta authority, when he and Nelson enter "an elegant suburban section where mansions were set back from the road by lawns" (267). Head and Nelson encounter the "artificial nigger" of the story's title, a "plaster figure of a Negro sitting bent over on a low yellow brick fence that curved around a wide lawn" (268). Head solemnly pronounces that "[t]hey ain't got enough real ones here. They got to have an artificial one" (269). Despite having walked through distinct racially segregated and unevenly developed areas of Atlanta, Head here fails to recognize that this wealthy suburb excludes *living* black southerners—and that to this degree, the city suburb is much like Head's rural home county. Nonetheless, this declaration of Atlanta's racial otherness allows the old man to reconcile the Heads to their own "home"—to a familiar sense of place that had been reduced to "nothing" (268) by the day's disastrous events. Upon returning to the country, Head feels he has achieved God's mercy and is ready to "enter Paradise" (270).

In an intriguing 1983 essay, H. R. Stoneback interpreted "sense of place" in O'Connor's "The Displaced Person" against the grain of criticism by C. Hugh Holman and Louis Rubin that assessed the story from the "Agrarian vision of experience." Stoneback argued that it is actually "the countryside [that] is hell, rather than Atlanta or New York, to name just two of the urban 'non-places' against which O'Connor characters (and readers) frequently direct their topophobia." Adapting Stoneback's polemical perspective to "The Artificial Nigger," one might argue that Head, in his brief moment of penitence, fails to see that Atlanta's sewer system is not the entrance to hell but rather "a kind of Purgatory, the required displacement [from the false rural Eden] in the rite of passage to grace." Instead, Head banishes his guilt by using the "artificial nigger" to redeem his country homeplace as a racial, rural Paradise. The reader, however, remains cognizant of the contrast between Head's moment of penitential despair in Atlanta, and his final, frantic desire to recover his worldly home as Eden. As such, the end of the story is stingingly ironic: by abandoning the urban purgatory and returning to his rural sanctuary, Head is living on bad faith.[21]

It should be noted, however, that, even when mapping capitalist development and urban segregation, O'Connor is not really focusing on *Atlanta's* "sense of place." She is more concerned with interrogating the presumed virtues of the rural South. This is also true of "The Life You Save May Be Your Own" (1953) and "A Circle in the Fire" (1954), two other stories that briefly cite Atlanta. Here too, O'Connor's white, rural characters define their own smug, complacent sense of place by rhetorically inventing Atlanta as an otherly dystopia. To this extent, O'Connor utilizes Atlanta to undermine the foundational Agrarian conception of place. Ultimately though, it is not only because the city is refracted through the distorted rural perspectives of Head and others that O'Connor's stories only obliquely reveal the material reality of 1950s Atlanta. O'Connor's radical sense of place is finally subservient to, even submerged by, her overwhelming religious beliefs. It should be apparent from Stoneback's language, not to mention my own, that it is difficult not to reach for religious terminology when discussing O'Connor's post-Agrarian southern cartographies. What Lewis Simpson calls O'Connor's "compelling aesthetic of revelation" eventually renders material, social geographies as irrelevant when compared to the "true country" of spiritual faith.[22]

Uncreative Destruction: Inner-City Atlanta in Donald Windham's The Dog Star

In 1998, as the hype surrounding *A Man in Full* went into overdrive (see the start of Chapter 9 for details), an advertisement in *Brightleaf* magazine splashed the headline "Stop crying Wolfe . . . read the *other* novel about Atlanta." Surprisingly, the advertisement was not referring to *Gone with the Wind*. Athens-based Hill Street Press was promoting its reprint of a book first published in 1950, Donald Windham's debut *The Dog Star*. Usurping *Gone with the Wind*'s status as *the* Atlanta novel was certainly an audacious promotional move. Unfortunately, Windham's own afterword to the new edition put things into a sobering historical perspective. Windham recalled that "[o]ne

---

21. H. R. Stoneback, "'Sunk in the Cornfield with His Family': Sense of Place in O'Connor's 'The Displaced Person,'" *Mississippi Quarterly* 36, no. 4 (fall 1983): 547, 555.

22. Lewis P. Simpson, *The Brazen Face of History*, 248; O'Connor, "The Displaced Person," in *The Complete Stories*, 214.

of my goals, of course, had been to portray Atlanta." But when his publishers decided to concentrate promotional activities there, "[t]he reaction of the city that had loved *Gone with the Wind* did not increase [the original publisher] Doubleday's enthusiasm." Moreover, Windham continues, "the next few times I visited the city, there was no copy in the Atlanta Carnegie Public Library." One of the more obvious ironies surrounding *Gone with the Wind* is that this epic expression of the capitalist New South Creed was published, and sold millions of copies, during the Depression. The irony is redoubled when one considers that, despite depicting the depressed inner city of the 1930s, *The Dog Star* completely failed to reconfigure the literary-cinematic image of Atlanta as a place of "magnolias and beautiful ladies" and/or the "*locus classicus* of the New South spirit."[23]

To be fair, the *Brightleaf* advertisement seems knowing in its irreverence. But Hill Street Press's claim that *The Dog Star* is "a landmark classic of southern literature" (on the back cover) does rather stretch the paratextual rhetoric. The reality is that there is not a single mention of Windham in monumentalizing tomes like *The History of Southern Literature* (1985); not one critical essay about *The Dog Star* has appeared. Yet *The Dog Star* deserves serious reconsideration, not only because the book challenged the narrative cartography of Atlanta popularized by Mitchell (and Selznick), but also because its representation of inner-city poverty and urban redevelopment anticipates aspects of *Peachtree Road, A Man in Full,* and *Those Bones Are Not My Child.*

The Dog Star opens with the teenage protagonist Blackie Pride returning to Atlanta. Blackie is fleeing the rural reform school where his best friend, Whitey Maddox, has just committed suicide. It soon becomes clear that, back in the city, Blackie is severely alienated from his family and friends. He has been changed utterly by his relationship with the antisocial but (apparently) strong and self-reliant Whitey. Arriving at his mother's house, Blackie recalls Whitey's world-weary maxim: "Home is the place where you don't feel at home" (12). Rejecting as sentimental the homesickness he felt while at the school, "now he felt as though the place he wanted to be no longer existed in the world" (13). Believing Whitey's "inheritance," a legacy of "strength and greatness and indifference," to be "his most important possession in the world" (45), Blackie mimics Whitey by ostracizing himself from everyone he

---

23. *Brightleaf: A Southern Review of Books* 2, no. 1 (winter 1998): 50; Donald Windham, "Afterword," in *The Dog Star* (1950; reprint, Athens: Hill Street Press, 1998), 225–26. All subsequent page references to *The Dog Star* will be incorporated into the main text.

knows: "now he did not belong with them" (17). Having thus dispossessed himself from family and friends, Blackie self-consciously embarks upon a search for "Whitey's place in the city" (57). But this search inevitably founders on the fact that Blackie associates Whitey with the County Farm School. Hence, "when he tried to imagine Whitey in the city the image faded, lost all its details" (56). Because "Whitey's place" can in fact only be found within his own experience, and not in the objective material landscape of Atlanta, eventually Blackie takes his "inheritance" to its grimly logical conclusion and, like Whitey, commits suicide.

Such images of placelessness, homelessness, and dispossession might locate *The Dog Star* in various ways. It may seem to be a novel "about the tragic alienation of youth," as Hill Street Press has promoted the new edition. It might seem to be existential in the "vulgar" mode critiqued by Edward Soja, "entrapped in pure contemplation of the isolated individual." Or, if we locate Blackie's "situation of being-in-the-world" within the social geography of Atlanta, *The Dog Star* may appear to be a neo-Agrarian indictment of urban life. Yet as it turns out, neither the novel, nor its image of Atlanta, is quite so easy to situate. Without taking a neo-Agrarian tack, it is important to emphasize the sociospatial (as opposed to adolescent or vulgarly existential) basis of Blackie's alienation: his fractured familial and social life in inner-city Atlanta. We learn that Blackie's father was "killed in a wreck as he started out on his first honest job" (27). Since then, Blackie's alcoholic mother has struggled in vain to sustain the family in one of the "newer cheaper and smaller houses" (9) located near the Techwood public housing project (the first of its kind in the United States, completed under the auspices of the New Deal in 1935). Blackie's older sister Pearl, a single mother, is living in a duplex on Baker Street while "working as a waitress in one of those stands on Ponce de Leon" (11), and his younger brother Caleb is living with two old women who act as his foster parents. Significantly, the narrative suggests a similar sociospatial basis for Whitey's otherwise seemingly abstract sense of isolation. Whitey once told Blackie that "he never had felt attachment for his family," recounting how, as a fourteen-year-old, he hitchhiked to California and back to Florida (55). Part of Blackie's tragedy is that, idealizing his friend's "strength and greatness and indifference," he never really recognizes the social background of Whitey's suicide.[24]

Rather than returning to school, Blackie resolves to find work in Atlanta

---

24. Soja, *Postmodern Geographies*, 131.

to obtain "the space and freedom which money creates" (70). At this point, Windham introduces a narrative strategy that vividly emphasizes the sociospatial relations that delimit Blackie's quest for "freedom" through self-reliance. Blackie "get[s] a job with a wrecking company tearing down houses" (104) for the Techwood renewal project. Pondering the contrast between his childhood summers in the park and "work[ing] all year round, like any man, twelve months a year," Blackie initially finds the idea "endless and fascinating" (105). But soon after starting work at the demolition site, Blackie becomes alienated by and from the reality of manual labor. He observes one of his older workmates: "numb from the heavy work," the man's hands move "as though they were tongs." Worse, "[t]he houses were so old and rotten that they fell apart . . . during the morning a man's leg had been crushed beneath a roof which had fallen without warning" (107). Blackie revises his original idealism: the work has become "endless but not fascinating. There was no climax or satisfaction" (116).

Blackie decides to quit his job: the "space and freedom which money creates" has proven to be an illusion. Most obviously, full-time work only hinders his existential quest for total self-sufficiency: "the money made him no more able to pursue adventure as long as he was working." But it is also important that Blackie's labor involves the literal *destruction*, rather than the *creation*, of space. It is true that, by clearing free land for the construction of Techwood Homes, the wrecking company is involved in the social *reconstruction* of Atlanta. Moreover, as a public-housing project funded by the federal government, this is not precisely the capitalistic "creative destruction" that David Harvey defines as typical of modernist urban development.[25] Nonetheless, division of labor dictates that Blackie is not involved in the constructive side of this sociospatial process. Consequently, all sense of his own use-value, his productivity, is transferred to the cash nexus itself: "All he *made* was money" (123, my italics). When the disillusioned Blackie decides to hand in his notice, the narrative pointedly segues Blackie's burgeoning nihilism into the destruction of Atlanta's built space: "He returned to work with a wild elation. All of the joy of destruction welled up in him. He stood on the floor beams of a second story pulling out a windowframe and . . . threw it with a joy of sheer energy down through the plaster ceiling below. Dry plaster and lathing

---

25. Harvey, *The Condition of Postmodernity*, 16–17. As we shall see in Chapter 8, this New Deal scheme differs from the business-driven creative destruction—the so-called urban renewal—of Atlanta during and after the 1960s.

exploded about the iron bar as it fell . . . giving him such pleasure to watch that he momentarily regretted being free of the job. But a few minutes before five he climbed down from his place and on the stroke of the hour he bolted" (123). The association between individual and social destruction serves to suggest that, for all his faith in economic "freedom," Blackie's social (and spatial) options are severely limited. This scene provides the sociospatial context and catalyst for Blackie's subsequent adoption of uncreative (self-)destruction as his way of being in—or against—the world.

Having quit his job, Blackie concentrates fully on living out his idealized image of Whitey's isolation and becomes more belligerently antisocial than ever. He estranges his older girlfriend, Mabel, and his oldest friends, Dusty and Hatchet. This pair and their accomplices subsequently attack and seriously injure Blackie while he is walking down a street "unaware of the empty dirty city about him as though he were the center of a universe which moved as he moved" (165). Briefly, the attack actually dispossesses Blackie of his "inherited" image of Whitey. Blackie recognizes and bemoans his willful isolation: "Why had he allowed himself to become helpless and alone?" Moreover, having been numbed by and alienated from his manual labor at Techwood, Blackie now feels physical pain that causes him to repossess his own body: "His body seemed the only thing in this world which was real and was his. He touched it gently, weeping for it, so innocent and so wronged" (169). But Blackie suddenly realizes that he has not been dispossessed of everything: his assailants did not take his money (his wages from the Techwood job). Counting the bills, Blackie recovers his earlier belief that economic independence guarantees existential survival: "The forty dollars was all there. . . . All his growing love and pity were metamorphosed instantly into bitterness and pride. He had triumphed over them after all" (170).

Blackie decides to use the money to get out of Atlanta altogether. But economic "freedom" again proves to be a form of false consciousness. Blackie is drawn back to Atlanta because "[h]e was afraid that the sons of bitches would think that he had run out of town because he was afraid" (178). This spatial turn back to Atlanta may suggest that the social reality of inner-city life is inescapable, existentially or economically. Yet it is also notable that the narrative never invents the rural South as a sanctuary, a benevolent agrarian antithesis of Atlanta. The County Farm School is less a "farmers' academy" (34), as Whitey once tried to dismiss it, than a strictly organized site of surveillance, discipline, and punishment. The rural landscape is also depicted in a distinctly *anti*pastoral fashion: during Blackie's initial escape from the

County Farm School back to Atlanta, he looks out upon "gnarled and warped" branches, "withered sticks with poison" (8). Now, having left Atlanta again, Blackie finds himself in a rural hinterland that is "the forlorn midst of nowhere" (179). Blackie senses that "[h]e had been a fool to think that the world would be any different away from the city. The whole world was the same, the whole world" (180). These lines might be read as the apotheosis of Blackie's universalized sense of displacement, his all-encompassing alienation. Yet the true tragedy may be that, for all inner-city Atlanta's grim social reality, it was at least the source of those social relations, the everyday familial love and comradeship, that Blackie has sloughed off in order to honor Whitey's image. To this degree, *The Dog Star* anticipates (minus the religious overtones) O'Connor's stories of the 1950s: if Atlanta is no dream of Arcady, then neither is rural Georgia a neo-Agrarian utopia.

In a somewhat mannered coda to *The Dog Star*, Caleb Pride seems destined to follow the doomed path of both Blackie and Whitey. We see Caleb fleeing Atlanta like his brother before him. Disturbingly, the narrative seems inclined to naturalize social alienation and economic poverty: "[w]ith the rhythm of water and blood, of things which have happened countless times before and will happen countless times again," torrential rain falls equally on Caleb and a "group of Negro children" who live on the border between Atlanta (Howell Mill Road) and the country. Yet there remains a twist: having "intended to run away, never return to the city," Caleb discovers that "the strangeness of the country frightened him" (220). By returning to the city, Caleb may still be turning back to a fate like Blackie's. But there also remains the possibility that Caleb may yet find succor, even salvation, in the kinds of social relations that Blackie so aggressively rejected: "He was lonely and he wanted comfort even if he had to return to the city where people did not understand" (220–21). It is the final torque to a novel that provides an unsparing portrait of poverty and alienation in Depression-era Atlanta yet refuses to dismiss inner-city, everyday life in neo-Agrarian terms.

The Emergence of the Postsouthern "International City"

Contemporary Atlanta remains characterized by certain historical and narrative continuities with the imaginary cities of Scarlett O'Hara (the 1870s), Blackie Pride (the 1930s) and Mr. and Nelson Head (the 1950s). It is useful, however, to consider Atlanta's social, economic, and spatial development since the 1960s in somewhat different terms. After 1961, boosters began to promote Atlanta as something more than the "New York of the South" or the capital of the "New South": now, they claimed, Atlanta was a "national city." Before the decade was out, Atlanta was being advertised as an "international city" and as "the World's Next Great City." In the second half of this chapter, I want to reconfigure Lewis P. Simpson's original, literary-historical notion of the postsouthern along economic and geographical lines to emphasize the capitalist logic behind the boosters' rhetorical and material reinvention of Atlanta as a "national" and "international" city.

In 1961, under the direction of its president, Ivan Allen Jr. (the son of the author of *Atlanta from the Ashes*), the Chamber of Commerce set out its grand vision of Atlanta as a "national city." This national identity would be defined according to Atlanta's growing ability to exert "a powerful economic force far beyond its normal regional functions." In a related move the same year, the chamber resurrected the "Forward Atlanta" campaign of the 1920s. This latest generation of Atlanta's private-public "power structure" (sociologist Floyd Hunter's famous term) were even more ambitious than Allen Sr. and his colleagues. The chamber hired a New York advertising agency to orchestrate "Forward Atlanta II," a campaign that was, as *National Geographic* later noted, a "spectacular success [in] selling Atlanta to the Nation as a good place to do business." As *Atlanta Journal* editor Jack Spalding observed in 1965 (by which time Allen Jr. had been mayor for three years), the goal of the city's civic-corporate leadership was to transform the provincial "Atlanta, Ga." into national "Atlanta, U.S.A." By 1969, more than four hundred of the top five hundred largest American industrial corporations had located operations in Atlanta. According to the chamber's own entirely economic criteria, such statistics confirmed Forward Atlanta II's "spectacular success" in promoting—even inventing—the "national city."[26]

Toward the end of the 1960s, the Chamber of Commerce began to advertise Atlanta as "The World's Next Great City." At times, such sloganeering seemed almost entirely rhetorical, with little reference to any material reality. In 1971, Atlanta Airport was renamed Hartsfield *International* Airport

---

26. Rutheiser, *Imagineering Atlanta*, 49; William S. Ellis, "Atlanta, Pacesetter City of the South," *National Geographic* 135, no. 2 (February 1969), 249, 250. The term "power structure" was first used by Hunter in his influential *Community Power Structure: A Study of Decision Makers* (Chapel Hill: University of North Carolina Press, 1953). Hunter showed how the decision makers in Atlanta's political and commercial affairs came from a privileged elite of wealthy white businessmen. See Allen, *Atlanta Rising*, 39. Spalding's article, from the 4 April 1965 *Atlanta Journal-Constitution* magazine, is quoted in Allen, *Atlanta Rising*, 136.

on the tenuous basis that Eastern Airlines had established a connection to Mexico City. In 1977, a massive new convention center situated downtown was named the Georgia *World* Congress Center (GWCC). If the local and the global were jarringly juxtaposed in the very name of the new complex, the city went further by locating GWCC on *International* Boulevard, formerly the more prosaic Cain Street.[27]

Atlanta's promoters were also quick to use a faddish neologism like "Sun Belt." Urban historian David Goldfield has remarked that "Sun Belt sophistry . . . has replaced the New South Creed as the prevailing rhetorical ruse in the region." As a "useful case study" of such "Sun Belt sophistry," Bradley Rice identifies a campaign organized by the Metropolitan Atlanta Council for Economic Development (MACFED). Rice observes that "[i]f entrepreneurs were searching for the Sunbelt, Atlanta's promoters wanted them to find it in Georgia's capital city. One of MACFED's booklets crowed, 'The Sun Belt, with Atlanta as its centerpiece, has surged into overwhelming economic significance.' The booklet urged business people to 'come find your place in the Sun Belt.' An ad placed in numerous business-oriented periodicals carried on the theme, saying, 'If you're looking for a place in the Sunbelt, you really can't afford to go anywhere else.'" It might be said that terms like "Sun Belt" and "international city" epitomized the semiotic logic of late capitalism. Such seemingly abstracted language was inextricable from—was intended to facilitate—the material redevelopment of Atlanta as a center of global finance and multinational corporate investment. Indeed, the extravagantly named Georgia World Congress Center *did* help the city became a leading site for corporate conventions; the grandly titled Hartsfield International Airport *did* (eventually) establish Atlanta as an important node in an increasingly globalized network of flows (of people and of capital).[28]

As the influx of national and transnational capital increased precipitously, it furthered the radical transformation of Atlanta's local, material geography. Atlanta was advertised as a prime investment site in the European business press, and boosters embarked on trade junkets to the commercial capitals of Europe and Asia. Such promotional maneuvers helped to ensure that the "mixed-use developments [MXDs] planned for downtown in the late

---

27. See Rutheiser, *Imagineering Atlanta*, 66, 190.

28. Bradley Rice, "Searching for the Sunbelt," in Raymond A. Mohl, ed., *Searching for the Sunbelt: Historical Perspectives on a Region* (Knoxville: University of Tennessee Press, 1990), 219; Goldfield is quoted on 218.

1960s and completed in the early 1970s" were often financed by transnational capital. To cite two prominent examples, the Atlanta Center was funded by Kuwaiti petrodollars, while Tom Cousins's predictably named Omni International—complete with an "international bazaar"—attracted substantial European investment. Moreover, multinational corporations were increasingly the tenants of Atlanta's MXDs. In 1969, *National Geographic* had noted the number of national businesses relocating to Atlanta. A follow-up feature in July 1988 noted that Atlanta "has become a top corporate-relocation center" for multinational corporations: "431 of the Fortune 500 industrial companies have offices in Atlanta, not to mention 134 firms from Japan."[29]

The global corporate redevelopment of Atlanta was largely unaffected by the accession to local political power of African Americans, consolidated by Maynard Jackson's election as mayor in 1973. A new "urban regime" of white business interests and black political power continued to encourage Atlanta's burgeoning status as a site for capitalist investment. This was especially the case during the 1981–89 mayoral reign of Andrew Young (which I will discuss at more length in Chapter 8). Ultimately, despite the rhetorical shift from "national" to "international," and the political shift from white to black, "economic force" remained as much the defining element of Atlanta's identity in the 1970s and 1980s as it had in the 1960s.[30]

But dissenting voices did emerge to challenge the boosters' masternarrative—what Rutheiser calls the "advertiser's monologue"—of a thriving "international city." Indeed, it became possible to reconfigure critically the boosters' own "national" or "international" economic criteria so as to question why the local populace, and even the local power structure, appeared to be losing control of the city's built space. By the 1970s, as Truman Hartshorn observed in *Metropolis in Georgia: Atlanta's Rise as a Major Transaction Center* (1976), the city was becoming "less dependent on the state and region and more on national and global business." Even sources that usually served as the media for the boosters' message began to express some concern. *Atlanta* magazine was founded by the Chamber of Commerce in 1961, and quickly attracted promising local writers like Pat Conroy and Anne Rivers (later Anne Rivers Siddons). Though the later, privately relaunched *Atlanta* remained

---

29. Rutheiser, *Imagineering Atlanta*, 165, 180–81; Erla Zwingle, "Atlanta: Energy and Optimism in the New South," *National Geographic* 174, no. 1 (July 1988), 6.

30. Clarence N. Stone, *Regime Politics: Governing Atlanta, 1946–1988* (Lawrence: University Press of Kansas, 1989), ix.

"more celebrative than investigatory," a 1981 article asked, with startling directness, "Who Owns Atlanta?" The author, Neil Shister, noted that "most of the prime properties in town are controlled by interests head-quartered elsewhere: New York, Dallas, Boston, Toronto, Hamburg, Amsterdam, Al Kuwait." The article concluded in terms that might have made Andrew Lytle say I told you so: "Atlanta has become a city owned by absentee landlords." The perturbing (and rather less boostable) local economic realities that came with global investment in and ownership of Atlanta's property and capital became starkly evident in the 1980s. In that decade, two of the city's most established financial institutions and "major members of the downtown power structure," Life of Georgia and the National Bank of Georgia, were bought out by Dutch and Saudi interests—even as twenty of the world's largest banks were opening branches in Atlanta.[31]

This dizzying transformation, even revolution, in the "ownership" of Atlanta epitomizes what has come to be seen as a defining characteristic of economic globalization, first identified by Jean-François Lyotard in 1979: the ascendancy of "new forms of the circulation of capital that go by the generic name of *multinational corporations* [and which] imply that investment decisions have, at least in part, passed beyond the control of the nation-states"—let alone city governments or civic-corporate "urban regimes." And

31. Rutheiser, *Imagineering Atlanta*, 11; Truman A. Hartshorn et al., *Metropolis in Georgia: Atlanta's Rise as a Major Transaction Center* (Cambridge, Mass: Ballinger, 1976), 14; Rutheiser, *Imagineering Atlanta*, 50; Shister quoted in Numan V. Bartley, *The Creation of Modern Georgia*, 2nd ed. (Athens: University of Georgia Press, 1990), 225; Rutheiser, *Imagineering Atlanta*, 181. For Lytle on "the absentee-landlordism of capitalism," see Chapter 1. An openly neo-Agrarian critique of Atlanta was provided in the same year by southern literary scholar Fred Hobson in a collection of essays attributed to "Fifteen Southerners" and titled *Why the South Will Survive*. The title and tenor of the volume was consciously in the Agrarian grain, and Hobson's essay, "A South Too Busy to Hate," took the Agrarians' distaste for Atlanta to its logical, more explicit limit. Hobson noted that "the Agrarians would wince at the term" Sun Belt, and echoed Ransom's attack (in *I'll Take My Stand*) on "the local chambers of commerce [that] exhibit the formidable data of Southern progress" by identifying "public relations" as "the compelling Southern vice" in the post–civil rights movement period. With more specific reference to Atlanta, Hobson observed aphoristically that "Peachtree Street succeeds Tobacco Road," and worried that Atlanta epitomized a "Sunbelt" that "held only to the integrity of the dollar." For Hobson, even Atlanta's (in the southern context) liberal attitude toward race relations was motivated by money: this was a city "too *busy* to hate," rather than "[t]oo humane, honorable, ethical, or even courteous." See Hobson, "A South Too Busy to Hate," in Fifteen Southerners, *Why the South Will Survive* (Athens: University of Georgia Press, 1981), 45–46, 49.

yet, despite the dominance of multinational corporations in the development of the so-called international city, and the implications that this has for a local "sense of place," international Atlanta continues to be all too uncritically boosted. As Charles Rutheiser remarks: "To the imagineers at Central Atlanta Progress and the Chambers of Commerce, the activities and investments of foreign corporations are clearly the most important and easily demonstrable criterion of Atlanta's global significance."[32]

Rutheiser's own *Imagineering Atlanta* (1996) is the most thoroughgoing critique of "the politics of place in the city of dreams." Rutheiser reconsidered Atlanta within the context of the burgeoning interdisciplinary critical debate over the production of space under postmodern capitalism (see Chapter 2). Particularly valuable is Rutheiser's discussion of Peachtree Center, the core of the self-styled "private urban renewal program" through which architect-developer John Portman dominated the production of Atlanta's "new downtown" between 1959 and 1992. Rutheiser makes the basic but compelling point that Atlanta's Peachtree Center was the testing ground for Portman's trademark "'atrium' hotel that Fredric Jameson has taken as the hyperspatial totem of late capitalism." For Rutheiser, the effacement of "local cultural-historical context" from Peachtree Center's hermetic hyperspace results in "the apotheosis of contemporary Atlanta's generic urbanism and sense of placelessness." Peachtree Center also provides a telling example of the transition of Downtown Atlanta's development and ownership from the local to the global. Having been funded initially by the likes of Atlanta developer Ben Massell and the Texan real estate magnate Trammel Crow, Peachtree Center passed to lenders from New York and Japan when Portman went bankrupt in 1990. Borrowing a page from both Rutheiser and Jameson, I will discuss Portman's role in the capitalist production of Atlanta's social geography in Chapters 9 and 10.[33]

If it is true that Atlanta's "sense of placelessness" is related to the privatization of Downtown's previously residential and public space, it becomes tempting to compare Atlanta with *non*southern cities that exhibit a similar capitalist spatial logic: New York and, especially, Los Angeles, which not only Jameson has identified as the archetypal postmodern, late-capitalist city. The risk here is that, despite ostensibly offering an oppositional narrative, critics will fail to

---

32. Lyotard, *The Postmodern Condition*, 5; Rutheiser, *Imagineering Atlanta*, 72.

33. Portman quoted in Allen, *Atlanta Rising*, 169; Rutheiser, *Imagineering Atlanta*, 161, 163; Allen, *Atlanta Rising*, 243.

sufficiently distinguish their skeptical viewpoints from the boosters' breathless desire to *celebrate* Atlanta's (claimed) affiliation with the very same cities. In particular, there is a danger of repeating the boosters' rhetorical obfuscation of the local inequalities that still exist within supposedly "(inter)national" Atlanta. While Rutheiser posits that Atlanta can be seen as "paradigmatic of . . . ageographic and generic urbanism," he also insists that "Atlanta also represents a unique conjuncture of universals and particulars, and describes a reality quite unlike either New York or Los Angeles." Rutheiser takes care to chart the specific, local character of residential spatial inequality in Atlanta, social realities that have been obscured by the narrative and material "imagineering" of a "national" and "international" commercial metropolis.[34]

Rutheiser also recognizes that these local particulars are often characterized by "historical continuities." In other words, the racial segregation and uneven development of contemporary Atlanta is not merely a postmodern, late capitalist phenomenon; frequently, it is also the latest version of an established "southern" system of sociospatial inequality. Rutheiser's phrase "Jim Crow in twenty-first-century drag" is rhetorically excessive, but metropolitan Atlanta's *sub*urban residential space is distinctly marked by *re*segregation. An area like Cobb County can seem "characteristically southern" in the attitudes its white populace exhibits toward inner-city Atlanta. As whites have moved out in droves, into the previously rural heartland of Cobb, the population of the city of Atlanta has declined to less than four hundred thousand, the clear majority of whom are poor African Americans. Rutheiser notes that "[d]espite . . . the construction of a number of glitzy new mixed-use developments, such as John Portman's Peachtree Center, white suburbanites . . . viewed the urban core in terms not too far removed from those used by Flannery O'Connor characters." Another recent commentator, Peter Applebome, has suggested that Cobb is "the perfect distillation of the two trends driving American demography": "suburbanization" and "Southernization." Applebome is referring here to the sheer growth of the suburban population in the South but, as his discussion of "Newtland" (Cobb was Newt Gingrich's power base) reveals, the terms might also describe the (sub)urban reconstitution of identifiably "southern" forms of racial segregation.[35]

34. Rutheiser, *Imagineering Atlanta*, 4, 6–7.
35. Rutheiser, *Imagineering Atlanta*, 5, 6, 98, 52; Peter Applebome, *Dixie Rising: How the South Is Shaping American Values, Politics and Culture* (1996; reprint, New York: Harvest, 1997), 26.

In the 1980s and the 1990s, metropolitan Atlanta experienced a further, *post*suburban form of development. Many neologisms were coined to define this new sociospatial phenomenon, but journalist Joel Garreau was most successful in popularizing one in particular, "edge city." Garreau had, in fact, already discussed Atlanta in his book *The Nine Nations of North America*, published in 1981. Then, Garreau was so perturbed by the Omni International's disorienting hyperspace—his experience eerily anticipates Jameson's bewildered walkabout in Portman's Bonaventure in Los Angeles—that he tried to recover a familiar, small-town "sense of . . . knowing your place" that he hoped would redeem "Dixie" from the "Atlanta-ization of every comfortable town." Yet just a decade later, Garreau was back in Atlanta reporting upon another radical reconfiguration of the city's social geography. In his introduction to the best-selling *Edge City: Life on the New Frontier* (1991), Garreau posits that edge cities are nothing less than Americans' "attempt at Utopia." Supposedly, edge cities have superseded both suburbanization and "the malling of America" because "we have moved our means of creating wealth, the essence of urbanism—our jobs—out to where most of us have lived and shopped for two generations." In this "restorative synthesis" of the urban, utilitarian machine and the rural garden—and of the homeplace, the marketplace, and the workplace—Garreau optimistically envisions a return to "our relationship to the land" and an opportunity to "reunite our fragmented universe." In short, edge cities seemed to offer just the kind of sense of place that, if not traditionally "southern," could at least curtail the Atlanta-ization of Dixie.[36]

Garreau's chapter-length case study of Atlanta opens optimistically. He identifies "four full-blown Edge Cities in the Atlanta area": Perimeter Center, Midtown, Cumberland Mall-Galleria, and Buckhead-Lenox Square Mall. He shows that, because all four of these edge cities were built north of Downtown, and because the emerging black middle class mostly resides in these edge cities (rather than, as in the past, in the urban core of the city of Atlanta itself), there has been a qualified erasure of "[p]sychological barriers long thought to separate Atlanta into the 'white' Northside and the 'black' Southside." Garreau also celebrates the significant economic progress of those middle-class African Americans (whether Atlanta natives or not) who have sought "the white-collar jobs of high technology and the Fortune 500" with "corporations [which] tend to be headquartered in Edge City." But Garreau's

---

36. Garreau, *The Nine Nations of North America*, 159–60, and *Edge City: Life on the New Frontier* (New York: Anchor, 1991), xxiii, 4, 14, xxiii.

utopian vision ultimately comes into conflict with the realities of race and class in Atlanta. He recognizes that much of the city's built space continues to be constructed along a very real "color line": "you still get almost all the predominantly black [urban] neighborhoods over on the Southside." What is more, Garreau and some of his interviewees are disturbed that, where *racial* segregation has been reduced by the growth of the black middle class, it has simply been replaced by further *economic* segregation. Another "color line" is imposed: in the choice words of Stephen Suitts of the Southern Regional Council, "people are not judged by the color of their skins, but by the color of their money." Ruefully, Garreau acknowledges that edge cities are less in the utopian American grain than historically continuous with the racial segregation and uneven development that has always characterized Atlanta.[37]

Getting Beyond Mitchell and O'Connor Country

So how exactly have southern novelists—and by extension, southern literary critics—responded to the emergence of postsouthern, "international" Atlanta? And how has contemporary "southern literature" depicted the local, historical continuities of racial segregation and uneven development? As Rutheiser rightly observes, Flannery O'Connor's representation of urban/suburban segregation remains resonant precisely because "beneath the shiny surface of the boosters' celestial Atlanta" there (still) exists "one of the poorest and most racially segregated central cities in the United States." Yet since O'Connor's premature death in 1964, Atlanta has remained largely absent from southern literature and southern literary criticism.[38]

Not surprisingly, Walker Percy offered some of the most acute observations on both Atlanta's redevelopment and the representational limits of "southern literature." In 1978, Percy began his essay "Going Back to Georgia" by noting the extent of change in the state capital, "especially if one had been used to the Atlanta of the 1930s." Percy intimated the extent to which this new metropolis challenged preconceived notions of southern "place" when he mused: "You drive through Atlanta . . . and take a look around, and up, and you wonder, what is this place? Is this a place?" Like Rutheiser later, Percy identified contemporary Atlanta's sense of placelessness with mixed-use

37. Garreau, *Edge City*, 156, 145, 156, 154, 162. See also Rutheiser, *Imagineering Atlanta*, 63, on how a third of all black households in Atlanta lived in poverty by 1990 (double the number from 1980).

38. Rutheiser, *Imagineering Atlanta*, 3.

developments. Percy predicted that the "Atlanta of the Omni and the Peachtree Plaza" would become part of "an ever more prosperous Southern Rim stretching from coast to coast, an L.A.-Dallas-Atlanta axis." Of course, Percy was not wrong in predicting that "the Atlanta of the Omni" would be this Southern Rim's "media center." But even Percy could never have foreseen that Ted Turner's CNN—initially dismissed as the "Chicken Noodle Network" but by the early 1990s transmitting across the globe from the Omni, now known as CNN Center—would expand far beyond the Southern Rim to guarantee "Atlanta's symbolic capital as a major city of global importance."[39]

Percy slyly registered his own distaste for Atlanta's transformation, and the civic-business boosterism that promoted and propelled it, in terms that echoed John Crowe Ransom: "I avoid the Chamber of Commerce word 'progress' because it does not do sufficient justice to the ambiguity of the change." Yet despite—or because of—his personal distaste for the corporate cityscape, Percy recognized the need for a new literature to represent contemporary Atlanta. What is more, he insisted that Agrarian presumptions and prejudices should not burden this new literature. In "Novel Writing in an Apocalyptic Time" (1986), Percy "notice[d] a certain tentativeness in young Southern fiction writers—as if they still had one foot in Faulkner country, in O'Connor country, in Welty country, but over there just beyond the interstate loom the gleaming high-rises of Atlanta." Percy hoped that the contemporary southern novelist would "not try to become a neo-Agrarian" and thereby avoid the challenge to represent this new built spatial form. But of course, Percy himself never wrote a novel about Atlanta. Indeed, if one recalls how Percy played out Binx Bolling's retreat from the postsouthern suburbs of New Orleans, it is perhaps not surprising that he never turned his fictional attention to Atlanta. If O'Connor's fiction enacts a leap of faith beyond material reality into the spiritual "true country," so Percy's dystopian vision of Atlanta's role in "the not wholly desirable future of the region" is consistent with his own Catholic-inflected metanarrative of civilization's decline into an atheistic, even apocalyptic postmodernity.[40]

39. Walker Percy, "Going Back to Georgia," in *Signposts in a Strange Land*, 26, 28, 31; Rutheiser, *Imagineering Atlanta*, 71. "Southern Rim," a term coined in 1975 by Kirkpatrick Sale, signified a region stretching from Florida to California that was broadly synonymous with most contemporaneous definitions of the Sun Belt.

40. Percy, "Going Back to Georgia," 26–27; Percy, "Novel Writing in an Apocalyptic Time," 166–67; "Going Back to Georgia," 31.

In 1972, the leading southern literary critic C. Hugh Holman published an intriguing essay "The View from the Regency Hyatt" (sic). In this pioneering piece, Holman anticipated many later critics by noting that, contrary to prior presumptions, there is no such thing as "a monolithic South." Holman's essay was also important because it challenged, however delicately, the prevailing (neo-Agrarian) tendency to exclude "critical social realism" from the southern literary canon. But when Holman introduced his titular, totemic image of contemporary Atlanta—John Portman's first ever atrium hotel, the Hyatt Regency, completed in 1967—his argument became especially interesting. Toward the end of the essay, Holman asks "is the South as social subject any longer relevant?" Holman is really reworking that most hackneyed yet enduring of debates: is the South still distinctly different from the rest of the nation? But rather than directly answering this question, Holman asks another, and in doing so introduces the conundrum of contemporary Atlanta. He wonders: "Can one take the glass-enclosed elevator to the twenty-second floor of the Regency Hyatt in Atlanta and look out upon a world distinctively different from what he might see in New York, Chicago, or Los Angeles?" As it turns out, the answer is provided not by Holman himself, but by the omnipresent doyen of southern literary criticism. Holman writes: "As Louis Rubin pointed out to me, within two blocks of the Regency Hyatt you can find street evangelists extolling their primitive religions in tone and manner that make you think Hazel Motes of *Wise Blood* has come back to life."[41]

Holman's visual perspectives on Atlanta anticipate spatial theorist Michel de Certeau's discussion of the contrasting views from the top and the bottom of New York's World Trade Center. Invoking de Certeau's terminology, one might say that the southern literary critic resists the spectacle of the "panorama-city" by getting back "down below": at street level, "the South" survives in all its grotesque glory. Yet one suspects that O'Connor herself might have been bemused to hear that, on his way to religious redemption, Haze Motes also saved "the South as social subject" from the specter of capitalist Atlanta. There is a lurking suspicion that Holman, for all his emphasis on "critical social realism," is yet evading the *economic* reality of the South's radical redevelopment, so explicitly symbolized in the Hyatt Regency. Not unlike Allen Tate in "The New Provincialism," Holman acknowledges, "to the

41. C. Hugh Holman, "The View from the Regency Hyatt," in *The Roots of Southern Writing: Essays on the Literature of the American South* (Athens: University of Georgia Press, 1972), 96, 99, 106–7.

extent to which the southern renascence assumed such an agrarian way of life, that renascence ended with the Second World War." But by citing Atlanta's O'Connoresque evangelists alongside other familiar signifiers of regional identity, Holman—unlike Tate, but much like Rubin throughout the 1970s (see Chapter 2)—reassures the reader that "the South" will survive, yet again. Having stepped tentatively into one of the gleaming high-rises of Atlanta, Holman finally seems more comfortable with his feet planted in O'Connor country.[42]

In a 1990 essay that I discussed in Chapter 2, Julius Rowan Raper proclaimed that "the skylines of Atlanta, even Durham, show us we are becoming the Postmodern South. Consequently, a Postmodern Southern Literature appears as inevitable as the movements that came before." Yet there remains a critical reluctance to look beyond "neo-Agrarian" notions of the southern "sense of place." In his introduction to *The Future of Southern Letters* (1996), John Lowe posits that: "The rural past has been eclipsed by an ever-expanding urban present, centered on high-finance, high-tech wheeling-dealing, which takes place in high-rise postmodern skyscrapers, hub airports, and gigantic shopping malls." Contemporary Atlanta encompasses these three examples of postmodern capitalist urban space. But of all the essays included in *The Future of Southern Letters*, only Lowe's own interview with the poet Brenda Osbey refers directly, and briefly, to contemporary Atlanta. *The Future of Southern Letters* is suggestive of how contemporary southern writers and critics have remained reluctant to extend O'Connor's protopostsouthern skepticism toward the neo-Agrarian, literary-critical construction of southern "place." Southern letters still tends to disregard present and "future" sociospatial realities in nostalgic remembrance of place past.[43]

Representing the Postsouthern "International City"

I have observed that there are continuities between Atlanta's earlier attachment to the New South Creed, which Rutheiser calls the "master myth of Atlanta history," and the city boosters' enthusiastic practice of "Sunbelt sophistry." But rather than continuing to see post-1960s Atlanta as a "Sun Belt" or "New South" city, or as an agglomeration of "edge cities," in Chapters 8 to 10 I will use the term postsouthern "international city." As I noted in

---

42. De Certeau, *The Practice of Everyday Life*, 93; Holman, "The View from the Regency Hyatt," 107.

43. Raper, "Inventing Modern Southern Fiction: A Postmodern View," 9–10, 17; John Lowe, introduction to Lowe and Humphries, eds., *The Future of Southern Letters*, 3–4.

Chapter 2, terms like "Sun Belt" or "New South" (or "*New* New South") are boosters' buzzwords, and there is a risk of uncritically recapitulating such terms. Carl Abbott observes pertinently that "the idea of a Sunbelt allowed the South to escape its own history and to transform instantly from a 'backward' to a 'forward' region." One catches resonant echoes here of the New South philosophy of Scarlett O'Hara. Furthermore, the term "Sun Belt" fails, or refuses, to convey the more troubling aspects of global capital's role in the radical reconstruction of Atlanta's local social geography. Of course, my own term echoes another, Atlanta-specific promotional slogan. But I suggest that, by putting suitably skeptical quotation marks around "international city," and by prefacing it with "postsouthern," we can begin interrogating the narrative representation (and material construction) of capitalist Atlanta. If "*postsouthern*" signifies the postmodern, capitalist redevelopment of "the South," it also retains its etymological root: "southern." "Postsouthern" thus prudently reminds us of the local, historical continuities of racial and economic inequality that remain within the "international city."[44]

I began this chapter by discussing Ellen Douglas's reconception of "Sense of Place" through an ecocritical worldview. I have suggested, however, that, in order to consider the sociospatial reality of postsouthern "international" Atlanta, it is useful to adopt a rather different planetary perspective: capitalist globalization. The contemporary "southern writer" (and southern literary critic) might usefully put into practice what human geographer Doreen Massey has called a "global sense of place." Such a perspective should help us to perceive and represent both the *local* and the *global* realities of contemporary Atlanta. We need to pay attention to both the bewildering effects of Atlanta's rise to prominence as a hyperspatial hub within the abstract matrix of global capital flows, and the local, material "geography of social relations" in which the city's residents practice their everyday lives. At the very least, the novels discussed in Chapters 8 to 10 offer an excellent opportunity to consider how contemporary novelists *have* taken up the unenviable task of mapping the postsouthern "international city."[45]

---

44. Rutheiser, *Imagineering Atlanta*, 14; Carl Abbott, "New West, New South, New Region: The Discovery of the Sunbelt," in Mohl, ed., *Searching for the Sunbelt*, 16.

45. See Massey, "A Global Sense of Place," in Trevor Barnes and Dick Gregory, eds., *Reading Human Geography: The Poetics and Politics of Inquiry* (London: Arnold, 1997), 315–23.

8. Urban Renewal and Mixed-Use Developments: Place and Race in Anne Rivers Siddons's *Peachtree Road* and *Downtown*

In his introduction to *The Future of Southern Letters* (1996), John Lowe advances his revisionist review of the southern literary canon by introducing the "conundrum" of "[p]opular *women* writers." Two noncanonical themes—Atlanta and popular southern women's writing—come together when Lowe refers to *Peachtree Road* (1988) by "current holder of the 'popular' southern historical novel crown," Anne Rivers Siddons. By citing a "popular" Atlanta-based novel like *Peachtree Road,* Lowe's reworked map of southern letters moves into largely uncharted territory. Yet this new critical cartography remains sketchy. Ultimately, Lowe's introduction inadvertently highlights the fact that almost every other essay in *The Future of Southern Letters* ignores Atlanta (see Chapter 7), and not one of the other contributors even mentions Siddons.[1]

Assessing *Peachtree Road* at the time of its publication, Bob Summer was more willing to embrace Siddons's novel as the future of southern letters. Indeed, Summer began his *Atlanta Journal-Constitution* review by referring to one (sadly anonymous) southern literary critic who dared to follow Walker Percy in proposing contemporary Atlanta as the perfect subject for post–Southern Renascence writers:

> A couple of years ago, a leading critic of what is called Southern literature was asked at a literary symposium if there was anything in the South to write about that had not already been appropriated by William Faulkner, Flannery O'Connor, Eudora Welty and other noted writers of previous generations.
>
> Oh yes, he replied. . . . Look at what has happened in Atlanta since World

---

1. Lowe, introduction to *The Future of Southern Letters*, 6. The only published scholarship on Siddons is Lamar York's survey of her first three novels, "From Hebe to Hippolyta: Anne Rivers Siddons' Novels," *Southern Literary Journal* 17, no. 2 (spring 1995): 91–99. *Peachtree Road* was Siddons's fifth novel, and her second set in Atlanta; see also the horror story *The House Next Door* (1978).

War II and especially in the 1960s and '70s, the venerable critic admonished, a drama he contended surpassed Sherman's burning and the city's rebuilding. Yet he added, Margaret Mitchell's *Gone with the Wind* remains the Atlanta novel.

Fully a decade before the hullabaloo over Tom Wolfe's *A Man in Full*, Summer declared that in *Peachtree Road* Siddons had produced "the Atlanta novel for our time." Even more effusively, novelist and Atlanta native Pat Conroy termed *Peachtree Road* "*The* Southern novel for our generation."[2]

Peachtree Road charts the turbulent life of rebellious southern belle Lucy Bondurant, as narrated by Lucy's cousin Shephard Gibbs ("Gibby") Bondurant III. But Summer's extravagant claims for *Peachtree Road* were largely based upon the impressive manner in which Siddons (like Mitchell in *Gone with the Wind*) constructs a grand narrative of Atlanta's social development. The sweep of *Peachtree Road* is such that it maps the shift from the New South city of the 1930s to what I have defined as the postsouthern "international city"—the metropolis of transnational capital and mixed-used developments constructed between the 1960s and the 1980s. Siddons is not a postsouthern parodic writer in the manner of Percy or Ford: she does not deliberately set out to critique southern literary-historical shibboleths such as "sense of place." Yet simply by focusing upon Atlanta, *Peachtree Road* (like *Gone with the Wind* before it) challenges neo-Agrarian critical cartographies of Faulkner, O'Connor, and Welty country.[3]

However, it is not the aim of this chapter to legitimize Siddons's "popular" novel as a suitably "literary" representation of Atlanta. Rather, I want to show how *Peachtree Road* constructs a certain idealized—and ideological— vision of the city's past. In a tenth-anniversary foreword to the novel, Siddons explicitly eulogized the "short, supercharged decade of the Sixties" and celebrated the city of that time as "an Atlanta as surely gone with the wind as the one young Margaret Mitchell wrote of . . . but to me, no less beautiful and seductive than that one" (no page number). The ideology

---

2. Bob Summer, "*Peachtree Road* Is Journey through Modern Atlanta," *Atlanta Journal-Constitution*, 16 October 1988, M10; Pat Conroy quoted on the cover of Anne Rivers Siddons, *Peachtree Road: Tenth Anniversary Edition* (1988; reprint, New York: HarperPaperbacks, 1998). All subsequent page references to *Peachtree Road* will be incorporated into the main text.

3. In a 1986 interview, Siddons explained that "sense of place" had been crucial to southern writers by trotting out the familiar references to the Confederacy's defeat and the burden of Reconstruction: "It's more than a matter of geography. We died for this land. We lost the war and lived as an occupied people. That never happened to the rest of the country." See Don O'Briant, "Profile on Peachtree," *Atlanta Journal-Constitution*, 26 January 1986, M4.

underpinning this nostalgia can be traced through the text's detailed but selective rendering of Atlanta's actual redevelopment. This is not to insist that Siddons's historical novel must necessarily answer what Georg Lukács once called "[t]he question of historical truth in the artistic reflection of reality" by rigidly conforming to factual, verifiable details of Atlanta's historical geography. Yet Siddons herself very clearly cleaves to "the mimetic-realistic impulse" of the traditional historical novel, despite what Fred Pfeil calls the "larger crisis of mimetic narrative and representation" that characterizes a "new moment in capitalist culture." So, to the degree that Siddons's "mimetic-realistic" text claims representational authenticity regarding recent Atlanta history and geography—whether through the author's own anniversary foreword, or through the character-narrator Gibby, who just happens to be a published historian—it is worth querying such narrative authority. Or to put it another way, precisely because Siddons's (to cite Lukács again) "realistic, literary means of expression for portraying [the] spatio-temporal (i.e. historical) character of people and circumstances" *is* so closely related to actual people, events, and places in Atlanta, it becomes possible to interrogate *Peachtree Road*'s ideological bias. The selective representation of Atlanta's (supposedly declining) "sense of place" between the early 1960s and the late 1980s in both *Peachtree Road* and *Downtown* (1995) supports an idealized image of the white power structure that ruled the city during the 1960s. *Peachtree Road* in particular is an important textual map of Atlanta's postsouthern, transnational redevelopment, but it is necessary to explicate the more problematic aspects of the novel's politics of place.[4]

Place, Race, and Real Estate: Buckhead and Southeast Atlanta, 1961

During his childhood, Gibby Bondurant is almost entirely confined to the wealthy, all-white enclave of Buckhead in north Atlanta. As such, Gibby is utterly unaware of the economic, racial, and spatial inequality that defines the city during the 1940s and 1950s. Even though the family's black servants populate young Gibby's narrow domestic geography, he grows up with an ideology of racial difference that ingenuously precludes economic

---

4. Lukács, *The Historical Novel*, 15; Fred Pfeil, "Fiction after History," in *Another Tale to Tell: Politics and Narrative in Postmodern Culture* (London: Verso, 1990), 50–51; Lukács, *The Historical Novel*, 18. Pfeil's remarks relate to Jean-François Lyotard's point that "capitalism inherently possesses the power to derealize familiar objects, social roles, and institutions to such a degree that the so-called realistic representations can no longer evoke reality except as nostalgia or mockery." See Lyotard, *The Postmodern Condition*, 74; also see Chapter 2 above.

class. He recalls that "I did not think of them as poor. I thought of them as Negroes. The one had nothing to do with the other" (26). Even during the occasional trip with the family servants to "pick up our laundry from Princess in Capitol Homes, or to fetch Amos from Pittsburgh, or Lottie, our cook, from Mechanicsville," he never really comprehends the chasmic contrast between the economic geographies of north and southeast Atlanta. Secure in his own secluded sense of place, young Gibby never ponders how the servants' everyday lives oscillate back and forth across the color line of segregated Atlanta: "I got no sense, from these visits [to the southeast slums], that people really lived in those places. They were, instead, destinations that provided the great houses of Buckhead with their provender" (203). Though Gibby never knew it, Princess and Lottie lived out a version of what bell hooks calls the historical African American "tension between service outside one's home, family, and kin network, service provided to white folks" and the "construction of a homeplace" of their own, "however fragile and tenuous."[5]

As a young adult, Gibby does come to realize that the world of Buckhead's white leisure class is made by the labor of slum-dwelling black servants. However, it is not until December 1961, when Gibby takes another motorized tour of the city, that he is fully exposed to the exploitative nexus of place, race, and real estate that inextricably connects the Bondurants with their servants, and Buckhead with southeast Atlanta. This time, Gibby travels not with Shem Cater, the Bondurants' own chauffeur, but with mayor-elect Ben Cameron and Glenn Pickens, the son of the Cameron family's live-in servants. The mayoral limousine traverses the extremes of Atlanta's unequal geography. Departing from Peachtree Road, the car passes first through downtown sites of white political and economic power—"Five Points, the epicenter of the business and financial district" (534) and Mitchell Street, where City Hall and the state capitol are situated (535). Only afterward do they enter the "the bowels of the city" (536): southeast Atlanta. Initially, Gibby is no more able to gain a visual "sense" of "those places" on the Southside than he was during his childhood visits. He recalls how "I had been down into the Southeast before, usually with Shem Cater in the Chrysler, to fetch or return one or another of my family's servants, but to *my blind white eyes*, the streets on which the Negroes lived were much like the Negroes themselves: they all looked alike" (535, my emphasis). Having proceeded through slum neighborhoods including

---

5. Bell hooks, "Homeplace: A Site of Resistance," in *Yearning: Race, Gender, and Cultural Politics* (Boston: South End Press, 1990), 42.

"Summerhill, Peoplestown, Joyland" (535), "Mechanicsville and Pittsburgh" (538), the tour terminates in Pumphouse Hill, a block of especially rundown tenements in Cabbagetown. At this point, Cameron discloses the devastating information that, unbeknown to Gibby, prompted the tour in the first place. The mayor-elect tells Gibby that "[y]our family owns" Pumphouse Hill (541). Thus it is that Gibby finally learns and *sees* how his family's privileged existence in Buckhead is built upon rent received from poor black Atlantans. Gibby's mother Olivia—who has "let the money pour in" from Pumphouse Hill despite having "never put a penny of my capital into it"—is finally revealed (to Gibby at least) as an absentee landlord. Gibby's (mind's) eye still cannot quite perceive the tenants themselves. However, he can now trace the relation between the tenants' abstract rent and the material construction of Olivia's (and his) own home. He can even map this nexus of place, race, and real estate on to the makeup of his mother's ostensibly "self-reliant" body—a body that suddenly reveals, in Patricia Yaeger's phrase, "the contradictions inherent in and hidden by elite southern space." As Gibby recalls it, "I thought of . . . what the hopeless misery of those silent, invisible wretches in the cold beds of Pumphouse Hill had bought her, and how little of that misery would ever penetrate these creamy white walls, or her creamy white skin" (543).[6]

For his part, Ben Cameron has earmarked Gibby to take over the Bondurant family business and renovate the Pumphouse Hill property. Cameron has long been telling Gibby that "real estate [is] an honorable way to make a living, and done right, a way to give something back to the community" (276). Frank Bascombe might approve the sentiment. But beyond such platitudes of civic duty, Cameron is also keenly aware of the wider political implications: by renovating Pumphouse Hill, Gibby might yet save a business-oriented city—and a Buckhead-based white power structure—imperiled by the prospect of racial and political unrest. It is, then, a tragic (or melodramatic) irony that Pumphouse Hill's dilapidated tenements are set alight by arsonists on the evening after the limousine tour. Moreover, Olivia has the gall to tell the assembled media that "[i]t's not my property! . . . my son owns it!" (545). Hence, Olivia's status as absentee landlord is never exposed to a wider public

---

6. Patricia Yaeger, *Dirt and Desire: Reconstructing Southern Women's Writing, 1930–1990* (Chicago: University of Chicago Press, 2000), 226. I am borrowing here from Yaeger's discussion of Ellen Gilchrist's story "The President of the Louisiana Live Oak Society," in which, Yaeger notes, "Robert's parents live in a house built from and dependent on the capital . . . wrestled from the ghetto, and yet they define themselves as utterly self-reliant."

gaze, and Gibby is branded a "Buckhead Slum Lord" by the *Atlanta Constitution*. Moreover, at this moment of crisis, Cameron explicitly states his primary obligation to the white power structure. He tells Gibby that "we're letting you hang" (rather than his mother, the supposedly honorable southern belle) in order to save "[a]ll of us out here in Buckhead. To save Buckhead itself, and the way of life that's all we know" (548).

Through the tour from Peachtree Road to Pumphouse Hill, Siddons constructs a vivid narrative cartography of the racial segregation and uneven economic development that characterized Atlanta circa 1961. However, it is worth taking particular note of the narrative twist whereby Cameron asks that Gibby accept his status as "Slum Lord" and social pariah, for this twist will resurface in another troubling turn to the novel's spatial (and racial) politics. But before that, the depiction of one black neighborhood featured during the tour—Summerhill—begins to reveal other problems with the text's politics of place.

Place, Race, and Urban Renewal: Summerhill, 1961–66

Reading *Peachtree Road* alongside nonfictional accounts of Atlanta, it soon becomes apparent that Siddons's Ben Cameron is, as historian Gary Pomerantz notes, "a thinly veiled version of Ivan Allen Jr.," the mayor of Atlanta between 1962 and 1970. Like Allen, Cameron takes office in 1962, having previously been vice-president and president of the city's Chamber of Commerce. As I noted in Chapter 7, Allen instigated the chamber's program to reinvent Atlanta as a "national city"; similarly, Cameron has formulated the "formal plan of growth and progress for the city that he felt would literally transform it into one of the country's great urban centers" (386). Indeed, Cameron's "six-point program" is identical to the "Six-Point Plan" outlined by the Allen-led Chamber in 1961: "keep the public schools open, build a vast new network of local freeways, implement a new program of urban renewal, erect a world-class auditorium-coliseum and stadium, get a rapid-transit system rolling and tell the country about it in an ambitious, if chauvinistic, public relations effort called Forward Atlanta" (393).But Siddons's fictional account is selective in its representation of the historical and geographical *consequences* of Allen's "Six-Point Plan"—particularly the harsh realities of "urban renewal."[7]

7. Gary M. Pomerantz, *Where Peachtree Meets Sweet Auburn: A Saga of Race and Family* (1996; reprint, New York: Penguin, 1997), 526. Allen's Six-Point Plan as "summed up in one piece of literature later published by the Chamber of Commerce" is reprinted in Ivan Allen

As Glenn Pickens drives the limousine through Summerhill in December 1961, Cameron "gesture[s] toward a nest of streets to the right" and informs Gibby that this is "where the new freeway will go through, and where the stadium will go, we hope" (537–38). Thus, three aspects of Cameron's "six-point program"—the proposals to construct freeways, "erect a world-class . . . stadium," and "implement a new program of urban renewal"—coalesce in this corner of southeast Atlanta. When Gibby asks what will happen to the residents of the area, however, Cameron admits that it is a "[g]ood question. I'm sure they'd like to know the answer." Cameron soberly acknowledges that the redevelopment of Atlanta's urban space is inextricable from the racialized problem of residential displacement: "Holy Christ. We can raise eighteen million for a new stadium, and the housing authority can pledge fifty million to wipe out the slums in a decade, but they can't seem to relocate a single black family whose house they knock down." Cameron also implies that, during his mayoralty, urban-planning policy will be reformed to include resident relocation, neighborhood renovation, and new public housing. Surveying Summerhill from the limousine, Cameron tells Gibby: "We've got to do better than this. We've got to do a lot better" (538). Yet when Cameron enters office only a month or so after the journey through Summerhill, any reference to the pernicious effects of the stadium's construction disappears from Gibby's narrative. This is notable because, during the Ivan Allen era, Atlanta Stadium was built adjacent to Summerhill, and "urban renewal" did, as Cameron anticipates in the novel, cause severe displacement of the local black population.

Geographer David Smith has observed that "[t]he strategy adopted by [Atlanta's] city government . . . involved more than urban renewal in the usual sense of specific projects designed to clear and/or rehabilitate areas of dilapidated housing." Atlanta's urban-renewal program was ultimately intended to facilitate the private redevelopment of the declining central business district (CBD). The destruction of mostly black residential neighborhoods and the construction of Atlanta–Fulton County Stadium became part of this larger strategy. As Smith comments, "[t]he growing concentration of severely

---

and Paul Hemphill, *Mayor: Notes on the Sixties* (New York: Simon and Schuster, 1971), 32–34. Siddons met Ivan Allen at a party shortly after the publication of *Peachtree Road*. The ex-mayor complimented Siddons on her novel, but admonished her, "It wasn't a 'Five-Point Plan' I had as mayor, it was a 'Six-Point Plan'" (Pomerantz, *Where Peachtree Meets Sweet Auburn*, 526–27). Perhaps Siddons was too polite to point out that, on this detail, *Peachtree Road* was an accurate fictional "reflection" of historical reality.

deprived people," mostly African Americans, in the slums "around the C.B.D. posed a threat both to existing capital investment and to the profitability of future development."[8] Consequently, as political scientist Clarence Stone explains, "[o]ne of the main objectives of the city's renewal program [was] the creation of buffers between the city's commercial cores and nearby low-income residential areas."[9] It was here that the value became evident of an urban-renewal "strategy [that] involved major public works projects associated with civic 'boosterism' [like] the Atlanta-Fulton County Stadium."[10] Stone emphasizes that the stadium "could have been located elsewhere with less residential dislocation." However, it was deliberately designed and situated as a "buffer" between the corporate real estate of Downtown and the surrounding poor slums (that is, those slums which survived outright demolition).[11] In his memoirs, Ivan Allen describes how he decided that the stadium would be located at Washington-Rawson, an area "cleared of its decaying slum houses." Allen recalled that there were "no immediate plans for use" of Washington-Rawson. In fact, the site remained unused because, as Smith notes, the mayor had made an agreement with "conservative businessmen" and "real estate interests" not to construct public housing on urban renewal land.[12]

By the time Atlanta–Fulton County Stadium was hastily completed in 1965, it had become more than just a "buffer" against the supposed threat that the slums posed to CBD regeneration. Though the stadium itself was built on the Washington-Rawson site, further land was required for car parking, resulting in the displacement of no fewer than 10,000 of the 12,500 residents in nearby Summerhill. Such "urban renewal" of largely black neighborhoods led critics to dub the policy "Negro removal." Yet most critics accepted that, considered on their own terms, the slums deserved to be condemned. Black civil rights organizations such as the Urban League tended to support the razing of slum areas as the "implicit stipulation was that replacement housing

8. David M. Smith, "Inequality in an American City: Atlanta, Georgia, 1960–1970," Occasional Paper No. 17, Department of Geography, Queen Mary College, University of London, January 1981, 51, 48.

9. Clarence N. Stone, *Economic Growth and Neighborhood Discontent: System Bias in the Urban Renewal Program of Atlanta* (Chapel Hill: University of North Carolina Press, 1976), 177.

10. Smith, "Inequality in an American City," 51.

11. Stone, *Economic Growth*, 177–78.

12. Ivan Allen, *Mayor*, 155–56; Smith, "Inequality in an American City," 53. The "conservative businessmen" objected to funds being spent on public housing; the "real estate interests" feared they would lose potential commissions and profits from private development.

would be provided."¹³ But as Smith observes, "[t]he basic problem was the failure to rehouse most of the people displaced by the renewal and redevelopment projects." Between 1958 and 1968, as many as seventy-five thousand black Atlantans were displaced from their homes. Between 1957 and 1967, twenty-one thousand housing units were demolished in central Atlanta—but only five thousand new public housing units were constructed. Ivan Allen himself later observed that in Summerhill circa 1966, "[t]here were around ten thousand poor Negroes crammed into 354 acres." Yet Allen's memoirs do not admit that the new stadium and parking lot had displaced thousands of these poor blacks. Instead, Allen blithely claims that the stadium was "the single structure that signified our arrival as a national city."¹⁴

The historical-geographical reality of "Negro removal" that resulted from the construction of Atlanta–Fulton County Stadium is never represented explicitly in *Peachtree Road*. Instead, Gibby, like Ivan Allen, celebrates the stadium's symbolic status in the development of the "major-league city": "In Atlanta, we were almost precisely where Ben and the Club thought we should be. The new major league stadium was begun and built in a record fifty-one days, and the Milwaukee Braves became the Atlanta Braves, and the NFL Falcons came to town, and we played ball." The fictional narrative echoes Allen's memoirs even more closely when Gibby proudly recalls that, during the 1960s, Atlanta was "the second highest city in the country in terms of new construction" (634). Gibby subsequently launches into an admiring litany of the hotels, malls, office buildings, apartment houses, bars, and restaurants built concurrently with the new stadium. Only when pausing to begin a new paragraph does Gibby mention that "Atlanta's momentum did not come cheap. Near-riots simmered in the bright, hot days and the thick nights" (635).¹⁵

With this reference to "near-riots," the historical-geographical relationship between "urban renewal" and "Negro removal" makes a subterranean reappearance in Gibby's narrative, for Siddons once more seems to base the relevant fictional scene upon an incident from the Allen era. As Charles

13. Stone, *Regime Politics*, 63. On "Negro removal," see Rutheiser, *Imagineering Atlanta*, 154, and Stone, *Regime Politics*, 68.

14. Smith, "Inequality in an American City," 52; Ivan Allen, *Mayor*, 33, 152. Statistics from Frederick Allen, *Atlanta Rising*, 162, and Smith, "Inequality in an American City," 51.

15. "Major league city" was Allen's favorite sporting synonym for "national city" (Pomerantz, *Where Peachtree Meets Sweet Auburn*, 340); see also note 29 below. "During 1964 we had the nation's second greatest gain in the primary index of growth: new construction" (Ivan Allen, *Mayor*, 130).

Rutheiser recounts, "[i]n the summer of 1966, anger with 'negro removal' and the slow pace of replacement housing construction sparked a number of civil disturbances in the area around the stadium." These protests came to a head on 6 September 1966, when a white policeman shot a black robbery suspect in Summerhill. The local population, galvanized by SNCC (the Student Nonviolent Coordinating Committee), gathered to protest at the highly symbolic stadium site. Mayor Allen went to the scene to appeal for calm, "was rocked off the top of a police car as he tried to address the street throng," and eventually "instructed the police to use tear gas."[16]

This is how *Peachtree Road* represents this fraught historical moment: "During one particularly spectacular confrontation he [Mayor Cameron] climbed atop a parked car, a surging sea of angry, frustrated black faces at his feet, his coppery head a target for any murderous fool within a mile radius, and pleaded through a borrowed bullhorn for order. He finally got it—and his photograph in the newspapers of an entire nation—before he was toppled from the car and ended up in Piedmont Emergency with a sprained ankle and a hole in the seat of his pants. But Atlanta did not blossom into flames as Detroit and Watts and Pittsburgh and other cities did in those summers, and as Ben himself said, that was worth a considerable chunk of a mayor's ass" (635). The novel briefly recapitulates the same scene on two other occasions (93, 270). Yet Gibby never explains *why* black Atlantans are protesting, or suggests that the residents of Summerhill had good reason to be aggrieved. As such, *Peachtree Road* elides the historical role that, as Frederick Allen puts it, "his [Mayor Allen's] new stadium might have played in triggering the unrest in Summerhill." Indeed, the novel does not actually locate the "near-riot" in Summerhill. Gibby's most substantial account of the scene is undated and unlocated (634–35); on one of the two other occasions, he recalls that the mayor "stood atop an automobile in Mechanicsville" (270). By fictionally "displacing" Cameron and the "surging sea of angry, frustrated black faces" from Summerhill, *Peachtree Road* further mystifies the problematic relationship between the fictional scene and the historical incident. Moreover, this displacement obscures the dramatic and historical irony of Cameron's words, "[w]e've got to do better than this"—declaimed while driving through Summerhill, past the prospective site of the stadium, in 1961. In reality, by proceeding with the construction of the stadium at the direct expense of Summerhill, and by failing to provide sufficient replacement housing, the mayor of Atlanta failed to "do a

---

16. Rutheiser, *Imagineering Atlanta*, 154; Stone, *Regime Politics*, 70.

lot better" by poor black Atlantans. To the extent that *Peachtree Road* suggests that the mayor single-handedly averted Atlanta's racial (and spatial) problems, Siddons seems to be producing—to adapt Fredric Jameson's formulation—symbolic narrative resolutions to real historical-*geographical* problems.[17]

Certainly, *Peachtree Road*'s depiction of Cameron's actions during the "spectacular confrontation" captures the personal bravery (or folly) of Allen's foray into Summerhill. The local SNCC activist Hosea Williams later recalled, "I couldn't believe some white man had that nerve. . . . He [Allen] had the guts of a lion." However, the implication that the mayor's actions alone prevented Watts-style rioting is the apogee (or nadir) of the novel's hagiographic image of Allen. Indeed, the narrative emphasis on the mayor's heroics, rather than on the "urban spectacle" enacted by the "angry, frustrated" black residents, recalls Lukács' critique of "the Romantic practice . . . of placing 'great men' at the center of . . . historic portrayals and of characterizing them by means of historically attested . . . anecdotes." As the novel's representation of the "near-riot" narrows into a repeated anecdote about the mayor's heroism, the reality of "Negro removal" is further obscured. Ultimately, the historical, material consequences of "rais[ing] eighteen million for a new stadium" and razing a black neighborhood are erased from *Peachtree Road*.[18]

Place, Race, and the "International City": Buckhead, 1970s–80s

Throughout *Peachtree Road*, Gibby regularly turns his disapproving gaze upon the corporate capitalist cityscape of contemporary (i.e., late 1980s) Atlanta. Early on, Gibby observes pithily that "[s]ome of our downtown and midtown structures . . . are very tall. That, to my eye, is all they are: tall." Gibby's dystopian view of the contemporary "megalopolis" gains particular intensity because the "towers of commerce that have made us the hub of the Sunbelt" (7) are no longer restricted to downtown. Gibby's beloved Buckhead has also become a prime site for commercial development.

Early on, Gibby observes that "Buckhead has always been known, proudly, as the wealthiest unincorporated suburb in America." In fact, Buckhead

---

17. Frederick Allen, *Atlanta Rising*, 149; Fredric Jameson, *The Political Unconscious: Narrative as Socially Symbolic Act* (London: Methuen, 1981).

18. Hosea Williams quoted in Pomerantz, *Where Peachtree Meets Sweet Auburn*, 348; Lukács, *The Historical Novel*, 80. David Harvey describes how "urban spectacle[s]" in the 1960s included "[c]ivil rights demonstrations, street riots, and inner city uprisings," and derived from "the seething mill of urban discontent that whirled around the base of modernist urban renewal and housing projects." See Harvey, *The Condition of Postmodernity*, 88.

was officially incorporated into the city of Atlanta in 1952, and Gibby comments that this "remains to many Buckheaders still alive a catastrophe of only slightly less magnitude than the one wrought by General Sherman" (49). Yet it is clear that, from Gibby's perspective, the "catastrophe" of 1952 is as nothing compared to what one might call Buckhead's incorporation into the "international city." Worse, to be incorporated into/by the spatial logic of multinational capital is also to be creatively destroyed. Gibby provides a vivid sketch of developers' scorched-earth policy toward residential Buckhead and its radical reconstruction as an edge city: "along Peachtree Road itself . . . the fine old houses of my youth stood empty or were coming down, falling to prissy, ridiculous, and hugely expensive, ersatz Federal 'townehomes' or thrusting glass condominium towers; to thirty- and forty-story office towers and hotels and great 'mixed-use' developments. . . . To the north, out Peachtree Road into and past Brookhaven . . . another mini city like the one in midtown was rising, its towers squeezed onto land that went, in some instances, for $3 million an acre" (726–27).[19]

The transnational creative destruction of Buckhead's built space by "the Arabs and the Lebanese and the Japanese and Germans and South Americans"—not to mention the "Yankees" (728)—is so voracious that Gibby finds the Bondurant house itself under siege. He observes that "only a scant square block of Peachtree Road where my own home stood was still inhabited by the old houses and their original families. Past us toward downtown not another private home stood" (727). Gibby learns from Carter Rawson, fellow former "Buckhead Boy" turned world-famous real-estate developer, just how zealously national and international speculators have sought his property: "Everybody with any money in all fifty states and about ten countries has been after your place" (757).

In Chapter 3, we saw how Percy's Binx Bolling searches for a metaphysical "spirit-presence of place" that might offer refuge from the proliferation of postsouthern suburbia. Similarly, Gibby Bondurant strives to salvage the mystical "place-magic" ("mine from birth") of residential Buckhead (57). Binx found sanctuary in New Orleans's Garden District; Gibby has been ensconced in the summerhouse at 2500 Peachtree Road since the "Slum Lord" scandal of 1961. But whereas the Garden District circa 1960 remained relatively

19. Rutheiser remarks wryly: "In a rhetorical turn that gives a rather literal twist to [Joseph] Schumpeter's notion of 'creative destruction,' the sacking of Atlanta [by Sherman] is now ritually invoked as point of reference and justification for virtually every municipally sanctioned spasm of demolition and displacement" (*Imagineering Atlanta*, 19).

untouched by real-estate development, 1980s Buckhead's metaphysical "place-magic" is being materially transformed. Hence, as much as Gibby clings to the "scant square block of Peachtree Road," he also retreats into a *mental* space: the 1940s/1950s Buckhead of his memories. He dismisses the new "business district" by focusing his mind's eye upon the old "residential Buckhead . . . insulated from the sweat, smells and cacophony of the city proper, to the south, by layers of money." For Gibby, this exclusive enclave, not the corporate, convention-centered Downtown, is—or was—the authentic Atlanta: "Visitors visit on Peachtree Street. Atlanta lives—or did—on and just off Peachtree Road" (32–33).

Gibby's mental map is most vividly illustrated when he recounts his nightly "run[s] through a landscape that existed forty-odd years ago" (39). During these jogs, Gibby envisions "my own personal Buckhead" by "see[ing] it now through the scrim of childhood" (33). This is a disingenuous point of view in that it allows Gibby to elide his epiphany that the domestic leisure of Buckhead's white elite was built upon the labor and rent capital of black Atlantans. Now, rather than recalling the nexus of place, race, and real estate between Buckhead and southeast Atlanta, Gibby fuzzily invokes "the children in my crowd" following the black "gardeners and yardmen of all these old estates" (40). His mind's eye envisions him "running through the dazzling shower from the hose held by Leroy Pickens, the Camerons' driver." Yet Gibby cannot entirely avert his gaze, or his narrative, from either the (literal) signs of land speculation—"I do not see the Sotheby and Harry Norman and Buckhead Brokers signs" (41)—or the material reality of the buildings themselves. He observes ruefully that "the monolithic and hideous Buckhead Plaza is going up now (unseen, unseen!)" (47).

Clearly, Gibby is scathingly critical of the creative destruction of Atlanta, and especially of residential Buckhead. However, his powerful critique of transnational capitalist redevelopment is based on a selective nostalgia for that era when Atlanta was ruled by "Ben Cameron and his tough, aristocratic new power structure" (393)—a time when Buckhead was still the white elite's residential base. This bias informs Gibby's reluctance to admit any "historical continuities" between the white power structure's invention of a "national city" in the 1960s, and the production of the "international" Atlanta of the 1970s and 1980s.[20]

---

20. On historical continuities in Atlanta's politics of place, see Rutheiser, *Imagineering Atlanta*, 5; also see Chapter 7.

Rutheiser describes how "[t]he wave [of real estate development in Buckhead] turned into a flood following the city's annexation of Buckhead in 1952 . . . a number of the city's major downtown developers assembled large tracts of land for subdivisions, commercial strips, and shopping malls." Evidently, Buckhead's residents had reason to regret the "catastrophe" of 1952. But the pace and scope of creative destruction really increased during the 1960s, when Buckhead "was overwhelmed by . . . strip, community, regional, and super-regional shopping centers." In that decade, records Rutheiser, "local developers in league with national partners built the first office buildings and mixed-use developments along Peachtree and Piedmont Roads." Yet Gibby never mentions any commercial construction in Buckhead *after* Lenox Square Mall, built in 1959 (476), and *before* those hateful "office towers and . . . 'mixed-use' developments" erected during the 1970s and 1980s. In other words, his narrative never suggests that residential Buckhead was *already* being massively redeveloped *during* the "Ben Cameron" era.[21]

By neglecting to depict the commercialization of residential Buckhead during the 1960s, Siddons is able to maintain *Peachtree Road*'s idealized image of Cameron, the Buckhead-based white power structure, and residential Buckhead itself. Instead, Gibby's (decline) narrative emphasizes the creative destruction of residential Buckhead during the 1970s and 1980s. Indeed, Gibby explicitly attributes the decline of his Northside neighborhood to the political downfall of the white power structure. He complains that "the city had eaten Buckhead"— "ever since the decade of Ben and the Club had ended . . . and the political and economic base and mix of the city had changed" (728). The implication is that Buckhead's radical reconstruction is attributable to a *post*-1960s power structure comprising local black politicians and global capital.[22]

Gibby observes that "[t]he city Ben Cameron had left behind him . . . was a city of severely curtailed white influence, aristocratic or otherwise." By the late 1970s, the scions of the white power structure, the "Buckhead Boys" of his own generation, are "by no means the only money in town now, or even the most substantial." This is not only because the economic influence

21. Rutheiser, *Imagineering Atlanta*, 123–24.

22. This emphasis on historical *discontinuities* "generically" defines *Peachtree Road* as a "historical novel" in the classic sense "insofar as it offers (or purports to offer) us no less than the inner experiential feel of times [the Allen era], spaces [residential Buckhead], and perceptual modes [the benevolent worldview of the white power structure] far different, decisively Other, from our own" (Pfeil, "Fiction after History," 51).

of the local Buckhead elite has been superseded by national and global capital. It is also because "political power and governmental influence" (729) has passed to black Atlantans. The black mayor of 1980s Atlanta is none other than Glenn Pickens, the son of the Cameron family's live-in servants and the man who chauffeured Gibby and the mayor-elect in December 1961. More than twenty years later, Pickens is "proving to be a very good mayor indeed . . . an international mayor for an international city." Gibby's words of praise may suggest that Mayor Pickens and contemporary Atlanta gloriously fulfill the "international" rhetoric first deployed by Atlanta's civic boosters in the 1960s. However, Pickens is seen by the old white power structure as "far too inclined to advocate the razing of the city's old homes and businesses to accommodate the inexorable mercenary army of high rises marching north out Peachtree Road" (752). Such is the ill feeling among certain members of the old elite that they see Pickens not as "an international mayor for an international city" but as "Ben Cameron's chauffeur boy" (753).

Gibby is quick to distance himself from such overtly racist views. He also notes that "the fabled Club of the Sixties . . . would be the first to acknowledge [that they had] been dethroned by the very people they sought to attract—and also by those they did not: the businessmen of the world and the concerted Atlanta black community" (751–52). At such points, as Summer notes, Gibby exhibits what reviewer Bob Summer identified as "an ambivalence that enhances his narrator's voice with a perceptive credibility." Gibby even speculates that, if mentally fit, Cameron himself might have found post-1960s Atlanta's "transformation exhilarating" (728).[23] Yet such moments of ambivalence are isolated. Generally, Gibby expresses agreement with the old Buckhead elite's dim view of Atlanta's latest reconstruction: "I *was* glad that he [Cameron] could not see the physical changes in his city" (753). Gibby recites a series of binary oppositions that rhetorically distinguish Ben Cameron's "real city" from Glenn Pickens' "international city": youth/arrogance, ambition/venality, energy/uproar (394). Gibby also posits that Pickens' "megalopolis" no longer provides the ordered, total sense of place that the white power structure's political and economic preeminence (supposedly) guaranteed. He claims that "[i]t would not be a city of unity and purpose and whole-

23. Summer, "*Peachtree Road* Is Journey through Modern Atlanta," M10. By the late 1970s, the ex-mayor is afflicted by amnesia—perhaps a suitable symbol of the novel's omission of Buckhead's redevelopment during the 1960s.

ness of ethos that he [Pickens] straddled. Atlanta was too big for that now, too fragmented, too much a city of parts and factions and interests." Though Gibby justifiably points to suburban white flight as evidence of contemporary Atlanta's racial disunity, he is once again forgetting that 1960s Atlanta, if not so sprawling, was similarly "fragmented" by inequality. Most provocatively of all, Gibby suggests that "in the city proper, the blacks who were left did not move with one body, mind and voice, as Ben and the Club had done, but snarled and jostled in warring packs" (730). Gibby does believe that Pickens will bring political "cohesion" to this concrete jungle—but only because the current mayor was "groomed by Ben Cameron" (730). Disturbingly, this racialized image of social Darwinism ameliorated by white paternalism is merely a portent of the power relationship that Siddons constructs between Cameron and his protégé—a relationship that plots the final twist in *Peachtree Road*'s politics of place.

Presiding over and actively encouraging the transnational capitalist redevelopment of Atlanta in the 1980s, the fictional Pickens approximates Andrew Young, the former civil rights activist who was mayor of Atlanta between 1982 and 1990. As mayor, Young was heavily criticized for sanctioning the razing of historical buildings. He famously dismissed one old house that had become a focus for preservationists as a "hunk of junk," and argued that "Atlanta has no character, we are building it now." Young's antipreservation policy was partly motivated by the belief that, in Rutheiser's words, "Atlanta's historic buildings were inimically bound up with the history of racialized inequality and that to preserve them was to somehow preserve and legitimate the memories of those times along with those spaces." However, it was also in keeping with his "unashamedly Reaganite vision of trickle-down economics" that Young enthusiastically encouraged corporate real-estate development and "gutted neighborhood participation in the planning process." One critic commented that Young "never met a building permit he didn't like": city hall issued twenty thousand building permits within three years of Young's becoming mayor.[24]

Thus it is noteworthy when *Peachtree Road* enacts a *departure* from Pick-

24. Rutheiser, *Imagineering Atlanta*, 186, 182; Frederick Allen, *Atlanta Rising*, 232. It should be noted, however, that Gibby mentions both Andrew Young *and* Glenn Pickens as "young lieutenants" (459) to Martin Luther King in the 1960s. In his perceptive review of the novel, Phil Garner observed that: "When it's time to deal with Atlanta's first black mayor, Maynard Jackson [who served from 1974 to 1982], Siddons chooses to fictionalize him and his times virtually out of existence." See *Atlanta*, December 1988, 62.

ens's fictional image of Young. Gibby discovers that the mayor is *preventing* the razing of the Bondurant house through unique zoning restrictions. However, Pickens is not doing this because he personally wants to protect what remains of white, residential Buckhead from corporate development. Indeed, the mayor warns Gibby: "Ben Cameron was able to save your asses out in Buckhead until he got sick . . . I'm not in the business of saving Buckhead asses." Pickens zones the Bondurant house only because Cameron wanted Gibby to receive belated compensation for his role as patsy in the 1961 "Slum Lord" scandal. Pickens explains to Gibby that "[t]he city owes you. You took a bad beating back then after the [Pumphouse Hill] fire . . . So this is an old debt. But don't thank me, because it's Ben Cameron you owe, not me" (760). *Peachtree Road* thus presents the preservation of Gibby's family home not as a benevolent gesture by Mayor Pickens but as a final heroic flourish from ex-mayor Cameron. In order to celebrate Cameron this one last time, the narrative foregrounds the troubling paternalistic relationship between Cameron and Pickens—troubling not only in the superficial sense that it seems a misleading fictional "reflection" of Andrew Young.[25] The paternalistic maneuverings behind Pickens's ascension to political office become apparent when the black mayor explains to Gibby just why he is willing to enforce zoning restrictions around 2500 Peachtree Road:

> I owe him [Ben Cameron] as much as you do. If I didn't, Buckhead would be solid high rise right now. You think your tax base is anything like what I could make for this city out of that residential real estate out there? No, Ben took me aside when I was getting ready to graduate from high school and said he'd pay my way through college and law school, and take care of my dad for the rest of his life, and he'd make me mayor one day, if I'd do everything he said to, because we were going to have a black mayor as sure as gun's iron, and it ought to be somebody like me . . . And in exchange for all that, I was to spare this little hunk of Buckhead real estate that his and your houses sat on when the developers got after it. (760–61)

---

25. Mayor Young often claimed that his vision of "Public Purpose Capitalism" and "public-private partnership" derived from previous mayors, including Ivan Allen. Indeed, Young praised Allen for transforming Atlanta into a "Big League city" through the construction of Atlanta–Fulton County Stadium. But (New Orleans–born) Young never had a white "mentor" like Allen. See "Andrew Young's State of the City Address, 1989," in Escott and Goldfield, eds., *Major Problems in the History of the American South*, vol. 2, *The New South*, 621–22.

That ex-mayor Cameron is identified as the real force behind the preservation of the Bondurant house further emphasizes that, by contrast, Mayor Pickens is (by his own admission) politically responsible for Buckhead's transformation from "residential real estate" to "solid high rise." Ultimately, Cameron's insistence that Pickens spare "this little hunk of Buckhead real estate" is not only figured as a favor on behalf of the long-suffering Gibby. It is also transfigured into the ex-mayor's last stand against the redevelopment of the white power structure's traditional homeplace—a final act of resistance against the present black mayor's prodevelopment policy.[26]

Toward the end of the novel, while on the way to Lucy's funeral in Oakland Cemetery, Gibby tells Ben's wife Dorothy Cameron that the "preposterous sunstruck towers" of Downtown "might as well be the back of the moon to me" (748–49). It is appropriate that Gibby uses the same lunar spatial metaphor to describe late 1980s Downtown that, circa 1961, he used to describe Pumphouse Hill in Cabbagetown: "This was literally [sic] the back of the moon to me" (539). For finally, both of these built landscapes—the slums of the 1960s and the "international city" of the 1980s—are incomprehensible to Gibby. This may be why Gibby never identifies the (ironic) similarity between the creative destruction of poor, black Summerhill, and the creative destruction of rich, white Buckhead. In the narrative's present, Gibby seems to have regressed into the state of ignorance that he exhibited before the limousine tour of 1961. He admits that he has "not seen Cabbagetown since a bitter cold day more than twenty-five years ago" (6): the day that he discovered the nexus of place, race, and real estate between north and southeast Atlanta. During the 1980s, Gibby is so preoccupied with the razing of residential Buckhead that he shows no awareness that poverty-stricken, black inner-city neighborhoods still exist within the "international city." Instead, Gibby flirts with a rather grotesque sense of place that will allow him to escape "international" Atlanta altogether. He envisions joining Lucy among the "ordered world" of "Atlanta's favored dead" at Oakland Cemetery—the one place where "Old Atlanta" has kept at bay the "trash and tackpots" (4–5).[27]

---

26. Gibby does eventually sell the Bondurant house to Carter Rawson (815)—but only to spite his Aunt Willa, the sole remaining sentient occupant of the house, for Willa's lifelong mistreatment of her late daughter Lucy.

27. We never learn whether the Bondurant family still owns the Pumphouse Hill property in the late 1980s.

A Palimpscestuous Postscript: Downtown

Siddons's ideological affiliation with the white power structure of 1960s Atlanta was made explicit in an essay published in the same year as *Peachtree Road*. In "The Maturing of a City: Atlanta Comes of Age" (1988), Siddons recalled the 1960s from the perspective of her time as a writer and editor for *Atlanta* magazine. She asserts that "Ivan Allen shone over those days like a young sun and was the spokesman for a decade and a generation," and recounts the time when the mayor "stood atop a car during an incipient riot in the black Summerhill neighborhood before he was toppled, talking, talking." As Phil Garner observed pointedly in (of all places) *Atlanta*, "Maturing of a City" extends in "nonfiction form" *Peachtree Road*'s celebratory "central image" of the white power structure.[28]

The reference to *Atlanta* magazine in "Maturing of a City" also recalls the prologue to *Peachtree Road*, where Gibby Bondurant quotes verbatim an article published in one "*Cityscope* magazine." *Cityscope*'s female journalist breathlessly depicts "*the power structure of that youngest and least typical Southern city, the movers and shakers, the 'club'*" who took Atlanta "*to the brink of what became known at the end of the incendiary 1960s as 'the next great international city'*" (13–15). It is possible that, in the figure of the "intense female journalist, who was not one of us [the Buckhead elite] but would have died to be," Siddons signals and even satirizes both her ideological affinity with the white power structure, and her background as a journalist-cum-booster for *Atlanta*. Yet it is telling that, although Gibby regards the *Cityscope* article as "overheated and romantic in the extreme," he also believes it encapsulates "a kind of oversimplified truth" (13). Indeed, Gibby's own narrative, with its hagiographic nostalgia for the "white power structure," can be seen as an epic extension of the *Cityscope* feature.[29]

Extending the somewhat surreal intratextuality of Siddons's writing, "The

---

28. Siddons, "The Maturing of a City: Atlanta Comes of Age," in Dudley Clendinen, ed., *The Prevailing South: Life and Politics in a Changing Culture* (Atlanta: Longstreet Press, 1988), 146, 145; Garner, 63.

29. Going beyond even Mayor Allen's hyperbole, a 1964 article in *Atlanta* magazine declared that major-league baseball would "complete the transformation of Atlanta from a semi-southern into a full-fledged national and international city." See Furman Bisher, "A Major League Boost for the Economy," *Atlanta*, August 1964, 46. Frederick Allen identifies this as the first published reference to Atlanta's supposed "international" status. Anne Rivers's name first appears as a senior editor of *Atlanta* in the December 1964 issue. In the March 1965 issue, she contributed a cover story on the city's building boom.

Maturing of a City" actually quotes almost verbatim numerous passages from Gibby's narrative in *Peachtree Road*. This bizarre self-plagiarism goes even further in *Downtown* (1995). In this novel, Smoky O'Donnell, a former journalist for Atlanta's Chamber of Commerce magazine *Downtown*, quite literally rewrites Gibby's hagiography of Cameron and the Buckhead elite. When Smoky recounts her first encounter with "the legendary Ben Cameron, mayor of Atlanta" and his colleagues at the Commerce Club, she declares without a trace of irony that "[i]n that moment I fell in love with the power structure of the city."[30] The text also reproduces one of the excitable litanies that appears in both *Peachtree Road* and "The Maturing of a City" as Smokey's ode to Old Atlanta (75). By *Downtown*, the language of Siddons and her character-narrators has become increasingly interchangeable and broadly indistinguishable from the breathless rhetoric of the city's boosters.

Most disquieting, though, is *Downtown*'s (double) take on the nexus of place, race, and real estate in 1960s Atlanta. In 1967, Smoky joins photographer Lucas Geary for her first trip into southeast Atlanta. Smoky and Geary take the same geographical—and narrative—route that Gibby, Cameron, and Pickens took in 1961. This time, it is Geary rather than Cameron who astonishes the narrator with his knowledge of "the geography and ethnology of these dismal black habitats" (167). But as we have seen, southeast Atlanta's "geography and ethnology" altered radically between December 1961 and the summer of 1967. Yet linguistically there are only slight differences between what Cameron and Geary say while passing through Summerhill—most obviously, in grammatical tense. In historical-geographical terms, however, these shifts have significant semantic ramifications. When mayor-elect Cameron "gestured toward a nest of streets to the right" in 1961, Gibby gazed upon "miserable little houses" (537). When Geary "gesture[s] to the right" in 1967, Smoky catches "a glimpse of the blue bowl of the new stadium." Whereas Gibby asked Cameron "[w]here will those people go?" (538), Smoky asks Geary "[w]here did the people go?" (168). In 1961, Cameron admitted that the stadium would be built on the site of a black neighborhood but said that he had no idea where the residents who lived on the site would be relocated. In 1967, Geary, repeating Cameron's words almost exactly but in the past tense, is unable to say what did happen to the displaced residents.

Geary does refer to a mayoral initiative to construct new public housing

---

30. Anne Rivers Siddons, *Downtown* (1994; reprint, London: Warner Books, 1995), 142, 76. All subsequent page references will be incorporated into the main text.

and regenerate those communities that have survived: "Ben Cameron has started, but it's going to take way too long." Yet even after the Summerhill riot of September 1966, the Allen administration's postprotest goals—"neighborhood improvements" and "an adequate supply of new low- and moderate-income housing"—faltered. In November 1966, the mayor appointed a Housing Resources Committee to oversee the construction of seventeen thousand new units of public housing over the next five years. Allen also included Summerhill—indeed, the entire Southside—in the federally funded Model Cities scheme. However, once "the threat of civil disordered receded," and influenced by "worries in the business community that subsidized housing would serve as a magnet for the poor and hasten the day that Atlanta would become a black majority city," the Allen administration returned to its pre-1966 policy. Only a few public housing units were built in Peoplestown. To answer Smoky's question, "Where did the people go?"—southeast Atlanta's displaced persons continued to gravitate toward the remaining, overcrowded slums. The result was that "conditions in the Model Cities zone deteriorated further."[31]

It is also notable that the otherwise garrulous Geary never mentions the riots of September 1966, even though he and Smoky are driving through Summerhill in the summer of 1967. Geary observes that "Atlanta's going to be lucky if somebody doesn't literally light a fire under it this summer" (168), yet overlooks the historical riots in Summerhill *last* summer. *Downtown* does seem to allude to Mayor Allen's encounter with the Summerhill rioters on 6 September 1966 when Smoky recapitulates *Peachtree Road*'s anecdote about the mayor's heroism. This time, the incident is at last (as it never is in *Peachtree Road*) located in Summerhill, but even now Smoky only refers vaguely to a "past incendiary summer" (179), rather than the *last* incendiary summer. To further mystify matters, Smoky's sometime paramour Brad Hunt situates what is apparently the same incident "down in Vine City a few years ago" (141). Finally then, *Downtown*'s "palimpscestous" relation to *Peachtree Road* further exposes the historical-geographical lacunae lurking within Siddons's (meta)narrative cartography of Atlanta.[32]

31. Stone, *Regime Politics*, 72–73, and Rutheiser, *Imagineering Atlanta*, 154.
32. I am adapting this term from Tim Crimmins's work on the "palimpscestuous" historical geographies of Atlanta. See Tim Crimmins, "The Atlanta Palimpsest: Stripping Away the Layers of the Past," *Atlanta Historical Journal* 26 (1982): 13–32.

In 1998, Anne Rivers Siddons moved away from Atlanta. She explained to the *Atlanta Journal-Constitution* that "Atlanta had a very specific feel to it in the 60s. It doesn't have that feel anymore." For Siddons, Atlanta had lost its sense of place because "[a]nything at all left of what the city was when it was neighborhoods has been torn down." Symbolically enough, developer Blaine Kelley had recently submitted an application for permission to raze the 1924 Georgian Revival house that had served as Siddons's model for the Bondurant mansion in *Peachtree Road*. Kelley planned to build condominiums on the site. Siddons moved to Charleston because, she said, "more historic buildings have been saved here [Charleston] than in any other big city. And here they celebrate the past. They don't pretend it never happened." That prototypical Atlanta land speculator Scarlett O'Hara would surely have disapproved of Siddons's gravitating to those "boring" Old South cities, Charleston and Savannah. Gibby Bondurant, though, would understand.[33]

33. See Don O'Briant, "Anne Rivers Siddons: Novelist Counting on New Surroundings to Refresh Her Writing," *Atlanta Journal-Constitution*, 25 June 1998, D1; and O'Briant, "Siddons: I Don't Want to Live in This Mess," *Atlanta Journal-Constitution*, 25 May 1997, K3. Siddons told O'Briant, "I gravitate now to the graceful, slower, older cities that won't change like Charleston or Savannah." Compare this statement with Scarlett's opinion that "Atlanta couldn't possibly be so boring as Charleston and Savannah had been." Mitchell, *Gone with the Wind*, 139.

9. Placing the Postsouthern "International City": Atlanta in Tom Wolfe's *A Man in Full*

The publication of Tom Wolfe's *A Man in Full* in November 1998 focused attention upon Atlanta as Anne Rivers Siddons's *Peachtree Road*, for all its popularity, never did—indeed, as no novel had since *Gone with the Wind*. A little over ten years earlier, Wolfe's ambitious and commercially successful debut novel *The Bonfire of the Vanities* (1987) had been heralded for its "brilliant evocation of New York's class, racial, and political structure in the 1980s." When news emerged that Wolfe's long-awaited follow-up would similarly analyze the social forces at work in Atlanta, and that the U.S. hardback first edition print run would be 1.2 million copies, there was a sense that this was more than a merely literary phenomenon. *A Man in Full* was a cultural and economic event, and nowhere more so than in Atlanta itself.[1]

At one level, *A Man in Full* became prime cultural capital: local boosters saw the novel as a tool to promote tourism and their own image of the "international city." Despite prepublication rumblings about the novel's controversial contents, the Atlanta Convention & Visitors Bureau invited the author to breakfast because "[w]e have a cultural tourism initiative in this city [and w]e feel Tom Wolfe is certainly a major novelist with a blockbuster book coming out this fall." As an example of how "[c]ultural tourism [was] winning out over a self-conscious image" in Atlanta, more than one booster noted how Savannah residents "forgot all the anger" toward John Berendt's *Midnight in the Garden of Good and Evil* (1994) when "they saw how much tourism they were getting." As sociologist John Shelton Reed observed, this was "the old Atlanta spirit!" Nor did it go unnoticed that Wolfe had turned his fictional focus upon Atlanta after his big book about New York, *the* "global city." The Brooklyn-based cultural critic Nelson George chided Atlantans for expressing anxiety about *A Man in Full*: "Come on, now. Wolfe wrote about Atlanta like it was a major city in this world."[2]

---

1. Quote from *Publishers Weekly* on the back cover of Tom Wolfe, *The Bonfire of the Vanities* (1987; reprint, London: Picador, 1990).

2. Maria Saporta, "ACVB to Welcome Author of New Controversial Book," *Atlanta Journal-*

But in the months before publication, many civic leaders and boosters remained implacably worried that Wolfe's novel would damage Atlanta's carefully honed image as an "international city." The Buckhead Coalition, a business group led by Sam Massell—the ex-mayor who had introduced the slogan "the world's next great city" in 1971—withdrew Wolfe's invitation to speak at their annual meeting when advance reports suggested that the novel was an exercise in "Buckhead bashing." There was particular concern regarding rumors that Wolfe paid close attention to real-estate development. Commentators in the *Atlanta Journal-Constitution* speculated as to which of the local developers had provided the model for Wolfe's mooted central protagonist. John Portman commented, "I'm sure his [Wolfe's] characters are composites," while fellow "real estate baron Charles Ackerman, who met with Wolfe several times," admitted that "[w]e've kidded about who's in the book at parties." But other developers were more obviously perturbed: Portman's great rival Tom Cousins "refused to comment, remember[ing] how Wolfe skewered New York bond traders in *The Bonfire of the Vanities*" and fearing that Atlanta real-estate developers would suffer a similar fate.[3]

The novel also prompted skeptical discussion about Atlanta's continuing status as a literary "nonplace." The city's limited presence in southern and American letters jarred with its chiefly economic claims to "international" status. In his review of *A Man in Full*, Reed noted the contrast between the "World-Class, Major-League City" announced on signs at Hartsfield International Airport, and the paucity of fictional representations of Atlanta. Reed sagely noted that "all this coverage [of *A Man in Full* in the *Journal-Constitution*] could only remind readers how long it has been since the last bestseller about this pushy, acquisitive New South city—which raises the question of why Atlanta produces or even attracts so few good writers, which raises the question of what 'world-class' really means." In the *Journal-Constitution* itself,

---

Constitution, 27 October 1998, B3; former city-planning director Leon Eplan quoted in Don O'Briant, "A Wolfe at Our Door?: Writer's Friends Say Atlanta Will Emerge Unscathed from New Novel about Race and Real Estate," *Atlanta-Journal Constitution*, 24 September 1998, D1; John Shelton Reed, review of *A Man in Full*, by Tom Wolfe, *Southern Cultures* 5, no. 2 (summer 1999), http://www.unc.edu/depts/csas/socult/revs/sc52rev1.htm; Nelson George quoted in Don O'Briant, "*Full* Visit: Lots of Dining, No Whining: Where's the Mayor? Bill Campbell Has Been Noticeably Absent at Wolfe Gatherings," *Atlanta Journal-Constitution*, 20 November 1998, G6.

3. Saporta, "ACVB to Welcome Author of New Controversial Book," B3; O'Briant, "A Wolfe at Our Door?" D1.

there emerged an unusual air of introspection, even self-flagellation, when Don O'Briant invited novelists and prominent citizens to give their views as to why "Atlanta has been largely ignored by the literati." Siddons reiterated her nostalgia for an earlier Atlanta, while another local novelist, Terry Kay, criticized the sense of impermanence that arose in "a city that is continually destroying itself."[4]

Though Kay's words seem bracingly scathing when compared to the boosters' rhetoric, they imply that the large-scale real-estate redevelopment or (to use a term Kay hints at) creative destruction of Atlanta is inherently antithetical to "serious" or even interesting fiction. Tom Wolfe evidently disagreed with this view. As O'Briant put it, Wolfe "practically salivated over the prime literary territory he discovered" in the city. With characteristic hubris, the author himself commented that "[t]here should be 25 or 50 novels about Atlanta by now. What are these novelists doing?"[5]

As it transpired, Cousins's concerns were not unfounded. Wolfe does use his man at the center, real-estate magnate Charlie Croker, to emphasize the role of land speculation and real-estate development in metropolitan Atlanta. This chapter considers how *A Man in Full* represents the capitalist production of place in the so-called international city. I will draw upon social and spatial theorists such as Fredric Jameson and Manuel Castells to elucidate Wolfe's investigation of Atlanta's "international" image: an image that has (as we saw in Chapter 7) been largely defined by the boosters, according to the city's burgeoning role within a finance-capitalist world-system. This chapter also considers Wolfe's depiction of the local and material politics of place that result from the speculative development and division of Atlanta's social geography.

I want to begin by considering an important scene in which Charlie Croker observes Atlanta from his private plane. The flight path of the Gulfstream Five (G-5) charts how, as Charles Rutheiser has observed, "the cutting edge of [land] speculation has shifted" away from Downtown and Midtown into "the outer tier of metropolitan counties," where "edge cities" have risen. But more interestingly, this panoramic set piece also suggests how Charlie's *visual* sense of Atlanta is inextricable from his status as a capitalist developer.[6]

4. Reed, review of *A Man in Full*; O'Briant, "Looking for Atlanta," *Atlanta Journal-Constitution*, 30 October 1998, K1.

5. O'Briant, "Looking for Atlanta," K1; O'Briant, "Full Visit," G6.

6. Rutheiser, *Imagineering Atlanta*, 77.

Mapping MXDs from a G-5: Charlie Croker's Visual Sense of Place

When Charlie first looks down from the window of the G-5, he consciously focuses upon the towers of Downtown, Midtown, and Buckhead because these (phallic) structures emphasize his exclusive status as one of the powerful (male) producers of Atlanta's corporate cityscape:[7]

> Charlie knew them [the skyscrapers] all by sight. He knew them not by the names of their architects—what were architects but neurotic and "artistic" hired help?—but by the names of their developers. There was John Portman's seventy-story glass cylinder, the Westin Peachtree Plaza, flashing in the sun. (Portman was smart; he was his own architect.) There was Tom Cousins's twin-towered 191 Peachtree . . . There was Charlie's own Phoenix Center; and, over there, his MossCo Tower; and over there, his TransEx Palladium. . . . Many was the time that the view from up here in the G-5, looking down upon the towers and the trees, had filled him with an inexpressible joy. *I did that! That's my handiwork! I'm one of the giants who built this city!*[8]

Fredric Jameson has stated that, under the postmodern cultural logic of late capitalism, "aesthetic production today has become integrated into commodity production generally" and that, "[o]f all the [postmodern] arts, architecture is the closest constitutively to the economic, with which, in the form of commissions and land values, it has a virtually unmediated relationship." Such an argument seems substantiated by Charlie's dismissive view of the architect and his celebration of the capitalist developer. From Charlie's perspective, the architect is less an artist than commissioned "help," while Atlanta's towers are evacuated of any aesthetic, auratic quality by the developer's fetishizing gaze. Indeed, the architectural artwork has been superseded by monumental mixed-use developments (MXDs) attributed entirely to the developers themselves, "the Creators of Greater Atlanta" (69). Tellingly, Charlie admires the man whom Jameson deems the doyen of postmodern hyperspace, John Portman—"a businessman as well as an architect and a

---

7. All of the main protagonists in *A Man in Full*, except Charlie's ex-wife Martha, are male. Hence, ways of seeing Atlanta in the novel are expressed through what the feminist geographer Gillian Rose has termed "the masculine gaze." In this chapter, I will emphasize that this masculine gaze is much more powerful—indeed, proprietorial—when augmented by economic power. See Rose, *Feminism and Geography: The Limits of Geographical Knowledge* (Cambridge, U.K.: Polity Press, 1993), Chapter 5.

8. Tom Wolfe, *A Man in Full* (London: Jonathan Cape, 1998), 63. All subsequent page references will be incorporated into the main text.

millionaire developer, an artist who is at one and the same time a capitalist in his own right"—precisely because Atlanta's preeminent developer is also "his own architect."⁹

When Charlie "look[s] away from the buildings and out over the ocean of trees," however, he is forced to acknowledge that Atlanta is populated by *people,* and that these people do not reside in the corporate "islands" of Downtown and Midtown. Rather, "most of them" (63) live in the suburbs beneath all those trees—thus obscured from Charlie's omniscient gaze. But if Charlie cannot *see* the suburbs of Greater Atlanta, he can *mentally* map them. This is because Charlie himself was involved in their development; he rapturously recalls "[h]ow fabulous the building booms had been" in "those subdivided hills and downs and glens and glades" (63–64). As the semantic fusion of "subdivision" and "hills" subtly suggests, Nature has been penetrated by—coopted to—the capitalist development of Atlanta's residential real estate.

Charlie is also well aware that "most of them [the residents of Greater Atlanta] are white," whereas "[f]ewer than 400,000 people lived within the Atlanta city limits, and almost three-quarters of them were black" (63). But the developer clinically constructs his vision of both commercial and residential Atlanta according to property values. It is thus hardly surprising that, while Charlie concentrates his omniscient gaze upon Downtown's corporate towers, or mentally maps the suburban landscape of Greater Atlanta, he never focuses his (mind's) eye upon the unprofitable, profoundly racialized inner-city.

Charlie's gaze only shifts away from the suburban treetops when the plane turns and he sees Perimeter Center, "the nucleus around which an entire edge city . . . had grown" (64). Charlie's attention is engaged by Perimeter Center because he has begun to build his own edge city in Cherokee County, north of Atlanta. The project got underway when Charlie tried to purchase 150 acres of rural real estate, only to discover that speculators had already bought up south Cherokee, transforming the "trees and pastures" into "investor land." As Charlie's ex-wife Martha explains, this is "land that's too valuable to be devoted to farming or timber but not yet ready for developing. So investors buy it for a song, like Charlie thought he was going to, and then they just sit on it, waiting for the time when they can sell it for a big price for development" (511). Because land values have been inflated by such speculation, Charlie found that 150 acres would "cost approximately $4 million" (595).

---

9. Jameson, *Postmodernism,* 4–5, 44. Portman coauthored the tellingly titled *The Architect as Developer* (1976).

Wolfe here suggests the extent to which agricultural production in traditional, rural north Georgia has been replaced by finance-capitalist land speculation in contemporary, metropolitan Atlanta. To put it another way, the Agrarian sense of place, and of time, has been usurped. In "The Hind Tit," his contribution to *I'll Take My Stand,* Andrew Lytle attacked what he saw as an "effort to urbanize the farm . . .to convince the farmer that it is time, not space, which has value." Lytle optimistically hoped this "industrial" scheme would fail. In *A Man in Full,* however, preemptive speculation in the (sub)urban expansion of Atlanta into previously rural areas has produced precisely that form of "abstract" sociospatial relations that Lytle attacked, the "absentee-landlordism of capitalism." Moreover, the economic abstraction of Cherokee's former farm land is compounded by the fact that finance-capitalist property speculation is divorced from any mode of production, agricultural or otherwise; as Jameson argues via David Harvey, it is solely "oriented towards the expectation of future value . . . future profits from the use of the land." Finally then, and *pace* Lytle, rural space *has* been (de)valued by time—the future time of finance-capitalist profits from "investor land."[10]

Viewing this scene in relation to a familiar southern literary landscape, and recalling Walker Percy's words from a 1986 essay, one can say that large-scale land speculation and development has moved beyond the "gleaming high-rises of Atlanta" itself into "O'Connor country."[11] In Chapter 7 we saw how, in Flannery O'Connor's short story "The Artificial Nigger" (1955), Mr. Head defines a pastoral sense of place in his all-white home county in terms of its difference from black, urban Atlanta. At the end of the story, after a day-long encounter with the Atlanta enemy, Head and his grandson gratefully return to the rural, racial refuge that is their home. But in 1990s Georgia, the geographical boundary between Atlanta and the outlying counties of O'Connor country has been blurred by real-estate speculation. Furthermore, Charlie finally acquires the required acreage for his Concourse project by co-opting the white southern racism of Head's spiritual descendants. In unlikely cahoots with Ku Klux Klan member Darwell Scruggs (and populist black politician Andre Fleet), Charlie simulates a KKK rally and a subsequent civil rights march "protesting racism and de facto segregation in this old rural county that's practically all white" (511). This pseudoevent makes "the national news on television for a couple of nights" (510) and serves to

---

10. Lytle, "The Hind Tit," 211, 243; Jameson, "The Brick and the Balloon," 43.
11. Percy, "Novel Writing in an Apocalyptic Time," 166–67. See also Chapter 7 above.

devalue the investor land, enabling Charlie to buy it up at a knockdown price. If Wolfe's plot device seems improbable, we might usefully see it as an example of postsouthern parody—albeit with serious implications for the traditional southern "sense of place." The familiar rural racism of O'Connor's Head is played out in desultory, stylized fashion by the latecomer Scruggs; even then, the Klan's stand for white racial (and spatial) purity is exploited by a capitalist developer. Here is an irony that Scruggs does not appear to understand and that Head would have hated: if racial integration does not destroy Georgia's all-white rural enclaves, Atlanta real-estate development will. For not only Cherokee, but also Paulding and Forsyth Counties, are becoming metropolitan Atlanta.[12]

Yet Charlie receives his comeuppance for his shady dealings in rural real estate. Since he completed the construction of Croker Concourse, the developer's original speculations in Atlanta's spatial "futures" market have proven awry. Charlie complains that "[a] few years down the line somebody would make a fortune off what he had put together . . . but for now—*too far north, too far* from the old city, Atlanta itself" (65). Suddenly, the sight of his failing edge city reminds Charlie that his major creditors, PlannersBanc, are threatening to repossess all of his Atlanta properties—including the Concourse itself. The developer's gaze is no longer so imperious: "Did he dare open his eyes and look down? He didn't want to, but he couldn't help himself. Just as he feared, the G-5 was in the perfect spot for an aerial view of Croker Concourse. There it was . . . a preposterously lonely island sticking up out of that ocean of trees. Croker's folly!" (64–65). Charlie's proprietorial perspective on metropolitan Atlanta has been rendered so precarious by the prospect of bankruptcy and repossession that he is glad when the G-5 finally heads south to an old place—the neoantebellum sanctuary of his plantation, Turpmtime (to which I will turn later in this chapter).

Jameson has posited that "in the realm of the spatial, there does seem to exist something like an equivalent of finance capital, indeed a phenomenon intimately related to it, and that is land speculation." I have tried to show how the speculative shenanigans over investor land on the northern edge of metropolitan Atlanta exhibit this equivalence. I want now to focus on Charlie's

---

12. Land speculation on the rural, northern fringe of metropolitan Atlanta in the 1990s was such that one developer secured options on one-fifth of the land in Paulding County. Development included "the construction of high-priced luxury housing" in "the longtime Klan stronghold" of Forsyth County. See Rutheiser, *Imagineering Atlanta*, 77.

dealings with PlannersBanc, for here we find a further, deeper relation between (global) finance-capitalism and (local) land speculation.[13]

The Forty-ninth Floor of PlannersBanc Tower and the Space of Flows

Atlanta-based PlannersBanc supplied the loans that funded Croker Concourse. In total, PlannersBanc loaned $515 million (42) to Croker Global at a time when "big loans were spoken of as 'sales'" (44). In the "palmy days" when those loan "sales" were arranged,[14] the bank provided a forty-ninth-floor room with a view that, much like the G-5, indulged Charlie's omniscient, proprietorial gaze: "beyond the glass window walls, always exquisitely curtained against glare, all of Atlanta . . . was laid out before him. *(It's all yours, Charlie)*" (46). But the debt-ridden developer is no longer invited to the lavish confines of the executive floor. Charlie's descending status within PlannersBanc's customer hierarchy is symbolically enacted when the bank's Real Estate Asset Management Department conducts its emergency meeting with the developer in a "cunningly seedy and unpleasant" (36) room on only the thirty-ninth floor. At the start of this meeting, PlannersBanc's senior loan officer, Raymond Peepgass, observes of Charlie "[t]he fool seemed to think he was still one of those real estate developers who own the city of Atlanta" (35). The emergency meeting is designed to disabuse Charlie of this possessive attitude toward the city. Most explicitly, the Real Estate Asset Management team demands that Charlie sell some of his properties to start paying back the loans. But the bank also announces its dissatisfaction—and asserts its own superiority within the visual economy of Atlanta's corporate power structure—by obscuring Charlie's previously privileged, proprietorial view of the city from PlannersBanc Tower: "he should have been able to look out through the plate-glass wall and seen much of Midtown Atlanta. . . . But he couldn't. . . . It was the glare. He and his contingent had been seated so that they had to look straight into it" (36).

When the recalcitrant Charlie continues to default on the loans, PlannersBanc ups the pressure by focusing its own proprietorial gaze upon Croker Concourse itself. Tricked into watching a fake promotional video for his edge

13. Jameson, "The Brick and the Balloon," 26.
14. Wolfe may have based PlannersBanc's troubles with Croker on the "nonperforming" real-estate-loan crisis at Citizens and Southern Bank in 1978. The crisis derived from "the wide-open days when every officer in the bank was authorized to lend the legal maximum of $10 million without so much as a supervisor's okay." See Allen, *Atlanta Rising*, 203.

city, Charlie is subjected to PlannersBanc's panoptical (re)possessive view of his under-occupied MXD: "Now the camera lingered lovingly on the tower itself. . . . Looking through the window on this side you could see through the window wall on the far side . . . floor after floor after floor . . . because there were no tenants in them" (594). By this point, Charlie is deeply depressed by the commercial failure of the Concourse project and the prospect of repossession and bankruptcy. When the lawyer Roger White visits the developer's office on the thirty-ninth floor of Croker Concourse and comments upon the "[s]pectacular view!" (553), Charlie responds in an uncharacteristically reflective manner: "If you look at Atlanta real estate long enough, you'll notice there was a time, not all that long ago, when folks didn't care about views one way or the other. Views came cheap as the air and a lot cheaper than dirt. Then . . . folks discovered views, and that gave everybody one more thing to get competitive about" (553–54).

Charlie's despondency reveals that PlannersBanc's merciless financial pressure has finally destroyed his own possessive gaze. But his rueful musings also help us to understand another dimension to the capitalist production of place in Atlanta. This process has gone beyond the financial valuation of land ("dirt," in Charlie's down-home rubric) as real estate; beyond the Marxist problem of ground rent; and even beyond the material construction of MXDs. In what might be seen as a variation on Guy Debord's famous declaration that even the image has become integral to capitalist commodity exchange in "the society of the spectacle," Charlie suggests that people's optical experience of the city has been infiltrated by the commodity logic of land speculation— that the *visual sense* (of place) itself has narrowed to "spectacular views" of "Atlanta real estate." This is a telling critique coming from a man who, moving and working within the vertiginous cityscape of corporate Atlanta, has long since internalized the speculative, competitive spatial economy of "spectacular views" as his own existential-visual sense of place. If, as Roger observes, Charlie waxes like "the Old Philosopher" (554), it is because he not only stands to lose the property and capital he has accrued through land speculation; he also stands to lose his very way of seeing the city, even his way of being-in-the-world.[15]

Situated amid the prime corporate real estate of Atlanta, PlannersBanc Tower's symbolic capital serves as a material, spatial sign of PlannersBanc's

---

15. Guy Debord, *The Society of the Spectacle* (1967; reprint, New York: Zone Books, 1995).

immense resources of finance-capital.¹⁶ But there is one moment in *A Man in Full* when PlannersBanc Tower seems peculiarly *im*material. This is when, during a meeting of the Real Estate Asset Management Department, Ray Peepgass finds himself looking "[t]hrough the glass inner wall of [an] office": "he could look through other glass walls, into other offices, in toward the very core of the forty-ninth floor. And everywhere he looked, he could see the eerie luminous rectangles of computer screens, and across those screens blipped the two hundred to three hundred *billion* dollars that moved through Planners-Banc every day" (238). PlannersBanc's window walls effect an optical illusion: the erasure of the forty-ninth floor's local, material geography. The divisions between offices appear to have vanished. In this moment, Ray, despite working at the bank for years, loses any familiar physical or visual sense of place.

I suggest that Ray's dislocation arises because the glass walls of Planners-Banc Tower express, in barely mediated architectural form, what Jameson calls "the fundamental source of all abstraction," the money form: more particularly, the bank's dealings in massive amounts of international yet placeless finance-capital.¹⁷ Looking at the figures on the screens, Ray tries to comprehend the bank's daily billion-dollar dealings in material, spatial terms—"*mov[ing] through* PlannersBanc every day." The problem is that, as Jameson has observed, finance capital "separates from the 'concrete context' of its productive geography," becoming a "second degree" abstraction of the money form, which "always was abstract in the first and basic sense." So, unlike capital abstracted to only the first degree, the financial capital that Ray "sees" is not represented by any *material* sign, such as gold or paper money. Nor does it "move through" any physical location ("concrete context") in PlannersBanc—except as *numerical* signs on the computer screens (that is, if a computer screen "can properly be regarded as a place").¹⁸

In this charged moment, then, the supposedly solid architectural space of PlannersBanc Tower seems to have melted into air. At the very least, the

16. "Symbolic capital" is Pierre Bourdieu's term. See Harvey, *The Condition of Postmodernity*, on how symbolic capital, as "the collection of luxury goods attesting the taste and distinction of the owner," is actually transformed "money capital." I would add the qualification that, while PlannersBanc Tower does attest to "the taste and distinction of the owner," the bank does not work "deliberately to conceal" but rather flagrantly advertises (to customers like Charlie), its "money capital" resources (Harvey, *The Condition of Postmodernity*, 77–78).

17. Jameson, "The Brick and the Balloon," 25; see also 44 on the "abstract dimension or materialist sublimation of finance capital" in postmodern glass towers.

18. Jameson, "Culture and Finance Capital," in *The Cultural Turn: Selected Writings on the*

building appears to have attained a "second sense" of placelessness that approximates the "second degree" abstraction of finance-capital itself: the (albeit illusory) dematerialization of the forty-ninth floor's office space is compounded by the placelessness of figures on the screens. All told, Ray's momentarily defamiliarized view of the forty-ninth floor shows him that PlannersBanc is less a visible, physical locus (PlannersBanc *Tower* in Midtown Atlanta) than a node within the immaterial, transnational matrix of technologically mediated finance-capital exchange. To employ Manuel Castells's distinction, the forty-ninth floor is less a "space of places" than a "space of flows" within "a global network of capital flows."[19]

This brings us to Atlanta's status as an "international city." PlannersBanc's evident role in what Castells calls the "internationalization of the process by which capital circulates [through] widespread utilization of new information technologies" seems to bear out the boosters' rhetorical claims that Atlanta is an "international city." Indeed, the bank has semiotically shed its provincial "Old South" image, changing its name from the Southern Planters Bank and Trust Company to perform a more suitably *post*southern, "international" identity. Adopting the compound fashion of "NationsBank, SunTrust, BellSouth" and others, "PlannersBanc" is intended "to show how cosmopolitan, how international, how global [the bank] had become" (37–38). But such a definition of "international(ization)" is entirely economic, tied to the "international financial markets themselves, increasingly working in their own sphere according to a logic distinct from that of any national economy"—and distinct from *Atlanta's* local economy or social geography. In 1936, Allen Tate attacked a form of "finance capitalism . . . top heavy with a crazy jigsaw network of exchange value"; Tate was dismayed by the disorienting effect that this "remote" system had upon individual lives. Yet Tate could hardly have imagined PlannersBanc Tower's abstract "space of flows"—the apotheosis of placelessness in an "international city" increasingly defined by global finance-capital exchange.[20]

It is important to qualify that, however "placeless" the finance-capital in which PlannersBanc deals, such abstract economic power does impress

---

Postmodern, 1983–1998 (London: Verso, 1998), 142; Harvey, *Justice, Nature, and the Geography of Difference*, 246.

19. Jameson, "Culture and Finance Capital," 142; Manuel Castells, *The Informational City*, 348, 311.

20. Castells, *The Informational City*, 310–11, 339; Tate, "Notes on Liberty and Property," 115.

itself upon Atlanta's material geography. I have already cited the monumental case of PlannersBanc's own Midtown tower, which Castells might explain as an example of "the increasing tension between places and flows." In *The Informational City*, Castells emphasizes that, even though the *organization* of finance-capital exchange is placeless, *control* of finance-capital exchange is place-specific. Even if, as Castells suggests, Atlanta still seems regional by comparison with New York, the city's growing role in the centralized control of transnational finance-capital is revealed in "Manhattanized" towers like PlannersBanc. PlannersBanc Tower, then, is not simply symbolic capital *signifying* finance-capital; it also locates the *control* of finance-capital. Certain areas of Atlanta—Downtown, Midtown, and Buckhead—have thrived upon the dialectic between local, material place and transnational, abstract capital flows.[21]

One can make further connections between global finance-capital and local land speculation, between the abstract "space of flows" and the material "space of places," in *A Man in Full*. For PlannersBanc's involvement in billion-dollar exchanges of capital enhances the bank's own role in the production of Atlanta's corporate space *beyond* its Midtown tower. The most notable example of PlannersBanc's investment in Atlanta is, of course, Croker Concourse. Indeed, it is global capital speculation that makes PlannersBanc a *more* significant force in the Atlanta real-estate market than Charlie Croker. Whereas the rebranding of the "Southern Planters Bank and Trust Company" legitimately referred to the bank's dealings in global capital, "Croker Global" is an egotistical, entirely performative misnomer: as the Real Estate Asset Management Department meeting reveals, Charlie has no overseas operations (51). Despite Croker Global's synergetic expansion into wholesale food production, the corporation's capital resources are measly compared to those of the bank. PlannersBanc accrued multimillion-dollar debts through its disastrous dealings with Charlie and other developers—and yet the bank's resources are such that it is able to write off those debts, even as it prepares to seize Croker Global's various properties. Ultimately, it is this "international" economic power that enables PlannersBanc to exert its omniscient, possessive gaze over Charlie and his edge city.[22]

---

21. Castells, *The Informational City*, 171, 169–70, 346. See also Rutheiser, *Imagineering Atlanta*, 125, on Atlanta's "Manhattanization."

22. Rather aptly, PlannersBanc's international investments are never geographically located, but Peepgass's stewardship of a $4.1 billion loan package for Finnish government bonds (161) gives a hint of the extent and value of such investments.

From the Forty-ninth Floor to Underground Atlanta(s)

Discussing the "postmodern cartographies" produced by leftist cultural critics in recent years, Brian Jarvis has observed that "[Fredric] Jameson and [David] Harvey often appear mesmerized by the awesome incorporative power of late capitalism." Jarvis further notes that "Jameson's views of landscape often seem to come from *within* the centres of luxury and affluence" (the most famous example being Jameson's view from within Portman's Bonaventure Hotel in Los Angeles). From what we have seen of *A Man in Full* so far, it might seem that similar criticisms could be leveled at Tom Wolfe's literary map of postsouthern, "international" Atlanta. The breathless litanies of Downtown and Midtown MXDs ("There was John Portman's seventy-story glass cylinder," and so on) might suggest that *Wolfe* is mesmerized by the large-scale capitalist development of Atlanta. One wonders if the "spectacular views" of the city "from *within* the centres of luxury and affluence" (PlannersBanc Tower and Croker Concourse) merely reproduce, in omniscient narrative form, the possessive visual economy of a capitalist real-estate developer—or, as John Shelton Reed worried, an Atlanta booster.[23]

But *A Man in Full* does not only observe and represent Atlanta from within postmodern capitalist hyperspaces. As Reed noted, *A Man in Full* also reveals the "largely unknown parts of the city." Citing Michel de Certeau, one might say that Wolfe shows how the spectacle of the "panorama-city" from Croker Concourse or PlannersBanc Tower is the land speculator's own "optical artifact . . . a projection that is a way of keeping aloof." As we have already seen, Wolfe begins to critique the reifying visual ideology of capitalist land speculation via Charlie's remarks on the "spectacular views" of Atlanta real estate. But the novel also features those whom de Certeau would call "ordinary practitioners of the city [who] live 'down below,' below the thresholds at which visibility begins." Mapping MXDs from the G-5, Charlie may not have seen other Atlanta(n)s, but they are visible in *A Man in Full*.[24]

The sociospatial chasm between those "above" and those "down below" is evident in a brief encounter between PlannersBanc's chief executive Arthur Lomprey and an immigrant market-stall operator in Underground Atlanta, the Downtown commercial complex. Despite PlannersBanc's speculative influence on the "international" image and material development of Atlanta,

---

23. Brian Jarvis, *Postmodern Cartographies: The Geographical Imagination in Contemporary American Culture* (London: Pluto, 1998), 46, 48; Reed, review of *A Man in Full*.

24. Reed, review of *A Man in Full*; de Certeau, *The Practice of Everyday Life*, 92–93.

its senior employee is detached from the everyday lives of most citizens. We usually witness Lomprey within a particularly exclusive version of what V. S. Naipaul has called "the bubble in which the white professional people of Atlanta lived: the house, the air-conditioned car, the office . . . the luncheon club." In Lomprey's case, the rarified loci are the Piedmont Driving Club, the High Museum, and his forty-ninth floor office at PlannersBanc Tower. This office affords a panoramic view "north toward Buckhead, east toward Decatur, and south toward Downtown and, assuming you wanted to, the vague expanse of the lower half of the city" (606). There is here the implication that Lomprey's speculative gaze is much like Charlie's: it glazes over the poor, black Southside, which is decidedly not prime development land.[25]

Lomprey is, then, in unfamiliar surroundings when he purchases "a fake Patek Philippe watch from a Senegalese street vendor out in front of Underground Atlanta with $65 of his own money" (236). Lomprey buys the watch to acknowledge a particularly effective performance by the Real Estate Asset Management Department's "workout artiste," Harry Zale, who (literally) seized a thirty-thousand-dollar Patek Philippe watch from one of the bank's intransigent debtors. But Lomprey's jest achieves its effect not just by celebrating Harry's chutzpah; it also plays upon the incongruous image of PlannersBanc's chief executive undertaking a petty cash transaction with an immigrant market-stall operator. Put another way, the joke evokes the socioeconomic chasm between PlannersBanc's position in the global, finance-capitalist space of flows, and the local, immigrant-operated space of places that is Underground Atlanta.

There are two extended set-pieces in *A Man in Full* that more thoroughly depict other (under)ground-level Atlantas. The first of these is Roger White's limousine tour from Buckhead to Vine City with Mayor Wes Jordan; the second is Conrad Hensley's experience as a fugitive among the immigrant population of "Chambodia."

From Buckhead to Vine City

Roger White's tour emerges out of a conference with Mayor Jordan during which the two men discuss the rumor that Georgia Tech's star running back, Fareek Fanon, has raped Elizabeth Armholster, the daughter of the "chairman of Armaxco Chemical and about as influential a businessman as existed in Atlanta" (4). Wes identifies the larger social issues surrounding the

25. V. S. Naipaul, *A Turn in the South* (London: Penguin, 1989), 29.

impending scandal: "Okay, not to belabor the obvious, there are two Atlantas, one black and the other white. . . . You see all the towers in Downtown and Midtown—that's all white money, even though the city is 70 percent black, perhaps 75 percent black by now." But black Atlantans are fully aware of the city's sociospatial inequality—an awareness that, Wes suggests, arises from their own visual sense of place: "Our brothers and sisters in this city are not blind. . . . They see" (183).

The usually loquacious mayor admits to Roger that "[i]t's hard to put it [Atlanta's unequal geography] into words. . . . It's going to be a whole lot easier if I *show* you" (183). Interestingly, *A Man in Full* here echoes the scene in Siddons's *Peachtree Road* where mayor-elect Ben Cameron tells Gibby Bondurant, "I'd rather show you." In both novels, the mayoral limousines then proceed on a chauffeur-driven tour from Buckhead to a poor, black South Atlanta neighborhood. Because *A Man in Full*'s mayoral tour exhibits an intertextual, even "palimpscestous" relation to *Peachtree Road*'s earlier, equivalent journey (set in 1961), it becomes possible to map the historical continuities of racial segregation and geographical uneven development that survive within the "international city."[26]

Mayor Jordan first has chauffeur Dexter Johnson drive by the expensive Buckhead properties of Croker and Armholster. These houses are hidden on private, tree-lined roads away from the general public's gaze, yet their symbolic capital—or, in the novel's own Veblenese terms, "sheer homage to conspicuous consumption" (190)—attests to their owners' financial and social status. The mayor then directs Dexter to drive through Atlanta's decentered business districts (no longer focused around Five Points, as in 1961, but along Peachtree Street, between Midtown and Downtown). Here, the narrative offers another awe-inspiring perspective on the material geography of multinational capital: a "canyon" of skyscrapers "streaming past on either side of Peachtree [Street], which was *the* place to have a tower" (195). But Wes adds a commentary that *sees through* (rather than simply *"from within"*) this mesmerizing spectacle—a commentary that furthers the novel's critique of how the "national" and "international city" has been defined. The mayor observes incredulously that "[a]ll these towers were supposed to show you that Atlanta wasn't just a regional center, it was a national center." Wes points out International Boulevard, CNN Center, the Georgia World Congress

---

26. Siddons, *Peachtree Road*, 533.

Center, and International Plaza—the latter a monument to "Atlanta's greatest international coup: the 1996 Olympics"—as evidence of the boosters' attempts "to make Atlanta a *world* center, the way Rome, Paris and London have been world centers in the past, and the way New York is today" (195–96). Yet Wes tempers his skeptical view of this performative signification of "international" Atlanta, for he knows that the boosters' rhetoric is not entirely free-floating. However inflated, the rhetoric does refer to—is backed up by—the kind of financial investment that produces massive capitalist development which is conspicuously evident at a local, material level. Wes recognizes that the "business interests" *have* succeeded in transforming (this part of) Atlanta into a "*national* center"—according to their own economic criteria. The mayor also ventures that the boosters may yet make the globalization rhetoric an (economic) reality: "They may just pull it off, turn this town into *the world center* . . . They know how to generate money" (197).[27]

The tour subsequently takes a turn, however, that indicts both Atlanta's putative global status and its local politics of place. The limousine suddenly leaves behind "all the glossy pomposity of the center of the world" (197) when it enters the black neighborhood of Vine City. Roger's gaze shifts abruptly from the "world center" that is "the business interests' dream" (195) to witness a local poverty much like that which Gibby saw in 1961: "Three vacant lots in a row . . . overgrown with weeds and saplings. . . . Through the weeds on one side of the house he could see a pool of collected water, out of which protruded . . . *junk* . . . of every sort" (198). Wes explains that, as the black middle class moved to southwest Atlanta, "the folks that took our place weren't owners, they were renters . . . and the landlord gives up on making any money on the property and walks away from it" (199). Thus the neighborhood has gone into a precipitous decline. Vine City's nexus of place, race, and rent reveals continuities with *Peachtree Road*'s Pumphouse Hill (though there is no direct landlord-tenant relationship between Buckhead and Vine City, as there was between the Bondurants and their tenants). Like Gibby before him, Roger has needed a mayoral tour to visually and mentally map the contrast between "the top" and "the bottom" (202) of Atlanta: "Roger looked round about the Bluff . . . in his mind's eye he could see Armholster's Venetian pala-

---

27. On the "performative resignification" of Atlanta, including Cain Street's rebranding as International Boulevard, see Chapter 7.

28. In *Peachtree Road,* Gibby Bondurant offers a strikingly similar description of the poor,

zzo and Croker's pile" (204).[28]

Certain qualifications should be made, however, regarding this powerful depiction of Atlanta's historical-geographical uneven development. To do so it is useful to return to the start of the tour, and Mayor Jordan's disquisition on how commercial cartographies of Atlanta reproduce racialized ways of seeing (or *not* seeing) the city: "Did you happen to see any of those 'guides to Atlanta' they published for the Olympics? . . . The maps—the *maps!*—were all bobtailed—cut off at the bottom—so no white tourist would even *think* about wandering down into South Atlanta." Because such texts guided the white tourist's gaze toward what Rutheiser has termed the "ornamental nodes" of the Olympian "stage set [created] for visitors and viewers," the black-majority population of Atlanta was, as Wes notes, made "invisible" to "the rest of the world" (185). Indeed, the supposedly objective, omniscient views of the city offered in such tourist guides approximate nothing so much as the selective, speculative gaze of Charlie or Lomprey—perspectives that, as we have seen, ignore "the vague expanse of the lower half of the city."[29]

A Man in Full's mayoral tour can be seen as Wolfe's attempt to rectify or *re-place* the Olympian maps' ideological bias. The journey from Buckhead through Peachtree Street to Vine City appears to be a more authentic, even mimetic (narrative) cartography of the so-called international city. But it is important to realize that the reader still experiences Atlanta from a particular ideological point of view. Mayor Jordan's mapping, and lawyer White's reading, of the city emerge from a middle-class perspective. The two men grew up in Vine City but have joined the black middle-class flight to the West End (199); Roger is so estranged from his old neighborhood that he does not even recognize much of it (an effort not helped by English Avenue's dilapidated state). There are echoes here of James Baldwin's observations on the black middle class' post-1960s "limbo" from an increasingly ghettoized inner-city Atlanta. It is true that the two men enter a black neighborhood omitted from the Olympic maps, and that Wes wants to show Roger the contrast between the Buckhead background of Elizabeth Armholster and the ghetto youth of Fareek Fanon. Yet the mayor and the lawyer *do* seem to be "sightseeing" (183) in Vine City. Like the Olympic promotional texts, Mayor Jordan acts as a "guide to Atlanta"—albeit an *other* Atlanta—directing Roger's tourist gaze.

---

black neighborhoods he witnesses during his mayoral tour. See Siddons, *Peachtree Road*, 536.

29. Rutheiser, *Imagineering Atlanta*, 6.

Afterward, and like Mayor Cameron and Gibby Bondurant before them, Wes and Roger can go home again (in their case to the West End, rather than Peachtree Road).[30]

Moreover, if the reader experiences the tour through Roger's eyes (and his "mind's eye"), there is also a certain overlap between Wolfe's status as omniscient narrator and Wes's position as Roger's (our) guide. Wolfe perhaps slyly acknowledges this equivalence by having the mayor state, "I'm just trying to construct a narrative, you might say, and I'm just hoping it'll unfold naturally" (193). The title that Wolfe gives to this chapter, "The Lay of the Land," is taken from another of Jordan's laconic comments upon the tour's purpose and direction (187). The sense that Wes's autopolitan[31] tourist gaze–narrative overlaps with the omniscient author's is compounded if one knows that, while researching the novel, Wolfe drove through English Avenue with former city-planning director Leon Eplan. The implication here is not that Wolfe is a white bourgeois author and should therefore be disqualified from writing about black South Atlanta. Such a claim would be a simple-minded echo of Quentin Compson's undialectical claim to "southern" authenticity, which here becomes: "You can't understand South Atlanta. You would have to be born there." Nonetheless, Toni Morrison had a point when she observed that: "You have *Gone with the Wind*. . . . Then you have this Tom Wolfe book. And that's Atlanta. Boom. Over. . . . And I thought, 'No, no, no.' No one is talking about Atlanta from the point of view of these people who knew it—not the political way, not the way the marketers knew it, but on the streets, in the houses, in the schools." We should simply realize that, for all the power of Wolfe's map of "the lay of the land" between Buckhead and Vine City, we do not experience Atlanta "from the point of view" of those "on the streets, in the houses" of the black Southside. For such a perspective, one has to turn to another recent Atlanta novel (edited by Morrison): Toni Cade Bambara's *Those Bones Are Not My Child* (see Chapter 10).[32]

30. See James Baldwin, *Evidence of Things Not Seen* (London: Michael Joseph, 1985), 25–26, 37–38.

31. See Rutheiser, *Imagineering Atlanta*, 82: Rutheiser takes the term "autopolis" from H. L. Preston, *Automobile Age Atlanta: The Making of a Southern Metropolis, 1900–1935* (Athens: University of Georgia Press, 1979).

32. Valerie Boyd, "Toni Morrison Brings Friend's 'Bones' to Print," *Atlanta Journal-Constitution*, 17 October 1999, http://www.accessatlanta.com/partners/ajc/newsatlanta/bambara/morrison.html. On Wolfe and Eplan, see O'Briant, "A Wolfe at Our Door?" D1.

The Real International City: Chambodia

Conrad Hensley, the Californian former Croker Global warehouse laborer cum fugitive, arrives in Atlanta via a space of flows rather different from that which facilitates the immaterial movements of transnational capital. Conrad's journey from Oakland via Portland to Atlanta involves a sophisticated transportation network that more usually assists the passage of (often illegal) immigrants into and across the United States. Upon arriving at Hartsfield International Airport, Conrad is met by his contact Lum Loc and taken to Chamblee, located in the northeast section of metropolitan Atlanta. Chamblee, Doraville, and Clarkston, where around ten thousand Vietnamese, Cambodian, Laotian, and Hmong refugees settled during the 1980s, comprise a district that offers an alternative definition of Atlanta as an "international city"—defined by its multicultural population, not the globalization of finance capital flows.

Walking in Chamblee for the first time, Conrad is astonished to discover a commercial strip of small shops operated by Southeast Asian immigrants that runs along New Peachtree Road; as Gibby Bondurant might observe, this is certainly *not* the old Peachtree Road. Conrad eventually comes to Asian Square, which, as a modest but apparently popular public space appropriated by immigrants, contrasts with the simulated cosmopolitanism of Downtown's International Plaza (519). Indeed, as Rutheiser notes, on account of the burgeoning immigrant population "the stretch of Buford Highway near the cities of Doraville and Chamblee became known as 'Atlanta's *Real* International Boulevard.'" Chamblee's residents themselves celebrate their origins by unofficially renaming the town "Chambodia" (515).[33]

But although Chambodia allows these immigrants to maintain a place-specific sense of identity and community, and despite the international origins of the heterogeneous populace, the district is distinctly segregated from the "international city." Conrad is struck by how the built landscape of immigrant-owned businesses around Buford Highway is "another world" (519). Wes Jordan ostensibly "belabor[ed] the obvious" by referring to "two Atlantas"; ironically, however, and despite bringing into focus the black neighborhoods otherwise excluded from the official Olympic maps, the mayor's bipolar narrative cartography itself "rendered invisible" outlying areas like Chamblee and Doraville that, as Rutheiser observes, have complicated the "polar shades of American-born black and white." Yet, by a further grim irony,

---

33. Rutheiser, *Imagineering Atlanta*, 89.

the new Southeast Asian arrivals themselves, isolated on the northeast edge of the metropolis, are forced to map Atlanta in similarly binary terms. As Lum Loc notes: "This side, America. Other side, Chambodia" (518).[34]

Chambodians' status as second-class citizens is especially evident in their experience of police surveillance, which severely restricts their ability to achieve a mobile, social sense of place in Atlanta. As an escaped convict, Conrad is circumspect about walking around Chamblee, even though he has acquired a false driver's license and birth certificate. Nonetheless, he is better off than the Vietnamese illegal immigrants he lives with, who cannot alter their appearance. Police surveillance is so pervasive that most new arrivals are told that they "[c]annot always walk around doing nothing in Chambodia" until Lum Loc "give[s] them IDs and they get work" (518). Consequently, as Conrad witnesses, many immigrants' everyday lives are literally confined to the private rooms of rented accommodation: "The tiny living room was now packed with people, with Vietnamese—must be fifteen or sixteen of them at least. . . . The place was ripe with the smell of too many human bodies in a small space" (514–15). The contrast between this restrictive, all too physical sense of place, and the abstract space of PlannersBanc Tower, could hardly be starker.

Eventually, Conrad himself comes under police scrutiny during an excursion into Chamblee. There are few pedestrians—not only because the immigrants are careful not to be caught on the sidewalks, but also because the built landscape around Buford Highway epitomizes Atlanta's status as an autopolis. Hence, Conrad is conspicuous despite his respectable appearance and white skin; sure enough, he is soon pulled over by a police patrol car and asked where he is heading. Chambodia may be beyond or below the elevated worldview of a Croker or a Lomprey, but the locals *are* subjected to the gaze of state authority. In this instance, de Certeau's "pedestrian speech acts," informed by the belief that "the long poem of walking manipulates spatial organizations, no matter how panoptic they may be," seem like little more than a postmodern fantasy.[35]

Finally, Chambodians' unequal status within Atlanta is best exemplified by the labor market. Vietnamese immigrants invariably have to take "work on the assembly line" at the "[v]ery big chicken plant in Knowlton" (517). It is Brother, the eccentric poor white who rents Conrad a room in a decrepit

---

34. Rutheiser, *Imagineering Atlanta*, 88.
35. De Certeau, *The Practice of Everyday Life*, 97, 101.

antiques shop in "Old Chamblee," who explains the "place" that Southeast Asian immigrants occupy in the local job market, and how such labor relations have redefined Chamblee's demography: "It's 'at chicken plant in Knowlton. Won't no white man work there and no black man, either, these days. So they wants the Orientals, but they don't want 'em living in Knowlton, so they park 'em in Chamblee and Doraville" (626). Knowlton and Chamblee, then, are not merely peripheral parts of metropolitan Atlanta; they are also buckled onto "the Broiler Belt" of chicken-processing factories, the "latest industry of toil to reign in the South." Wolfe here provides *A Man in Full*'s most sobering example of how, out on the less glamorous edges of the postsouthern metropolis, beyond finance-sector employment in the space of flows, traditionally "southern" manual labor is still being performed. The only historical change is that the workers are not southern-born blacks but the newest and most truly international residents of the so-called international city.[36]

From Turpmtime to Oakland: Labor and Capital across Postsouthern America

A Man in Full does focus upon one older southern place that appears to have little or no connection to the "international city": Charlie Croker's plantation, Turpmtime. Charlie has convinced himself that he is the patriarch of Turpmtime through some "natural" selection of southern manhood: "this was the South. You had to be man enough to *deserve* a quail plantation" (9). In fact, the developer became "Cap'm Charlie"—as he enjoys being called by Turpmtime's black employees—through the rather more prosaic process of purchasing twenty-nine thousand acres of south Georgia real estate. Aboard the G-5 during the flight from his failing edge city to the sanctuary of Turpmtime, Charlie rhapsodizes over the aerial view of south Georgia's fecund landscape. But there is a telling limit to Charlie's pastoral fantasy. This limit is first evident when he looks out over a "breathtaking" peach orchard, "gorgeous beyond belief," only to conclude his meditations by "[w]onder[ing] who owns it?" (75). Shortly afterward, Charlie follows the eyes of his financial adviser Wizmer Stroock to a house "amid a swath of orchards"; focusing his own gaze, the developer muses that it "[m]ust cost a fortune to keep up a

---

36. See Harvey, *Justice, Nature, and the Geography of Difference*, 335. On the harrowing experiences of the local chicken-broiler industry's underpaid and generally nonwhite workforce, see also Jennifer Smith, "Workers Demand 'Poultry Justice,'" *Creative Loafing*, 15 April 2000, 27. (*Creative Loafing* is a free weekly newspaper published in Atlanta.)

place like that" (77). So it is that Charlie views plantation country in much the way that he mapped Atlanta's MXDs from the G-5—through the capitalist gaze of a real estate developer. South Georgia is not some residual oasis of a "natural" or premodern South that has somehow survived outside the nexus of capital and land speculation. Despite Charlie's rhetoric, Turpmtime is less "real life" (80) than real estate.

Charlie embellishes his own plantation's Arcadian image by contrasting it with the postsouthern metropolis: "When he was here at Turpmtime, he liked to shed Atlanta, even in his voice. He liked to feel earthy, Down Home, elemental; which is to say, he was no longer merely a real estate developer, he was . . . a man" (5). No matter that, according to Allen Tate, we "cannot pretend to be landed gentlemen two days of the week if we are middle-class capitalists the five others": Charlie's weekends as the "master of Turpmtime" (276), not his weekdays as a developer in Atlanta, make him feel like a man in full. This urban/Down Home dualism is disingenuous, however; the plantation's economic base is firmly rooted in Atlanta real estate. In various interviews at the time of *A Man in Full*'s publication, Wolfe explained how the genesis of the novel, and its location in Atlanta (rather than New York), derived from the moment when "[s]ome friends invited me to see a couple of plantations down in Georgia in 1989." Wolfe discovered that "[t]he plantations were owned largely by real-estate developers." It seems certain—though it is never explicitly stated in the novel—that Charlie, the son of poor whites from Baker County, bought Turpmtime on the back of his success as "one of the Creators of Greater Atlanta." What we do know for sure is that the plantation is far from self-sufficient: the capital that maintains Turpmtime's antebellum image can also be traced back to land speculation in Atlanta. At the emergency meeting in PlannersBanc Tower, Charlie claims that Turpmtime is an "experimental farm" and "the main testin' ground for our food division" (53). In fact, the meretricious upkeep of Turpmtime is written off to Croker Global's food division (74)—which the developer bought in 1987 on the basis of his success in the "booming" Atlanta real-estate market (72).[37]

It seems to be a particularly postsouthern irony: for Charlie to act like the "master of Turpmtime," the plantation requires capital accrued during

---

37. Allen Tate, "What Is a Traditional Society?" in *Essays of Four Decades*, 548; Harry Ritchie, "Tom Wolfe in Full," *Waterstone's Magazine* 15 (autumn 1998): 4. One of the friends who showed Wolfe around Georgia plantations was developer C. Mackenzie Taylor, cofounder of the Perimeter Center edge city that so engages Croker's omniscient gaze.

Charlie's everyday life as an Atlanta real-estate developer. But we might also note Charlie's affinity with another (fictional) entrepreneur whose role in the original Reconstruction of Atlanta provided the capital that enabled the creation of a similar, neoantebellum sense of place. As we saw in Chapter 7, it is Scarlett O'Hara's success as a New South timber merchant that enables her to reinvent Tara in the image of the Old South. PlannersBanc's Peepgass is more perceptive than he knows when he refers to Charlie's acting like "a son of the South Georgia sod" on "that ridiculous goddamned plantation of his, which he thinks is fucking Tara" (246). For like Scarlett with Tara, Atlanta real estate development has allowed "Cap'm Charlie" to imagineer Turpmtime—original, 1830s "Big House" and all—as a simulacrum of a "true antebellum Old South" (81) that never really existed.[38]

But whereas Tara remains merely a fetishized monument to an antebellum fantasy, Turpmtime has a subtle use-value that repays its debt to the Atlanta real-estate arm of Croker Global. Charlie uses the plantation's simulated Old Southernness to woo potential corporate tenants ("pigeons") to Croker Concourse and his other Atlanta MXDs. He knows that "Turpmtime might not be, strictly speaking, an experimental farm, but it had paid for itself many times over in terms of bagged pigeons, a point he didn't know quite how to get across to those small-brained niche-focused motherfuckers at PlannersBanc." PlannersBanc's own pliable loan salesman John Sycamore was subjected to "the Turpmtime Spell" (278), thereby facilitating a generous flow of loans to Croker Global. Charlie thus exhibits a nuanced understanding of the plantation's synergetic value to his Atlanta real estate. He certainly shows more nous than Stroock, who suggests his boss should sell Turpmtime because it appears to be "a non-core asset, not functionally integrated into the rest of the corporation" (68).

In *Gone with the Wind*, the loyal likes of Mammy and Pork gave Tara some semblance, however bathetic, of historical continuity between slavery and "free" labor. Croker's relationship with Turpmtime's black workforce appears to be that of a rather ludicrous latecomer playing out a part-time, postsouthern pastiche of what Richard King has called the "Southern family romance." Yet "the Turpmtime Niggers" perform a crucial role in the seduction of Charlie's real-estate clients: they provide an authentic sheen of slave-like labor to

---

38. On an economic and performative scale, "Cap'm Charlie's" conspicuous southernness far exceeds that of the Cudworths and Carringtons in the 1930s Tennessee of Robert Penn Warren's *A Place to Come To*. (See Chapter 3.)

the plantation's simulated Old South. The "Turpmtime Spell" that Charlie casts over his prospective MXD tenants includes a calculated, profoundly racist reconstruction of what King calls the old "Southern conception of itself" as master and slave knowing "their place": "[Croker] knew that the magic of Turpmtime depended on thrusting his guests back into a manly world where people still lived close to the earth, a luxurious bygone world in which there were masters and servants and *everybody knew his place*. He didn't have to say who Uncle Bud was. He merely had to say his name in a certain way, and one and all would realize that he was some sort of faithful old retainer, probably black" (277, my emphasis). If it is shocking that "Cap'm Charlie" requires his black employees to perform a minstrel-like image of antebellum slave labor (albeit for a cash wage), it is perhaps even stranger that these "real *country*" (55) people effectively work in the field, so to speak, of Atlanta real-estate development.[39]

Yet there remains one final spatial turn to the case of labor relations at Turpmtime—a turn that leads not only to Atlanta but also to California. Swayed by his romantic, proprietorial vision of southern land—and, to some degree, by his paternalistic sense of responsibility to the black employees— Charlie refuses to sell Turpmtime. Instead, he resolves to lay off 15 percent of the national workforce in Croker Global's food division. At this point, Charlie's peroration (during the emergency meeting at PlannersBanc) on "how Croker Global was today one of the biggest employers of unskilled black labor in that part of Georgia" (55) takes on dramatic irony. For among those Charlie lays off are the similarly "unskilled" (and not only black) laborers at a frozen-foods warehouse in Oakland—including Conrad Hensley. In this instance, even the mystified use-value of Turpmtime as a site for "bagging" corporate tenants of Atlanta real estate hardly justifies shifting the job cuts elsewhere, especially considering that the cuts occur in the one division of Croker Global, foods, that remains profitable (74). Ultimately, Charlie's desire to maintain his paternalistic, simulated, Old South sense of place at Turpmtime has an all too real impact on the lives of workers elsewhere in the Croker Global corporation and postsouthern America.[40]

* * *

39. King, *A Southern Renaissance*, 21.

40. Tellingly, Croker makes his final decision to "lay off 15 percent of the food division" (89) after catching a rattlesnake at Turpmtime, an incident that reaffirms his "Southern manhood."

In his famous essay "The Search for Southern Identity," C Vann Woodward contrasted a generally American "quality of abstraction," a "superiority to place, to locality, to environment" with what he—following his friend, the lapsed Agrarian Robert Penn Warren—saw as the South's "fear of abstraction." Woodward went on to cite the South's concrete focus on "place, locality, and community," as evidenced in the work and "experience of Eudora Welty of Mississippi." Yet neither Welty nor Warren ever confronted the degree of abstraction we find in *A Man in Full*. In Wolfe's postsouthern Atlanta, we witness a profoundly abstract sense of placelessness that derives from (to update Tate) a top-heavy focus on *transnational* finance-capitalism. Yet *A Man in Full* also emphasizes an apparent paradox of such abstract, placeless finance-capital: its power to create (and creatively destroy) the concrete geography of metropolitan Atlanta through the construction of monumental MXDs.[41]

As I noted earlier, Welty seems to have seen "real estate people" as at least partly responsible for the destruction of the South, and her fiction mostly returns to an era when a more familiar sense of place remained intact. By contrast, Wolfe focuses on contemporary Atlanta to show how land speculation and real-estate development have produced a locus unlike any of those earlier places we have called "southern." The rural landscape to the north of postsouthern Atlanta—O'Connor country—has been transformed into "investor land." Meanwhile, Charlie Croker uses his south Georgia plantation, an elaborate simulation of the antebellum South, to market Atlanta MXD office space to unsuspecting clients. All told, *A Man in Full* seems to suggest that there is no residual or unmediated "South" that has escaped the effects of speculative capitalist development.

But such a reading would be to elide the end of the novel, which has been evocatively and accurately described by Norman Mailer as "a mess, a *tidy* mess." Having been converted to Stoicism by his recently hired personal home-care assistant—none other than Conrad Hensley—Charlie Croker decides to surrender all his "worldly goods" to his creditors (722). There then follows a brief epilogue in which, as Mailer observes incredulously, "Charlie is not even present." Only in "a short paragraph" narrated by Mayor Jordan do we learn that Charlie has become a Stoic evangelist back home in Baker County and on "into the Florida Panhandle and southern Alabama" (732).[42]

41. Woodward, "The Search for Southern Identity," 23.
42. Norman Mailer, "A Man Half Full," *New York Review of Books*, 17 December 1998, 20. Wolfe cockily but not always convincingly responded to Mailer's criticisms, as well as those

Whatever the manifest problems with *A Man in Full*'s denouement, there are aspects that are particularly germane to my focus on the postsouthern sense of place(lessness). I suggest that Wolfe resorts to a peculiar kind of "spatial fix" in the epilogue. This term is usually understood to refer to "the absorption of excess capital and labor in geographical expansion . . . the production of new spaces within which capitalist production can proceed."[43] *A Man in Full*'s spatial fix involves the *textual* production of places—Baker County, the Florida Panhandle, and southern Alabama—that enable the narrative to escape the problem of capitalist spatial production in metropolitan Atlanta. Finally, Wolfe *does* appear to have been trapped within his own image of the "awesome incorporative power of late capitalism" to create, destroy, and unevenly develop a place. Having so thoroughly delineated the depressing limits imposed on everyday life in "other" Atlantas (Vine City and Chambodia), Wolfe seems to resort to an escapist anticlimax in which Charlie simply surrenders his properties to PlannersBanc and other creditors before disappearing down home into rural south Georgia. After seven hundred pages that suggest there is no southern "sense of place" unaffected by land speculation or real-estate development, the epilogue vaguely invokes a residual, rural "South" that—unlike Atlanta, the investor land of north Georgia, or the plantations to the south—somehow remains outside the realm of capital.

Charlie's conversion to Stoicism is bound up in *A Man in Full*'s troublesome ending. Wolfe does offer hints that we should be suspicious of the reborn Stoic's evangelical motives: Mayor Jordan mentions Charlie's ability to "talk . . . the bills out of your wallet" and his "syndication deal with Fox Broadcasting" (732). Ultimately however, Wolfe seems seriously to propose classical Stoicism as a moral counterpoint to the materialism of contemporary capitalist society. Like the Stoic philosopher Epictetus, Charlie comes to see being-in-the-world per se as a hindrance to "freedom." Such a yearning for transcendence evacuates the novel's earlier emphasis on *social* being mediated by and between processes local *and* global, abstract *and* material. It is telling that, upon resolving to proselytize the Stoic creed, Charlie (like Conrad) leaves Atlanta: the practical value of his new faith is therefore never tested *within* the capitalist metropolis. It is also notable that Croker the Stoic abnegates even that limited (if paternalistic) social responsibility he held as

---

of John Irving and John Updike, in "My Three Stooges," *Hooking Up* (London: Picador, 2000), 145–71.

43. Harvey, *The Condition of Postmodernity*, 183.

an Atlanta real-estate developer cum plantation owner. It is one thing for Charlie to renounce the commodity fetishism of "worldly goods"—"the Croker Global corporation, every last branch of it, my houses, my plantation"—for Stoic character, "the only real possession you'll ever have" (722–23). But his Stoic turn must also require him to abandon Turpmtime's black laborers to PlannersBanc's "worldly" economic motives. In leaving Atlanta, Charlie also appears to have departed from any form of social reality, whether materialistic or paternalistic: if Roger White is the epilogue's "man of the world," Charlie has become a "vessel of the Divine" (727).

Of course, Stoic philosophy is not new to the South; indeed, Charlie's Stoicism recalls the (albeit more aristocratic) worldview of Emily Cutrer in *The Moviegoer*. As is well known, Walker Percy based Emily on his cousin and guardian William Alexander Percy, whose conservative vision of the neoclassical Old South's decline led him (like Emily) to seek consolation in "the Stoic maxims of Marcus Aurelius."[44] There are, in fact, interesting parallels to the spatial turns played out in the epilogues to *The Moviegoer* and *A Man in Full*. At the end of Percy's novel, Binx Bolling, too, becomes less a "man of the world," a social being, than a "vessel of the Divine"—although his leap of faith is more Catholic than Stoic. But at the worldly level, both protagonists end up abandoning a postsouthern, capitalist landscape for a more familiar "southern" place. As we saw in Chapter 3, Binx escapes from the ever-expanding, mass-produced suburbs of New Orleans and reenters Emily's "southern" retreat, the Garden District. Charlie renounces the corporate landscape of Atlanta and returns to rural Baker County. If Binx and Charlie both experience alienation at different periods in the capitalist development of a (sub)urbanized post-South, both yet find some sort of sanctuary in a traditional southern "sense of place."

By depositing the reborn Stoic back in Baker County, well away from his earlier Atlanta-based economic tribulations, Wolfe finally (if fuzzily) privileges the rural South as one "worldly" locus that is freer than the postsouthern "international city." This is not to imply that, in reality, there is nowhere like Baker County, no (rural) place that has resisted large-scale land speculation. My point is that *A Man in Full*'s all-too "tidy" epilogue allows Wolfe to abandon postsouthern Atlanta and the complex issues of place, race, and (finance-) capital that he explored so effectively earlier in the novel.

44. King, *A Southern Renaissance*, 87.

10. Capitalist Abstraction and the Body Politics of Place: Toni Cade Bambara's *Those Bones Are Not My Child*

Between 1979 and 1981, Atlanta's black community was both torn asunder and brought together by the mysterious disappearance and death of a number of local African American children. Fresh from the critical success of her novel *The Salt Eaters* (1980), writer and Atlanta resident Toni Cade Bambara responded to the traumatic events going on around her, and fulfilled her unofficial role as southwest Atlanta's "writing lady," by embarking upon a novel about the so-called Atlanta Child Murders. Bambara became, by her own admission, obsessed with the missing-and-murdered case, and the manuscript grew incrementally. She continued to work on the novel into 1983 and 1984, even as media interest in the child murders receded dramatically following the arrest and imprisonment of a local black man, Wayne Williams. Ultimately, Bambara never completed the manuscript, which expanded to approximately eighteen hundred pages. *Those Bones Are Not My Child* did not appear in bookshops until 1999—four years after Bambara's death, and a few months after the publication of *A Man in Full*—and then only because of the diligent editorial work of Bambara's friend and fellow novelist Toni Morrison.[1]

The difficult history of *Those Bones Are Not My Child* meant that, although Bambara had begun the book as events were still unfolding, it was not the first *published* "Atlanta novel" to feature the child murders. In 1992, Marilyn Dorn Staats published *Looking for Atlanta*, a mass-market novel centered around Margaret Bridges, a Buckhead-born, self-confessed "lapsed Southern Belle" going through a midlife crisis in her new home in "Arcadia Heights: Atlanta's Most Exclusive New Suburban Subdivision."[2] Described by Anne Rivers

---

1. Bambara comments upon her role as the community's "writing lady" in the acknowledgments to the published book, which also indicate quite clearly the travails involved in writing *Those Bones*. See Toni Cade Bambara, *Those Bones Are Not My Child* (New York: Pantheon, 1999), 671. All subsequent page references will be incorporated into the main text.

2. Marilyn Dorn Staats, *Looking for Atlanta* (1992; reprint, New York: Warner Books, 1993), 11, 29. All further page references will be incorporated into the main text.

Siddons as perhaps "the single best-drawn Southern woman I've encountered in fiction,"[3] Margaret is almost as bewildered by the transformation of Atlanta as Siddons's own Gibby Bondurant—though unlike *Peachtree Road*, *Looking for Atlanta* plays the protagonist's response to the city's redevelopment primarily for laughs. The novel's more serious side has to do with the accidental death of Margaret's teenage daughter and its traumatic repercussions. Sporadically throughout the narrative, Margaret projects her mourning on to events elsewhere in the city. She comments that "I've become obsessed with the missing and murdered case. . . . I study the pictures of grieving mothers in the newspapers, watch them being interviewed on television, feel their anguish, know the sudden blankness that falls over their faces" (149). Margaret's response to the child murders is far more sympathetic than that of her wealthy white friends in the Buckhead Garden Club, who dismiss "[t]his so-called list of missing and murdered children [as] just another example of nigra paranoia," and reassure themselves with the thought that "[a]nyway, they're not killing children in Buckhead" (158). To this degree, *Looking for Atlanta* identifies the racial fault lines that remain in the city and which the child murders brought into media focus.

But the novel's representation of the missing-and-murdered case, and its impact on the city, is only conveyed from Margaret's perspective, "looking for Atlanta" from afar. This limited perspective is rather literally figured through the motif of Margaret gazing at the distant downtown skyline from a suburban rooftop in Arcadia Heights, accompanied by "my yardman" (23) Harold. Other than servants like Harold and the cook Annie D, Margaret, like Siddons's Gibby, knows no black Atlantans; also like Gibby, she finds it hard to imagine the servants' lives back home in southwest Atlanta, independent of their domestic labor in Buckhead and Arcadian Heights (215–16). At one point, Margaret observes that "nobody from Atlanta goes downtown anymore" (14), by which she really means no rich white people. When she does venture into the city, her somewhat understandably self-centered response to the child murders seems to merge with a familiar white southern hysteria concerning race and sexuality. Margaret's perception of downtown as a racialized locus of sexual violence even revives that most hackneyed southern-white myth, the predatory black buck: "A black man with a nervous Adam's apple and a suspicious bulge in his coat pocket—perhaps he was the serial killer

---

3. The Siddons quote appears alongside other blurbs and reviews on the inside cover of *Looking for Atlanta*.

the police were looking for in the case of Atlanta's missing and murdered children!—began picking at his teeth with a switchblade knife." Contemporary Atlanta is sufficiently "international" in its demographic makeup, however, that Margaret sees other nonwhite "others" as sexually menacing too: "In the elevator going down, a possible rapist posing as a Cuban aluminum-can collector plopped his bag right down next to me" (23).

The representation of the missing-and-murdered case in *Looking for Atlanta* is, then, both limited and troubling, channeled through Margaret's perspective and mediated by her preconceptions concerning race, gender, and labor (preconceptions that Margaret does at least, toward the end of the novel, recognize as problematic [199]). Ultimately, black Atlanta is only marginal to Staats's narrative map of the city. There is nothing in *Looking for Atlanta* to moderate Morrison's opinion that, before *Those Bones Are Not My Child*, no novel about Atlanta had even attempted to depict the city from an African American, inner-city, street-level perspective.[4]

While *Those Bones Are Not My Child* may have been a long time coming, it is an altogether different proposition from *Looking for Atlanta*—or, indeed, *A Man in Full*. Even before the novel proper begins, an autobiographical prologue constructs an intensely localized narrative cartography of a working-class, African American neighborhood in southwest Atlanta circa 1981. We witness the authorial figure "running down the streets of southwest Atlanta like a crazy woman"—running because "[a] cab can't jump the gully back of the fish joint and can't take the shortcut through the Laundromat lot" (8). The prologue's protagonist walks through the wooded lot because, in such secluded spaces, she might find evidence that will help solve the child murders: "You stub your toe on brown glass . . . you pry loose a crusty beer bottle . . . beneath the bottle is a rain-blurred Popsicle wrapper. *Late summer*, you figure, moving on, stooped over, eyes scanning the ground" (11–12). The narrator runs frantically because she is supposed to meet her twelve-year-old child (apparently Bambara's own daughter Karma) at school at a time and in a place where local youths were going missing and being found murdered.

The narrator muses to herself that "[l]ess than five months ago, you would not have been running alone . . . your whole neighborhood would have mobilized the second you hit the sidewalk": Mother Enid and Brother Chad, even "[t]he on-the-corner hard-heads." But by 16 November 1981, five months after the arrest of Wayne Williams, conciliatory signs have begun to

4. See Boyd, "Toni Morrison Brings Friend's *Bones* to Print."

appear in neighborhood windows: "Let the Community Mend Again" (8–9). *Those Bones Are Not My Child* exhaustively interrogates the official view that Williams was the single Atlanta Child Murderer.[5] But through its perspective on and from the southwest neighborhoods, Bambara's novel also critiques the imagineering of Atlanta as an "international city," a global capital of capital. Almost immediately, the prologue suggests the social, spatial, and representational lacunae between what Charles Rutheiser terms "[t]he 'official' mythology" or "advertiser's monologue"[6] of the "international city," and another Atlanta that the child murders bring (albeit slowly) "to citywide, nationwide and finally worldwide attention" (17): "Reporters everywhere were trying to make sense of what was happening in Atlanta. *Gone with the Wind* Atlanta. New International City Atlanta. Atlanta, Black Mecca of the South. Second Reconstruction City. Home of a bulk of Fortune 500 companies. Scheduled host of the World's Fair in the year 2000. Proposed site of the World University. Slated to make the Top Ten of the world's great financial centers" (18). This Gibby Bondurant–like litany of Atlanta's "world-class" economic and institutional potential is exposed not only by the international media's focus upon the child-murder case but also by Bambara's own oppositional narrative. Through the representation of another Atlanta—by mapping black neighborhoods and undeveloped wastelands on to the "international city"—*Those Bones Are Not My Child* reveals the tensions between the global (capital, and Atlanta's position in the global capitalist "space of flows") and the local (murder, and the resulting anguish and activism of the southwest's black community). Bambara's novel reveals how the hegemony of (finance) capital, even as it defines and shapes the "international city," abstracts the other Atlanta(s)—grimly symbolized and embodied by the missing and murdered children—out of existence. Through a grotesque body politics of place, Bambara critiques the economic imperative and definition of "international" Atlanta, and refocuses attention upon the missing and murdered children. Moreover, Bambara moves from such local politics of place, centered on the neighborhood and the body, to resituate "international" Atlanta within a world-system of inequality and exploitation.

5. Williams was charged with only two murders, and neither victim was a child. Upon Williams's conviction, the missing-and-murdered case was closed, although even the official list cited twenty-eight murders (alternative lists included many more).

6. Rutheiser, *Imagineering Atlanta*, 3, 11.

All That Is Solid "Fall[s] through a Door in the Air": Disappearing Bodies and Capitalist Abstraction

Marzala ("Zala") Spencer, the protagonist of *Those Bones Are Not My Child,* has "always prided herself on her knowledge of the city." When Zala was a girl, her father drove her around Atlanta, helping her to map familial and communal geographies: "he made certain that she understood that the Atlanta they had a stake in was not the mythical one drummed up in the guidebooks, the billboards, the newspapers ads, the novels, the glossy brochures with tables of figures and graphs and maps showing gray areas slated for 'demographic changes and redevelopment.' Atlanta, the real one, was documented in the sketchbooks, the scrapbooks, the photo albums, the deeds, family Bibles, in the memories and mouths of the elders, those who had stayed and those long since moved" (84). There is here a distinct echo of Mayor Wes Jordan's critique of authorized ways of seeing the city—guidebooks, maps and newspapers—that elide and erase the historical geography of an "other Atlanta." The difference is that Zala possesses a local knowledge of southwest Atlanta that outstrips the voyeuristic, "sightseeing" gaze of a middle-class black professional like Jordan or Roger White. Having said that, Bambara complicates any easy, absolute claims to *the* authentic view and representation of "Atlanta, the real one." In *A Man in Full,* Roger White knows corporate Downtown but loses all sense of place in Vine City, where he grew up. In *Those Bones,* Zala struggles to reconcile her highly detailed, relatively stable mental map of southwest Atlanta with the bewildering developmental flux of the central business district: she comes to understand "that the downtown area she's mastered at five, then remastered at ten" has become "a confusion of sawhorse barriers, open ditches, plank sidewalks, and sandy pathways for yellow Caterpillars carrying boulders in their maws" (85). According to Zala's father's binary logic, here we have one of those "gray areas slated for 'demographic changes and redevelopment'" that constitutes the *un*real Atlanta. Yet such large-scale creative destruction of Atlanta's social geography cannot simply be ignored. Zala discovers that, in order to attain a nuanced, local sense of place in the "international city," she must master and remaster not only the quotidian makeup of the southwest neighborhoods, but also the disorienting, large-scale land speculation and redevelopment that is occurring throughout metropolitan Atlanta.

The notion of a "real," noncommercial Atlanta, and of an "authentic," uncommodified knowledge or counternarrative of such a place, is problematized by the revelation that Zala's own working life is bound to the local boom industries of real estate and tourism. Because Zala works for a firm called Tour Atlanta, the "early training" by her father has become a valuable commodity, enabling her "to contribute to the Black tour company's information bank" (84). Nor is Zala the only member of the Spencer family involved in real estate. Her estranged husband Nathaniel ("Spence") co-owns a realty firm with his sister Delia, and Zala too works for the firm, again putting her youthful "training" to profitable use: after all, "[s]he knew what was where" (84). Hence, Zala's historical-geographical knowledge is not rooted in some residual "real" Atlanta that somehow survives outside and independent of the capitalist "international city"; textually, Bambara does not transfigure Zala's knowledge into a simple-minded aesthetic of antidevelopment.

Nevertheless, there is a distinction to be made between Zala and Spence. Whereas Zala tries to move and mediate between corporate Atlanta and the southwest's African American community, Spence has immersed himself in the former at the expense of the latter. Zala ponders how her husband has "been bitten by the Atlanta bug and started running around in business suits big-deal bragging, bar hopping, back slapping, power lunching with potential policyholders or real-estate investors" (75). So whereas Spence no longer knows "if the Institute of the Black World was still there on Chestnut Street, or if Atlanta U's poli-sci department was still a progressive enclave" (116), Zala has retained a critical relative autonomy from the "international city."

The novel proper opens just as Zala and Spence's everyday lives are brutally disrupted by the dawning realization that their son, Sundiata (Sonny), has disappeared. Inevitably, this traumatic event has radical implications for their respective attitudes toward Atlanta: Zala's critical autonomy is imperiled, while Spence must shake off the "Atlanta bug" in order to rejoin the southwest black community and join the search for Sonny and the other missing children. But even the family's domestic sense of place is changed utterly. At home, Zala and Spence feel that "the walls [are] moving in" upon them: "Inches, feet, yards foreshortened. The conventional laws of perspective shot. Their son at the vanishing point" (122). Walking the streets in search of Sonny, Zala "pictured herself of late treading the ground with the suspicion that any minute it might crack open and suck her under" (151). Yet for all the terror of such moments—this sense of being crushed by the walls of one's home, or swallowed up by the earth—the self, the body remains material, tangible, thus enabling Spence and Zala to maintain their subjectivity and their active search for Sonny. Elsewhere, though, the narrative begins to describe black bodies disappearing altogether. Shortly after imagining her own son "at the vanishing point," Zala thinks about those other black "[c]hildren [who] were sent on errands with no thought that a child could fall through a door in the air. Some said Jefferey Mathis had vanished in a puff of smoke before he reached the Star service station" (126). What is going on here?

Most obviously, this extended metaphor of dematerialization attempts to express something of the horror felt at the sudden, inexplicable absence of a loved one. The image captures the black community's—and Bambara's— struggle to comprehend and narrate ("Some said") such events. The seemingly literal disappearance "in[to] the air" of some mother's son becomes a kind of horror or ghost story, told and retold. But the novel also sets up this image of dematerializing black bodies in such a way that it intones and indicts "international" Atlanta itself, critiquing not only the way in which the city prioritized business and profit over the missing-and-murdered case, but also the distracting power of capital itself in a city increasingly defined by local land speculation and transnational financial exchange. This critique becomes clearer if one considers the social context within which Zala, the black community, and the novel itself tell and retell this tale of one black boy's mysterious disappearance: "For nothing had stopped. That was the bewildering thing. Children had been bludgeoned, shot, stabbed, and strangled, and nothing had stopped. Conventions came to town. . . . Newspaper and magazine articles put asterisks alongside the Fortune 500 branches in Atlanta. Suits were pressed, briefcases were polished. And nothing stopped" (126). Thus the narrative connects and contrasts Atlanta's pursuit of profit with the city's failure, even refusal, to pursue the missing-and-murdered case. The point is repeated elsewhere that, between 1979 and 1981, significant elements of Atlanta's civic-corporate power structure remained motivated by money—convention dollars (16, 152), real-estate development, and multinational corporate investment—despite, and in the midst of, the murder of at least twenty-seven African Americans. Zala meets an old man in Central City Park who wryly captures this mentality: "Only one kinda killing 'poze to talk about in the financial district" (168).

But beyond such economic *dis*tractions, disturbing as they are, this key scene also identifies, and begins to interrogate, the more complex issue of *ab*straction. I want to suggest that Jefferey Mathis's disappearance is related to what Fredric Jameson calls "the fundamental source of abstraction," the money form; more specifically, abstraction as a structural aspect and effect of finance-capitalist speculation. Mathis's sudden loss of materiality and subjectivity, expressed metaphorically as a "fall into air," also operates as an allegory of finance-capital and its perplexing formation in the postmodern era.[7]

Jameson has observed that capital no longer emerges from or refers back to (supposedly "disappearing") industrial modes of extraction and production. Rather, contemporary finance-capitalism exists largely within the "disembodied phantasmagoria" of the global stock market, its speculative "specters of value" detached from the subjective, productive labor of real people and the objective materiality of actual commodities—that is, those elements of capitalism that were once presumed to be necessary for speculation and profit. Instead, profit in the present era seems to be generated in and of itself via an increasingly globalized, technologically mediated network of capital circulation that (as we saw in Chapter 9) sociologist Manuel Castells has termed the "space of flows." In *Those Bones,* then, Mathis's dematerialization allegorizes the "disembodied phantasmagoria" of a money form that has somehow sloughed off both human relations and material geography (the "space of places") in order to circulate freely within an abstract space of flows. The mysterious tale of Jefferey Mathis becomes, in Jameson's suggestive phrase, a "postmodern ghost story, ordered by finance-capital spectralities." All that is solid "fall[s] through a door in the air."[8]

In a sense, the allegorical dimension of this scene makes it all the more disturbing: after all, the bleak fact remains that black children from Atlanta really *did* disappear and die. Later in this chapter I will consider Bambara's skillful negotiation of the problematic relationships between history and fiction, metaphor and the material body, and allegory and (black) subjectivity. But the key scene that I am focusing upon here is already complicated because it is not just allegorical; it also identifies a grotesque *equivalence* between disappearing bodies and capitalist abstraction. The bilious irony is that the lives and bodies of the very people who *cannot* participate in the "international city's" speculative economy are those that become as invisible and immaterial as finance capital itself.

7. Jameson, "The Brick and the Balloon," 25.
8. Jameson, "Culture and Finance Capital," 136, 142, 138, and "The Brick and the Balloon," 46; Castells, *The Informational City,* 348.

"At the Vanishing Point": Resisting Capitalist Abstraction

On 11 October 1980, while trying to map the killer's (killers') route, Spence and Zala find themselves in a "new neighborhood." Amid the new buildings and "partly bulldozed woods," the Spencers observe "a vacant house from a former time of mills and farms and company stores" (204). But rather than testifying to the historic sense of place that Zala's father taught and practiced, this remnant—one of a few remaining old buildings "slated for demolition" (205)—vividly emphasizes the extent to which agriculture and rural industry have been replaced by metropolitan land speculation. Rather than indicating "the coexistence of modes of production" that Jameson identifies in earlier societies (including the South depicted by Faulkner), the abandoned building alerts one to the nearly total redevelopment around it. Indeed, because the old houses are vacant, Zala herself must *invent*, in Jameson's phrase, the "popular memory . . . in vivid narrative form" that has been erased from the place itself: "She imagined boarders pausing there to chat with the mailman. . . . She pictured mill hands rising from sturdy chairs to spear potatoes from plain, chipped bowls" (204–5). But despite Zala's valiant efforts to offset the speculative imagineering of metropolitan Atlanta by envisioning the local particulars of working-class labor and leisure, it is clear that, as such "hitherto surviving enclaves of socio-economic difference have been effaced," other Atlanta citizens have begun to suffer from what Jameson would call a "waning of [their] sense of history" (or more properly, historical geography). This diminished historical-geographical consciousness is barely compensated for by the prevailing profit ethic: Zala identifies the new development as "a community-to-be for self-invented people unsaddled by nightmares and conflicting dogmas, people who could toss mamasay and preachersay over their shoulders with a pinch of coke and, applying one of Atlanta's upbeat sobriquets to their lifestyle ('City too busy to hate'), required nothing further to move ahead" (204).[9]

In this sequence, *Those Bones Are Not My Child* echoes a point well made in *A Man in Full:* the older, urban-rural boundary between Atlanta and the outlying counties of "O'Connor country" has been (creatively) destroyed by capitalist real-estate development. The scene also shows just why Atlantans who want to maintain their "knowledge of the city" must master and remaster the wider metropolitan geography of creative destruction. Something more

9. Jameson, *Postmodernism*, 405.

complex also happens here, however, and in a subsequent scene—Zala's trip to the Omni International mixed-use development—that brings into focus not only the material reality of capitalist spatial production, but also, once again, the abstracting effect of finance-capital itself. Attempting to navigate their way back home to southwest Atlanta, the Spencers suddenly realize that they have lost any sense of place: "Lost, they were safe for the moment. Zala squinted at the overcast sky for signs of a seam, for an entry into the other Atlanta where they'd been safe from moment to moment" (206). Here, Zala does not simply want to get back to the family's house on Thurmond Street. She wants to get back to "the other Atlanta," the one she knew before Sonny went missing. But as she processes these thoughts, Zala has stopped moving through Atlanta's actual built landscape. She has stopped actively trying to recover and recite (or reinvent) spatial histories of labor and everyday life. Instead, Zala is dreamily seeking some "seam" in the sky. In other words, she is shifting from the historical-geographical, the material, into the metaphysical, the abstract. To be sure, she may not conceive her thoughts in such grand terms: she just wants to get back to that time when her boy was still safe at home. But this "seam" in the sky seems less like a conduit back to some "other Atlanta" than the "door in the air" through which Sonny, Jefferey Mathis and numerous other black children have "disappeared." In this moment, Zala's mystical yearning for escape from the present is eerily akin to the dominant attitude in and of the "international city" itself—the impulse to ignore, even to de-realize, the child murders.

Most disturbingly, Zala's desire to disappear into a "seam" in the sky approximates the dematerializing (il)logic of finance-capitalism as it is mediated through the corporate geography and architecture of "international" Atlanta. On 19 December 1980, five months after Sonny's disappearance, Zala steps out of an elevator on to the twelfth floor of the Omni International: "Beyond was a wall of glass sun-splashed by the skylight. Behind the glass, blond desks floated on a creamy carpet with magenta zigzags. Zala got a good grip on her package and herself" (326). The glass window-walls produce the illusory sensation that the desks are coming detached from material space and floating in to air.

One recognizes this phenomenon from *A Man in Full*; in particular, the scene where Ray Peepgass loses his physical sense of place while looking through the glass window-walls on the forty-ninth floor of PlannersBanc Tower. Like Ray, Zala is experiencing capitalist abstraction at an epiphanic level of intensity. Like a suitably "floating" sign of finance-capital—itself a "second degree" abstraction of the money form—the desks seem to have "separate[d] from the 'concrete context' of [the Omni's] productive geography." Though the Omni is not an abstract "space of flows" on the scale of PlannersBanc—it is not a bank, the primary forum for the transnational flow of finance-capital—its construction was funded by national and international investors. One can even say, with only a little poetic license, that the Omni International was built on air. As well as buying up the land upon which the Omni was constructed, developer Tom Cousins and his consortium purchased "air rights" to the space above. Zala encounters these various forms of capitalist abstraction—the transnational investment and flow of global capital, the "second degree" abstraction of finance-capital, speculation in air (rights)—as they are mediated through the architectural form of the Omni itself. Zala's experience (circa 1980) elucidates somewhat the *economic* forces that inform and empower the Omni's status as "the home of every distracting environmental stunt that architecture has ever devised," as Joel Garreau conceived it (circa 1981). Though Garreau failed to identify explicitly the role of capitalist abstraction in the postsouthern "international city," he experienced the Omni as the hyperspatial antithesis of the southern "sense of knowing where you are and who you are . . . quite literally knowing your place, both geographic and your position in it."[10]

Stepping out of the elevator, Zala initially seems alert to the dematerial-

10. Jameson, "Culture and Finance Capital," 142; Rutheiser, *Imagineering Atlanta*, 163; Garreau, *Nine Nations of North America*, 158–60. Despite the international investment and the sheer scale, the Omni opened in 1975 as "nothing less than 'one of the worst real estate disasters in history'" (Rutheiser *Imagineering Atlanta*, 163). As Harvey Newman notes, the Omni and other Downtown MXDs "not only drove up the value of surrounding land but also generated an oversupply of office space in the downtown and contributed to the decline of areas between the megastructures" See Harvey K. Newman, *Southern Hospitality: Tourism and the Growth of Atlanta* (Tuscaloosa: University of Alabama Press, 1999), 176–77. The Omni was saved by Ted Turner in 1985, at which point it became CNN Center, an informational "space of flows" that demonstrated "the potential of technology to undermine existing place hierarchies within the global information order" (Rutheiser, *Imagineering Atlanta*, 70).

It would be wrong, however, to define the Omni only as a site of exorbitant land speculation and technofinancial abstraction. As James Baldwin noted in 1985, the Omni was located very close to "a sprawling, poor Black neighborhood, called Vine City." Baldwin observed ruefully that a black child from Vine City "can walk here [to the Omni] from his home in less than five minutes; some of the murdered children were last seen in this place." Thus Baldwin testified to the dizzyingly local inequality that still existed within the so-called international city. Baldwin, *Evidence of Things Not Seen*, 63.

izing effect of the Omni's glass walls. She gathers herself together to avert the sense of placelessness, of melting into air. Yet whereas even a loyal PlannersBanc employee like Ray Peepgass saw *through* the glass walls to the space of flows of global finance-capital exchange, the ostensibly more critical Zala is seduced: "'Glass,' she said, easing around the sofa. 'Glass, glass,' in case she hadn't given up on the dream of finding a permeable membrane to pass through to the other Atlanta where newspapers spoke of earthquakes in Italy, uprisings in Poland, the murder of a diet doctor in Scarsdale; the only hometown count the final score in the last Hawks game" (326). The glass towers seduce Zala because she still dreams of returning to "the other Atlanta" that she knew before Sonny went missing. But the dangers of such wishful thinking, and of surrendering her subjectivity, are more apparent than ever. Zala's fantasy of a "permeable membrane" or "seam" that takes her out of history, geography, and the awful responsibility of searching for her son, into a "dream" of an earlier time and place, is channeled through the glass walls of the Omni, a veritable ground zero—or vanishing point—of the money form. Indeed, from its economic base through its architectural form to its very name, the Omni International is the apotheosis of the "international city" itself: a phantasmagorical place where black children melt into air, where the only recognized "killing" occurs in the financial district, and where the only officially acknowledged hometown count is the final score from Omni Coliseum.[11]

Crucially, however, Zala eventually rejects the abstract fantasy that both the "seam" in the sky and the Omni's glass walls seem to offer. She reminds herself that "there was no place to dream anymore. . . . No place to dream and no way to live a rational life" (326). In other words, the "rational life" that

---

11. Zala and Ray's sense of melting into air also invites comparison across time and space with the disorienting experience of Frank Wheeler in Richard Yates's *Revolutionary Road* (1961). When Frank steps out of the elevator on to the fourteenth floor of the Knox Building in 1950s New York, the plate-glass partition walls, "corrugated to achieve a blue-white semi-transparency," produce the effect of a "wide indoor lake in which swimmers far and near were moving . . . some treading water . . . and many submerged, their faces loosened into wavering pink blurs as they drowned at their desks." The fact that Frank's experience of architectural semiabstraction does not reach the extreme levels experienced by Zala and Ray—desks do not float, but sink—may be related to the fact that, in the 1950s, capital remained more obviously tied to material production (the Knox Company produces computers) and physical geography rather than circulating freely in a financial space of flows. See Richard Yates, *Revolutionary Road* (1961; reprint, London: Methuen, 1986), 79.

her "other Atlanta" represents is irrecoverable for at least as long as (Sonny's part in) the missing-and-murdered case remains unresolved. Zala will not be seduced by the capitalist "city of dreams," whatever its guise. Instead, the Spencers, together with other southwest Atlanta community activists, will continue searching. In doing so, they begin to counter the way in which the hegemony of capital has obscured and abstracted the brutal reality of murder, and to offer another perspective on, another narrative of, the so-called international city. By narrating this search, and by reinscribing the materiality of black life and death through a body politics of place, Bambara, too, reconfigures the official cartographies of Atlanta.

Recovering and Representing Atlanta's "Throwaway Bodies"

In a letter that she sends to relatives abroad, Zala identifies a link between economic strength and narrative/vocal power. Using speech as a metaphor, she contrasts the financial might wielded by corporate Atlanta with the comparative economic weakness of local African Americans: "Convention dollars speak so much louder than an invisible community silenced by their very wealth of pigment and their very lack of dollars" (152). Yet it is also by speaking, by *naming* the local children, that the black community begins to challenge "the 'official' mythology," the "advertiser's monologue," and to make black children—whether safe, missing, or murdered—visible and even material again. The local storytellers may have been unable to recover Jeffrey Mathis from that "door in the sky," but the power and virtue of narrative in forming and maintaining community becomes apparent: "The boys were respectful. More, they looked grateful. For if someone called you by name, or only 'son,' 'junior,' 'boy,' even if they were scolding, then you were alive, alive to that community that named you" (313).[12]

By contrast, when the Atlanta authorities attempt to address the missing-and-murdered case, their narrative method remains oblique, obfuscating the grim reality. Local television runs repeatedly a public announcement featur-

12. For Bambara herself, the production of the novel was an extension of this process of "naming" and placing oneself (as well as others) in the local community that, as noted above, regarded her as its "writing lady." She has said elsewhere that "[w]riting is a legitimate way, an important way, to participate in the empowerment of the community that names me." Quoted in Farah Jasmine Griffin, "Toni Cade Bambara: Free to Be Anywhere in the Universe," *Callaloo* 19, no. 2 (1996): 229–30.

ing a jingle entitled "Let's Keep Pulling Together, Atlanta" in which "Black and white citizens of all ages [are seen] holding fast to a rope in a tug-of-war against an invisible team." It takes the "invisible [black] community" to get beyond this abstract (non-) representation of an "invisible team" to identify and vocalize the suppressed subtext, the murder of children: "what was being dragged up on the other end of that rope? The ten-second public announcement was supposed to be reassuring. It gave them the creeps" (461).

We are moving here from capitalist abstraction and the unspoken disappearance of black bodies to the material and textual recrudescence and recovery of the corporeal. In her recent revisionist study, *Dirt and Desire: Reconstructing Southern Women's Writing, 1930–1990*, Patricia Yaeger brings into focus the southern literary and social significance of the (almost always African American) "throwaway body." For Yaeger, the bleak archaeology of "digging children out of ditches" in "black literature about the South" also penetrates the complacent surface of the southern literary-critical "sense of place." Yaeger shows how "the depths of southern 'place' yield the remains of foundation-bearing black folks who lie beneath the earth (the subjects of lynching, shooting, drowning, murder, beating, suicide, being ignored, or being worked to death)." Discussing Sarah Wright's neglected novel *This Child's Gonna Live* (1969), Yaeger notes that the narrative "struggles to gather up the child's blasted remains. . . . This novel presents the black child as someone who's invaluable and yet becomes white culture's throwaway." Yaeger also reworks another southern literary-critical shibboleth, the grotesque. She insists "that the grotesque is a form of social protest steeped in local politics"—a form that, in southern literary texts, helps us to remember and recover throwaway bodies that have been subjected to racist violence.[13]

Bambara utilizes the grotesque body politics of place that *Dirt and Desire* describes. As in *This Child's Gonna Live*, the black community in *Those Bones Are Not My Child*, as well as the text itself, strives to recover the remains—"'Remains,' they [the Atlanta authorities] called the discoveries. . . . A tag is affixed to the toe that extends from the sheet. A mother backs away. *Those bones are not my child*" (12)—and to represent and revalue black bodies and being. Most redemptively, Sonny himself rematerializes in Miami—alive, although his body has been fouled by his experience (530), and he has become as deceptive and distracted as Atlanta itself (582). More morbidly, but no less powerfully, dead black bodies irrupt on to the pages of the novel, and

---

13. Yaeger, *Dirt and Desire*, 12, 20, xi, 224.

into the "international city": "Bacteria activated by the heat, swelling, the odor—any corpse looked like a homicide when it burst" (265). As a way of getting beyond contemporary capitalist abstraction, this intensely physical grotesquerie (with its suggestion of repressed subjectivity "bursting" forth, even in death) also gestures toward the grim historical continuity of African American death in the South. One thinks of Emmett Till, battered by his murderers and bloated by the Tallahatchie River, and of a terrifying anecdote from James Baldwin's meditation on the Atlanta child murders, *Evidence of Things Not Seen* (1985). Baldwin recalls how "[s]ome years ago, after the disappearance of civil rights workers Chaney, Goodman and Schwerner in Mississippi, some friends of mine were dragging the river for their bodies. This one wasn't Schwerner. This one wasn't Goodman. This one wasn't Chaney. Then, as Dave Dennis tells it, 'It suddenly struck us—what difference did it make that it wasn't *them*? *What are these bodies doing in the river?*'" Both Baldwin and Bambara provide case studies in "reverse autochthony." This is Yaeger's term for "a site where both grownups and children are hurled into water or earth without proper rituals, without bearing witness to grief, without proper mourning." Such scenes and sites of the grotesque serve to reconfigure our complacent southern literary-critical "sense of place" and to expose the subterranean reality of the *post*southern "City Too Busy to Hate."[14]

Another aspect of the grotesque body politics of place in *Those Bones Are Not My Child* is the critique of a material and economic equivalence between black bodies and waste. Yaeger argues that many southern texts featuring throwaway bodies "present 'place' not as the nostalgic location of 'sights and smells and seasons' [Eudora Welty's definition] but as a trash heap with profound economic resonance." For Yaeger, this economic resonance of waste in "place" refers to the African Americans who literally made the South, but whose bodies and very lives were discarded once their labor power waned.[15] But in *post*southern, "international" Atlanta, black bodies are immediately disposable because they have no such laboring use-value to an economy structured around land speculation and the abstracted exchange-value of globalized finance-capital. Bambara's novel identifies a relation between these waste bodies and wasteland, the dingy woods and empty lots that are excluded from Atlanta's speculative spatial economy. I have already referred to the moment in the prologue when the autobiographical narrator sifts through dirt-laden

14. Baldwin, *Evidence of Things Not Seen*, 99; Yaeger, *Dirt and Desire*, 17.
15. Yaeger, *Dirt and Desire*, 18.

beer bottles and Popsicle wrappers in a secluded "wooded lot" for evidence of child murder (9–10). This relation between throwaway bodies and useless land is signaled again when Zala perceives a trash-laden lot—the *spatial* waste of geographical uneven development—as a funeral pyre for the missing and murdered children: "Zala stared into the weeded lot and forced the dead bodies back into the shape of trash heaps" (164).

When we do witness ordinary black folk working in *Those Bones*, the images are sometimes no less disturbing: "In a vacant lot back of the MARTA station, children, stooped as if working a snatch-row, collected aluminum cans. . . . There was no play to their actions. . . . They worked as though the family budget depended on their seriousness." Though physically within the limits of the "international city," this abject locus falls outside the finance-capitalist space of flows. Indeed, the image of children "working a snatch-row" evokes neither opportunity nor hopeful subjectivity but rather the historical geography of slave labor. In such a wasteland, there is little to distinguish working with waste, the detritus of commodity consumption, and becoming waste oneself, as disposable as a Popsicle wrapper or a Coca-Cola can: "She [Zala] was thinking of the Jones boy, who'd been visiting from Cleveland. He'd disappeared while gathering cans with his Atlanta cousins, the papers said" (147).[16]

Those Bones Are Not My Child attempts to recover, revalue, and even rematerialize those black bodies that have been obscured from public life or reduced to waste by and within the postsouthern "international city" (and, Yaeger might add, by and within "southern literature"). It remains a problematic enterprise, however. First, Bambara must confront the relation between history and fiction, what she herself terms "the dodgy business of writing a novel about real events" (672). This is especially difficult when those "real events" revolve around a sensitive subject like the Atlanta Child Murders (as we have seen, Bambara most immediately attempts to deal with this difficulty through the autobiographical prologue). Second, Bambara is faced with the inherent difficulty—one that has been especially emphasized in postmodernism—of narrative representation. She must deal with the apparently abstract relation of language to material (not least spatial) reality, what Don DeLillo's *The Body Artist* describes as the "imaginary point, [the] nonplace where language intersects with our perceptions of time and space."[17] Third, if *Those Bones Are*

---

16. The narrative does at one point suggest that the missing-and-murdered case may be connected to *contemporary* plantations based on slave labor (600–601).

17. Don DeLillo, *The Body Artist* (London: Picador, 2001), 99.

Not My Child suggests that capital's hegemonic role in the "international city" circa 1979–81 turned black life, black bodies, into an abstraction, the novel risks simply reifying this logic. The grim irony here is that the power of the text's own images of capitalist abstraction are such that they threaten to override any attempt to re-inscribe the materiality and subjectivity of the fictional protagonists, or the historical victims.

Bambara most clearly tries to ameliorate these various problems through her characterization of the Spencer family. At the risk of being accused of "fictionalizing" a horrific historical-geographical reality, Bambara's focus upon the Spencers ensures that, as Valerie Boyd observes, "[t]he novel isn't about the infamous cases in an abstract way: It's about a particular family and what happens to its members when a son doesn't come home one Sunday in 1980." By mediating her historical-geographical representation of Atlanta through the Spencers' perspective, Bambara produces, in Mikhail Bakhtin's famous definition, a novelistic chronotope that is a "carefully thought-out, concrete whole." Through the agonizing days and months of Sonny's absence, time "thickens, takes on flesh, becomes artistically visible." So too, as the Spencers and their fellow community activists map Atlanta—thereby countering the moment when Zala seems to be floating into air at the Omni—"space becomes charged and responsive to the movements of time, plot and history."[18]

But the text must also deal with the more specific, highly sensitive issue of the murdered children themselves. In *Dirt and Desire,* Yaeger expresses serious reservations about narrative representations of the body that are "loaded with political and emotional anagrams of the social." Drawing on Slavoj Zizek's work, Yaeger warns that the tendency to see the grotesque—in the southern case, mutilated and murdered black bodies—as cultural allegory can detract from the materiality, the "brutal physicality," of the body itself. In Bambara's case—and, of course, my own—there is a serious danger of representing black bodies (dead or alive) as only the *allegorical* equivalent of waste in a culture of commodity consumption, or as merely a grotesque *metaphor* for capitalist abstraction. So what to do?[19]

Bambara once explained her narrative aesthetic as an attempt to get beyond the metaphorical to the material, the physical: "I'm trying to break

---

18. Boyd, "Toni Morrison Brings Friend's *Bones* to Print"; Mikhail Bakhtin, "Forms of Time and of the Chronotope in the Novel: Notes toward a Historical Poetics," in Michael Holquist, ed., *The Dialogical Imagination* (Austin: University of Texas Press, 1981), 84.

19. Yaeger, *Dirt and Desire,* 224, 228.

words open and get at the bones, deal with symbols as though they were atoms." This textual praxis approximates Bakhtin's vision of Rabelais as a novelist who wanted "word-linkages and grotesque images . . . to 'embody' the world, to materialize it, to tie everything in to spatial and temporal series, to measure everything on the scale of the human body." For Bakhtin, this process of embodiment helps us to see and make the world anew. But as Yaeger warns, black southern bodies have rarely been "the exuberant site of cultural renewal that a theorist of the grotesque such as Mikhail Bakhtin might imagine." Even if we believe that Bambara successfully "break[s] words open and get[s] at the bones," that her own "word-linkages and grotesque images" not only rematerialize bodies but also space and time in a city defined by capitalist abstraction, we are still left with Yaeger's provocative question: "What happens if we refuse to think about the grotesque as the objective correlative for civic decay?" What happens if we are forced to abandon sociocultural allegory and focus upon the mutilated and/or murdered bodies themselves?[20]

Bambara's struggle to make language material enough to represent and dignify the flesh and bones of Atlanta's dead children, even while guarding against "making the abjected body allegorical,"[21] is most powerfully apparent in her rendition of the Bowen Homes disaster. On 13 October 1980, a nursery exploded in the Bowen Homes neighborhood of southwest Atlanta, killing four children and a teacher. The authorities identified a faulty boiler as the cause of the explosion, and insisted that the incident was unrelated to the missing-and-murdered case. Nevertheless, alternative theories abounded. Once again Bambara, like Baldwin, invokes that lingering specter of southern history, racial violence: "It could've been summer '64, Neshoba County: missing—three civil rights workers . . . Chaney, Schwerner, Goodman" (288). The narrative also suggests that the explosion might be linked to a convention of international right-wing racists taking place in Atlanta that weekend. Yet in an extraordinarily evocative and sensitive sequence, the narrative homes in on the dead, dying, and wounded children themselves. Like the community witnesses left "to shape the story" on a private and local level in the wake of Mayor Maynard Jackson's public, political speech, *Those Bones Are Not My Child* tries to tell the Bowen Homes story "right, lest it dishonor those who'd

---

20. Bambara quoted in Janelle Collins, "Generating Power: Fission, Fusion, and Postmodern Politics in Bambara's *The Salt Eaters*," *MELUS* 21, no. 2 (summer 1996): 35; Bakhtin, "Forms of Time and of the Chronotope," 177; Yaeger, *Dirt and Desire*, 221, 229.

21. Yaeger, *Dirt and Desire*, 229.

lived through it and those who hadn't" (297). Striving to represent, but also respect, the material reality of mutilated bodies, Bambara refuses to transform them into "political and emotional anagrams of the social":

> A locket and chain torn from the neck ripped the skin of a toddler running with a slashed femoral artery through hot debris. Bawling babies crawled over blistered pacifiers, dropping scorched dolls on dump trucks smashed flat by scrambling knees cut on the metal edges of robots leaking battery juice. Soaked socks, torn drum skins, hands crawling at the mesh of playpens while tinny xylophones plunked eerily pinching fingers. Spines rammed by table legs busting the strings of ukuleles curling into black lumps. Teddy-bear stuffing like popcorn in the gritty air where glass spattered into the wounds of toddlers. Flashcards fluttered high against Venetian blinds clattering down on brightly painted furniture collapsed on a baby boy's life. (277)[22]

Toward a Global Sense of Place

In Part VI of *Those Bones Are Not My Child*, after Sonny has been found in Miami and reunited with his family, the narrative shifts to rural Alabama, where the Spencers recuperate in the company of Marzala's mother, Mama Lovey, and the other members of her bee-keeping cooperative. There is something of an intertextual echo here: as we saw in Chapter 9, *A Man in Full*'s epilogue enacts an abrupt (albeit offstage) shift from Atlanta to rural Georgia. According to the logic of my earlier argument about Wolfe's novel, we might well ask whether Bambara, too, is indulging in a version of the "spatial fix." Does *Those Bones* textually produce the retreat in Epps, Alabama, as

---

22. It is worth emphasizing, however, that Bambara's grotesque politics of place are not always in this material, corporeal mode—as the equally powerful and moving representation of Jefferey Mathis's disappearance should indicate. Indeed, the image of Mathis's dematerialization ("fall[ing] through the air") might even be termed a *post*southern form of the grotesque in that it is particularly appropriate to—but, crucially, also critical of—the role of finance-capitalist abstraction in the "international city." If, as I have suggested, the boy's mysterious disappearance becomes (in Jameson's words) a "postmodern ghost story, ordered by finance-capital spectralities," then it is significant that Bambara tells another such ghost story that relates directly to the Spencer family. One night, four months after Sonny's disappearance (and nine months before he is discovered in Miami), a breeze-like presence passes through the Spencer home and enters a pair of boots on the porch, so that it seems as if "an invisible boy were standing in them" (262). Thus Sonny's "ghost," like Jefferey Mathis's, continues to haunt the text and the "international city" itself, and Bambara's critical grotesquerie encompasses both the material and the spectral.

a residual space of resistance to, or at least escape from, the grotesque death and abstraction of Atlanta? One might even wonder whether the contrast between Mama Lovey's retreat (a member of the Federation of Southern Cooperatives) and the "international city" comes close to reconstructing the kind of neo-Agrarian opposition between hellish urban Atlanta/rural Eden that Flannery O'Connor dismantled in "The Artificial Nigger." In his long review of *Those Bones,* John Lowe commented, "The Edenic treatment of these scenes . . . provides a useful contrast to the urban scenes, which are appropriately hellish." Certainly, Epps seems to offer an idyllic sense of community. Mama Lovey's galvanizing presence reaffirms Toni Morrison's argument—an argument made with reference to earlier books by Bambara—that "[w]hat is missing in [African American] city fiction and present in village fiction is the ancestor. The advising, benevolent, protective, wise Black ancestor is imagined as surviving in the village but not in the city."[23]

But despite everything they have been through, the Spencer family returns to what Lowe calls the "city of torment." The narrative vividly states the Spencers' dilemma: "How could they go back to Atlanta? And how could they not?—it was home" (551). Moreover, having returned to Atlanta, Zala and Spence continue to search into the missing-and-murdered case. The Spencers keep searching even after Wayne Williams's trial has begun, and even though Zala's "co-workers in the bank tower went to considerable lengths to obscure certain aspects of reality from themselves. 'Which trial?' they would have asked" (608). In the process, the narrative shifts again from localized sites—corporeal, personal, familial, and communal—to the larger sociopolitical sphere. Consequently, alongside the *regional,* "southern" historical continuities of racism and murder, the narrative also provides a *transnational* perspective on race, class, and economic inequality.

One of the Spencers' friends and fellow community activists, Speaker, has a prominent role in the novel's polyphonic narration of race and class oppression across regional and national boundaries. Symbolically, Speaker offers his own counternarrative to the official mythology of "Lovely Atlanta" (171) from the center of the financial district. But when Speaker invokes the imprisonment to hard labor of seventy-year-old black female voter-registra-

---

23. See John Lowe, "City of Torment," *The World and I* 15, no. 2 (February 2000): 267–74; Toni Morrison, "City Limits, Village Values: Concepts of the Neighborhood in Black Fiction," in Michael C. Jaye and Ann Chalmers Watts, *Literature and the Urban Experience: Essays on the City and Literature* (Manchester, U.K.: Manchester University Press, 1981), 39.

tion workers in Pickens County, Alabama, one of his audience interrupts: "That's Alabama. . . . And this is Atlanta" (170). Though Speaker enters into the spirit of dialogical call-and-response with his audience, he upbraids the heckler's view. It is, in fact, a worldview very close to that which Baldwin called a "stubborn and stunning delusion"—the false consciousness of those who, believing the "international city's" own hype, could claim: *"I'm from Atlanta. I'm not from Georgia."*[24]

Speaker calls for a sense of solidarity against oppression within and *beyond* the place he calls the "Noose South" (173). He envisions a united black diaspora that encompasses the kind of transnational "Black Atlantic" geography conceptualized by Paul Gilroy:[25] "'Tell me we aren't a cosmopolitan people!' Speaker shouted. 'Tell me we aren't one big family with kinfolks scattered all over the world. Mississippi, Grenada, Alabama, Soweto, Brooklyn, St. Ann's Parish, Brixton, Bahia, Salvador, Christiansted, Mobile, Chattanooga—' he was breathless. 'Charleston, Frogmore, Mosquito Island, Kingston, Robbins Island, Parchman Farm Prison, the projects, ya mudder's kitchen, Catfish Row. Whatchu think?'" (170) Elsewhere, various characters ponder similarly "cosmopolitan" connections. Zala muses upon the New Cross "massacre" in Brixton, England (365), an event with disturbing parallels to the Bowen Homes explosion.[26] Spence connects Atlanta's own ghosts, the missing children, with those who have disappeared in Chile, Colombia, Argentina, Brazil, and Uruguay—"loved ones dragged from schools, from jobs, spirited away in the dead of night," their spectral images chalked on the walls of government buildings by the Women of the Disappeared (179).

Perhaps the novel's most interesting revelation of the connections between socioeconomic inequality within the "international city" and throughout the world takes place in another glass elevator, in another of Atlanta's Downtown developments, John Portman's Hyatt Regency hotel. We join Zala in a "glass car [that] floated down past vine-tangled balconies toward the city

24. Baldwin, *Evidence of Things Not Seen*, 2. Early on, before she knows Sonny has disappeared, Zala vaguely believes the child murders must be taking place in Alabama (41). As she later observes, "I kept telling myself it wasn't happening, not here. In Alabama or Mississippi maybe, but not here in Atlanta" (659).

25. Paul Gilroy, *The Black Atlantic: Modernity and Double Consciousness* (London: Verso, 1993).

26. In January 1981, a house in Lewisham, south London, was firebombed, killing thirteen black youths. The New Cross Massacre Action Committee was formed within days to protest against the perceived bias and deficiencies of the police investigation.

street below" (480). This sense of "floating" recalls Zala's experience of capitalist abstraction at the Omni International. But as the elevator descends to street level, the narrative perspective expands beyond local or even national limits. Wealthy tourists entering the elevator trade "roof stories" about various international travel destinations: Lima, Paris, Rio, Tokyo, and San Juan. One tourist observes distastefully the presence beyond downtown Lima of "corrugated lean-tos," and expresses relief "that no unruly *cholos* threatened their family-reunion holiday in Atlanta." Another tells how "in Rio the geography was the reverse; bandits lived in the hills with the poor and frequently came down from the favelas to raid the estates below" (480–81). *Those Bones* here reconfigures a conundrum posed by southern literary critic C. Hugh Holman in 1972. Holman asked: "Can one take the glass-enclosed elevator to the twenty-second floor of the Regency Hyatt [sic] in Atlanta and look out upon a world distinctively different from what he might see in New York, Chicago, or Los Angeles?" Holman worried that Atlanta was being transformed from an identifiably "southern" site into a homogenous national city.[27] But when Zala "look[s] out of the Hyatt Regency's glass elevator" (480) she not only envisions the vertiginous inequality that remains *within* the "international city," but also—by critically refocusing the wealthy tourists' complacent gazes—the uneven development that divides other global capitals of capital.[28] In Chapter 9, we saw how the very "lay of the land" between Buckhead and Vine City operated as an objective correlative of the socioeconomic difference between the "top" and the "bottom" of Atlanta. By introducing a comparative, transnational element to the geographical uneven development in and of various "international cities," Bambara expands Wolfe's narrative cartography to more explicitly global—and more explicitly critical—dimensions. In this defining scene, Bambara's protagonist moves toward what geographer Doreen Massey calls a "global sense of place." Zala becomes alert to how, in Massey's definition, "the geography of social relations" have become "increasingly stretched out over space"—by the globalization of "geographical uneven development" *between* nation-states, and by the commonality of inequality *within* various "international cities." Hence, the globalized production of

27. Holman, "The View from the Regency Hyatt," 106–7. See also Chapter 7 above.

28. Zala also sees the Hyatt-Regency itself as "gaunt" (480). In doing so she perhaps captures something of the Hyatt's hermetic alienation from nearby southwest Atlanta, just as Frank Bascombe's use of the same adjective caught the "disjunction from the surrounding city" of Detroit's Renaissance Center (another Portman project). See Chapter 5.

sociospatial inequality inadvertently generates possibilities for globalized solidarity and resistance: "a really global sense of place" of precisely the kind that locals like Speaker and Zala preach and practice.[29]

In *Those Bones Are Not My Child*, Toni Cade Bambara mediates between the material (body) and the abstract (capital); moves between the neighborhood (southwest Atlanta) and the "international city"; and makes connections between the local and global politics of class, race, and place. Bambara helps us rethink not only the southern literary-critical "sense of place," but also the largely economic criteria that inform the official definition of Atlanta as an "international city," a world center in the global space of capital flows. All told, Bambara's final, posthumously published novel is a fitting last testament to what bell hooks called its author's "wild mixture of down home basic blackness and a rare, strange all-over-the-place complex global consciousness."[30]

29. Massey, "A Global Sense of Place," 321, 323, 321.
30. Bell hooks, "Uniquely Toni Cade Bambara," *Black Issues Book Review* 2, no. 1 (January/February 2000): 16.

Epilogue: Against the Agrarian Grain, Taking the Transnational Turn

At the end of Part 1, I quoted David Harvey's claim that "[t]he preservation or construction of a sense of place" by individuals and social groups, in social reality and fiction, is more important than ever "in a phase of capitalist development in which the power to command space, particularly with respect to financial and money flows, has become more marked than ever before." In Parts 2 and 3 I have tried to show the various ways in which eight writers—from that original Agrarian white male Robert Penn Warren to an African American resident of "international" Atlanta, Toni Cade Bambara—have represented the capitalist spatial redevelopment of "the South." I have argued that these authors' narrative cartographies reconfigure radically the familiar neo-Agrarian, southern literary-critical conception of "place."[1]

By now it should be clear that I have focused primarily upon urban and suburban geographies because the mainstream southern literary-critical apparatus—including the foundational concept "sense of place"—has derived from an image of "the South" as predominantly rural and agricultural. I have taken a historical-geographical materialist approach to the socioeconomic production and abstraction of "place" because such an approach has been too often and easily sidelined from southern literary and cultural criticism, to the extent that even the Agrarians' own important emphasis upon the relationship between "capitalism and land" has been ignored. Nonetheless, a skeptic might reasonably ask: what about the *contemporary* rural South? The Agrarian ideal of agricultural, subsistence-based real property might be defunct—the Agrarians' "South" may be redundant—but what of the rural landscape that remains? Real estate may have displaced agricultural real property in Robert Penn Warren's small-town Alabama or Tom Wolfe's metropolitan Atlanta, but should we consider the forms of small farming that still survive, albeit not on the yeoman-subsistence model lovingly crafted by Andrew Lytle in "The

---

1. Harvey, *Justice, Nature, and the Geography of Difference*, 306, 247.

Hind Tit"? When a theorist like Fredric Jameson states that postmodernism has fully erased "precapitalist agricultures," the empirical evidence seems compelling enough. But might southerners still balk at Jameson's confident assertion that Nature itself has been effaced from postmodern America?[2]

In a provocative 1997 essay titled "Recognizing Rusticity: Identity and the Power of Place," Gerald Creed and Barbara Ching rebuke three spatial theorists whom I have cited throughout: Jameson, Harvey, and Edward Soja. Creed and Ching note that "[p]ostmodern social theory's stable reference point has been the city," at the almost total expense of the country. They observe that Jameson "feels no need to justify his equation of the postmodern with the urban," and assert that Soja simply offers a "variation on the Marxist distaste for rural idiocy." Ching and Creed argue that, not least because of urban(e) intellectual disdain for the "rustic margin," there has been a "radical embracing of that marginality by many people in order to contest the late twentieth century's hegemonic urbanity."[3]

Upon reading this from a (post)southern perspective, one is impelled to note that the *original* Agrarian movement was precisely a radical (radically reactionary) embracing of the rural South by *not* many people in order to contest the *early* twentieth century's increasingly hegemonic urbanity. Indeed, southern intellectual and literary-critical thought has been, until very recently, so disproportionately dominated by neo-Agrarianism that one cannot seriously claim that postmodern or postsouthern theory has marginalized the rural South—at least, not yet. Moreover, rather than constructing simplistic binary oppositions between the country and the city, it is important to recognize their dialectical links. I have emphasized the interaction between Nashville high society and the conspicuous performance of farming in *A Place to Come To*; explicated the economic nexus between Turpmtime and Atlanta real estate in *A Man in Full*; and discussed the social relations between southwest Atlanta and the Alabamian cooperative farm in *Those Bones Are Not My Child*. And yet it does seem plausible that, in striving to correct the fetishization of rusticity prevalent in southern thought and fiction, a postsouthern theoretical approach risks reproducing the city-centric logic of postmodern "place" theory. Thus I would like to take this opportunity to consider briefly

---

2. Jameson, *Postmodernism*, 366.

3. Gerald W. Creed and Barbara Ching, "Recognizing Rusticity: Identity and the Power of Place," in Creed and Ching, eds., *Knowing Your Place: Rural Identity and Cultural Hierarchy* (New York: Routledge, 1997), 7, 10, 5.

a couple of contemporary writers who have reconfigured rural, agricultural "place" against the Agrarian grain: Harry Crews and Barbara Kingsolver.

In the last few years, significant critical attention has finally been given to Harry Crews, who has been publishing regularly since his first story appeared in the *Sewanee Review* in 1963. Matthew Guinn has argued persuasively that Crews's work has been marginalized from a neo-Agrarian southern literary canon because it focuses upon the poor white, the subject of Stark Young's scorn in *I'll Take My Stand*. More than that, though, Crews's *A Childhood: The Biography of a Place* (1978) also exposes the ideological lacunae in the ostensibly less elitist Agrarian vision, developed during the 1930s, of the yeoman subsistence farmer as the man at the center of the proprietary ideal. For Crews's autobiographical narrative brings into focus the far more widespread reality of tenant farming. He describes how, in Bacon County, Georgia, circa 1927 (and things had not changed when Crews himself was born in 1935) there were in fact "very few landowners. Most people farmed on shares or standing rent." Crews proceeds to critique the arrival in Bacon County of tobacco, a "money crop," and the way in which the "illusion" of tobacco profits captivated men who had previously been subsistence (tenant) farmers.[4]

This critique might seem to be in the Agrarian mode of Lytle's "The Hind Tit" or John Crowe Ransom's 1931 essay "Land!" a jeremiad against "the substitution of the capitalistic or money economy for the self-subsistent or agrarian economy"—particularly the replacement on small farms of subsistence crops by money crops. However, unlike Lytle, Crews resolutely refuses to romanticize subsistence farming, or small farming generally, or to adopt a neo-Agrarian aesthetic of antidevelopment. Indeed, as Guinn has perceptively observed, Crews challenges the "rhetoric of tradition" that resonates in "The Hind Tit"—"[i]njunctions such as Lytle's to 'throw out the radio and take down the fiddle from the wall.'" As Crews points out, Bacon County's tenant farmers "loved *things* the way only the very poor can. They would have thrown away their kerosene lamps for light bulbs in a second. They would have abandoned their wood stoves for stoves that burned anything you did not have to chop. For a refrigerator they would have broken their safes and burned them in the fireplace, which fireplace they would have sealed forever

---

4. Harry Crews, *A Childhood: The Biography of a Place*, in *Classic Crews: A Harry Crews Reader* (New York: Touchstone, 1993), 26, 43. All subsequent page references will be incorporated into the main text.

if they could have stayed warm any other way" (132). For Lytle, the fiddle is, like corn and sallet, a magical anticommodity that symbolizes the southern agrarian way of life. By contrast, Crews shows that, for Bacon County's tenant farmers—by now displaced to urban, industrial Jacksonville, Florida, precisely because farming did not pay—modern, capitalist "*things*" have an aesthetic- and use-value that cannot be dismissed as mere commodity fetishism. This implicit (and elsewhere, explicit) critique of Lytle's Agrarian aesthetic of antidevelopment is all the more intriguing if one knows that "Mr. Lytle" was Crews's literary mentor.[5]

Crews shows how the concepts of "home place" (31) and private property were revered by Bacon County's small farmers despite, or because of, their experience of extreme poverty and their tenant status. But it is important to realize that from start to finish, *A Childhood* describes deliberately and self-consciously a place and people that no longer survive. Whereas Welty's *Losing Battles* was (as I argued in Chapter 2) perceived by certain critics as the "last great 'Southern' novel" because it represented a (textual) return to a sense of place based upon subsistence farming, Crews has no such nostalgic illusions about his memoir. So, the autobiography pointedly concludes, in 1956, with a poignant vignette that captures the adult Crews's own sense of *displacement* from Bacon County and tobacco farming. Ultimately, and as Crews warns early on, this "biography of place" depicts "a way of life gone forever out of the world" (22)—and to the extent that this way of life was no Agrarian idyll, he refuses to mourn.

The vicissitudes of contemporary farming figure heavily in Barbara Kingsolver's fine novel *Prodigal Summer* (2000), set in and around the failing agricultural community of Egg Fork, Kentucky. For starters, and from the viewpoint of wildlife biologist and National Forest guard Deanna Wolfe, *Prodigal Summer* problematizes the pastoral ideal of farmers at one with Nature. Deanna

---

5. Ransom, "Land!" 219; Guinn, *After Southern Modernism*, 13; Lytle, "The Hind Tit," 244. In an interview with Erik Bledsoe, Crews expresses his appreciation of Lytle; but also notes that "we were from very different Souths, and I don't think he ever realized that. His daddy sent him to France to study. His daddy was a planter that never touched a plow, never had his hands on a plow or stock. My family was the white trash way down at the end of the road from the big house." Such a starkly personal critique puts Lytle's theoretical focus upon the yeoman farmer (as opposed to Stark Young's emphasis upon the aristocratic planter) into sobering perspective. See "An Interview with Harry Crews," in Bledsoe, ed., *Perspectives on Harry Crews* (Jackson: University Press of Mississippi, 2001), 153.

decries the hunting and maltreatment of wild animals and the destruction of trees by Appalachian farmers. From another perspective, that of cantankerous old Garnett Walker and his ongoing feud with neighboring Nannie Rawley, *Prodigal Summer* narrates a debate over chemical/industrial farming versus organic farming. However, rather than simply constructing a binary opposition and coming out in favor of organic farming, Kingsolver develops a nuanced dialogue between the two neighbors' points of view. In the process, this dialogical imagination takes us beyond Agrarian assumptions. When Garnett ponders the agricultural use-value of a John Deere tractor as opposed to a mule, musing that "sometimes horsepower can do what horseflesh cannot," the novel recalls and reconfigures Allen Tate's famous distinction, in *I'll Take My Stand*, between "the complete horse" and "horsepower in general."[6] Tate conceived "horsepower" as a suitably distorted metaphor for the abstraction of the industrialized modern mind; but for Garnett, and the other local farmers, technology is necessary to sustain an agrarian way of life at all. Nor does Nannie's organic mode of production fit into the Agrarian (or Weltyan) ideal of family-centered subsistence farming operating largely outside the cash nexus. She sells her apples "to some company in Atlanta Georgia with a silly name," and, to Garnett's horror, employs immigrant Mexican pickers in lieu of the family or community members who did such work in the past (398).

The contemporary complexities of small farming are explicated most effectively in the story of Lusa Maluf Landowski, a self-proclaimed "Polish-Arab-American" (153) and former university researcher in natural science. When her husband Cole Widener is killed in a traffic accident, Lusa is suddenly marooned on the Widener family farm near Egg Fork. Cole's death while driving a delivery truck to North Carolina can be traced directly to the modern agricultural economy—specifically, to "the drop in [tobacco] price supports that had pressed him to take part-time work driving grain deliveries for Southern States" (50), an agribusiness corporation. Left with the debt-ridden "Widener place," and refusing to "grow *drugs* instead of food" while "half the world's starving" (124), Lusa wants to grow corn (108). Lytle would likely have approved the sentiment, but Lusa comes up against the harsh realities of modern "[f]arm economics" (124). Subsistence farming has become so unfeasible that the locals now "buy feed at Southern States and go to Kroger's

---

6. Barbara Kingsolver, *Prodigal Summer* (London: Faber and Faber, 2001), 84; Tate, "Remarks on the Southern Religion," 156–157. All subsequent page references to *Prodigal Summer* will be incorporated into the main text.

for a loaf of god-awful bread that was baked in another state" (294). However, their (literal) distaste for this situation does not mean that Egg Fork's unhappy farmers share Ransom's nostalgic, idealized vision of "the old self-subsistent way." Hardened farming members of the Widener clan have, with few regrets, left the land altogether to work in the nearby Toyota automobile plant (120–21)—further evidence that, despite its geographical isolation, Egg Fork is entangled in national and global trade and labor relations.[7]

Lusa eventually transcends the farming community's skepticism toward her urban, intellectual, and immigrant background. She does so by manipulating and even remapping the agricultural market economy so that it goes beyond the economic determinism of corporate agribusiness to encompass geographies, histories, and cultures that are decidedly not "southern" in any familiar sense. Lusa hatches a scheme to collect and raise goats (worthlessly overabundant in the local economy) and sell them to an Arab cousin in New York before Id-al-Fitr and Id-al-Adha, two Muslim holidays organized around goat feasts. By thus becoming a successful landowner and farmer, albeit an unorthodox one, Lusa negotiates a position for herself within the Widener family, and within the recognizably "southern" narrative geography of "the Widener place": "one long story, the history of a family that had stayed on its land. And that story was hers now as well" (440). But she also reconnects with her own family's "farming lineages" (45)—not in the American South, but in Poland (104) and Palestine (164). Ultimately then, if *Prodigal Summer* rescues a rural, agricultural "sense of place," it is not just post-Agrarian or even postsouthern: it is transnational.

There is much more that could be said about Kingsolver's rich and complex novel, not least from an ecocritical angle. (I doubt that many readers will come away from *Prodigal Summer* feeling that, for all its depressing revelations of despoliation and extinction, Nature has been entirely effaced.) As I bring this book to a close, however, I want to end by emphasizing the extent to which *Prodigal Summer*, like *A Man in Full* and *Those Bones Are Not My Child*, reveals that "place" in "the South" must be increasingly understood in a transnational context.

In Part 2, I applauded Richard Ford for comprehensively deconstructing those images and myths that supposedly have defined the distinctiveness of "the South" and "southern literature": community, (tragic) history, and "sense

---

7. Ransom, "Land!" 219.

of place," especially as it has been defined with comparative reference to "the North" as a purported "nonplace." I suggested that Ford rejects the residual hold of "the South" as an ideologically loaded locus in Walker Percy's protopostsouthern fiction so that, in *Independence Day*, Frank Bascombe speaks to us from the late-capitalist landscape of postsouthern America. Yet, having clinically dissected and disposed of the hoary shibboleths that supposedly define "the South" as different from "the North," *Independence Day* becomes entangled in even more pervasive and powerful myths of *national* identity. As we saw in Chapter 5, in *The Sportswriter* Frank Bascombe and his parents had no "sense of their *place*" in the historical geography of the (white) South. Frank's adolescent experience in Mississippi comprehensively repudiated the assumption of Faulkner's Gavin Stevens that "For every Southern boy fourteen years old . . . there is the instant when it's still not yet two oclock on that July afternoon in 1863" when General George Pickett led the charge at Gettysburg. Yet in *Independence Day*, Frank cheerfully requires his son Paul to read excerpts from Carl Becker's *The Declaration of Independence* as Independence Day approaches. So, whereas Frank could never have considered 3 July 1863 as a totemic expression of regional (or pseudonational) difference, he still believes that 4 July 1776 can operate as an organizing myth of national (as well as familial) coherence.[8]

To put it another way, having got beyond Faulkner and Welty country, Frank immerses himself in the self-consciously "American" language-landscape of Ralph Waldo Emerson. This is not to say that *Independence Day* caricatures Emerson as a simple-minded nationalist, or reduces Emersonian ideas of "self-reliance" and "independence" to vulgar versions of American individualism or exceptionalism.[9] Yet *Independence Day*'s extended musings upon "American-ness" tend to preclude consideration of social, economic, spatial, or human relations that go beyond the boundaries of the nation-state. (Frank's wry celebration of the Canadian welfare state is a notable exception.) This is perhaps most apparent in Frank's inclination to read the property market and demographic flows exclusively in a national framework. Frank exhibits a creditable understanding of African American migratory patterns and property ownership across the country, and it may be true that "real

---

8. William Faulkner, *Intruder in the Dust* (1948; reprint, New York: Vintage, 1972), 194.

9. As I demonstrated in Chapter 6, Ford interprets "independence," with careful reference to Emerson, in terms of social relations and connections with others, rather than as isolation or vulgar individualism.

estate prices [are] an index to the national well-being." But Frank demonstrates scant awareness that there are *trans*national flows of capital and people into the United States from beyond its borders. The early passing reference to "the workers all Cape Verdeans and wily Hondurans from poorer towns north of here" indicates Frank's broader failure to recognize that transnational migratory patterns provide the cheap labor in action so close to home—that this part of Haddam, at least, is the world the immigrants made.[10]

Having praised Ford's thoroughgoing embrace and practice of "the postsouthern turn" across three chapters, it is not my intention to turn around and score him in these final few paragraphs. My point is that there are conceptual limitations to Lewis P. Simpson's term "postsouthern America"—not least as I myself have used the term to read *Independence Day*. If the implications of Simpson's term were startling for southern literary studies circa 1980, it is increasingly apparent that complex relationships of capital, land, and place (as well as community, family, and so on) are no longer played out only between regions, within the nation. This is why the work of Wolfe, Bambara, and Kingsolver is particularly important: these writers have, in different ways and to varying degrees, begun to resituate "the South" and to reformulate attendant ideas of "place" within the transnational frameworks of capital, migration, and labor.

In the last few years, there has been much talk of a "transnational turn" in American Studies. As Robert Gross has recognized, economic globalization—"the far-ranging transformation of the world economy over the last two decades [by] transnational corporations [spreading] around the globe"—looms large in any definition or discussion of "transnationalism." I have

---

10. Ford, *Independence Day*, 5, 3. See Chapter 6 for further discussion of the opening paragraphs of the novel. Frank's ignorance of sociopolitical processes beyond the borders of the nation-state is perhaps even more pronounced in *The Sportswriter* (though arguably less significant given that ideas of American identity are less explicit than in *Independence Day*). When octogenarian neighbor Delia Deffeyes asks his opinion on "what our government's doing to the poor people in Central America," Frank responds blankly, "I've been out of town a couple of days, Dee" (*The Sportswriter*, 217). Frank's inability to remember who is president—he confuses Ronald Reagan with another actor, Richard Chamberlain (*The Sportswriter*, 218)—suggests that Frank's complacent immanence in the capitalist landscapes of postsouthern America has spilled over into Reaganite amnesia/ignorance about the United States' imperialist activities beyond its national borders. (*The Sportswriter* was published in the year that the Iran-Contra scandal broke.)

noted (especially in my analysis of Atlanta and its literary representations) that there is compelling evidence that "the South" is now comprehensively integrated into a globalized economy dominated by multinational corporations that have transcended or circumvented the physical boundaries of the nation-state. To recall only one resonant example, we have seen how *A Man in Full* suggests and satirizes the South's relocation within this global economic context by describing the semiotic transformation of the Southern Planters Bank and Trust Company into PlannersBanc, a more suitably postsouthern, "international" term that testifies to the bank's growing role in the transnational flow of capital.[11]

Transnationalism is not *only* about global capital flows, however; nor is it simply synonymous with the "provincialism" that Allen Tate attributed to the erasure of regional cultures by both capitalist and socialist world-systems. As Gross observes, "'Transnationalism' captures a world of fluid borders, where goods, ideas, and people flow constantly across once-sovereign space." Of course, the image of a transnational flow of people into the South should—to put it mildly—give pause for uneasy thought. After all, the South has an inauspicious history of transatlantic trade in people *as* goods—a history that all too often has been absent from "southern literature." Indeed, one might well worry that the labor of present-day immigrants perpetuates this identifiably southern history of exploitation, albeit without slavery's blatant coercion. In Chapter 9, with reference to *A Man in Full* and the denizens of Chambodia employed in a chicken-processing plant on the periphery of the "international city," I quoted Harvey's observation that "the Broiler Belt" of chicken-processing factories constitutes the "latest industry of toil to reign in the South." Labor historian Leon Fink recently has provided further evidence that the historical-geographical continuities of southern labor have taken a transnational turn with the hiring of cheap immigrant workers in poultry plants throughout the region. In his book about "the *nuevo* New South" of the 1990s, *The Maya of Morganton,* Fink constructs a detailed case study of a labor dispute in Morganton, North Carolina, involving hundreds of poorly paid Guatemalan and Mexican immigrants at a poultry plant called Case Farms.[12]

So one would do well not to come across as utopian when talking about

---

11. Robert Gross, "The Transnational Turn: Rediscovering American Studies in a Wider World," *Journal of American Studies* 34, no. 3 (2000), 378–79.

12. Gross, "The Transnational Turn," 378; Leon Fink, *The Maya of Morganton: Work and Community in the Nuevo New South* (Chapel Hill: University of North Carolina Press, 2003).

the transnational South. Yet transnational immigrant flows do promise to reconfigure "the South" in radical, and even hopeful, ways. I have argued that *A Man in Full* is valuable because it offers an alternative conception of Atlanta as an "international city" defined by immigrant cultures, not the global "space of flows" of finance-capitalism. Bambara's work, meanwhile, bears out Gross's observation that "older minorities, notably, African Americans, [are] reconceiv[ing] themselves in international terms": *Those Bones Are Not My Child* gains much of its power from the "cosmopolitan consciousness" of both the author and her characters, and the transnational connections made between the local and the global politics of class, race, and place. Elsewhere, in the admittedly rather slight story "Madame Bai and the Taking of Stone Mountain," Bambara sketches the sense of solidarity *within* Atlanta itself, during the missing-and-murdered saga, between an African American protagonist and two political refugees from Jordan and Vietnam. It is possible, then, to take a stand: if not in the Agrarian grain, then against the exploitative forces and purely economic definitions of "globalization" or "transnationalism," and for radically revised conceptions of community and solidarity. For example, in *The Maya of Morganton*, Fink demonstrates how the Maya poultry workers reconfigured "community" within and despite the context of economic "globalization"—that is, "the increasing fluidity" not only of capital flows and investments, but also of labor markets—by maintaining connections to Guatemala even while making new friendships and alliances in North Carolina. Here we encounter a notably transnational way of achieving, in Jameson's words, "the practical reconquest of a sense of place." Turning back to fiction with Fink's formulation of globalized community in mind, one can say that, like the Maya of Morganton, the southeast Asian immigrants of *A Man in Full*'s Atlanta rework familiar southern conceptions of "community." Everyday life in Chambodia may be highly contingent, subject to police surveillance and exploitative employment practices, but—as the self-consciously bourgeois white American Conrad Hensley discovers—the residents still demonstrate solidarity in adversity.[13]

It will be intriguing to see how these transnational geographies and demographies develop as the twenty-first century proceeds apace, and how they are depicted in the narrative cartographies of contemporary (post)southern

---

13. Gross, "The Transnational Turn," 378; Bambara, "Madame Bai and the Taking of Stone Mountain," in *Deep Sightings and Rescue Missions* (New York: Pantheon, 1996), 27–44; Fink, *The Maya of Morganton*, 3; Jameson, *Postmodernism*, 51.

fiction. One should probably resist the temptation to make predictions: after all, no-one could have scripted the bewildering boom-and-bust of Bernie Ebbers's WorldCom, a "global" corporation the name of which even Tom Wolfe might have thought beyond parody, and based not in Atlanta but in Barry Hannah's hometown of Clinton, Mississippi, "where [Ulysses S.] Grant had once stabled his horses in a chapel in the midst of giant cedars. Now its suburbs defined it. Pine forests ripped down for the blocky bunkers of new businessmen and computer Christians fleeing the blacker Jackson to the east."[14] One can at least hope that writers will emerge from the region's new transnational populations to rewrite "the South" again in unexpected and exciting ways.[15] And though predictions are perilous, it does not seem entirely foolhardy to conclude by venturing a premise for future debate: that nearly a quarter-century after Lewis P. Simpson coined the term, to tell about the postsouthern, and to map postsouthern geographies, is increasingly and necessarily also to take the transnational turn. Only then can one develop a sufficiently critical, global "sense of place."

14. Barry Hannah, *Yonder Stands Your Orphan* (London: Atlantic Books, 2001), 217.

15. As Maureen Ryan has recently demonstrated, one distinctive (yet eclectic) ethnic group of "outsiders with inside information" on the region has already emerged in contemporary southern fiction: the Vietnamese who populate stories and novels by Robert Olen Butler, Wayne Karlin, Mary Gardner, and Lan Cao. See Ryan, "Outsiders with Inside Information: The Vietnamese in the Fiction of the Contemporary American South," in Suzanne W. Jones and Sharon Monteith, eds., *South to a New Place: Region, Literature, Culture* (Baton Rouge: Louisiana State University Press, 2002), 235–252.

Bibliography

Abbott, Carl. "New West, New South, New Region: The Discovery of the Sunbelt." In *Searching for the Sunbelt: Historical Perspectives on a Region,* edited by Raymond A. Mohl. Knoxville: University of Tennessee Press, 1990.

Agar, Herbert, and Allen Tate, eds., *Who Owns America?: A New Declaration of Independence.* 1936. Reprint, Wilmington, Del.: ISI Books, 1999.

Allen, Frederick. *Atlanta Rising: The Invention of an International City, 1946–1996.* Atlanta: Longstreet Press, 1996.

Allen, Ivan, and Paul Hemphill. *Mayor: Notes on the Sixties.* New York: Simon and Schuster, 1971.

Applebome, Peter. *Dixie Rising: How the South Is Shaping American Values, Politics and Culture.* 1996. Reprint, New York: Harvest, 1997.

Bakhtin, Mikhail. "Forms of Time and of the Chronotope in the Novel: Notes toward a Historical Poetics." In *The Dialogical Imagination,* edited by Michael Holquist. Translated from the Russian by Carolyn Emerson and Michael Holquist. Austin: University of Texas Press, 1981.

Baldwin, James. *Evidence of Things Not Seen.* London: Michael Joseph, 1985.

Bambara, Toni Cade. "Madame Bai and the Taking of Stone Mountain." In *Deep Sightings and Rescue Missions: Fictions, Essays and Conversations,* edited by Toni Morrison. New York: Pantheon, 1996.

———. *Those Bones Are Not My Child.* New York: Pantheon, 1999.

Bartley, Numan V. "The New Deal as a Turning Point." In *Major Problems in the History of the American South,* vol. 2, *The New South,* edited by Paul Escott and David Goldfield. Lexington, Mass: D. C. Heath, 1990.

———. *The Creation of Modern Georgia.* 2nd ed. Athens: University of Georgia Press, 1990.

Baudrillard, Jean. *Simulations.* Translated from the French by Paul Foss, Paul Patton, and Philip Beitchman. New York: Semiotext(e), 1983.

Bellah, Robert, et al. *Habits of the Heart: Individualism and Commitment in American Life.* New York: Perennial, 1986.

Bingham, Emily, and Thomas Underwood, eds. *The Southern Agrarians and the New Deal: Essays after "I'll Take My Stand."* Charlottesville: University Press of Virginia, 2001.

Bisher, Furman. "A Major League Boost for the Economy." *Atlanta,* August 1964: 45–47.

Bledsoe, Erik. "An Interview with Harry Crews." In *Perspectives on Harry Crews*, edited by Erik Bledsoe. Jackson: University Press of Mississippi, 2001.

Bloom, Harold. *The Anxiety of Influence: A Theory of Poetry.* New York: Oxford University Press, 1973.

Bone, Martyn. "'All the Confederate Dead . . . All of Faulkner the Great': Faulkner, Hannah, Neo-Confederate Narrative and Postsouthern Parody." *Mississippi Quarterly* 54, no. 2 (spring 2001): 197–211.

———. "Were Farms Necessary?: The Agrarian Question." *Mississippi Quarterly* 56, no. 3 (summer 2003): 421-37.

Bonetti, Kay. "An Interview with Richard Ford." *The Missouri Review* 10, no. 2 (1987): 71–96.

Boyd, Valerie. "Toni Morrison Brings Friend's *Bones* to Print." *Atlanta Journal-Constitution*, 17 October 1999, http://www.accessatlanta.com/partners/ajc/newsatlanta/bambara/morrison.html.

Cass, Michael. Foreword to *A Requiem for the Renascence: The State of Fiction in the Modern South*, by Walter Sullivan. Athens: University of Georgia Press, 1976.

Castells, Manuel. *The Informational City.* Oxford: Blackwell, 1989.

Ciuba, Gary M. *Walker Percy: Books of Revelations.* Athens: University of Georgia Press, 1991.

Cobb, James C. *The Selling of the South: The Southern Crusade for Industrial Development, 1936–1990.* 2nd ed. Urbana and Chicago: University of Illinois Press, 1993.

Collins, Janelle. "Generating Power: Fission, Fusion, and Postmodern Politics in Bambara's *The Salt Eaters*." *MELUS* 21, no. 2 (summer 1996): 35–47.

Conkin, Paul K. *The Southern Agrarians.* Knoxville: University of Tennessee Press, 1988.

Cowley, Malcolm. "Going with the Wind." In *Recasting: "Gone with the Wind" in American Culture*, edited by Darden Asbury Pyron. Miami: University Presses of Florida, 1983.

Creed, Gerald W., and Barbara Ching. "Recognizing Rusticity: Identity and the Power of Place." Introduction to *Knowing Your Place: Rural Identity and Cultural Hierarchy.* New York: Routledge, 1997.

Crews, Harry. *A Childhood: The Biography of a Place.* In *Classic Crews: A Harry Crews Reader.* New York: Touchstone, 1993.

Crimmins, Tim. "The Atlanta Palimpsest: Stripping Away the Layers of the Past." *Atlanta Historical Journal* 26 (1982): 13–32.

Daniel, Pete. "Federal Farming Policy and the End of an Agrarian Way of Life." In *Major Problems in the History of the American South*, vol. 2, *The New South*, edited by Paul Escott and David Goldfield. Lexington, Mass: D. C. Heath, 1990.

Daniel, Robert. "Eudora Welty's Sense of Place." In *Southern Renascence: The Literature of the Modern South*, edited by Louis D. Rubin and Robert D. Jacobs. Baltimore: Johns Hopkins University Press, 1953.

Davidson, Donald. "A Mirror for Artists." In *I'll Take My Stand: The South and the Agrarian Tradition*, by Twelve Southerners. 1930. Reprint, Baton Rouge: Louisiana State University Press, 1977.

———. "Dilemma of the Southern Liberals." In *The Southern Agrarians and the New Deal: Essays after "I'll Take My Stand,"* edited by Emily Bingham and Thomas Underwood. Charlottesville: University Press of Virginia, 2001.

———. "*I'll Take My Stand*: A History." *American Review* 5 (1935): 301–21.

———. "Current Attitudes toward Folklore." In *Still Rebels, Still Yankees and Other Essays*, edited by Lewis P. Simpson. 1957. Reprint, Baton Rouge: Louisiana State University Press, 1972.

———. "Still Rebels, Still Yankees." In *Still Rebels, Still Yankees and Other Essays*.

———."Why the Modern South Has a Great Literature." In *Still Rebels, Still Yankees and Other Essays*.

———."Agrarianism and Politics." *Review of Politics* 1 (April 1939): 114–25.

———. *Southern Writers in the Modern World*. Athens: University of Georgia Press, 1958.

Debord, Guy. *The Society of the Spectacle*. 1967. Reprint, New York: Zone Books, 1995.

De Certeau, Michel. *The Practice of Everyday Life*. Berkeley: University of California Press, 1984.

DeLillo, Don. *The Body Artist*. London: Picador, 2001.

Dickey, James. "Notes on the Decline of Outrage." In *South: Modern Southern Literature in Its Cultural Setting*, edited by Louis D. Rubin and Robert D. Jacobs. Garden City, N.Y.: Dolphin Books, 1961.

Dreiser, Theodore. *Sister Carrie*. 1900. Reprint, Harmondsworth: Penguin Classics, 1986.

Douglas, Ellen. "Neighborhoods." In *A Place Called Mississippi: Collected Narratives*, edited by Marion Barnwell. Jackson: University Press of Mississippi, 1997.

Duncan, Christopher. *Fugitive Theory: Political Theory, the Southern Agrarians, and America*. Lanham, Md.: Lexington Books. 2000.

Dupuy, Edward. "The Confessions of an Ex-Suicide: Relenting and Recovering in Richard Ford's *The Sportswriter*." *Southern Literary Journal* 23, no. 1 (fall 1990): 93–103.

Dwyer, Richard. "The Case of the Cool Reception." In *Recasting: "Gone with the Wind" in American Culture*, edited by Darden Asbury Pyron. Miami: University Presses of Florida, 1983.

Ehrenreich, Barbara. "Realty Bites." *New Republic*, 18–25 September 1995, 48–51.

Egerton, John. *The Americanization of Dixie: The Southernization of America*. New York: Harper and Row, 1974.

Ellis, R. J., and Graham Thompson, "Interview with Richard Ford." *Over Here: A European Journal of American Culture* 16, no. 2 (winter 1996): 105–25.

Ellis, William S. "Atlanta, Pacesetter City of the South." *National Geographic* 135, no. 2 (February 1969): 246–81.

Escott, Paul D., and David Goldfield, eds. *Major Problems in the History of the American South*. Vol. 2, *The New South*. Lexington, Mass: D. C. Heath, 1990.

Faulkner, William. *Absalom, Absalom!* 1936. Reprint, New York: Vintage International, 1993.

———. *The Hamlet*. 1940. 3rd rev. ed. New York: Vintage, 1964.

———. "Delta Autumn." In *Go Down, Moses*. 1942. Reprint, New York: Vintage, 1973.

———. *Intruder in the Dust*. 1948. Reprint, New York: Vintage, 1972.

———. *Requiem for a Nun*. 1951. Reprint, New York: Vintage, 1975.

———. *The Mansion*. 1959. Reprint, New York: Vintage, 1965.

Fink, Leon. *The Maya of Morganton: Work and Community in the Nuevo New South*. Chapel Hill: University of North Carolina Press, 2003.

Folks, Jeffrey. "The Risks of Membership: Richard Ford's *The Sportswriter*." *Mississippi Quarterly* 52, no. 1 (winter 1998–99): 73–88.

Ford, Richard. *A Piece of My Heart*. 1976. Reprint, London: Harvill, 1996.

———. "Walker Percy: Not Just Whistling Dixie," *National Review* 29 (13 May 1977): 558–64.

———. *The Sportswriter*. 1986. Reprint, London: Harvill, 1996.

———. "My Mother, In Memory." *Harper's* 275 (August 1987): 44–57.

———. "Heartbreak Motels." *Harper's* 279 (August 1989): 12–15.

———. "An Urge for Going: Why I Don't Live Where I Used to Live." *Harper's* 284 (February 1992): 60–68.

———. "S.O.P." *Aperture* 127 (spring 1992): 64.

———. *Independence Day*. 1995. Reprint, London: Harvill, 1996.

Ford, Richard, et al. "A Stubborn Sense of Place." *Harper's* (August 1986): 35–45.

Garner, Phil. Reviews of Anne Rivers Siddons's *Peachtree Road* and Dudley Clendinen's *The Enduring South*. *Atlanta* (December 1988): 61–63.

Garreau, Joel. *The Nine Nations of North America*. New York: Avon, 1981.

———. *Edge City: Life on the New Frontier*. New York: Anchor, 1991.

Gilroy, Paul. *The Black Atlantic: Modernity and Double Consciousness*. London: Verso, 1993.

Gleason, William. *The Leisure Ethic: Work and Play in American Literature, 1840–1940*. Stanford: Stanford University Press, 1999.

Godden, Richard. *Fictions of Capital: The American Novel from James to Mailer*. Cambridge: Cambridge University Press, 1990.

———. *Fictions of Labor: William Faulkner and the South's Long Revolution*. Cambridge: Cambridge University Press, 1997.

Graff, Gerald. "American Criticism Left and Right." In *Ideology and Classic American Literature*, edited by Sacvan Bercovitch and Myra Jehlen. Cambridge: Cambridge University Press, 1986.

Gray, Richard. *The Literature of Memory: Modern Writers of the American South*. London: Edward Arnold, 1977.

———. *Writing the South: Ideas of an American Region.* 1986. Reprint, Baton Rouge: Louisiana State University Press, 1998.

Gretlund, Jan Nordby. *Eudora Welty's Aesthetics of Place.* Odense, Denmark: Odense University Press, 1994.

Griffin, Farah Jasmine. "Toni Cade Bambara: Free to Be Anywhere in the Universe." *Callaloo* 19, no. 2 (1996): 229–31.

Gross, Robert. "The Transnational Turn: Rediscovering American Studies in a Wider World." *Journal of American Studies* 34, no. 3 (2000): 373–93.

Guagliardo, Huey. "A Conversation with Richard Ford." *Southern Review* 34, no. 3 (summer 1998): 609–20.

Guinn, Matthew. *After Southern Modernism: Fiction of the Contemporary South.* Jackson: University Press of Mississippi, 2000.

Hannah, Barry. *Yonder Stands Your Orphan.* London: Atlantic Books, 2001.

Hartshorn, Truman A., et al. *Metropolis in Georgia: Atlanta's Rise as a Major Transaction Center.* Cambridge, Mass: Ballinger, 1976.

Harvey, David. *The Condition of Postmodernity.* Oxford: Blackwell, 1989.

———. *Justice, Nature, and the Geography of Difference.* Oxford: Blackwell, 1996.

Hobson, Fred. "A South Too Busy to Hate." In Fifteen Southerners, *Why the South Will Survive.* Athens: University of Georgia Press, 1981.

———. *Tell about the South: The Southern Rage to Explain.* Baton Rouge: Louisiana State University Press, 1983.

———. *The Southern Writer in the Postmodern World.* Athens: University of Georgia Press, 1991.

———. "Surveyors and Boundaries: Southern Literature and Southern Literary Scholarship after Mid-Century." *Southern Review* 27, no. 4 (winter 1992): 739–55.

Hoffman, Frederick J. "The Sense of Place." In *Southern Renascence: The Literature of the Modern South,* edited by Louis D. Rubin and Robert D. Jacobs. Baltimore: Johns Hopkins University Press, 1953.

———. *The Art of Southern Fiction: A Study of Some Modern Novelists.* Carbondale and Edwardsville: Southern Illinois University Press, 1967.

Holditch, W. Kenneth. "On the Fine Edge of Disappearing: Desperation and Despair in *A Piece of My Heart.*" In *Perspectives on Richard Ford,* edited by Huey Guagliardo. Jackson: University Press of Mississippi, 2000.

Holman, C. Hugh. "The View from the Regency Hyatt." In *The Roots of Southern Writing: Essays on the Literature of the American South.* Athens: University of Georgia Press, 1972.

Hooks, bell. "Homeplace: A Site of Resistance." In *Yearning: Race, Gender, and Cultural Politics.* Boston: South End Press, 1990.

———. "Uniquely Toni Cade Bambara." *Black Issues Book Review* 2, no. 1 (January/February 2000): 14–16.

Hornby, Nick. *Contemporary American Fiction.* New York: SMJ, 1992.
Hutcheon, Linda. *A Poetics of Postmodernism.* London: Routledge, 1988.
Jameson, Fredric. *The Political Unconscious: Narrative as Socially Symbolic Act.* London: Methuen, 1981.
———. *Postmodernism, or, the Cultural Logic of Late Capitalism.* London: Verso, 1991.
———. "The Brick and the Balloon: Architecture, Idealism and Land Speculation." *New Left Review* 228 (March/April 1998): 25–46.
———. "Culture and Finance Capital." In *The Cultural Turn: Selected Writings on the Postmodern, 1983–1998.* London: Verso, 1998.
Jancovich, Mark. *The Cultural Politics of the New Criticism.* Cambridge: Cambridge University Press, 1993.
Jarvis, Brian. *Postmodern Cartographies: The Geographical Imagination in Contemporary American Culture.* London: Pluto, 1998.
Jones, Anne Goodwyn. *Tomorrow Is Another Day: The Woman Writer in the South, 1859–1936.* Baton Rouge: Louisiana State University Press, 1980.
Justus, James. Foreword to *Southern Writers at Century's End,* edited by Jeffrey Folks and James Perkins. Lexington: University Press of Kentucky, 1997.
Karl, Frederick. *William Faulkner: American Writer.* 1989. Reprint, New York: Ballantine Books, 1990.
Kazin, Alfred. *On Native Grounds.* 1942. Garden City, N.Y.: Doubleday Anchor, 1956.
Kennedy, Richard S. Preface to *Literary New Orleans: Essays and Meditations.* Baton Rouge: Louisiana State University Press, 1992.
King, Richard H. *A Southern Renaissance: The Cultural Awakening of the American South, 1930–1955.* New York: Oxford University Press, 1980.
———. "The 'Simple Story's' Ideology: *Gone with the Wind* and the New South Creed." In *Recasting: Gone with the Wind in American Culture,* edited by Darden Asbury Pyron. Miami: University Presses of Florida, 1983.
Kingsolver, Barbara. *Prodigal Summer.* 2000. Reprint, London: Faber and Faber, 2001.
Kreyling, Michael. "*The Fathers:* A Postsouthern Narrative Reading." In *Southern Literature and Literary Theory,* edited by Jefferson Humphries. Athens: University of Georgia Press, 1990.
———. *Inventing Southern Literature.* Jackson: University Press of Mississippi, 1998.
Lawry, Edward G. "Literature as Philosophy: *The Moviegoer.*" *The Monist* 63, no. 4 (October 1980): 547–57.
Lawson, Lewis. *Still Following Percy.* Jackson: University Press of Mississippi. 1996.
Lowe, John. Introduction to *The Future of Southern Letters,* edited by John Lowe and Jefferson Humphries. New York: Oxford University Press, 1996.
———. "City of Torment." Review of *Those Bones Are Not My Child* by Toni Cade Bambara. *The World and I* 15, no. 2 (February 2000): 267–74.
Lukács, Georg. *The Historical Novel.* 1962. Reprint, Harmondsworth: Peregrine Books, 1969.

Lyotard, Jean-François. *The Postmodern Condition: A Report on Knowledge*. Manchester, U.K.: Manchester University Press, 1984.

Lytle, Andrew. "The Hind Tit." In *I'll Take My Stand: The South and the Agrarian Tradition*, by Twelve Southerners. 1930. Reprint, Baton Rouge: Louisiana State University Press, 1977.

———. "The Small Farm Secures the State." In *Who Owns America?: A New Declaration of Independence*, edited by Herbert Agar and Allen Tate. 1936. Wilmington, Del.: ISI Books, 1999.

———. "How Many Miles to Babylon." In *Southern Renascence: The Literature of the Modern South*, edited by Louis D. Rubin and Robert D. Jacobs. Baltimore: Johns Hopkins University Press, 1953.

Mailer, Norman. "A Man Half Full." *New York Review of Books*, 17 December 1998, 18–23.

Majeski, Sophie. "Richard Ford: The *Salon* Interview." http://www.salon1999.com/weekly/interview960708.html.

Marx, Karl, and Frederick Engels. *The Communist Manifesto*. 1848. Reprint, London: Verso, 1998.

Massey, Doreen. "A Global Sense of Place." In *Reading Human Geography: The Poetics and Politics of Inquiry*, edited by Trevor Barnes and Dick Gregory. London: Arnold, 1997.

McKinney, John C., and Linda Bourque, "The Changing South: National Incorporation of a Region." *American Sociological Review* 36, no. 3 (June 1971): 399–412.

McMurtry, Larry. Review of Richard Ford's *A Piece of My Heart*. *New York Times Book Review*, 24 October 1976, 16.

Milne, Drew. "Introduction Part II: Reading Marxist Literary Theory." In *Marxist Literary Theory*, edited by Terry Eagleton and Drew Milne. Oxford: Blackwell, 1996.

Mitchell, Margaret. *Gone with the Wind*. 1936. Reprint, London: Pan Books, 1974.

Mohl, Raymond A., ed. *Searching for the Sunbelt: Historical Perspectives on a Region*. Knoxville: University of Tennessee Press, 1990.

Morrison, Toni. "City Limits, Village Values: Concepts of the Neighborhood in Black Fiction." In *Literature and the Urban Experience: Essays on the City and Literature*, edited by Michael C. Jaye and Ann Chalmers Watts. Manchester: Manchester University Press, 1981.

Murphy, Paul V. *The Rebuke of History: The Southern Agrarians and American Conservative Thought*. Chapel Hill: University of North Carolina Press, 2001.

Naipaul, V. S. *A Turn in the South*. London: Penguin, 1989.

Newman, Harvey K. *Southern Hospitality: Tourism and the Growth of Atlanta*. Tuscaloosa: University of Alabama Press, 1999.

Nixon, H. C. "Whither Southern Economy?" In *I'll Take My Stand: The South and the Agrarian Tradition*, by Twelve Southerners. 1930. Reprint, Baton Rouge: Louisiana State University Press, 1977.

———. "From Tenancy to the Forefront." In *The Southern Agrarians and the New Deal*, edited by Emily Bingham and Thomas Underwood. Charlottesville: University Press of Virginia, 2001.

O'Briant, Don. "Profile on Peachtree." *Atlanta Journal-Constitution*, 26 January 1986, M4.

———. "Siddons: I Don't Want to Live in This Mess." *Atlanta Journal-Constitution*, 25 May 1997, K3.

———. "Anne Rivers Siddons: Novelist Counts on New Surroundings to Refresh Her Writing." *Atlanta Journal-Constitution*, 25 June 1998, D1.

———. "Looking for Atlanta." *Atlanta Journal-Constitution*, 30 October 1998, K1.

———. "A Wolfe at Our Door?: Writer's Friends Say Atlanta Will Emerge Unscathed from New Novel about Race and Real Estate." *Atlanta Journal-Constitution*, 24 September 1998, D1.

———. "*Full* Visit: Lots of Dining, No Whining: Where's the Mayor?: Bill Campbell has Been Noticeably Absent at Wolfe Gatherings." *Atlanta Journal-Constitution*, 20 November 1998, G6.

O'Brien, Kenneth. "Race, Romance, and the Southern Literary Tradition." In *Recasting: "Gone with the Wind" in American Culture*, edited by Darden Asbury Pyron. Miami: University Presses of Florida, 1983.

O'Brien, Michael. "A Heterodox Note on the Southern Renaissance." In *Rethinking the South: Essays in Intellectual History*. Baltimore: Johns Hopkins University Press, 1988.

O'Donnell, George Marion. "Looking Down the Cotton Row." In *Who Owns America?: A New Declaration of Independence*, edited by Herbert Agar and Allen Tate. 1936. Reprint, Wilmington, Del.: ISI Books, 1999.

O'Connor, Flannery. "The Artificial Nigger." In *The Complete Stories*. 1971. Reprint, London: Faber & Faber, 1990.

———. "The Displaced Person." In *The Complete Stories*.

———. "A Late Encounter with the Enemy." In *The Complete Stories*.

Owsley, Frank. "The Irrepressible Conflict." In *I'll Take My Stand: The South and the Agrarian Tradition*, by Twelve Southerners. 1930. Reprint, Baton Rouge: Louisiana State University Press, 1977.

———. "The Pillars of Agrarianism." *American Review* 4 (March 1935): 529–47.

Percy, Walker. "Carnival in Gentilly." *Forum* 3 (1960): 4–18.

———. *The Moviegoer*. 1961. New York: Vintage International, 1998.

———. *The Last Gentleman*. 1966. New York: Ivy, 1989.

———. "Going Back to Georgia." In *Signposts in a Strange Land*, edited by Patrick Samway. London: Bellew, 1991.

———. *Lost in the Cosmos: The Last Self-Help Book*. 1983. London: Arena, 1984.

———. "Novel Writing in an Apocalyptic Time." In *Signposts in a Strange Land*, edited by Patrick Samway. London: Bellew, 1991.

———. "Why I Live Where I Live." In *Signposts in a Strange Land*, edited by Patrick Samway. London: Bellew, 1991.
Pfeil, Fred. "Fiction after History." In *Another Tale to Tell: Politics and Narrative in Postmodern Culture*. London: Verso, 1990.
Pomerantz, Gary M. *Where Peachtree Meets Sweet Auburn: A Saga of Race and Family*. New York: Penguin, 1997.
Pyron, Darden Asbury, ed. *Recasting: "Gone with the Wind" in American Culture*. Miami: University Presses of Florida, 1983.
———. "The Inner War of Southern History." In *Recasting: "Gone with the Wind" in American Culture*, edited by Darden Asbury Pyron. Miami: University Presses of Florida, 1983.
Ransom, John Crowe. "Reconstructed but Unregenerate." In *I'll Take My Stand: The South and the Agrarian Tradition*, by Twelve Southerners. 1930. Reprint, Baton Rouge: Louisiana State University Press, 1977.
———. "Land! An Answer to the Unemployment Problem." *Harper's* (July 1932): 216–24.
———. "Happy Farmers." *American Review* 1 (October 1933): 513–35.
———. "The Aesthetics of Regionalism." *American Review* 2 (January 1934): 290–310.
———. "Modern with the Southern Accent." *Virginia Quarterly Review* 11 (April 1935): 184–200.
———. "The South Is a Bulwark." *Scribner's* 99 (May 1936): 299–303.
———. "Fiction Harvest." *Southern Review* 2 (1936–37): 399–418.
Raper, Julias Rowan. "Inventing Modern Southern Fiction: A Postmodern View." *Southern Literary Journal* 22, no. 2 (spring 1990): 3–18.
Reed, John Shelton. Review of Tom Wolfe's *A Man in Full*. *Southern Cultures* 5, no. 2 (summer 1999): http://www.unc.edu/depts/csas/socult/revs/sc52rev1.htm
Reed, Richard. "Real Estate in *Look Homeward, Angel*." *Southern Literary Journal* 19, no. 1 (fall 1986): 46–55.
Rice, Bradley. "Searching for the Sunbelt." In *Searching for the Sunbelt: Historical Perspectives on a Region*, edited by Raymond A. Mohl. Knoxville: University of Tennessee Press, 1990.
Ritchie, Harry. "Tom Wolfe in Full." *Waterstone's Magazine*, 15 (autumn 1998): 2–9.
Rock, Virginia. "Twelve Southerners: Biographical Essays." In *I'll Take My Stand: The South and the Agrarian Tradition*, by Twelve Southerners. 1930. Reprint, Baton Rouge: Louisiana State University Press, 1977.
Romine, Scott. "Where Is Southern Literature?: The Practice of Place in a Postsouthern Age." *Critical Survey* 12, no. 1 (spring 2000): 5–27.
———. *The Narrative Forms of Southern Community*. Baton Rouge: Louisiana State University Press, 1999.
Rose, Gillian. *Feminism and Geography: The Limits of Geographical Knowledge*. Cambridge, U.K.: Polity Press, 1993.

Rouse, H. Blair. "Time and Place in Southern Fiction." In *Southern Renascence: The Literature of the Modern South*, edited by Louis D. Rubin and Robert D. Jacobs. Baltimore: Johns Hopkins University Press, 1953.

Rowe, John Carlos. "The Economics of the Body in Kate Chopin's *The Awakening*." In *Kate Chopin Reconsidered: Beyond the Bayou*, edited by Lynda S. Boren and Sara DeSaussure Davis. Baton Rouge: Louisiana State University Press, 1992.

Rubin, Louis D. "Thomas Wolfe in Time and Place." In *Southern Renascence: The Literature of the Modern South*, edited by Louis D. Rubin and Robert D. Jacobs. Baltimore: Johns Hopkins University Press, 1953.

———. "Introduction to Torchbook Edition (1962)." In *I'll Take My Stand: The South and the Agrarian Tradition*, by Twelve Southerners. 1930. Reprint, Baton Rouge: Louisiana State University Press, 1977.

———. "Fugitives as Agrarians: The Impulse behind *I'll Take My Stand*." In *William Ellis Shoots a Bear: Essays on the Southern Literary Imagination*. Baton Rouge: Louisiana State University Press, 1975.

———. "Introduction: Library of Southern Civilization Edition (1977)." In *I'll Take My Stand: The South and the Agrarian Tradition*, by Twelve Southerners. 1930. Reprint, Baton Rouge: Louisiana State University Press, 1977.

———. *The Wary Fugitives: Four Poets and the South*. Baton Rouge: Louisiana State University Press, 1978.

———. "The American South: The Continuity of Self-Definition." In *The American South: Portrait of a Culture*, edited by Louis D. Rubin. Baton Rouge: Louisiana State University Press, 1980.

———. "Scarlett O'Hara and the Two Quentin Compsons." In *Recasting: "Gone with the Wind" in American Culture*, edited by Darden Asbury Pyron. Miami: University Presses of Florida, 1983.

———, ed. *The American South: Portrait of a Culture*. Washington: Voice of America Forum Series, 1979.

Rubin, Louis D., and Robert D. Jacobs, eds. *Southern Renascence: The Literature of the Modern South*. Baltimore: Johns Hopkins University Press, 1953.

———. Introduction to *South: Modern Southern Literature in Its Cultural Setting*, edited by Louis D. Rubin and Robert D. Jacobs. Garden City, N.Y.: Dolphin Books, 1961.

Rubin, Louis D., and C. Hugh Holman, eds., *Southern Literary Study: Problems and Possibilities*. Chapel Hill: University of North Carolina Press, 1975.

Rutheiser, Charles. *Imagineering Atlanta: The Politics of Place in the City of Dreams*. New York: Verso, 1996.

Ryan, Maureen. "Outsiders with Insider Information: The Vietnamese in the Fiction of the Contemporary American South." In *South to a New Place: Region, Literature, Culture*, edited by Suzanne Jones and Sharon Monteith. Baton Rouge: Louisiana State University Press, 2002.

Saporta, Maria. "ACVB to welcome author of new controversial book." *Atlanta Journal-Constitution*, 27 October 1998, B3.
Shelton, Frank. "Richard Ford (1944–)." In *Contemporary Fiction Writers of the South: A Bio-Bibliographical Sourcebook*, edited by Joseph Flora and Robert Bain. Westport, Conn.: Greenwood Press, 1993.
Siddons, Anne Rivers. *The House Next Door*. 1978. New York: HarperPaperbacks, 1995.
———. *Peachtree Road: Tenth Anniversary Edition*. 1988. Reprint, New York: HarperPaperbacks, 1998.
———. "The Maturing of a City: Atlanta Comes of Age." In *The Prevailing South: Life and Politics in a Changing Culture*, edited by Dudley Clendinen. Atlanta: Longstreet Press, 1988.
———. *Downtown*. 1994. Reprint, London: Warner, 1995.
Simmons, Philip. *Deep Surfaces: Mass Culture and History in Postmodern American Fiction*. Athens: University of Georgia Press, 1997.
Simpson, Lewis P. "What Survivors Do." In *The Brazen Face of History: Studies in the Literary Consciousness of America*. Baton Rouge: Louisiana State University Press, 1980.
———."The Closure of History in a Postsouthern America." In *The Brazen Face of History*.
———. *The Fable of the Southern Writer*. Baton Rouge: Louisiana State University Press, 1994.
Smith, David M. "Inequality in an American City: Atlanta, Georgia, 1960–1970." Occasional Paper No. 17, Department of Geography, Queen Mary College, University of London, January 1981.
Smith, Jennifer. "Workers Demand 'Poultry Justice.'" *Creative Loafing*, 15 April 2000, 27.
Smith, Stephen. "The Rhetoric of Southern Humor." In *The Future of Southern Letters*, edited by John Lowe and Jefferson Humphries. New York: Oxford University Press, 1996.
Soja, Edward. *Postmodern Geographies: The Reassertion of Space in Critical Social Theory*. London: Verso, 1989.
Staats, Marilyn Dorn. *Looking for Atlanta*. 1992. Reprint, New York: Warner Books, 1993.
Stone, Clarence N. *Economic Growth and Neighborhood Discontent: System Bias in the Urban Renewal Program of Atlanta*. Chapel Hill: University of North Carolina Press, 1976.
———. *Regime Politics: Governing Atlanta, 1946–1988*. Lawrence: University Press of Kansas, 1989.
Stoneback, H. R. "'Sunk in the Cornfield with His Family': Sense of Place in O'Connor's 'The Displaced Person.'" *Mississippi Quarterly* 36, no. 4 (fall 1983): 545–55.

Sullivan, Walter. *Death by Melancholy: Essays on Modern Southern Fiction.* Baton Rouge: Louisiana State University Press, 1972.

———. *A Requiem for the Renascence: The State of Fiction in the Modern South.* Athens: University of Georgia Press, 1976.

Summer, Bob. "Peachtree Road Is Journey through Modern Atlanta." Review of Anne Rivers Siddons's *Peachtree Road*. *Atlanta Journal-Constitution*, 16 October 1988, M10.

Tate, Allen. "Remarks on the Southern Religion." In *I'll Take My Stand: The South and the Agrarian Tradition*, by Twelve Southerners. 1930. Reprint, Baton Rouge: Louisiana State University Press, 1977.

———. "Notes on Liberty and Property." In *Who Owns America?: A New Declaration of Independence*, edited by Herbert Agar and Allen Tate. 1936. Reprint, Wilmington, Del.: ISI Books, 1999.

———. "The New Provincialism." In *Essays of Four Decades*. Chicago: Swallow Press, 1969.

———. "The Profession of Letters in the South." In *Essays of Four Decades*.

———. "A Southern Mode of the Imagination." In *Essays of Four Decades*.

———. "What Is a Traditional Society?" In *Essays of Four Decades*.

Twelve Southerners. *I'll Take My Stand: The South and the Agrarian Tradition.* 1930. Reprint, Baton Rouge: Louisiana State University Press, 1977.

Urgo, Joseph. "Faulkner's Real Estate: Land and Literary Speculation in *The Hamlet*." *Mississippi Quarterly* 48, no. 3 (summer 1995): 443–57.

Walker, Elinor Ann. *Richard Ford.* New York: Twayne, 2000.

Warren, Robert Penn. "The Briar Patch." In *I'll Take My Stand: The South and the Agrarian Tradition*, by Twelve Southerners. 1930. Reprint, Baton Rouge: Louisiana State University Press, 1977.

———. "Literature as a Symptom." In *Who Owns America?: A New Declaration of Independence*, edited by Herbert Agar and Allen Tate. 1936. Reprint, Wilmington, Del.: ISI Books, 1999.

———. "William Faulkner." In *William Faulkner: Three Decades of Criticism*, edited by Frederick J. Hoffmann and Olga Vickery. 1960. Reprint, New York and Burlingame: Harbinger, 1963.

———. *A Place to Come To.* London: Secker and Warburg, 1977.

———. "The South: Distance and Change; A Conversation with Robert Penn Warren, William Styron, and Louis D. Rubin, Jr." In *The American South: Portrait of a Culture*, edited by Louis D. Rubin. Washington: Voice of America Forum Series, 1979.

Weaver, Richard. "Aspects of the Southern Philosophy." In *Southern Renascence: The Literature of the Modern South*, edited by Louis D. Rubin and Robert D. Jacobs. Baltimore: Johns Hopkins University Press, 1953.

Webb, Max. "Binx Bolling's New Orleans: Moviegoing, Southern Writing, and Father Abraham." In *The Art of Walker Percy: Stratagems for Being*, edited by Panthea Reid Broughton. Baton Rouge: Louisiana State University Press, 1979.

Welty, Eudora. "Death of a Traveling Salesman." In *A Curtain of Green*. 1943. Harmondsworth: Penguin, 1947.

———. "Some Notes on River Country." In *The Eye of the Story: Selected Essays and Reviews*. 1979. Reprint, London: Virago, 1987.

———. "Place in Fiction." In *The Eye of the Story: Selected Essays and Reviews*.

———. *Losing Battles*. 1970. Reprint, London: Virago, 1986.

———. "Growing Up in the Deep South: A Conversation with Eudora Welty, Shelby Foote, and Louis D. Rubin, Jr." In *The American South: Portrait of a Culture*, edited by Louis D. Rubin. Washington: Voice of America Forum Series, 1979.

———. "The State of Letters: Louis Rubin and the Making of Maps." *Sewanee Review* 97, no. 2 (spring 1989): 253–60.

Westendorp, Tjebbe. "*A Place to Come To*." In *Robert Penn Warren: A Collection of Critical Essays*, edited by Richard Gray. Englewood Cliffs, N.J.: Prentice-Hall, 1980.

Wheen, Francis. *Karl Marx*. 1999. Reprint, London: Fourth Estate, 2000.

Wilson, Charles Reagan. "Place, Sense of." In *The Encyclopedia of Southern Culture*, edited by Charles Reagan Wilson and William Ferris. Chapel Hill: University of North Carolina Press, 1989.

Windham, Donald. *The Dog Star*. 1950. Reprint, Athens, Ga.: Hill Street Press, 1998.

Wolfe, Tom. *The Bonfire of the Vanities*. 1987. Reprint, London: Picador, 1990.

———. *A Man in Full*. London: Jonathan Cape, 1998.

———. "My Three Stooges." In *Hooking Up*. London: Picador, 2000.

Woodward, C. Vann. "The Search for Southern Identity." In *The Burden of Southern History: Enlarged Edition*. 1968. Reprint, Baton Rouge: Louisiana State University Press, 1989.

Wright, Gavin. *Old South, New South: Revolutions in the Southern Economy since the Civil War*. 1986. Reprint, Baton Rouge: Louisiana State University Press, 1996.

Yaeger, Patricia. *Dirt and Desire: Reconstructing Southern Women's Writing, 1930–1990*. Chicago: University of Chicago Press, 2000.

Yates, Richard. *Revolutionary Road*. 1961. Reprint, London: Methuen, 1986.

York, Lamar. "From Hebe to Hippolyta: Anne Rivers Siddons' Novels." *Southern Literary Journal* 17, no. 2 (spring 1995): 91–99.

Young, Andrew. "Andrew Young's State of the City Address, 1989." In *Major Problems in the History of the American South*, vol. 2, *The New South*, edited by Paul Escott and David Goldfield. Lexington, Mass: D. C. Heath, 1990.

Young, Stark. "Not in Memoriam, But in Defense." In *I'll Take My Stand: The South and the Agrarian Tradition*, by Twelve Southerners. 1930. Reprint, Baton Rouge: Louisiana State University Press, 1977.

Young, Stephen Flinn. "Post-southernism: The Southern Sensibility in Postmodern Sculpture." *Southern Quarterly* 27, no. 1 (fall 1989): 41–60.

Young, Thomas Daniel. *The Past in the Present: A Thematic Study of Modern Southern Fiction.* Baton Rouge: Louisiana State University Press, 1981.

Zukin, Sharon. *Landscapes of Power: From Detroit to Disney World.* Berkeley: University of California Press, 1991.

Zwingle, Erla. "Atlanta: Energy and Optimism in the New South." *National Geographic* 154, no. 6 (July 1988): 3–29.

Index

Abbott, Carl, 169
Absalom, Absalom! (Faulkner), 70, 142
Ackerman, Charles, 193
Agrarianism: and the proprietary ideal, viii–ix, 7, 9, 10–11, 16–17, 33–34, 41, 123, 125, 133, 135, 142, 245; and race, 3–4, 16; as anticapitalism, 5–6; and Marxism, 9, 49; and the New Deal, 15, 33; challenged by Robert Penn Warren, 55–64; challenged by Richard Ford, 119, 122, 123; as anti-Atlanta, 141–42; challenged by Flannery O'Connor, 152; challenged by Harry Crews, 245–46; challenged by Barbara Kingsolver, 247–48. *See also* Davidson, Donald; *I'll Take My Stand*; Lytle, Andrew; Neo-Agrarianism; Nixon, Herman; Owsley, Frank; Ransom, John Crowe; Tate, Allen; Warren, Robert Penn; *Who Owns America?*; Young, Stark
Alabama: in *A Place to Come To*, 56–58, 62–63; in *Those Bones Are Not My Child*, 237–38, 239; compared to Atlanta, 239
Allen, Frederick, 149, 179
Allen, Ivan, Jr., 158, 175–80, 186n, 188, 190
Allen, Ivan, Sr., 141, 147, 148
Applebome, Peter, 163
Arkansas: in *A Piece of My Heart*, 76–81, 88
"Artificial Nigger, The " (O'Connor), xii, 150–52, 197–98, 238
Atlanta, xi–xiv, 110; and the postmodern South, 44, 168; and southern literature, 139–40, 142, 146–48, 165–69, 193–94; as "international city," 140, 157–65, 168–69, 171, 181–82, 184, 187, 188, 192, 194, 202–8, 210–12, 221, 222, 223–24, 225, 230–31, 233–34, 239–41; as "space of flows," 140, 202–3, 205, 212, 222, 226, 229n; and "sense of placelessness," 140, 162, 165–66, 201–2, 216, 230; and the Civil War, 140; and the New South, 141; compared to New York, 141, 158, 162–63, 167, 192, 203, 207, 240; compared to Chicago, 141, 167, 240; and the "Atlanta Spirit," 141, 147–48, 192; in *Gone with the Wind*, 143–48; in Flannery O'Connor's work, 149–52; and racial segregation, 150–51, 163–64, 169, 172–75, 176–80, 182, 185, 187, 190, 196, 206–9, 210–11, 220; in *The Dog Star*, 152–57; and creative destruction, 155, 181, 182, 183, 194, 216, 217, 223, 227; as "national city," 158, 175, 178, 188n29, 240; "power structure" of, 158, 172, 174–75, 182, 183–84, 187, 188, 189; international investment in, 159–61, 181, 225; urban renewal of, 162, 175–80, 189–90; compared to Los Angeles, 162–63, 166, 167, 240; edge cities in, 164–65, 196–97; and postsouthernism, 168–69; in *Peachtree Road*, 171–87; Anne Rivers Siddons' view of, 171, 188, 191; in *A Man in Full*, 192–218; capitalist abstraction in, 201–2, 225–26, 228–31, 233, 235; immigrants in, 204–5, 210–12, 221; in *Those Bones Are Not My Child*, 219–41; and Atlanta Child Murders, 219–41; compared to Alabama, 239; compared to other "international cities," 240

Bakhtin, Mikhail, xiii, 235–36
Baldwin, James, 208, 229n, 233, 237, 239
Bambara, Toni Cade, xiii–xiv, 51, 140, 209, 219–41, 243, 250, 252
Bankhead, John, 11
Becker, Carl, 249
Bellah, Robert, 123

Berendt, John, 192
Bingham, Emily, 33
Birringer, Johannes, 49
Bloom, Harold, 97
Bonetti, Kay, 102
Bonfire of the Vanities, The (Wolfe), 192, 193
Bourdieu, Pierre, 201n16
Bourque, Linda, 36
Boyd, Valerie, 235
Brooks, Cleanth, 11
Brown, Norman, 40

California: in *A Piece of My Heart*, 76, 78, 80; in *A Man in Full*, 210, 215
Camus, Albert, 107
"Carnival in Gentilly" (Percy), 66n17
Cass, Michael, 37
Castells, Manuel, xii, xiii, 140, 194, 202–3, 226
Certeau, Michel de, 118, 124, 127, 130, 167, 204, 211
Chicago: in *A Place to Come To*, 61–62; attacked by Donald Davidson, 61, 69, 89; in *The Moviegoer*, 69–71, 128; in *A Piece of My Heart*, 81–85, 87; in *Sister Carrie* (Dreiser), 105; compared to Atlanta, 141, 167. *See also* Illinois
Childhood: The Biography of a Place (Crews), xiv, 245–46
Ching, Barbara, 244
"Circle in the Fire, A" (O'Connor), 152
Community: Donald Davidson's definition of, 17; Allen Tate's critique of "world community," 19; Louis Rubin on the South's loss of, 27; Walter Sullivan on the destruction of, 36; Thomas Daniel Young on the decline of, 37; Frank Bascombe's postsouthern revision of, 119; as "lifestyle enclave," 123, 129; and real estate, 125–31; and race, 126–28; and transnational immigration, 252
Conkin, Paul, viii, 5, 7, 9, 11, 17, 32–33, 49n41
Connecticut: in *Independence Day*, 119, 128–31
Conroy, Pat, 160, 171
Cousins, Tom, 160, 193, 194, 229

Cowley, Malcolm, 146
Creed, Gerald, 244
Crews, Harry, xiv, 43, 245–46
Crimmins, Tim, 190n32
Crow, Trammell, 162

Daniel, Pete, 15
Daniel, Robert, 38, 40
Davidson, Donald, xi, 9–10, 15, 16–17, 20, 25, 28, 30, 31, 36, 48, 50n41, 61, 63, 68, 69, 89, 122, 126, 131, 141, 148
Debord, Guy, 200
DeLillo, Don, 234
Detroit: in *The Sportswriter*, 105–10, 120, 128, 240n27. *See also* Michigan
Dickey, James, 29
"Displaced Person, The" (O'Connor), 151
Dog Star, The (Windham), xii
Douglas, Ellen, vii, 139–40, 169
Downtown (Siddons), xiii, 140, 172, 188–90
Dreiser, Theodore, 105
Dupuy, Edward, 86, 103, 104, 112, 113
Dwyer, Richard, 146

Ebbers, Bernie, 253
Egerton, John, 36n17, 105
Ehrenreich, Barbara, 124–25
Emerson, Ralph Waldo, 131, 249
Engels, Frederick, xiii
Eplan, Leon, 209

Faulkner, William, viii, xi, 20, 21–23, 25, 27, 48, 50, 75–77, 82–83, 84, 85–86, 87, 88, 91, 96, 97, 142, 144, 146, 166, 227, 249
Fink, Leon, 251–52
Flags in the Dust (Faulkner), 97
Florida: in *The Sportswriter*, 114–15; in *Independence Day*, 117; in *A Childhood: The Biography of a Place*, 246
Folks, Jeffrey, 94, 97n, 108, 112, 118
Ford, Richard, x–xi, 51, 75–136, 171, 248–49
Foucault, Michel, 47
Garner, Phil, 185n, 188
Garreau, Joel, 103, 164–65, 229

Gaston, Paul, 141
George, Nelson, 192
Georgia: racial segregation of, 163; in *A Man in Full*, 197–98, 212–15, 216; in *A Childhood: The Biography of a Place*, 245–46. See also Atlanta
Gilroy, Paul, 239
Gingrich, Newt, 163
Gleason, William, 141
Go Down, Moses (Faulkner), 77–78
Godden, Richard, ix, 7, 16, 21, 22, 39, 77
"Going Back to Georgia" (Percy), 165
Golden Apples, The (Welty), 40
Goldfield, David, 159
Gone with the Wind (Mitchell), xii–xiii, 142–48, 149, 152, 171, 192, 209, 214
Grady, Henry, 141
Graff, Gerald, 50n41
Grant, Ulysses S., 107
Gray, Richard, 4, 5, 17, 148
Gretlund, Jan, 39, 83n10
Gross, Robert, 250–51
Guagliardo, Huey, 99
Guinn, Matthew, 76, 88, 103, 109, 124, 125, 130, 245

Hamlet, The (Faulkner), viii, 21–23, 35, 102
Hannah, Barry, 43, 45, 46n35, 253
Hartsfield, William, 149
Hartshorn, Truman, 160
Harvey, David, x, 48–50, 51, 106, 124, 126, 155, 180n18, 197, 201n16, 204, 243, 251
"Heartbreak Motels" (Ford), 104
Hegel, Georg, 24
Heidegger, Martin, 68n, 107
Heilman, Robert, 34
Hemingway, Ernest, 98n5
Historical-geographical materialism, 45–46
Hobson, Fred, 25, 81, 93n, 98, 101, 105, 114, 133, 161n
Hoffman, Frederick, 29, 33, 34, 38
Holditch, Kenneth, 78–79
Holman, C. Hugh, 151, 167–68, 240
Hooking Up (Tom Wolfe), 216n42

hooks, bell, 173, 241
Hornby, Nick, 89, 91, 93n
Hunter, Floyd, 158
Hutcheon, Linda, 46, 56

I'll Take My Stand (Twelve Southerners), viii, 3–10, 16, 30–32, 55, 141, 148, 161n, 245, 247
Illinois: in *The Moviegoer*, 69–71, 110, 134; in *The Sportswriter*, 95. See also Chicago
Independence Day (Ford), xi, 92, 116, 117–36, 249–50
Intruder in the Dust (Faulkner), 249
Irving, John, 216n42

Jackson, Maynard, 160, 237
Jacobs, Jane, 84
Jacobs, Robert D., 25–29
Jameson, Fredric, x, xiii, 47–48, 50, 51, 67, 98, 109, 162, 164, 180, 194, 195, 197, 198, 201, 204, 226, 227, 237n, 244, 252
Jancovich, Mark, 6n7
Jarvis, Brian, 204
Jones, Anne Goodwyn, 72
Jones, Madison, 40
Justus, James, 38

Kay, Terry, 194
Kazin, Alfred, 14
Kelley, Blaine, 191
Kentucky: in *Prodigal Summer*, xiv, 247–48; in "Notes on Liberty and Property" (Tate), 13
King, Martin Luther, Jr., 185n
King, Richard, 6, 143, 144–45, 147, 214–15
Kingsolver, Barbara, xiv, 246–48, 250
Kreyling, Michael, vii, ix, 3, 28n, 30, 43–44, 45, 47–48, 57, 75, 84, 86, 99
Labor: in *A Piece of My Heart*, 79–81; in *The Sportswriter*, 94–95; in *Independence Day*, 120, 250; in *The Dog Star*, 155–56; in *A Man in Full*, 211–12, 214–15; and transnational immigrants in the South, 211–12, 251–52; in *Those Bones Are Not My Child*, 227, 233–34

Lancelot (Percy), 91, 136
"Land! An Answer to the Unemployment Problem" (Ransom), 10–11, 13, 14, 33, 35, 245
Land speculation and development: in *A Place to Come To*, 57–58, 62; in *The Moviegoer*, 65–67, 73, 114; in *The Sportswriter*, 101–2, 106–7, 108, 114; in *Independence Day*, 118, 120–36; in *Gone with the Wind*, 143–46; in Atlanta, 159–65; in *Peachtree Road*, 174–75, 180–87; in *A Man in Full*, 193, 194, 195–99, 212–15, 216; in *Those Bones Are Not My Child*, 223–24, 225, 227–28
Last Gentleman, The (Percy), 55, 99, 135
"Late Encounter with the Enemy, A" (O'Connor), 149–50
Lawry, Edward, 68n
Lefebvre, Henri, 47, 107, 120n7
"Life You Save May Be Your Own, The" (O'Connor), 152
Looking for Atlanta (Staats), 219–21
Losing Battles (Welty), ix, 40–41, 246
Lost in the Cosmos (Percy), 86, 104
Louisiana: in *The Moviegoer*, 64–69, 71–74; in *Independence Day*, 135. See also New Orleans
Lowe, John, 168, 170, 238
Lukàcs, Georg, 50n41, 148, 172, 180
Lyotard, Jean-François, 45, 46, 161
Lytle, Andrew, viii, 4, 7, 8, 10, 12, 13, 18, 20, 25–26, 31, 40, 48, 49, 57, 161, 197, 243, 245–46

Macherey, Pierre, 148
"Madame Bai and the Taking of Stone Mountain" (Bambara), 252
Mailer, Norman, 216
Man in Full, A (Tom Wolfe), xiii, 140, 152, 153, 171, 192–218, 219, 221, 223, 227, 228, 248, 251, 252
Mansion, The (Faulkner), 22–23, 35–36
Marx, Karl, xiii
Massell, Ben, 162

Massell, Sam, 193
Massey, Doreen, xii, 169, 240
"Maturing of a City, The" (Siddons), 188
McKinney, John C., 36
McMurtry, Larry, xi, 75–76, 80, 84, 88, 92, 135
Michigan: in *The Sportswriter*, 95–96, 105–10, 115, 122. See also Detroit
Mississippi: in *The Sportswriter*, xi, 93–96; in *A Piece of My Heart*, 87, 88–90; Richard Ford's view of, 91; in *Independence Day*, 134
Morrison, Toni, 209, 219, 221, 238
Moviegoer, The (Percy), x–xi, 55–56, 64–74, 77, 79, 80, 87, 93, 94, 104, 128, 134, 218
Murphy, Paul, 33
"My Mother, in Memory" (Ford), 83n11, 95n3

Naipaul, V. S., 205
Nashville: in *A Place to Come To*, 59–61
Neo-Agrarianism: in southern literary studies, 26–27, 31, 33–34, 40, 148, 167, 168, 243, 245; in southern literature, 40, 55, 166, 171; in *A Place to Come To*, 58; in *The Moviegoer*, 68; in *Independence Day*, 125; as critique of Atlanta, 161n; Walker Percy's criticism of, 166. See also Agrarianism
New Jersey: in *The Sportswriter*, xi, 98–105, 110–14; in *Independence Day*, 117–34, 136
New Orleans: in *The Moviegoer*, x, 64–67, 71–74, 104, 114, 166, 181; in *The Sportswriter*, 99; Walker Percy's view of, 99; Richard Ford's view of, 99. See also Louisiana
"New Provincialism, The" (Tate), 19–20, 38, 167
New York: in *The Sportswriter*, 113–14; compared to Atlanta, 141, 158, 162–63, 167, 192, 203, 207, 240
Newman, Harvey, 229n
Nixon, Herman, 8, 11n18
Nordan, Lewis, 45
"Novel Writing in an Apocalyptic Time" (Percy), 166

O'Briant, Don, 194
O'Brien, Kenneth, 143
O'Brien, Michael, 33n

O'Connor, Flannery, xii, 76, 91, 149–52, 157, 163, 165, 166, 167, 197–98, 238
O'Donnell, George Marion, 11–12
Odum, Howard, 36
Osbey, Brenda Marie, 168
Owsley, Frank, 3, 4, 6, 7, 8, 11, 15, 18, 26, 29, 33

Paine, Thomas, 22
Peachtree Road (Siddons), xii–xiii, 140, 153, 170–91, 192, 206, 207, 220
Percy, Walker, x, xi, 40, 43, 51, 55–56, 64–74, 75, 77, 86–87, 88, 90, 91, 93, 94, 96, 98–99, 104, 105, 117, 123, 135, 136, 165–66, 170, 181, 197, 218, 249
Percy, William Alexander, 218
Pfeil, Fred, 172, 183n22
Pickett, George, 249
Piece of My Heart, A (Ford), x–xi, 75–92, 93, 98, 102, 109, 115, 134, 135, 136
Place: in southern literary studies, vii, ix, 28–29, 123, 133, 139, 142, 148, 151–52, 168, 232–33, 241; and race in the South, 3–4, 27, 29, 69, 72, 73, 84–85, 134–35, 150–52, 172–75, 176–80, 182, 185, 187, 189–90, 196, 197–98, 206–9, 212, 214–15, 232–33; and capitalist abstraction, 13, 35, 41, 46, 48–49, 201–2, 216, 225–26, 228–31; in Eudora Welty's work, 38–42, 65, 81, 123, 233; in postmodern theory, 47–51, 162, 204, 243–44; and contemporary capitalism, 47–52, 64–69, 73, 109–10, 123–24, 134, 157–63, 181–82, 195–203, 214–15, 216–18, 222, 227–28, 229–31; as marker of the South's supposed difference from the North, 56, 59, 61–64, 69–71, 87, 88–89, 95, 98–100, 120, 216; as received notion of southern identity, 81–83; and class, 82–83, 90, 94–95, 101, 120; and race in New Jersey, 101, 120, 125–28; and race in Detroit, 109; and postmodern hyperspace, 109–10, 162–64, 195, 204, 229; Frank Bascombe's philosophy of, 118–19, 123–24, 128, 129–31, 132; *Those Bones Are Not My Child*'s body politics of, 222, 232–37; global sense of, 240–41, 253
"Place in Fiction" (Welty), ix, 38, 39, 40
Place to Come To, A (Warren), x, 55–64, 70, 74, 95, 96, 214n
Pomerantz, Gary, 175
Portman, John, 109, 162, 163, 164, 167, 193, 195, 204, 239
Postsouthernism: Lewis P. Simpson's coining of, ix, 42, 55; and postmodernism, 43; and parody, 43–44, 45, 46, 75, 76, 84, 85, 88, 91, 92, 98, 99, 114–15, 135, 171, 198; and capitalism, 44, 45–46, 65, 66, 73, 202, 204, 213; and the transformation of the South, 44, 46, 64–69, 71, 73–74, 202; and historical-geographical materialism, 46–47; and skepticism toward Agrarianism, 59–61, 62–63, 103; as alternative to "neo-Faulknerism," 75, 84, 85, 88, 92; limitations of in *A Piece of My Heart*, 76, 88–92; and class, 84, 94; contrasted in *The Moviegoer* and *The Sportswriter*, 93–95, 96, 97–100, 105–6; and intertextuality, 96–97, 135; and Frank Bascombe's philosophy of place, 119; and Atlanta, 168–69; and the rural South, 244, 248; and transnationalism, 248, 250–53; and conceptual limitations of, 250
Price, Reynolds, 43
Prodigal Summer (Kingsolver), xiv, 246–48
"Profession of Letters in the South, The" (Tate), 18–19
Pyron, Darden, 146

Ransom, John Crowe, viii, 3–6, 10, 11, 12n20, 14, 16, 17, 18, 26, 29, 30, 33n, 48, 49, 133, 141–42, 146–48, 161n, 166, 245, 248
Raper, Julius Rowan, 44, 45, 47, 119, 168
Reagan, Ronald, 250n
Reed, John Shelton, 192, 204
Reed, Richard, 23, 28n
Requiem for a Nun (Faulkner), 21n42
Rice, Bradley, 159
Romine, Scott, ix, 9, 24, 43, 44–45, 47, 59, 101

Rose, Gillian, 195n7
Rowe, John Carlos, 108
Rubin, Louis D., 9, 25–34, 37, 42, 62, 135, 143, 144, 151, 167–68
Rutheiser, Charles, 110, 140, 160, 162–63, 165, 168, 179, 183, 185, 194, 208, 210, 222
Ryan, Maureen, 253n15

Sale, Kirkpatrick, 166n39
Salt Eaters, The (Bambara), 219
Selznick, David, 149, 153
Shelton, Frank, 90
Sherman, William Tecumseh, 140, 141, 181
Shister, Neil, 161
Siddons, Anne Rivers, xii, 51, 140, 160, 170–91, 192, 206, 219
Simmons, Philip, 66n16, 73
Simpson, Lewis P., ix, xi, 42, 55, 74, 152, 250, 253
Smith, David, 176–78
Soja, Edward, x, 47, 50, 66, 69n, 107, 118, 120n7, 130, 154, 244
"Some Notes on River Country" (Welty), ix, 39–40, 65, 123, 139
"S.O.P." (Ford), 132n22
Sound and the Fury, The (Faulkner), 22, 87
South Dakota: in *A Place to Come To*, 61–62
"Southern Mode of the Imagination, A" (Tate), 20
Spalding, Jack, 158
Sportswriter, The (Ford), xi, 92, 93–116, 117, 119, 122, 125, 126, 128, 132, 133, 134, 135, 249
Staats, Marilyn Dorn, 219–21
Stone, Clarence, 177
Stoneback, H. R., 151
Suitts, Stephen, 165
Sullivan, Walter, ix, 26, 27, 28, 34–38, 40, 41–42, 45, 49, 50
Summer, Bob, 170–71
Sun Belt: and postsouthernism, 50–51, 168–69; and the economic redevelopment of the South, 50–51, 62, 92; Robert Penn Warren's view of, 62, 135; Richard Ford's view of, 91–92, 135–36; and Atlanta, 159, 161n, 180

Tate, Allen, viii, ix, 13, 16, 17–20, 23–24, 25, 26, 27, 28, 30, 35, 42, 45, 48, 49, 50, 52, 62, 70, 97, 147, 167–68, 202, 213, 216, 247
Taylor, C. Mackenzie, 213n
Thoreau, Henry David, 103, 132n22
Those Bones Are Not My Child (Bambara), xiii, 140, 153, 209, 219–41, 244, 248, 252
Till, Emmett, 233
Town, The (Faulkner), 35–36
Transnationalism: and postsouthernism, xiv, 248, 250–53; and the Black Atlantic, 239; and solidarity, 240–41, 252; and migration, 250–52; and global capitalism, 250–52; and labor, 251–52
Turner, Ted, 166, 229n

Underwood, Thomas, 33
Updike, John, 216n42
"Urge for Going, An" (Ford), 91–92
Urgo, Joseph, xi, 21, 22n46, 102

Venturi, Robert, 109
Vermont: in *Independence Day*, 121–23, 127; Donald Davidson's view of, 122

Walker, Elinor Ann, 84n12, 119n
"Walker Percy: Not Just Whistling Dixie" (Ford), 75, 91–92, 136
Warren, Robert Penn, viii, 3, 13, 16, 21–22, 25, 29, 30, 38–39, 48, 55–63, 95, 122, 135–36, 214n, 216, 243
Weaver, Richard, 25–26, 29, 31, 33, 34
Webb, Max, 72
Welty, Eudora, ix, xi, 33, 38–42, 65, 83n10, 123, 136, 139, 142, 166, 216, 233, 246
Westendorp, Tjebbe, 63
Who Owns America? (Agar and Tate, eds.), viii, 11–14, 16–17, 19, 24, 28, 29, 33, 34, 36, 55, 59, 148
"Why I Live Where I Live" (Percy), 98, 104
Wiener, Jon, 16

Williams, Hosea, 180
Williams, Wayne, 219, 221, 222n5, 238
Wilson, Charles Reagan, vii, 4, 135
Windham, Donald, xii, 152–57
Wise Blood (O'Connor), 150, 167
Wolfe, Thomas, 23, 28n
Wolfe, Tom, xii–xiii, 51, 140, 171, 192–218, 243, 250, 253
Woodward, C. Vann, 38–39, 216
Wright, Gavin, 8, 10, 12n21, 15, 16, 44, 77
Wright, Sarah, 232

Yaeger, Patricia, xiii, 174, 232–36
Yates, Richard, 230n
Young, Andrew, 160, 185–86
Young, Stark, 4, 8, 12, 245, 246n
Young, Stephen Flinn, 43
Young, Thomas Daniel, ix, 26, 34, 37–38, 42, 45, 49, 70–71

Zizek, Slavoj, 235
Zukin, Sharon, 109, 110n26

www.ingramcontent.com/pod-product-compliance
Lightning Source LLC
Chambersburg PA
CBHW082103250426
43661CB00079B/2619